Aristotle on the Apparent Good

Aristotle holds that we desire things because they appear good to us—a view still dominant in philosophy now. But what is it for something to appear good? Why does pleasure in particular tend to appear good, as Aristotle holds? And how do appearances of goodness motivate desire and action? No sustained study of Aristotle has addressed these questions, or even recognized them as worth asking. Jessica Moss argues that the notion of the apparent good is crucial to understanding both Aristotle's psychological theory and his ethics, and the relation between them. Beginning from the parallels Aristotle draws between appearances of things as good and ordinary perceptual appearances such as those involved in optical illusion, Moss argues that on Aristotle's view things appear good to us, just as things appear round or small, in virtue of a psychological capacity responsible for quasi-perceptual phenomena like dreams and visualization: *phantasia* ('imagination'). Once we realize that the appearances of goodness which play so major a role in Aristotle's ethics are literal quasi-perceptual appearances, Moss suggests, we can use his detailed accounts of *phantasia* and its relation to perception and thought to gain new insight into some of the most debated areas of Aristotle's philosophy: his accounts of emotions, *akrasia*, ethical habituation, character, deliberation, and desire. In *Aristotle on the Apparent Good*, Moss presents a new—and controversial—interpretation of Aristotle's moral psychology: one which greatly restricts the role of reason in ethical matters, and gives an absolutely central role to pleasure.

Jessica Moss is Professor of Philosophy at New York University.

OXFORD ARISTOTLE SERIES

General Editors
Julia Annas and Lindsay Judson

PUBLISHED IN THE SERIES

How Aristotle gets by in *Metaphysics* Zeta
Frank A. Lewis

The Powers of Aristotle's Soul
Thomas Kjeller Johansen

Aristotle on the Apparent Good
Perception, *Phantasia*, Thought, and Desire
Jessica Moss

Teleology, First Principles, and Scientific Method in Aristotle's Biology
Allan Gotthelf

Priority in Aristotle's Metaphysics
Michail Peramatzis

Doing and Being
An Interpretation of Aristotle's Metaphysics Theta
Jonathan Beere

Aristotle on the Common Sense
Pavel Gregoric

Space, Time, Matter, and Form
Essays on Aristotle's Physics
David Bostock

Aristotle on Teleology
Monte Ransome Johnson

Time for Aristotle
Physics IV. 10-14
Ursula Coope

Political Authority and Obligation in Aristotle
Andres Rosler

On Location
Aristotle's Concept of Place
Benjamin Morison

Aristotle on the Apparent Good

Perception, Phantasia, Thought, and Desire

Jessica Moss

OXFORD
UNIVERSITY PRESS

Great Clarendon Street, Oxford, OX2 6DP,
United Kingdom

Oxford University Press is a department of the University of Oxford.
It furthers the University's objective of excellence in research, scholarship,
and education by publishing worldwide. Oxford is a registered trade mark of
Oxford University Press in the UK and in certain other countries

© Jessica Moss 2012

The moral rights of the author have been asserted

First published 2012
First published in paperback 2014

All rights reserved. No part of this publication may be reproduced, stored in
a retrieval system, or transmitted, in any form or by any means, without the
prior permission in writing of Oxford University Press, or as expressly permitted
by law, or under terms agreed with the appropriate reprographics
rights organization. Enquiries concerning reproduction outside the scope of the
above should be sent to the Rights Department, Oxford University Press, at the
address above

You must not circulate this work in any other form
and you must impose this same condition on any acquirer

Published in the United States of America by Oxford University Press
198 Madison Avenue, New York, NY 10016, United States of America

British Library Cataloguing in Publication Data

Data available

Library of Congress Cataloging in Publication Data

Data available

ISBN 978–0–19–965634–9 (Hbk)
ISBN 978–0–19–870794–3 (Pbk)

Links to third party websites are provided by Oxford in good faith and
for information only. Oxford disclaims any responsibility for the materials
contained in any third party website referenced in this work.

For Cian, who has read it all,
and for Oscar and Una,
who do not have to read it.

Contents

Acknowledgements   ix
Introduction   xi
Abbreviations   xvi

PART I. THE APPARENT GOOD

1. Evaluative Cognition   3
   1.1 Desire and the good   3
   1.2 Practical cognition   9
   1.3 Practical cognition in the *de Motu Animalium*   11
   1.4 Practical cognition in the *de Anima*   16
   1.5 Non-rational finding-good   20

2. Perceiving the Good   22
   2.1 Practical cognition and pleasure   22
   2.2 Pleasure as value-perception   29
   2.3 Perceiving the good as such   30
   2.4 Just deflationary enough   41
   2.5 Higher modes of cognition   46

3. *Phantasia* and the Apparent Good   48
   3.1 *Phantasia* in action   49
   3.2 *Phantasia:* the basic conception and beyond   51
   3.3 Practical *phantasia*   57
   3.4 *Phantasia* and thought   64

PART II. THE APPARENT GOOD AND NON-RATIONAL MOTIVATION

4. Passions and the Apparent Good   69
   4.1 Doxastic vs. phantastic accounts of the passions   70
   4.2 The passionate part of the soul   71
   4.3 Passions in the *Rhetoric*   75
   4.4 Platonic precedent   85
   4.5 First doxastic objection: the contents of perception   87
   4.6 Second doxastic objection: accepting vs. believing   90
   4.7 Aristotle and the Stoics on *phantasia*, assent, and passion   92
   4.8 Aristotle and the Stoics on passions, *phantasia*, and belief   94

5. *Akrasia* and the Apparent Good 100
   5.1 A puzzle about *akrasia* 100
   5.2 *Akrasia* in *de Anima* III.9-10 103
   5.3 Ethical error and perceptual illusion 106
   5.4 Following appearances against knowledge 112
   5.5 The illusion account of *akrasia* 118
   5.6 *Nicomachean Ethics* VII.3 121
   5.7 Ignorance and struggle revisited 132

PART III. THE APPARENT GOOD AND RATIONAL MOTIVATION

6. *Phantasia* and Deliberation 137
   6.1 Rational desire 137
   6.2 Starting-points vs. calculations 141
   6.3 *Phantasia* and calculations 142

7. Happiness, Virtue, and the Apparent Good 153
   7.1 *Phantasia* and the starting-points of reasoning 153
   7.2 Virtue makes the goal right 155
   7.3 Virtue is non-rational 163
   7.4 Making the goal right 174
   7.5 *Phronesis* and ends 179
   7.6 The role of *phronesis* 191
   7.7 *Phantasia* and the goal 198

8. Practical Induction 200
   8.1 Induction and habituation 200
   8.2 Habituation and pleasurable perception: an argument from first principles 201
   8.3 Pleasure in perceiving the fine 206
   8.4 *Phantasia* of the goal 219
   8.5 Beyond *phantasia*: true supposition of the end 223

   Conclusion: Aristotle's Practical Empiricism 234

Bibliography 236
Index 243
Index Locorum 248

Acknowledgements

I have learned so much from so many people over the eight years it took me to write this book that I am not sure where to start. Certainly I owe thanks for excellent comments on various chapters at various stages from James Allen, Rachel Barney, David Bronstein, John Cooper, Klaus Corcilius, Jamie Dow, Malcolm Heath, Simon Keller, Gabriel Richardson Lear, Hendrik Lorenz, Wolfgang Mann, Anthony Price, Kieran Setiya, Damien Storey, Sergio Tenenbaum, Jennifer Whiting, Chris Young, and the anonymous referees for OUP; I also got lots of help from audiences at Pittsburgh, Texas, Toronto, USC, Leeds, Cambridge, and Oxford. Damien Storey was a wonderful indexer and proofreader. My gratitude to my colleagues at Oxford is particularly vivid because I see up-close how much else they have to do: David Charles, Angela Chew, Ursula Coope, Terry Irwin, Thomas Johansen, Chris Shields and Ralph Wedgwood each read large chunks of the book and gave me enormously helpful comments; Ben Morison and David Bronstein read and discussed the *de Motu Animalium* with me. The book owes a less direct but very large debt to my teachers: Sarah Broadie, John Cooper, Alexander Nehamas, and Allan Silverman guided me through ancient philosophy when I was a student, and remain excellent models. I have been lucky to have great undergraduate and graduate students in my seminars, reading groups, supervisions and tutorials on Aristotle at Pitt and Oxford: it has been a pleasure to learn with all of them. I am also sharply aware of my debt to other writers on Aristotle: although I have tried faithfully to footnote them, it would take too many footnotes to convey the extent to which I am here developing and expanding on and revising ideas others have had. While I have learned enormously from those I disagree with too, I want particularly to note here some authors whose views on Aristotle's ethics and psychology I see myself as championing: Deborah Achtenberg, John Burnet, Thomas Tuozzo, and Jennifer Whiting. The central claim of this book, that there is an important connection between *phantasia* and the apparent good, is explored in Heda Segvic's work; I wish very much I could have discussed these ideas with her. I am grateful to the AHRC for a grant which gave me time finally to finish the book, to my colleagues at Balliol and in the philosophy faculty at Oxford for granting me leave to use it, and to Adam Swift for handing down an excellent anti-procrastination technique so I didn't waste it. Very special thanks are due to Oscar and Una Dorr for helping me not rush to press with the half-baked ideas I had when I first started this project and at many points thereafter – and for being wonderful. Finally, and above all, I thank Cian Dorr. I can imagine no better philosophical critic, interlocutor, or model, and I shudder to think how much worse this book (to stick to that) would be without him.

Some of the material in this book has been published elsewhere, and I thank the publishers and editors for permission to reprint it. Parts of Chapter 1 and of an earlier version of Chapter 2 are published as "Aristotle's non-trivial, non-insane view that we always desire things under the guise of the good," in S. Tenenbaum ed., *Desire and the Good* (Oxford, 2010): 65-81. A version of Chapter 5 is published as "*Akrasia* and Perceptual Illusion," *Archiv für Geschichte der Philosophie* (2009) 91: 119-156. One section of Chapter 4 is based on "Pictures and Passions in the *Philebus* and *Timaeus*," in R. Barney, T. Brennan, and C. Brittain (eds.), *Plato and the Divided Self* (Cambridge, 2012), 259-280. Parts of Chapters 7 and 8 are published as "'Virtue Makes the Goal Right': Virtue and *Phronesis* in Aristotle's Ethics," *Phronesis* (2011) 65: 204-261.

Introduction

The object of desire and of wish is either the good or the apparent good (*phainomenon agathon*). And this is why the pleasant is desired, for it is an apparent good; for some believe it is, and to some it appears [so] although they do not believe it so. For *phantasia* and belief do not reside in the same part of the soul. (*Ethica Eudemia* VII.2 1235b26-29)

The cause of [perceptual illusions] is that the faculty in virtue of which the ruling part judges is not identical with that in virtue of which appearances (*phantasmata*) come before the mind. A proof of this is that the sun appears only a foot in diameter, though often something else contradicts the *phantasia*. (*de Insomniis* 460b16-20)[1]

These two passages, one drawn from Aristotle's ethical works, the other from his psychological works, present parallel accounts of two apparently disparate phenomena: motivational conflict on the one hand, and the experience of optical illusion on the other. Aristotle implies that both involve a clash between how one rationally judges things to be and how things appear. In the optical case, the relevant appearances are visual appearances: ways things look. In the ethical case, they are what we might call evaluative appearances: appearances of things as good or bad.

Talk of things appearing good is pervasive in a philosophical tradition which stretches from Plato to the present, a tradition which holds that we desire things insofar as they appear good to us.[2] Aristotle very much belongs to this tradition, and talk of the apparent good is particularly prominent in his works. In his psychological works the apparent good surfaces as the goal of all actions driven by appetite, human and animal. In his ethical works it plays a major role in the explanations both of human motivation and of moral error: we all strive for what appears good to us, but only to the virtuous person does what is truly good appear so. In fact, I shall argue, the apparent good is a notion absolutely central to Aristotle's accounts of desire, pleasure, emotion, deliberation, and virtue – in short, to some of the most important and most debated areas of his psychology, philosophy of action, and ethics.

But what is it for something to appear good? What is the relation between such appearances and ordinary perceptual appearances? Why does pleasure in particular appear good, as Aristotle claims in the first passage above (and as many would agree)? And how does what appears good motivate desire and action?

---

[1] Translations throughout are mine unless otherwise noted.
[2] Famous modern proponents of this view include Donald Davidson and Elizabeth Anscombe; as the few who argue against the view emphasize, it is widely and often uncritically accepted by philosophers historical and contemporary.

For some philosophers, talk of the apparent good is loose or metaphorical: that something appears good to someone means just that she believes it good, or perhaps that its appeal is particularly vivid to her. For others appearing good may be a primitive notion. I want to show that Aristotle's case is different: his texts provide the resources for a substantive theory of apparent goodness. The parallels between the two passages quoted above suggest – and other passages confirm – that we should take the 'apparent' in 'apparent good' quite literally. They imply that Aristotle holds that things appear good to us, just as things appear large or small, in virtue of a psychological capacity responsible for quasi-perceptual phenomena like dreams, visualization, after-images and optical illusions: *phantasia* (conventionally but misleadingly translated 'imagination').[3] And things falsely appear good to us when *phantasia* misrepresents the world, just as in cases of perceptual illusion.

If this is right, then we can reach a better understanding of Aristotle's notion of apparent goodness by applying the account Aristotle gives of *phantasia* and its role in motivation – an account we find in the psychological works – to the notion of the apparent good as it figures in his ethical theory. The project of this book is to do just that. I will argue that while no account of the apparent good is explicit in the ethical works, these works assume an account that we can derive from the psychological works. An appearance of goodness is a motivating representation through *phantasia*, which derives from previous perception of its object as pleasant, and forms in turn the basis for thoughts about goodness.

This may seem a stretch: surely, some will protest, Aristotle's talk of *phantasia* in the first passage above is metaphorical, or at least broad; he does not intend the word in the technical sense developed in the *de Anima* and other psychological works, nor does he intend his various mentions of things appearing good in the ethical works to have any special connection with quasi-perceptual appearance. Aristotle, just like us, often talks of how things appear as a way of talking about how people believe things to be, perhaps implying that the beliefs in question are pre-reflective or in need of examination: consider, for example, the famous *phainomena* of *EN* VII.1, appearances which are surely intellectual rather than perceptual.

This is true; nonetheless, there is a general reason to suspect that his talk of the apparent good is specially connected with *phantasia*. Looking at the notion of the apparent good across the corpus, we will see that Aristotle uses it in two ways: to explain motivation in general, and more narrowly to explain mistaken motivation. Meanwhile, a close look at *phantasia* in the psychological works will reveal that it plays two main explanatory roles that correspond closely to these. Through *phantasia*, we can represent objects of perception or of thought to ourselves when those objects are not present: that is, through *phantasia* objects of perception or thought appear to us in their

---

[3] A more literal translation, given the root in φαντάζεσθαι – to appear or be made apparent – would be 'appearance-awareness' or 'being-appeared-to,' but as these are awkward I will usually leave the word and its cognates untranslated. I give a detailed account of *phantasia* in Chapter 3.

absence. Such appearances are necessary for motivation (as well as for thought): through them we can represent something not yet present to perception and thereby come to have it as a goal. But they can also play a potentially harmful role, when through *phantasia* we misrepresent the objects of perception. This is what occurs when we experience perceptual illusions; it is also, I shall argue, what happens in ethical error – what happens when we act or feel as we should not.

Thus we have reason to take seriously the connections between *phantasia* and the apparent good. When we do, I want to show, we gain new insight into some of the most important areas of Aristotle's practical philosophy: the roles of desire and cognition in action, the nature of the passions, the role of intellect in *akrasia*, the relation between character and intellect, the mechanism of ethical habituation, and the scope of practical reasoning. Most generally, we get a new and controversial interpretation of Aristotle's moral psychology, one on which he holds a view I will call Practical Empiricism.

It is well known that Aristotle holds that the content of all theoretical thought is ultimately derived from perception: as the medieval philosophers paraphrased his view, "There is nothing in the mind that was not previously in the senses." My analysis of the apparent good will show that he holds a similar view of practical thought: thought about what one should do, what is good. Just as ordinary perception is at the basis of all theoretical cognition, so practical perception – which I will analyze as pleasurable or painful perception of things as good or bad – is at the basis of all practical cognition. Pleasurable perceptions give rise through the work of *phantasia* to appearances of goodness, which in turn form the basis for our thoughts about goodness – and thereby for even our most rational desires.

This interpretation of Aristotle as a practical empiricist will be controversial in two important, and related, ways. First, it gives an absolutely central role to pleasure in human motivation, and thereby in human virtue. Second, it greatly restricts the role of rational, intellectual thought in Aristotle's ethics, for it entails that *phantasia* – a non-rational form of cognition, i.e. one that we share with lower animals, and that belongs to a non-rational part of the human soul – plays roles that others have claimed can only be played by intellect.

The book is divided into three parts. Part I explicates the notion of evaluative appearance implicit in the psychological works. Chapter 1 argues that the *de Anima* and *de Motu Animalium*'s discussions of locomotion show that there is a special form of cognition crucial to all action: evaluative cognition. Chapter 2 offers an account of the most basic form of such cognition, evaluative perception, arguing that Aristotle construes pleasurable and painful perception as genuine cognition of value. Chapter 3 turns to *phantasia*, a very vexed topic: although Aristotle claims that *phantasia* plays a necessary role in all action (and all thought), interpreters disagree over its nature, its scope, and even over whether Aristotle provides a unified account of it at all. I argue that he does, and defend an account of *phantasia* which differs from recent ones in its minimalism: *phantasia* can do everything Aristotle attributes to it while being simply what he evidently defines it as, a faculty of preserving and reproducing perceptual experiences. I then use this account to show that *phantasia*'s crucial role in action involves preserving and reproducing the pleasurable, or painful, motivating aspects of perceptions of value. This yields an account of the apparent good: for something to appear good to an agent is for that agent to have a pleasurable, motivating appearance of that thing through *phantasia*.

The rest of the book shows how this notion of evaluative *phantasia* is at work in Aristotle's views about human motivation and human virtue. The aim is not only to show continuity between the ethical and psychological works, but also to use the philosophy of action derived from the psychological works in Part I to illuminate important debates and puzzles about Aristotle's ethical views.

Part II examines non-rational human motivation. Chapter 4 takes on a long-standing debate about Aristotle's account of the passions, the non-rational emotions and desires central to ethical character. Using the analysis of the apparent good developed in Chapter 3, I argue that when Aristotle describes fear, shame, pity and other emotions as involving appearances of things as good or bad, he means this to be taken literally: passions are based on evaluative *phantasia*. Chapter 5 focuses on appetites, and in particular on Aristotle's account of *akrasia*, weakness of will. Here I use Chapter 3's analysis of the apparent good to show that the *de Anima* contains an overlooked account of *akrasia*; I then argue that recognizing this account helps us to solve the interpretative problems that have plagued the more famous account in the ethical works.

Part III argues that evaluative *phantasia* plays a crucial role even in our distinctively rational, distinctively human motivations: decision ($\pi\rho oa\acute{\iota}\rho\epsilon\sigma\iota\varsigma$) about what promotes our ends, and wish ($\beta o\nu\lambda\acute{\eta}\sigma\iota\varsigma$) for our ends themselves. Chapter 6 shows that practical reasoning (deliberation) relies on evaluative *phantasia*. Chapter 7 shows that when Aristotle says that we wish for what appears good to us, he means this in the technical sense: wishes are for ends, and each person's view of the end is a function of her non-rational character; therefore it is *phantasia* rather than intellect which provides us with our goals. Chapter 8 explains this by developing the Practical Empiricism thesis. Ethical habituation shapes character, as Aristotle argues, because it involves repeated pleasurable perception of virtuous activity, which gives rise via *phantasia* to a general appearance of virtuous activity as good. Intellect conceptualizes this general appearance, but the content comes from non-rational cognition. Thus even our most distinctively human and distinctively virtuous desires are grounded in *phantasia* and thereby, ultimately, in evaluative perception – in pleasure.

I should add that this book, although long, is much shorter – or at least covers much less ground – than the book I originally intended to write. That book would have traced the link between pleasure, *phantasia*, and apparent goodness through Plato, Aristotle, Epicurus, and the Stoics; it would have shown that the views I here attribute to Aristotle have important precedents in Plato and an important afterlife in the Hellenistic philosophers, and that these connections illuminate each philosopher's views. I would still like to write that book some day, but in the meantime Chapter 4 goes a small way toward making the point with reference to Plato and the Stoics, and I can refer the reader to my published work on Plato for more detailed arguments that he holds views very similar to the ones discussed here: that the non-rational part of the soul is the seat of perception and appearance-reception, and that it is subject to evaluative appearances which explain its passions and desires.[4]

One final note: it is a major commitment of this book that Aristotle's ethical views are deeply linked to his psychological views, and that research into the connections between the two will be profitable in understanding the ethics. Some might, however, think this a philosophically dispiriting claim. Many of the details of Aristotle's psychology, and particularly of his account of perception, are arcane, empirically falsifiable, or otherwise suspect; if his ethics turns out to be deeply rooted in his psychology one might then think that his ethics turns out to be less fruitful for contemporary philosophy than has been so widely thought. But this does not follow. Aristotle's moral psychology as I will interpret it is, physiological details aside, very much a going one. In particular the idea that perceptual imagination is tightly linked with our emotions, plays a major role in the formation of our characters and in our deliberations, and is to a large extent independent of rational thought, is as alive now as it was when Aristotle (following Plato) developed it.[5] If Aristotle were around today he would doubtless study moral psychology not only from the armchair but also from the psychology lab; I see every reason to think, however, that the hypotheses he would be testing would be the very ones he actually endorsed (and surely he would find a way, perhaps without too much effort, to interpret his data to confirm them). Moreover, much of what we will see in his psychology is *a priori*: questions about what counts as awareness of the good, for instance, and where to draw the line between reasoning and the non-rational. Thus I am hopeful that as one consequence of my main arguments in this book it will emerge not that Aristotle's ethics is hamstrung by an outdated psychology, but instead that Aristotle is as worth listening to about psychology, at least moral psychology, as he is about ethics.

---

[4] See especially my 2006, 2008, and 2012.
[5] See for example recent work on the role of imagery in emotion and character by cognitive therapists, summarized in Hackmann, Bennett-Levy, and Holmes 2011, psychologists' discussions of "System 1" and "System 2," and Tamar Gendler's work on "alief" (e.g. Gendler 2008).

Abbreviations

APo.	*Analytica Posteriora (Posterior Analytics)*
de An.	*de Anima (On the Soul)*
EE	*Ethica Eudemia (Eudemian Ethics)*
EN	*Ethica Nicomachea (Nicomachean Ethics)*
HA	*Historia Animalium (History of Animals)*
Insomn.	*de Insomniis (On Dreams)*
MA	*Motu Animalium (On the Movement of Animals)*
Mem.	*de Memoria (On Memory)*
Met.	*Metaphysica (Metaphysics)*
PA	*de Partibus Animalium (On the Parts of Animals)*
Phys.	*Physica (Physics)*
Pol.	*Politica (Politics)*
Rhet.	*Rhetorica (Rhetoric)*
Sens.	*de Sensu (On the Senses)*
Somn.	*de Somno et Vigilia (On Sleep and Waking)*
Top.	*Topica (Topics)*

PART I

The Apparent Good

1

Evaluative Cognition

1.1 Desire and the good

My aim in Part I of this book is to give an account of Aristotle's notion of the apparent good. I will argue that all motivation involves an appearance of the desired object as good (or of the rejected object as bad).[1] Moreover, these appearances are the work of quasi-perceptual *phantasia*, derived from pleasurable perception.

Before making the case for this claim, however, I want to establish a more general one: that on Aristotle's view all motivation involves at least *some* form or other of finding-good – some form or other of evaluative cognition. That is the task of this chapter.

By 'cognition' I mean to capture what Aristotle calls κρίσις, from κρίνειν: to discern, discriminate, or judge – one of the activities that distinguishes humans and animals from plants (*de An.* 432a16). Aristotle holds that there are three capacities through which creatures exercise κρίσις: perception and *phantasia*, common to humans and animals, and intellect or thought, which is distinctively human.[2] (It is worth emphasizing that on this use of the term there is nothing specially rational or intellectual about cognition: even a simple animal who lacks any mental powers more sophisticated than the sense of touch counts as a cognizer. 'Cognition' may sound exclusively intellectual to some ears, but I use it, along with the more idiomatic 'finding,' for lack of a better general term.[3] I should also note that I will use the verbs 'cognize as' and

---

[1] Like Aristotle, I will for the most part focus on desire, pleasure, and the apparent good, but I mean my conclusions – as he evidently does his (see especially *de An.* 431a8-12, discussed in Chapter 2) – to apply *mutatis mutandis* to aversion, pain and the apparent bad.

[2] For all three as κριτικά see *MA* 700b19-21, discussed below; cf. *de An.* 427a17-22: "thinking and understanding seem to be just like perceiving something, for in both cases the soul discerns (κρίνει) and recognizes (γνωρίζει) something of the things that are." Some interpret Aristotle as denying that *phantasia* is κριτικόν, at *de An.* 428a3 ff., but the manuscripts have "[*phantasia*] is one of the capacities or states by which we κρίνομεν (cognize, discern) and achieve truth or falsehood": it is Ross who inserts an ἆρα before this line (and Bywater a ζητῶμεν εἰ), turning the assertion into a question, and then taking Aristotle to answer the question in the negative. And while Aristotle does certainly deny that *phantasia* is identical to any of the other κριτικά (perception, belief, knowledge, intellect), he just as explicitly affirms that it can be true or false (428a10); hence this interpretation must be flawed. Moreover, given how explicit and unambiguous *MA* 700b20 is, we have no reason to amend the mss. at *de An.* 438a3. The analysis of *phantasia* I give in Chapter 3 will further support the claim that it is κριτικόν.

[3] There is moreover a tradition of using the Latin *cognitio* to translate Aristotle's κρίσις in the relevant sense: see Aquinas' commentary on the *de An.* at e.g. 622, where *cognitio* applies both to intellect and to perception. (Aquinas elsewhere uses *apprehensio* for the same purpose.)

'find' non-factively: one can cognize something as F, i.e. find it F, even if it is not F.) My claim in this chapter, then, is that all motivation depends on the agent's finding the desired object good through one or another cognitive capacity.

We have already encountered the main evidence for this claim in the Introduction, in Aristotle's characterization of the object of desire as "the good or the apparent good (*phainomenon agathon*)." This is a claim he makes repeatedly, and in many different contexts:

The object of desire (ὀρεκτόν) always moves, but this is either the good or the apparent good. (*de An.* 433a27-29)

What causes movement in the first place is the object of desire and the object of thought... And we must suppose that the apparent good also holds the place of a good, and also the pleasant, for it is an apparent good. (*MA* 700b23-29)

Without qualification and in truth the object of wish is the good, but for each person it is the apparent good. (*EN* III.4 1113a23-24)

These passages characterize the object of desire (ὄρεξις) as the good or as the apparent good. The discussion surrounding the *EN* passage on one particular species of desire, wish (βούλησις), is the most explicit. Here Aristotle argues that the unqualified object of wish is the good — i.e. the genuinely good; each person wishes for what appears good *to her*, however, and therefore only virtuous people wish for what is really good (*EN* 1113a15-31). Thus, although he draws little attention to the ambiguity, 'apparent' here plays two roles: to call something an apparent good is to show both (a) that it subjectively appears good to a particular agent, and (b) that this appearance may be false.

If his use is consistent, then in saying in other passages that the object of desire is the good or the apparent good, he means that while some desires are for things genuinely good, and others for things merely apparently good, every desire is for something that appears good to the one who desires it: 'apparent' in this context always carries the sense of subjective appearance, as well as indicating the possibility of error. Other passages confirm that the subjective appearance sense is intended by making the even stronger claim that we desire things *because* they appear good to us:

The object of desire (ὀρεκτόν) and the object of wish (βουλητόν) is either the good or the apparent good. And this is why (διό) the pleasant is an object of desire, for (γάρ) it is an apparent good... (*EE* VII.2 1235b25-27)

The apparent fine (καλόν) is the object of appetite (ἐπιθυμητόν), whereas the really fine is the primary object of wish (βουλητόν). But we desire on account of (διότι) it seeming [to be fine], rather than it seeming on account of our desiring.[4] For thought is the starting-point. (*Met.* 1072a27-30)

---

[4] Ὀρεγόμεθα δὲ διότι δοκεῖ μᾶλλον ἢ δοκεῖ διότι ὀρεγόμεθα. We could also translate: "We desire because we think [it fine], rather than so thinking because we desire." (The passage does not specify the content of the thinking or seeming, but we have to fill in δοκεῖ with something, and the references in the previous lines to the fine, genuine and apparent, provide the only clear antecedent.)

The pleasant is desired *because* (γὰρ) it is an apparent good; objects are desired *because* (διότι) they seem fine (here in the *Met.* passage Aristotle uses 'fine' instead of 'good,' but *MA* 700b25-26 shows that he sometimes uses the two terms interchangeably when characterizing the object of desire).

I will argue in Chapter 3 that the variants on 'appear' (φαίνεσθαι) in all these passages are meant in a narrow, technical sense: the apparent good is what appears good quasi-perceptually through *phantasia*. For now, however, I want to focus on a more general point: if the goal of all action and desire is the apparent good, then every desire and action requires *some* form of awareness of its object as good. Whenever someone desires some object, she does so because she finds that object good, through some mode of cognition or other. It is only by being cognized as good that something becomes an object of desire.

This is the *prima facie* interpretation of the "apparent good" passages quoted above, and it has a fair amount of support from interpreters (see below). Nonetheless it will be worth arguing for at some length, as I do in this chapter, for many will find it plainly wrong.

A striking feature of Aristotle's view of desire, inherited from Plato, is the distinction between rational desires – distinctively human desires involving distinctively human forms of cognition – and non-rational desires, the appetites and other passions which we share at least to some extent with lower animals, and which can conflict with rational desires in the human soul. (I will have more to say about Aristotle's understanding of this distinction later on; what I have said here should serve to fix the terms' reference. Note that 'rational' on this use is descriptive rather than normative: one can have mistaken or bad rational desires.) Rational motivations – wish, and its quasi-desiderative cousin decision (προαίρεσις) – are indeed for things the agent finds good, as the *EN* passage on wish in particular makes clear (1113a23-24, with the surrounding lines). But rational motivations have this feature, many will protest, precisely because they are rational. Consider how Aristotle distinguishes the two types of desire in the *Rhetoric*:

We do some things on account of rational (λογιστικὴν) desire, others on account of non-rational (ἄλογον). For wish is desire for the good (for no one desires anything but what he supposes to be good), but anger and appetite are non-rational desires. (*Rhet.* 1369a1-4)

Elsewhere, he explicitly distinguishes appetite from decision and wish on the grounds that appetite is for the pleasant instead of the good (*EN* III.2 1111b17; cf. *Topics* 146b36-147a8). And he describes akratics – incontinent or weak-willed people who act on appetite against rational decision – as choosing the pleasant "instead of the things they themselves believe (δοκοῦντα) good" (*EN* IX.4 1166b9): the desires they act on are in direct conflict with their judgments about what is good.

Thus Aristotle seems to introduce the category of appetite in part to show that some desires are not for things *qua* good. His point is widely understood to be that recognizing something as good requires intellectual capacities available only to humans, and indeed only to the rational part of the human soul.[5] And many will find this obviously correct: only reason can work out that something is good, as opposed to merely pleasant, and therefore only reason-based desires can be for the good.[6]

What then should we make of the "apparent good" passages quoted above, which seem to show that all desire is for what the agent finds good? One response would be to deny that appearances of goodness are distinct from desires: to say that the pleasant is an apparent good, for instance, is just to say that it is an object of desire. But this is a hard fit with the causal language we find in passages like *Met.* 1072a27-28 and *EE* 1235b25-27, quoted above: to say that the pleasant is an object of desire *because* it is an apparent good is to imply that there is at least what Aristotle would call a difference in being between those two properties.[7] (It is also a hard fit with the *MA* and *de An.* texts I discuss below, which, I will argue, confirm this causal account.) Another response may seem promising, however: one might deny that 'apparent good' carries the sense of subjective appearance at all. Irwin proposes a very different reading, as follows:

> ...'apparent good' need not refer to something's appearing *as* good, but may instead refer to the good that appears, even if it appears as something other than good – as pleasant, for instance... When the animal acts to get what appears to it, the appearance must be in general an appearance of its good – an appearance of something that is in fact good for the animal, though not necessarily an appearance of it *as* good. (Irwin 1990, 332)

Thus a thirsty slug seeks water not because water appears good to it, but because water appears to be water, or appears pleasant. That is, the claim that desire in general (and appetite in particular) is for the apparent good is merely an *extensional* claim about the object of desire: the things we desire are things which are (a) in fact good, and moreover (b) apparent to us – i.e. things of which we are in one way or another aware. Nature designs creatures to desire things which are in fact good for them, and so teleologically it is correct to say that desire is for the good, but this implies nothing about how the creatures themselves view the objects they desire.

A recent paper by Corcilius (2011) deploys this same extensionalist strategy in tackling the claim which will be our focus in Chapter 2, and which we can take for now as a specific version of the claim that the object of appetite appears good: that in perceiving something pleasant one "perceives the good as such" (*de An.* 431a11).[8] Although Aristotle

---

[5] For this account see e.g. Irwin 1990, 331-32, citing in support *Pol.* 1253a15-18 (which I discuss in Chapter 2): only humans have perception of the good and bad.

[6] Irwin supplies Aristotle with an explanation of why this should be so: "To conceive my good, as opposed to my pleasure, I have to be able to deliberate, and to compare the results of different actions" (1990, 336).

[7] For brief discussion of David Charles' interpretation on which desiring a pleasure and having an appearance of it as good are, while "different in being," identical activities, see Chapter 2.3.

[8] Later I will argue that there is a difference between perceiving something as good and having an appearance of something as good: the latter is a function of *phantasia*. But since *phantasia* derives its content from perception (see Chapter 3), and since both are non-rational forms of cognition, the distinction does not matter for our present purposes.

is often taken to be saying here that we have appetites for what we perceive *as* good, Corcilius argues that he must mean instead that we have appetites for things which are (a) in fact good, and moreover (b) perceived by us (as something or other).

If these extensional readings are correct, then the "apparent good" passages give no evidence that non-rational motivation involves any kind of cognition of things *as* good, and thus in no way conflict with Aristotle's characterization of appetite as for the pleasant rather than for the good. Is this enough to justify the extensionalist strategy? I think not.

First, Aristotle's use of the phrase 'apparent good' (φαινόμενον ἀγαθόν) in the passages where he discusses it at length is clearly and unambiguously intensional. *EN* III.4 1113a23-31, the passage on the object of wish quoted in part above, explicitly explains the claim that wish is for the apparent good as meaning that we wish for things that appear good to us; this is also the clear implication of *Top.* 146b36-147a4 (which also elaborates a similarly intensional use of the phrase 'apparent pleasant').[9] Thus it would be at best highly misleading of Aristotle to characterize the object of appetite, and of desire in general, as the 'apparent good' without meaning to suggest that here too the agent in some way finds the desired object good. The extensional reading is not only strained, but uncharitable.

Second, the extensionalist faces a glaring problem in accounting for error: not everything desired is in fact good, and Aristotle surely means to point this out in saying that the object of desire is either the good *or* the apparent good. The extensionalist might take him to mean that the object of desire is either something in fact good (e.g. wholesome water) or something that appears to be something in fact good (e.g. tainted water that appears wholesome), but this is to stretch the phrase 'apparent good' perhaps intolerably far. Moreover, this strategy cannot help us with the akratic: to say that the akratic goes for what appears to be something that is in fact good for him – pastries masquerading as vegetables, perhaps – would be to ignore the distinctive and problematic feature of *akrasia*, namely that the akratic goes for something he himself correctly thinks *not* good.[10] Consider a passage on the kind of motivational conflict involved in *akrasia*, from the *de An.*:

[A]ppetite [moves one] on account of the now; for the presently pleasant appears both without qualification pleasant and good without qualification, from a failure to look to the future. (*de An.* 433b8-10)

---

[9] Here Aristotle argues that one should define wish as desire for the apparent good rather than the good, and appetite as desire for the apparent pleasant rather than the pleasant, "For often what is [really] good or pleasant escapes the desirers' notice, so that [what they desire] is not necessarily good or pleasant, but only apparently so (πολλάκις γὰρ λανθάνει τοὺς ὀρεγομένους ὅ τι ἀγαθὸν ἢ ἡδύ ἐστιν, ὥστ' οὐκ ἀναγκαῖον ἀγαθὸν ἢ ἡδὺ εἶναι ἀλλὰ φαινόμενον μόνον)."

[10] Irwin does not mean to apply his analysis to akratic appetites, but only to those of lower animals. In the texts that characterize the object of appetite as the apparent good, however – see especially *MA* 6 and *de An.* III.10, both quoted below – Aristotle seems unconcerned to draw any distinctions between human and animal appetites.

I see no way to read this passage as making the merely teleological point that nature designs creatures to desire the pleasant, and does so because the pleasant is (normally) in fact good, and moreover is something apparent (something manifest or easily apprehended). It is not, as the extensionalist reading would require, that the presently pleasant is something in fact without qualification good, which is moreover apparent: rather, it is something which *appears* to be without qualification good although it in fact is not – and which is desired because it appears good.[11]

Third, and I think decisively, when Aristotle says the pleasant is desired *because* it appears good (as e.g. at *EE* VII.2 1235b25-27, quoted above) he evidently means to be saying something more explanatory than that the pleasant is desired because it appears pleasant. This is particularly clear in the *de An.* passage quoted just above, where appetite is moved to pursue a pleasure not merely because it appears pleasant, but also because it appears good ("both...and"). Even if these turn out to be two ways of making the same point (that is, even if the 'and' should be read as epexegetical – and I will argue in Chapter 5 that it should), it is notable that Aristotle considers the second worth mentioning. He evidently thinks that the appearance of the object as good plays a role in explaining why it is desired.

There is a strong case to be made for the intensional reading of Aristotle's claim that desire is for what appears good, then, but it seems to conflict badly with his views of non-rational cognition and non-rational desire. Should we therefore take it that he overstated his case in the "apparent good" passages? Should we conclude that he wavered on the nature of appetite, sometimes construing it as for what subjectively appears good and sometimes not? Or can we instead find a way to attribute to him a coherent overall view?

This would be a challenge: we would have to find an interpretation which accommodates both the face-value reading of the apparent good passages and the motivations for rejecting it – an interpretation which allows that all desires are for what the agent finds good, while also explaining the difference between rational and non-rational desires in such a way that it makes sense to say, in some contexts at least, that appetites are for the pleasant instead of for the good.

In the remainder of this chapter, I argue that the challenge must be met: the notion that desire depends on finding-good is not confined to a few passages, but plays a crucial role in Aristotle's most detailed accounts of motivation. In Chapter 2, I turn to show how the challenge can be met – how we can accommodate Aristotle's distinction between rational and non-rational desires.

The view I will be attributing to Aristotle is a radical one. There are plenty of philosophical theories which draw a special connection between desires and judgments of value: take for example the view, sometimes called motivational internalism, that the thought 'ϕ-ing would be good,' construed as the recognition that one has *reason* to ϕ,

---

[11] I give a more detailed account of this passage, and in particular of the phrase 'without qualification good,' in Chapter 5.

normally motivates one to ϕ, and thus that the resulting desire to ϕ depends on an evaluative cognition. But such views apply only to a restricted set of desires: desires that are specially rational in the sense of being responsive to reasons recognized as such.[12] These desires are construed as dependent on evaluative cognition, but this is by stark contrast with desires of another type which are not: whims, urges, attractions, and, paradigmatically, appetites like hunger and thirst.[13] What I want to show is that for Aristotle there is no such distinction. There is of course something special about the distinctively human, distinctively rational desires that play a crucial role in ethical action. What is special about them is not that they depend on evaluative cognition, however, for that is true even of appetites; instead it is that the evaluative cognition on which they depend is rational.

1.2 Practical cognition

If we want to know whether or not Aristotle thinks motivation dependent on evaluative cognition, the natural direction to turn is to the two texts in which he discusses the psychology of motivation: the question he puts as "What in the soul is the mover" (*de An.* 432a18-19), or "How the soul moves the body, i.e. what is the origin of animal movement" (*MA* 700b10-11). In these two texts, *MA* 6-11 (passage 1 below) and *de An.* III.9-11 (passage 2), Aristotle seeks to identify the psychological causes of locomotion (κίνησις κατὰ τόπον), or more generally of acting (τὸ πράττειν).[14] When a human or animal voluntarily moves her body in the pursuit of some goal, what is the efficient cause within the agent of that movement? Both texts give the same broad answer: the chief mover is desire (ὄρεξις: *de An.* 433b10-12, 27-29; *MA* 703a5), but there is something else that plays a necessary role in motivation too: either perception, or *phantasia*, or thought – that is, some form or other of cognition.

We see that the things which move the animal are thought and *phantasia* and decision and wish and appetite. And all these can be reduced to intellect (νοῦς) and desire (ὄρεξις). For both

---

[12] See for example Nagel's distinction between motivated and unmotivated desires (1970, 29), or Schiffer's distinction between reason-producing and reason-following desires (1976, 197 ff.).

[13] See Schiffer on thirst (1976, 198) and Nagel on hunger (1970, 29). Hume makes a similar point about hunger in the *Treatise*, where he notably construes most other desires along the lines I will attribute to Aristotle: "the passions...are founded on pain and pleasure, and...in order to produce an affection of any kind, 'tis only requisite to present some good or evil...DESIRE arises from good consider'd simply, and AVERSION is deriv'd from evil" (*A Treatise of Human Nature*, II.iii.ix).

[14] At *MA* 701a34, quoted in 1e below, Aristotle says he has been offering an account of how animals are brought "to move and to act" (κινεῖσθαι καὶ πράττειν). Certainly there are differences between locomotion and action: arguably one can act without locomoting (e.g. in issuing a decree from the throne, or in catching a fly on one's tongue), and arguably one can locomote without acting (for Aristotle sometimes uses πρᾶξις in a strict sense which applies only to distinctively rational action: *EE* II.8 1224a28-30 and *EE* V/*EN* VI.2 1139a20). But given *MA* 701a34's casual equation of the two, it should be clear that Aristotle is not attending to those differences here, and we should thus recognize a broad sense of 'action' which covers everything Aristotle means to be explaining in these accounts. This will be confirmed by what we see below: he is clearly explaining not only animal locomotion but also deliberated human action, πρᾶξις even in the strictest sense.

phantasia and perception (αἴσθησις) hold the same place as intellect, for they are all cognitive (κριτικά). (*MA* 700b17-21)

The object of desire (ὀρεκτόν) moves by being thought or by being presented through *phantasia* (τῷ νοηθῆναι ἢ φαντασθῆναι). (*de An.* 433b12)

The proximate cause of the movement is desire, and this comes to be through perception or through *phantasia* and thought. (*MA* 701a34-36)

... it is pretty much at the same time that the creature thinks it should move forward and moves, unless something else impedes it. The affections (πάθη) suitably prepare (παρασκευάζει) the organic parts, and desire (ὄρεξις) the affections, and *phantasia* desire. This itself comes about either through thought (νοήσεως) or through perception. (*MA* 702a15-19)

Insofar as the animal is capable of desiring (ὀρεκτικόν), this much is it capable of moving itself. But it is not capable of desiring without *phantasia*. (*de An.* 433b27-29)

The animal is moved and travels in virtue of desire or decision (ὀρέξει ἢ προαιρέσει), when something has been altered in accordance with perception or *phantasia*. (*MA* 701a4-5)

Cognition therefore can be practical as well as theoretical: it can be a cause of action, when it joins in the right way with desire. But what sort of cognition is practical cognition? And how precisely do cognition and desire combine to cause action – what role does each play? I want to show that, just as the "apparent good" passages lead us to expect, practical cognition is evaluative: it identifies objects as good, thereby rendering them objects of desire. But this will take some work. For both the *MA* and *de An.* discussions are difficult and confusing, and while many interpreters argue or assume that they present practical cognition as evaluative (see citations below), there is evidence in both texts which seems to support a very different account of motivation: one on which desire sets the goals, while cognition merely discerns means to those ends. (One might call this interpretation a Humean one, but this would be in some ways misleading; I will call it simply an instrumental-cognition interpretation.[15]) On this interpretation, motivation, or at least non-rational motivation, can occur without any evaluative cognition – any finding-good – at all. And this may seem to throw us back on the extensional reading of the apparent good passages after all.

In what follows I provide analyses of both texts which show that while they do allow practical cognition an instrumental role, they also characterize it as essentially evaluative. Just as the thought which underlies a wish is thought of an object as good, so too the pleasurable perception or *phantasia* which underlies an appetite is perception or *phantasia* of an object as good.

---

[15] A Humean view of motivation might allow a non-instrumental role for perception and imagination, and even belief, while restricting reasoning to a purely instrumental role. Hume himself evidently did just this, as noted in footnote 13 above: he held that most desires are founded on impressions or ideas about pleasure or pain (see *Treatise* I.3.10 and II.3.9).

1.3 Practical cognition in the *de Motu Animalium*[16]

The *MA* very explicitly presents practical *intellect* as playing two roles in the generation of action: first identifying something as good, and then working out the means to achieve it. Intellect contributes to action by being both instrumental and evaluative. At least that is what Aristotle says in one passage (*MA* 701a6-25, the passage on the practical syllogism quoted below as 1c). The rest of the discussion of locomotion is confusing, however, and it is not obvious how to reconcile it with this view of practical intellect. I want to show that it nonetheless provides a coherent account, with two important features. First, it consistently presents intellect as causing action by playing both evaluative and instrumental roles. Second, it draws no relevant distinctions between intellect and the lower forms of cognition (perception and *phantasia*): these lower forms act parallel to intellect in both its roles. And thus – although Aristotle is certainly not as clear about the distinction between the two roles as one would like him to be, and may hold that both roles are often condensed into one cognitive act – cognition in general, not just rational cognition, is practical by being evaluative as well as by being instrumental.[17]

The discussion is confusing because it seems to give its guiding question – "How does the soul move the body, i.e. what is the origin (ἀρχή) of animal motion?" (700b10-11) – several different answers. It begins with a very general account, in a passage we saw in part at the beginning of this chapter:

1a. All animals both move and are moved for the sake of something, so that this is the limit of all motion for them: the that-for-the-sake-of-which. And we see that the things that move the animal are thinking and *phantasia* and decision and wish and appetite. But all these reduce to intellect (νοῦς) and desire (ὄρεξις). For both *phantasia* and perception hold the same place as intellect: for all are cognitive (κριτικά), while they differ in the ways discussed in other works. Wish and spirited desire and appetite are all desire, and decision shares in thinking and desire. (700b15-23)[18]

There are two movers, desire and cognition – with intellect as the paradigm species of cognition. (Note that here and throughout both the *MA* and *de An.* discussions of motivation Aristotle evidently uses νοῦς to denote a cognitive capacity, like perception, rather than in the special sense of 'intelligence,' an intellectual virtue, which we find for instance in *EE* V/*EN* VI. In fact, the way he places νοῦς alongside perception and *phantasia* here, along with his casual shifts between νοῦς and terms like διάνοια (see below), indicate that he is often using it as a general term for all distinctively human cognition, fallible thoughts and beliefs included. I will thus translate it as 'intellect,' meaning this as

---

[16] My understanding of this text owes a lot to discussions with David Bronstein and Ben Morison, and to Malcolm Heath (which is not to say that they agree with me).

[17] The *MA* text is less discussed than the *de An.*, but recent work has taken on the issues I here address. For readings on which non-rational practical cognition (in particular *phantasia*) is purely instrumental, see Nussbaum 1978, Essay 5, and Schofield 2011; for a reading on which all practical cognition is evaluative, see Labarrière 2004.

[18] Translations of the *MA* are loosely based on Nussbaum's (1978).

a suitably general term.) Moreover, all three forms of cognition play at least roughly the same role: *phantasia* and perception "hold the same place" as intellect (τὴν αὐτὴν χώραν ἔχειν, 700b20).

The next lines shift from the psychological causes of motivation to its objects:

1b. As a result, what causes movement in the first place is the object of desire and object of thought (διανοητόν). But not every object of thought, but the *telos* of things doable (πρακτόν). Wherefore the mover is this kind of good, but not every fine thing... And one must suppose that the apparent good holds the place of the good (ἀγαθοῦ χώραν ἔχειν), and the pleasant, for it is an apparent good. (700b23-29)

The apparent good "holds the place of the good" in the explanation of locomotion: that is, it too can function as the goal or that-for-the-sake-of-which which 1a declared the ultimate cause of all animal locomotion. Given that 1b's identification of the *telos* as a good is in keeping with many other passages (see citations and discussion in Chapter 2), we can spell out Aristotle's thinking in these lines as follows. First he makes an unqualified statement, relying on his standard connection between good and goal: something can be a goal and object of desire for an agent just in case it is good for the agent. Then he considers an objection: sometimes agents desire goals that are not good for them, e.g. pleasant things. Then he offers a response: the pleasant can be a goal because it shares an important feature with the good: it is an apparent good. But there was another simplification in the first lines of 1b: the goal is not always the object of thought (διανοητόν), because not every animal is capable of thought.[19] Does Aristotle address this simplification too? He does, and with the same word, *apparent*.[20] I argued in section 1 that Aristotle standardly uses the phrase 'apparent good' to do double-duty: to indicate not only the possibility of error but also the subjective nature of the appearance. In this passage, at least, we can be more specific about the second sense: Aristotle has in mind appearances through *phantasia* (and perhaps perception). For, especially given the parallel between *phantasia* and perception "holding the same place" as intellect (1a) and the apparent good "holding the place" of the good (1b), the implication is clear: the object of desire is either a good that is grasped by intellect, or an apparent good grasped by *phantasia* (or perhaps perception).

Should we however read the claim that the object of desire is the good or apparent good as intensional rather than merely extensional – as entailing that practical intellect, *phantasia* or perception cognize things *as* good? Certainly in the case of intellect we

---

[19] And, as I will argue in later chapters, not every human desire is based in thought.
[20] Some will try to read 1b's description of the pleasant as the apparent good as applying only to humans, on the grounds that only humans are capable of evaluative cognition. I address this kind of objection more generally in Chapter 2, but for now we can note that Aristotle here means to be offering a general account of animal locomotion, that he signals no restriction of the "apparent good" clause to humans, and indeed on the contrary that – if my interpretation here is correct – one of his motives for introducing that clause is precisely to widen the application of his first statement to non-human animals, those incapable of thought.

should, for this passage is closely followed by the explicit statement of the two-roles account:

1c. How is it that one when thinking (νοῶν) sometimes acts and sometimes doesn't act, and [sometimes] moves, but sometimes doesn't move? It seems that something happens very similar to what happens to those thinking and reasoning about unchanging things [i.e. in theoretical reasoning]. But there the *telos* [goal, end] is a proposition (θεώρημα) (for whenever one thinks the two premises, one thinks and puts together the conclusion), but here from the two premises the conclusion becomes the action – as for example whenever one thinks that *every human being must walk* (βαδιστέον), *and that one is a human being*, straightaway one walks, or that *no human being should now walk, and one is a human being*, straightaway one stays still. And one does both things, if nothing prevents or compels one. "*I must make something good, a house is good*": one makes a house straight away. "I need a covering, a cloak is a covering; I need a cloak. *What I need, I should make. I need a cloak;* I should make a cloak." And the conclusion, that one should make a cloak, is an action. One acts from the starting-point. If there is to be a cloak, it's necessary for this to be first, and if this, then this. And this one does straight away. That the conclusion is the action is clear. *And the productive premises come about through two forms, through the good and through the possible* (αἱ δὲ προτάσεις αἱ ποιητικαὶ διὰ δύο εἰδῶν γίνονται, διά τε τοῦ ἀγαθοῦ καὶ διὰ τοῦ δυνατοῦ). (*MA* 701a7-25, emphases mine)

Here we are told that intellect is practical in part by identifying things as good. If we are to take seriously the parallel between intellect and non-rational cognition implied by the "holds the same place" passages, then we should conclude that the same is true for *phantasia* and perception.

I will offer more evidence that this is the right reading of the *MA* when we consider the later part of its discussion in Chapter 2, but first we must consider the lines which immediately follow 1c, which may seem to contradict the interpretation outright:

1d. But just as with some of those who ask questions, so here thought does not pause at all to consider the second premise, the obvious one (τὴν ἑτέραν πρότασιν τὴν δήλην οὐδ' ἡ διάνοια ἐφιστᾶσα σκοπεῖ οὐδέν). For example, if walking is good for a human being, that oneself is a human being one doesn't spend time on. Wherefore also whatever we do without calculating, we do quickly. For whenever one is active with perception or *phantasia* or intellect toward the that-for-the-sake-of-which, what one desires one does straightaway. For in the place of (ἀντ') questioning or thinking there comes the activity of desire. "I must drink," says appetite; "This is drink," says perception or *phantasia* or intellect (ποτέον μοι, ἡ ἐπιθυμία λέγει· τοδὶ δὲ ποτόν, ἡ αἴσθησις εἶπεν ἢ ἡ φαντασία ἢ ὁ νοῦς); straightaway one drinks. (701a25-33)

Taken in isolation, the last lines of this passage seem to speak unambiguously in favor of the interpretation on which practical cognition is purely instrumental: it is desire that sets the end, and cognition's only role is to identify a means of achieving it. A tempting reading reconciles this with 1c by saying that premises of the good – end-setting evaluations – only a play a role in rational motivation; when appetite is at issue, it motivates without any reference to the good at all. Someone who accepts this reading will find confirmation in the lines which follow, and which are evidently meant as a summary of 1a-d:

1e. In this way, then, animals set out to move and to act, desire being the proximate cause of the movement, and this coming about either through perception or through *phantasia* and thought (γινομένης ἢ δι' αἰσθήσεως ἢ διὰ φαντασίας καὶ νοήσεως). (701a33-36)

A general desire like 1d's appetite for drink is converted, by means of an instrumental cognition like "This is drink," into a specific desire of the kind that directly causes locomotion. On the instrumentalist reading, that is cognition's only role.

The fact is, however, that this cannot be Aristotle's view – as even someone inclined toward the extensionalist interpretation of the "apparent good" passages should agree.[21] For Aristotle characterizes appetites not as brute desires or blind urges toward drink or food, but instead as desires for the pleasant (*de An.* 414b5-6, *EN* III.2 1111b17). He thinks that creatures have appetites for food and drink *because* they find them pleasant:

All animals have appetite for food because they have perception of the pleasure that arises from food. (*PA* 661a6-8; cf. *de Sensu* 436b16-18, *Topics* 146b9-12)

Even in the case of appetitive motivation, then, there must be some correlate of intellect's "premise of the good": a cognition of an object as having some characteristic which renders it desirable, namely as being pleasant. A blind drive interpretation, on which appetite impels a creature to pursue drink independently of the creature in any way finding drink attractive, should not even be on the table. And thus 1d's "This is drink" should not be taken to give an exhaustive account of cognition's role in appetitive motivation.

Moreover, I will argue in Chapter 2 that the remainder of the *MA*'s discussion of locomotion confirms that practical cognition always has an evaluative aspect. Here is a brief preview of that argument: The lines that follow 1e show that cognition leads to action by bringing with it certain material changes, heatings and chillings; these are the material aspects or effects of pleasure and pain; therefore practical cognition is essentially pleasurable (Chapter 2.1); moreover, Aristotle construes pleasurable cognition as evaluative cognition.[22] Therefore we should accept the reading of the *MA* implied by the "holds the same place" passages: all motivation involves evaluative cognition.

What then are we to make of the drink passage, the last lines of 1d? I propose an alternative reading, or rather two variants on an alternative reading; I am not sure which Aristotle had in mind, and I admit that both are speculative, but something along these lines is necessary to accommodate the point that appetite is for the pleasant, and to make the passage fit with the rest of the *MA*'s discussion.

The first lines of 1d show that the drink case is presented as an example of acting μὴ λογισάμενοι: not having reasoned or calculated (701a28). It certainly looks to involve a

---

[21] I am grateful to Terry Irwin for making me see this point about the proponent of the extensionalist reading.
[22] Chapter 2.2-5 makes this case for perception, Chapter 3 makes it for *phantasia*, and chapters 6-8 make it for thought.

syllogism: "I must drink" looks just like "I must make something good" and other first premises in 1c's examples, and "This is drink" plays the same general role as the "premises of the possible" in 1c: it shows how to put the imperative into effect. In denying that this is a case of reasoning, then, Aristotle does not mean that it lacks elements that correspond to the premises involved in practical reasoning. What he is denying instead is shown by the first lines of 1d: just as in some cases there is no "pausing to consider" the second premise, here there is no pausing to do any considering at all – no need for "questioning or thinking" (701a31) – for *both* elements are obvious. That is, there is no more need to reason out a premise of the good than to reason out a premise of the possible: both are equally obvious. Instead of having to reason out "If I am to get a drink then I must first find a river," for example, one simply sees or imagines or thinks of some water.[23] And instead of having to reason out "Drinking is good for me," one simply sees or imagines or thinks that this is so. (According to the analysis I give in the next two chapters, one can have such a cognition simply by having a pleasurable perception, memory, or anticipation of drink.)

If this is right, then in the drink passage Aristotle does not bother to mention the element that corresponds to a premise of the good at all, but it is nonetheless there in the background, the work of one or another of the cognitive faculties. What he mentions is only the effect of that evaluative cognition, namely the appetite for drink, to which he here (misleadingly) attributes words that sound just like a premise of the good.

In fact, we might even take Aristotle's idea to be that here evaluation and non-evaluative representation are combined in one cognitive act. The facts are so obvious, and there is thus so little need for calculation ("thinking and questioning"), that there are not even two separate premise-like elements at all: instead, everything that intellect has to reason out in the syllogism cases is captured here by "This is drink," cognized in a special, evaluative way. One's body is in a certain condition: depleted of liquid. One sees (remembers, thinks of) some water ("This is drink," says perception, *phantasia* or thought). One thereby acquires a desire to drink – a desire that "comes to be through" the cognition. This occurs because, given one's bodily condition, the awareness of the water as drink is a special kind of awareness: not the bare registering of a fact, but an evaluative representation.

This suggestion may seem odd, but it in fact has a lot to recommend it. First, if Aristotle thinks that the evaluative and instrumental roles of practical cognition are often both condensed into one act, this explains why he draws so little attention to the distinction between these roles outside the *MA*'s passage on the practical syllogism (1c). Second, it fits particularly well with the physiological account of practical cognition we get in the remainder of the *MA*'s discussion – but we will come to that in Chapter 2.

---

[23] I am not at all sure how *phantasia* or intellect could provide the information "This is drink" in a way that renders drinking *immediately* possible, without involving deliberation. Perhaps Aristotle's idea is that they do so in conjunction with perception, as e.g. when one sees a well and remembers (through *phantasia*) or thinks that there is water inside.

For now, we have seen that the *MA*'s discussion of how desire and cognition cause action shows not only that practical intellect is practical in part by being evaluative, but also that all forms of practical cognition "hold the same place" as intellect in causing action – and thus that even non-rational motivation depends on evaluative cognition. In the next section, I show that this is confirmed by Aristotle's other main discussion of motivation, in the *de An.*

1.4 Practical cognition in the *de Anima*

De Anima III.9 seeks to identify the psychological causes of locomotion. It rules out the nutritive and perceptive faculties; it seems then to rule out intellect and desire as well, on the grounds that each can override the other. But III.10 shows the situation to be more complex:

2a. It is apparent then, at any rate, that there are two movers, desire or intellect (νοῦς), if one classifies *phantasia* as a sort of thinking (νόησιν).

b. For many follow *phantasiai* [plural] contrary to knowledge, and in the other animals there is neither thinking nor reasoning, but *phantasia*.

c. Therefore both of these cause locomotion, intellect and desire – intellect, that is, that calculates for the sake of something, i.e. practical intellect; this differs from theoretical intellect in its end. And all desire is for the sake of something: for that which is the object of desire is the starting point of practical intellect, and what is last is the starting point of the action. So that these two reasonably appear to be movers, desire and practical thought. For the object of desire moves, and on account of this thought moves, because its starting point (ἀρχή) is the object of desire.

d. And when *phantasia* moves it doesn't move without desire. So the mover is one and is the faculty of desire.[24] For if two things, intellect and desire, moved, they would move in accordance with a common form. But as it is, intellect doesn't appear to move without desire. For wish (βούλησις) is desire, and whenever one is moved in accordance with reasoning, one is moved in accordance with wish.

e. But desire moves contrary to reasoning [too]: for appetite is a kind of desire. While intellect is always correct, however, desire and *phantasia* can be correct or not correct. Wherefore (διό) while the object of desire always moves, this is either the good or the apparent good...

f. Since desires arise that are opposed to one another, and this happens when the *logos* and the appetites are opposed, and this occurs in those who have perception of time – for intellect orders one to hold back on account of the future, but appetite [orders? moves?] on account of the now; for the presently pleasant appears both without qualification (ἁπλῶς) pleasant and good without qualification, from a failure to look to the future –

g. the mover will be one in form, the desiderative faculty, insofar as it is desiderative, but before everything the object of desire, for this moves, itself unmoved, by being thought or represented by *phantasia* (φαντασθῆναι)... (*de An.* III.10 433a9-b12)

---

[24] Reading ὀρεκτικόν at 433a21 with one group of manuscripts; another group has ὀρεκτόν, object of desire. Nothing in my argument hinges on this dispute.

Cognition and desire are both movers (2a) – not, as one might have concluded from the last lines of III.9, because each sometimes causes action on its own, but rather, as is most clear from 2g, because they somehow cause action together: desire moves with the aid either of intellect or of *phantasia*.[25] (Thus when Aristotle speaks of intellect motivating us to do something he means that it does so *via* rational desire (wish) (2d); when he speaks of "following *phantasia*" (2b) he means following desire that is guided by *phantasia* (2d).)

How do desire and cognition jointly cause action?[26] 2c seems to characterize practical intellect as instrumental reasoning; this, in combination with 2a's and b's implication that *phantasia* plays a role roughly parallel to that of intellect, may suggest that desire sets the end, and cognition determines the means. But 2c identifies practical intellect as "intellect that calculates for the sake of something" in order to distinguish it from theoretical intellect: the point may be not that it is instrumental, but that unlike theoretical reason its function is to bring something about. When we look at the wider context, moreover, we find something very different from a purely instrumental-cognition account.

In 2e Aristotle makes the claim that has been my focus: that the object of desire is "the good or the apparent good." In 2c the starting-point (ἀρχή) of practical reasoning was identified with the object of desire; now the object of desire is identified with the good or apparent good. But this, by simple transitivity, makes 2c a version of a thesis we find in the ethical works:

Practical syllogisms have a starting point: "Since the end and the best is of such a sort . . . " (*EE* V/ *EN* VI.12 1144a31-33)

Practical reasoning starts from an object of desire, but this is to be understood as something the agent finds good (or even 'best'). Thus practical reasoning does supply means to ends, but it begins by doing something very different: identifying something as an end in the first place, by judging it good.[27] In other words, the *de An.* works with the same "two roles" account of practical intellect which we saw in the *MA*'s practical syllogism passage above (1c).

---

[25] It is notable that perception seems to have dropped from the list we found at *MA* 700b19-21 (quoted in 1a above); I will return to this point in considering the differences between the different forms of practical cognition in Chapter 3.

[26] The evaluative-cognition reading of this chapter that I will defend has wide support: it is sometimes argued for, and sometimes simply assumed. For variations on it in recent literature, see Hudson 1981, Charles 1984, 89, Richardson 1992, Freeland 1994, Segvic 2002, and Destrée 2007. Alexander of Aphrodisias interpreted Aristotle in this way and incorporated the view into his own theory of action: see e.g. his *de Fato* 178, 184, and *Mantissa* 172 (quoted in Chapter 2). But it has not been clearly shown how to accommodate 2c's implications that practical intellect is purely instrumental, nor have the possibilities for an instrumentalist reading of the rest of the passage been thoroughly examined, and so I think it worth defending the evaluative cognition reading once again. My argument overlaps at some points with those of Richardson and Hudson.

[27] Compare a slightly later passage from the *de An.*, which characterizes the first premise in practical reasoning as "Such a person should (δεῖ) do such a thing" (434a16-19). As I explain in Chapter 2, Aristotle treats "one should φ" and "φ-ing is to-be-done" in these contexts as interchangeable with "φ-ing is good."

The first lines of 2e further confirm that practical intellect is in part evaluative. Aristotle presents the claim that the object of desire is "the good or the apparent good" as a consequence of the difference between the two forms of practical cognition: intellect is always correct but *phantasia*, like desire, is sometimes not correct, and this is why (διό) the object of desire is either the good or the apparent good. (I discuss the sense in which intellect is always correct, and give a more detailed reading of this passage, in Chapter 5.) The natural inference is that the object of desire is either what is apprehended as good by intellect, correctly, or what appears good through *phantasia*, perhaps falsely.[28] It is also natural to read the case of motivational conflict in 2f as dramatizing just this difference: intellect orders one to hold back from some merely apparent good, while appetite urges one toward it, and does so because it "appears good," i.e. is apprehended as good by *phantasia* – just the sort of case described in 2b as "following *phantasiai* contrary to knowledge."

One might attempt to defend an instrumentalist account by giving an extensionalist reading of 2e-f on which they make no reference to the agent desiring objects *as* good: the point would be simply that when one uses intellect one hits on what will be genuinely beneficial, while when one relies on *phantasia* one might be led astray. (My intellect can, for example, reason out that abstention from the fifth beer will give me more pleasure in the long run, thereby focusing my desires on a genuine good; meanwhile the beer might *appear* very pleasant, and so if I let my desires be guided by *phantasia* they will push me toward a merely apparent good.) But we have seen ample evidence that intellect contributes to motivation by judging things good, and 2e in fact confirms that claim. For unless it is part of practical intellect's function to identify things as good, we cannot explain why intellect's being "always correct" should guarantee that the object of intellectual desire is the genuine, rather than merely apparent, good. Someone with desires for bad ends may deliberate perfectly correctly about how to obtain what she wants, but the object of her desire will for all that not, by Aristotle's lights, be anything more than apparently good. Aristotle himself explicitly recognizes this possibility in *EE* V/*EN* VI.10: the akratic or base person can deliberate correctly about how to get what she wants, but will thereby attain something bad (1142b18-20).[29]

---

[28] (This is a widespread reading of the passage: see for example Simplicius' commentary, and Richardson 1992.) We should thus take it that desire's being "correct or not correct" is not an independent phenomenon alongside *phantasia*'s being such, in need of further explanation, but a consequence of desire being sometimes guided by infallible intellect, sometimes by fallible *phantasia*. I will argue below that intellect-guided desire is wish, and *phantasia*-guided desire appetite; I will also address the apparent overstatement in the claim that intellect is infallible.

[29] The possibility of correct deliberation toward bad ends also plays a crucial role in the discussion of *akrasia* in *EE* VI/*EN* VII.2 and 9. If someone decides against pursuing a given end on the grounds that it is bad, but then acts according to her calculations about how to achieve that end, she is still akratic – still in some sense acting contrary to her practical reasoning; if we interpret Aristotle as restricting practical intellect to means-end reasoning we leave no room for this idea. (For this point, see Hudson's analysis of 2e-f: Hudson 1981, 124–25). Moreover, someone who reasons correctly about how to achieve something bad and then abandons her deliberation is in a sense acting irrationally, but she does not count as akratic: the akratic is one

What about *phantasia*? Just like 1a with its claim about "holding the same place," 2a and b imply that it plays the same kind of role in causing action that intellect does: that is why it can substitute for intellect, in animals, or oppose intellect, in people (in cases of *akrasia* and *enkrateia*, incontinence and continence). This already suggests that *phantasia* too operates in part by finding objects good. And indeed, this is just what we find in the last lines of 2f, where appetite pushes one toward some pleasant thing *because* that thing appears (φαίνεται) pleasant and good. I have argued above that the passage is naturally read as attributing the appearance in question to *phantasia*; thus the lines show that through *phantasia* we are aware not only of things like "There is cake around the corner," but also of things like "The cake is pleasant and good."[30] There remain many questions about how a non-rational capacity like *phantasia* could receive such an appearance, and I will address them in the chapters that follow; for now, I want simply to emphasize that this is what Aristotle says.

Thus *de An.* III.10 characterizes practical cognition as not only instrumental but also evaluative. 2e tells us that the object of desire is either what is thought good by intellect or what appears good through *phantasia*; 2f reinforces this with a causal claim: objects are desired *because* they are cognized as good. We have a wish for something because we think it good; we have an appetite for something because it appears good to us through *phantasia*.

And thus the *de An.*, like the *MA*, confirms the face-value reading of Aristotle's claims that the object of desire is the good or the apparent good: all desire is for something the agent finds good, and therefore all motivation depends on evaluative cognition.

There remains a question as to precisely how it does so, and here I think both discussions are open to two different readings. On the first, motivation begins with evaluative cognition, which generates desire for its object. On the second, motivation begins with desires, but these desires are desires for something good; therefore the instrumental cognition which focuses desire on a particular object (and thus gets the body moving) is *inter alia* cognition of something as a way of fulfilling that desire – that is, is *inter alia* cognition of something as good. I am not sure which of these options best represents Aristotle's view, nor am I sure that he consistently held one rather than the other, or even clearly distinguished between them. What I want to stress, however, is common to both. Whether Aristotle thinks that practical cognition's role is to focus pre-existing desire-for-the-good onto a specific goal or to generate desire in the first place, he is committed to the idea that all motivation crucially involves evaluation. All practical cognition, not just the rational variety, is practical in part by being evaluative – whether this is in addition to its being instrumental, or by way of being instrumental.

who acts contrary not to just any practical reasoning, but to "*true logos* and *correct* decision" (1151a34), emphasis mine. Thus 'true *logos*' must mean not whatever correctly achieves a given end, but more narrowly what correctly achieves a good end. See also Anscombe 1965.

[30] I offer a more detailed discussion of this passage, and defense of this interpretation, in Chapter 5.

Even if its role is restricted to finding means to satisfy desires, it does so not merely by recognizing things as, e.g., drinks or predators, but by recognizing them as good or bad. This is what makes practical cognition practical – what ties it to desire and thus to action.

1.5 Non-rational finding-good

I have argued that Aristotle construes all desire as dependent on evaluative cognition. This is the point of his claims that desire is for the "apparent good," which we saw must be read intensionally; it is confirmed by his most detailed discussions of the relation between cognition and desire, in the *MA* and *de An.* accounts of motivation. Thus we should take the point as established. On Aristotle's view, all desires are for what the agent finds good. All desires are based on evaluative cognition (where this means either that cognition generates such desires, or that it focuses them onto specific objects). Rational desires are based on rational evaluative cognition – intellect; non-rational desires are based on non-rational evaluative cognition – perception or *phantasia*. Appetites are for the pleasant, but they are for the pleasant *because* it appears good (see 2f from the *de An.* and 1b from the *MA*).

But as we saw in the first section of this chapter, Aristotle sometimes makes claims which seem to conflict with this – claims which provide the motivation for the extensionalist reading of the apparent good claims and the instrumental-cognition readings of passages 1 and 2. At *EN* III.2 1111b17 he explicitly distinguishes appetites from rational desires on the grounds that the former are for the pleasant instead of for the good; other passages imply the same (see quotations in section 1). And this would seem to imply that only intellect can grasp the good: practical intellect judges things good, while practical perception and *phantasia* merely represent things as pleasant.

Can we reconcile these claims, and attribute to Aristotle a coherent view of non-rational desire? I want to show that we can. What we need to find is an account of the claim "appetites are for the apparent good" which steers a clear path between two extremes, as follows.

Clearly we need to avoid a reading of this claim on which appetites are for what the agent finds good in precisely the same way that rational desires are – in other words, a reading on which appetites are based on intellectual cognition (thoughts) of things as good. This would be to collapse the difference between appetites and rational desires, ignoring all the evidence that appetites are independent of evaluative beliefs (see section 1).

One might try to escape this difficulty by retreating to an extremely deflationary reading of the claim: perhaps 'appears good' as a characterization of the object of desire could be construed as mere metaphor, meaning nothing more than 'is attractive,' or 'is pleasant.' We have already seen that Aristotle characterizes evaluative cognition as essentially motivating; in Chapter 2, I will argue that he also characterizes it as essentially pleasurable. And thus it may seem that we should cash out the notion of appearing good, with respect to appetites, entirely in non-cognitive terms – as a conative or affective state, or both, but not literally a cognitive one. But this will not do either. For we have seen that Aristotle takes himself to be making a substantive, explanatory claim when he says that appetites are for the pleasant because it appears good. Practical perception and *phantasia* "hold the same place" as practical intellect: they evaluate objects, leading us to desire them. And these claims cannot stand if we simply reduce the appearance of goodness to pleasure or to desire.

What we need, then, is an account of the claim that appetites are for the apparent good which is just deflationary enough: not so robust as to make the implausible claim that appetites are for what we think good, but not so weak as to undermine the causal, explanatory claim Aristotle is evidently making when he says that we desire the pleasant because it appears good. In the next chapter I will argue that we find just what we require through a closer analysis of the idea that the pleasant – the object of appetite – appears good. This might be interpreted to mean simply that when we take pleasure in something, we thereby come to find it good, but Aristotle is often taken to hold a stronger view: that to feel pleasure in something *is* to find it good, i.e. that pleasure is a mode of value-cognition. I will defend that interpretation, arguing that even perceptual pleasure – the most basic form of pleasure, and that which forms the basis for non-rational appetites – counts as literal, though very primitive, cognition of value.

2

Perceiving the Good

I want to establish two claims about the relation between the pleasant and the apparent good. First, Aristotle links the two more closely than has been generally recognized: his view is not simply that the pleasant appears good, but that evaluative cognition – cognition through which things appear good, or indeed are otherwise cognized as good – is itself essentially pleasurable. Second, this is no incidental attribute of evaluative cognition: instead, pleasurably cognizing something *is* cognizing it as good.

I mean these claims to apply to all forms of cognition, and will argue for them with respect to *phantasia* and thought in Chapters 3 and 6. My focus in the present chapter will be solely on perception, however, and this for three reasons.

First, it is here that an extensionalist reading of the "apparent good" claims is most appealing. It is all very well to talk about thinking things good, but to talk about tasting or smelling or hearing something as good – and thus to say that appetites for pleasant food and the like are always desires for what one finds good – may sound much more like metaphor. What is needed to show that even appetites are for what literally appears good, then, is an argument that pleasurable perception is cognition of value. (In fact I will argue in Chapter 3 that many appetites are based on *phantasia*, but we will see that this entails that they are indirectly based on perception: we have appetites for things which appear good to us now because we previously perceived things of the same kind as good.)

The second reason for focusing on perception is one that will be crucial for the whole of my interpretation of Aristotle. Perception is on Aristotle's view not only the simplest form of cognition, but also the fundamental form: it is from perception, in one way or another, that all thoughts and *phantasiai* ultimately derive (see Chapters 6 and 7). This is widely recognized as being Aristotle's view of theoretical cognition, but I shall argue in the remainder of the book that he takes it to apply to practical cognition as well: he embraces Practical Empiricism. Thus if we want to understand what it is for something to appear good through *phantasia*, or what it is to judge rationally that something is good – two notions absolutely central, I will argue, to Aristotle's conception of human action and ethical virtue – we must begin by understanding what it is to perceive something as good.

2.1 Practical cognition and pleasure

In the previous chapter we examined the *MA*'s discussion of practical cognition; I argued that such cognition must always be at least in part evaluative, although the last lines we examined, 1d's drink syllogism, seem at first to present it as solely instrumental. I want now to show that the rest of the *MA*'s discussion provides further evidence against the instrumental-cognition reading.

If practical cognition were purely instrumental then there need be no intrinsic difference between practical and theoretical cognition: Aristotle could hold that all exercises of cognition are of the same type, but depending on the use to which they are put (finding means to achieve a goal vs. merely receiving information) count either as practical or theoretical. What we find in the latter part of the *MA*'s discussion, however, shows that Aristotle presents the cognition that causes action as being of a special kind. Practical cognition as he here characterizes it is essentially pleasurable or painful, and hence essentially motivating. (This may seem a rather different point from what I need to confirm my arguments in Chapter 1, but I will argue in the rest of the chapter that this in fact amounts to the view that it is evaluative.)

After 1e (see Chapter 1.3), Aristotle makes something of a fresh start, now introducing physiological factors into the causal account of locomotion:

1f. For just as automata move when a small change has occurred, the cables being released and the pegs knocking against one another... so too do animals move. For those kinds of functioning parts have the same nature as the sinews and bones... When these are released and slackened the creature moves... But in the animal the same part has the capacity to become both larger and smaller and to change its shape, as the parts expand because of heat and contract again because of cold, and alter. *Phantasiai and perceptions and thoughts (ἔννοιαι) alter the parts.* For perceptions are at once a kind of alteration, and *phantasia* and thinking have the power of the actual things. (701b1-19, emphasis mine)

Automata (Aristotle probably has in mind some kind of puppets) move without undergoing qualitative change; animals move when their parts change size and shape because they have been heated or chilled. The heating and chilling are caused in their turn by "*phantasiai* and perceptions and thoughts," i.e. by cognition. Thus the claim is that cognition causes physical alterations which in turn cause large-scale bodily movements. A later passage gives the same account, although this time only with reference to perception rather than to cognition more generally:

When *on account of (διά) perception* the area around the origin [of the "movement-imparting soul" – sc. the heart] is altered and changes, the adjacent parts change with it, expanding and contracting, so that by these means animal motion necessarily comes about. (*MA* 702b21-25, emphasis mine)

Notably, neither of these passages mentions desire at all. Given all the evidence we have seen that desire is crucial to locomotion it is clear that we must take their accounts as elliptical, and 1e has shown us how to fill in the gap: desire is the proximate cause of locomotion, and "comes to be" through cognition (cf. 702a17-19). By omitting to mention desire in these two passages, however, Aristotle puts the emphasis on practical cognition's power to cause bodily changes, and thereby confirms 1e's implication that cognition is the beginning of the causal chain. How are we to explain this power? It will help to know what we are to make of the changes themselves, the heating and chilling that lead to expansion and contraction and thereby to locomotion, and on this point we get significant help from the lines that follow 1f:

1g. For in a certain way the thought form of the pleasant or frightening[1] is like the actual thing itself. That is why we shudder and are frightened just thinking of something. All these are affections (πάθη) and alterations; and when bodily parts are altered some become larger, some smaller.... Now the origin of motion is, as has been said, the object of pursuit and avoidance in the practical sphere (τὸ ἐν τῷ πρακτῷ διωκτὸν καὶ φευκτόν). Of necessity (ἐξ ἀνάγκης) heating and chilling attend (ἀκολουθεῖ) the thought and the *phantasia* of these things.[2] For the painful is avoided, and the pleasant pursued, and the painful and pleasant are nearly all accompanied by (μετὰ) some chilling and heating (but we don't notice this happening concerning very small things). (*MA* 701b19-702a1)[3]

The perceptions or *phantasiai* or thoughts that lead to locomotion – practical cognitions – somehow bring with them heating or chilling, which in turn sets off other changes that lead to locomotion. Perhaps, as 'perceptions are at once a kind of alteration' may indicate, heating and chilling are the material aspects of the cognition itself; perhaps they are separate, efficient-causal effects. I do not see any clear way to decide which of these Aristotle intended.[4] What matters most for my purposes, however, comes through on either reading. Even if the heating and chilling are separable effects of the cognition rather than its matter, they are necessary effects: "*Of necessity* heating and chilling follow the thought and the *phantasia* of these things." (This seems to conflict with the 'nearly all' (παντὰ σχεδὸν) in the next line, but that must therefore be meant as a tentative caveat, withdrawn in the parentheses that

---

[1] Excising θερμοῦ ἢ ψυχροῦ ἢ ("hot or cold or") with Nussbaum, although the sense of the text need not be affected if we leave it in: it is clear from context that Aristotle's main concern here is with the pleasant and frightening, and that if he did write in 'hot or cold' as well, he did so only to give related examples of the way thoughts preserve the character of their objects.

[2] Perception is omitted here, but this is not meant to show that it is not "attended by" heating and chilling: rather, the point is that that goes without saying, while Aristotle needs to emphasize that what holds for perception holds also for thought and *phantasia*. (See 1f: all forms of cognition have the same effects on the bodily parts, "for perceptions are at once a kind of alteration and *phantasia* and thinking have the power of the actual things"). I will argue in later chapters that *phantasia* and thought derive the relevant powers from perception itself.

[3] The lines I have omitted show how the immediate changes lead eventually to large-scale movement: "It is not difficult to see that a small change occurring in an origin sets up great and numerous differences at a distance – just as, if the rudder shifts a hair's breadth, the shift in the prow is considerable. Furthermore whenever an alteration occurs around the heart in accordance with heat or cold or some other affection (πάθος), even if in an imperceptible part of this, it produces a great difference in the body with blushing and pallor, and shuddering and trembling and the opposites of these" (701b24-32).

[4] A line quoted above – the alterations occur "on account of" (διά) the perceptions (702b21) – may support the efficient-causal reading, but perhaps the alterations Aristotle has in mind here are the contractions and expansions caused by the heating and chilling, which would be consistent with the latter being the material aspects of perception. In general we might fairly say that Aristotle is not overly concerned with distinguishing between relations of identity, constitution, and causation in this part of the *MA*.

follow.) All cognition has some material aspect,[5] but the material aspect of practical cognition is special: it includes or necessarily induces heatings and chillings – and thereby leads to locomotion. This is confirmed by a later passage:

Heatings and chillings are responsible for (αἰτίαι) the movements [that lead to locomotion] . . . For thought and *phantasia*, as was said earlier, present the forms of the things that produce [the alterations]. (*MA* 703b14-20)

But what are these heatings and chillings – what does Aristotle have in mind? The text makes clear that they are closely connected to pleasure and pain. The objects of the cognition which brings on heating and chilling are named as "the pleasant and frightening," and a few lines later as "the painful and pleasant" (701b20, 36); what follows reveals the second identification to be the most general one (which fits well with Aristotle's definition of fear as a response to things *qua* painful).[6] In fact 1g seems to say not merely that the painful and pleasant are among the objects of pursuit and avoidance, but that *all* such objects are painful or pleasant. For Aristotle argues that (a) heating and chilling necessarily follow the cognition of the objects of pursuit and avoidance, and then supports this with the claim that (b) the pleasant and painful are followed by heating and chilling; if there are other objects of pursuit and avoidance not mentioned here, then (b) can hardly support the necessity claim in (a). In later chapters I will argue that this is precisely Aristotle's view. Here however we are confining our attention to appetites, and it is uncontroversially Aristotle's view that the objects of appetitive pursuit and avoidance are the pleasant and painful.

Thus practical perception – our focus here – is always perception of the pleasant and painful. And while one might use the phrase 'perception of the pleasant and painful' to mean ordinary perception of something that is in fact pleasant or painful – on which use it would be accurate to say that a sick or depressed or un-hungry creature who sees its favorite food without feeling any particular affect or motivation is still perceiving something pleasant – Aristotle's use is clearly different. 1g mentions frightened shudders as an example of the chilling that accompanies practical cognition, and in the next lines, Aristotle illustrates the point that "the painful and pleasant are nearly all accompanied by some chilling and heating" as follows:

1h. This is clear from the affections/passions (παθήματα).[7] For daring and fears and lusts and the other bodily painful and pleasant [passions/states] are accompanied by heating or chilling, some

---

[5] Even thought has a material aspect, since it cannot occur without a *phantasia* (*de An.* 431a14-17, 432a3-9). Aristotle does suggest at some points that there is a form of thought that is purely immaterial (*de An.* III.4), but this is theoretical rather than practical thought.

[6] (See e.g. *Rhet.* 1382a21.) The interpretation of the heatings and chillings we find for example in Michael of Ephesus' commentary thus seems well justified: "Our nerves and parts . . . become bigger during pleasures by the agency of the well-mixed heat, and again contract . . . in fears on account of the cooling" (commentary on the *MA*, 119.7-10).

[7] Aristotle must mean either the passions he goes on to mention in the next sentence or the physical aspects or accompaniments of them.

of a part and some of the whole body. Memories and expectations, using such things as images, are sometimes less and sometimes more responsible for the same things [i.e. heatings and chillings]. (702a3-7)

The most prominent members of the class of heatings and chillings are thus the familiar physical aspects of pleasurable or painful emotions and desires: warm flushes and tingles, cold shivers and chills. (The class also includes the smaller, less noticeable relatives of these, as we see from the comment on the rudder: Aristotle's claim is that whenever we have a practical cognition we experience heating or chilling, but sometimes these reactions are so subtle that we barely register them. This serves at least to make the necessity claim more plausible.) Indeed, Aristotle seems to mean that heating and chilling are literally the material components of the psychological experiences of pleasure and pain.[8]

This shows that in talking of cognition of the pleasant and the painful (as at 1g; cf. *de An.* 431a8–10, quoted below, on perception of the pleasant and painful) what Aristotle has in mind is a form of cognition that is itself pleasurable or painful: the enjoyable tingly perception or anticipation of a sweet taste, the nasty chilling apprehension of danger, and so on.[9] Once we recognize that the kind of cognition at issue in the *MA*'s account of locomotion has this special feature of being pleasurable or painful, we see why it is essentially practical. For on Aristotle's not implausible view, pleasure and pain always have motivational consequences:

Perception, then, is analogous to simply stating or thinking. But whenever the perceptible thing is pleasant or painful, the soul, *as if affirming or negating, pursues or avoids it.* (*de An.* 431a8-9, emphasis mine)

Wherever there is perception there is also pain and pleasure, and wherever these are there is of necessity appetite too... (*de An.* 413b23-24; cf. 414b1-6)

Feeling pleasure in something leads us to desire it; feeling pain in something leads us to be averse to it. I will have more to say about the relation between pleasure and desire

---

[8] Comparing these passages with other texts provides further evidence for this interpretation. 1h claims that passions are "accompanied by" (μετά) heating and chilling, while elsewhere Aristotle says that all passions are accompanied by pleasure and pain (pleasure and pain "attend" (ἕπεται) the passions: *EN* 1104b14-15, *EE* 1220b12-14, *Rhet.* 1378a19-22; see discussion in Chapter 4). Moreover, 702b21-5 locates the physical changes entailed by practical cognition in the area around the heart (it does not explicitly describe these changes as heatings and chillings but it is natural, given 1h, to include them in its picture); a passage we will return to from the *PA* locates pleasure and pain in that region: "The movements of pleasures and pains and in general of every perception (αἱ κινήσεις τῶν ἡδέων καὶ τῶν λυπηρῶν καὶ ὅλως πάσης αἰσθήσεως) appear to begin from there [the heart] and terminate there" (*PA* 666a11-13). Furthermore, the *de An.* identifies the physical aspect of anger as the boiling of the blood around the heart (403a31-b1), while the *Rhet.* defines anger as a painful passion (1378a30-31).

[9] I am here leaving indeterminate the relation of the pleasure or pain to the cognition (cf. note 4): for all Aristotle says here, the idea could be that the cognitions are intrinsically pleasurable and painful, or that pleasure and pain follow them as necessary effects. The crucial claim for my purposes is that a given episode of cognition cannot count as cognition of the pleasant or painful – and thus cannot be an instance of practical, motivating cognition – without giving rise to pleasure or pain.

below, but for now what I wish to emphasize is simply that on Aristotle's view there is a necessary link between pleasurable or painful awareness and motivation. And this, we can now see, is just what he means to capture in the causal-chain passages of the *MA*, which provide the physical correlate of that psychological claim: heating and chilling cause alterations and expansion and contraction, and thereby lead to locomotion.[10]

In fact there is an important oversimplification in this position as I have stated it: Aristotle does recognize what we would call purely aesthetic perceptual pleasures, ones that induce no appetites and no locomotion (see e.g. *de Sensu* on the pleasant smells of flowers, which "contribute not at all to appetite" (443b29), and *EN* III.10's distinction between the pleasures of sight and sound and those of taste and touch). Moreover he explicitly recognizes pleasures, very pleasurable ones indeed, of purely theoretical thought. Thus it will not do to say that cognition is practical simply in virtue of being pleasurable. The main point I am arguing for is that practical cognition is essentially pleasurable (or painful); I am not however sure how to make room on Aristotle's view for the fact that cognition can be pleasurable without thereby being practical. There does seem to be a tension in Aristotle's position here (rather than merely in my statement of it), for both the *de An.* passages quoted just above and the *MA*'s causal account of action imply that pleasurable cognition necessarily induces motivation.[11]

I suspect that the right thing for him to say is this. Pleasure is indeed by its nature essentially motivating, but not necessarily appetite- or action-inducing. In some cases, pleasurably perceiving or contemplating something motivates us simply to carry on perceiving or contemplating it: for example, "the pleasures that come from contemplating and learning will make us contemplate and learn all the more" (*EN* VII.12 1153a22-23). What explains this is the difference between the objects of theoretical and practical cognition, and the corresponding difference in their ends. The objects of theoretical cognition are things that cannot be changed or acted on, while the objects of practical cognition are things that are πρακτά, doable or to-be-done. (Both *MA* 700b25-26 and *de An.* 433a28-30, lines I elided from passages 1 and 2, stipulate that the object of practical cognition is not just any good or fine thing, but the practical (πρακτόν) good or fine, which, as I argue below, Aristotle understands as the to-be-done.[12]) Thus even though the pleasure we feel in theoretically contemplating or perceiving something registers the object's attractiveness and appeal, the only way we have to respond to this attractiveness is to keep on cognizing it; in the practical case,

---

[10] Given what we have seen about the relation between heating and chilling and pleasure and pain, it would thus be natural to take the alteration of the bodily parts, or their expansion and contraction, as the material aspects or necessary material effects of desire, but I see no conclusive evidence that this is Aristotle's intention, and will leave the point as a speculation.

[11] The second passage quoted, *de An.* 413b23-24, could be interpreted as saying that all creatures with the capacity for perception also have the capacity to experience pleasure and pain and also the capacity for appetite, which would be consistent with some episodes of pleasurable perception not leading to appetite. But the first passage (431a8-9) seems to be making the stronger claim that whenever a creature pleasurably perceives something it is thereby motivated to pursue it, and so too does the *MA*.

[12] See also *EE* V/*EN* VI.2 1139a6-8 on the differing objects of theoretical and practical thought.

however, we respond by doing something. To put it another way, theoretical cognition has its end in itself, and therefore so do its pleasures; practical cognition, meanwhile, is for the sake of some goal (see 2c from the *de An.*), and therefore so too are the pleasures that attend it.[13] Pleasure in the smell of a flower does not make us want to do anything other than go on smelling the flower, but pleasure in the smell of food gives us a goal outside what we are doing at the moment: it makes us want to eat the food.

I am not sure how the *MA*'s account of the role of pleasure in locomotion should accommodate these distinctions, but I suppose Aristotle's claim would be that only registering something as to-be-done brings about the heating or chilling kind of pleasure (after all, one rarely blushes at the beauty of a rose, or of the Pythagorean theorem), and that this explains why the pleasures of theoretical cognition do not lead to action. In other words, there is a distinctive kind of pleasure which characterizes the distinctive kind of cognition we are concerned with here: practical cognition of something as a goal.

There are interesting questions to be pursued about the pleasures of theoretical cognition, but I will leave the subject at that. For my main point is that what we see in the *MA* makes clear that even if pleasure and motivation attach to some exercises of theoretical cognition, they are essential and necessary features of practical cognition – and this should be decisive against the pure instrumental-cognition reading. Sometimes when we see, smell, imagine, or think of some object, our awareness is pleasurable or painful, in a way that thereby disposes us to pursue the object or avoid it. Whether this occurs only when we are already actually desiring to obtain or avoid something, as on the second interpretation of practical cognition canvassed in Chapter 1, or whether it can precede and generate desire or aversion, as on the first, the cognition itself is a special one: pleasurable or painful, accompanied by heating or chilling, and by its very nature inseparable from desire for its object. It is thus essentially different from, and cannot be reduced to, non-practical cognition. If on a given occasion an agent's cognition of a sweet smell (e.g.) is pleasurable, heating, and desire-inducing, then this cognition is essentially different from the cognition she might have of an identical smell on an occasion when it fails to motivate her – when, for instance, she is too full or too sick to want food, or has become too temperate to be tempted by unhealthy treats.

Thus the *MA* first presents practical cognition as evaluative (see Chapter 1: every episode of motivation has a cause equivalent to an intellectual "premise of the good"), and then presents it as essentially pleasurable or painful (and hence essentially motivating). One might think that these are two separate points, but we have already seen that on Aristotle's view pleasure and evaluation are closely linked: the pleasant appears good. We need now to investigate more closely the relation between feeling pleasure in something and finding it good. I will argue that at least in the case of perception – saving higher modes of cognition for later chapters – pleasurably cognizing something

---

[13] On the differing ends of theoretical and practical thought see also *EE* V/*EN* VI.2 1139a35-36.

is finding it good. Before I proceed, it is worth noting one benefit this will have regarding the texts we examined in the previous chapter: it will explain why outside the *MA*'s passage on the practical syllogism Aristotle draws no attention in his discussions of practical cognition to the distinction between evaluative and non-evaluative practical cognition. For at least with reference to perception it will confirm the suggestion I raised above in relation to the "This is drink" passage (1d): that in many cases, the two roles which Aristotle assigns to practical cognition are combined in one cognitive act. If pleasurably tasting some water counts as perceiving the water as good, then one episode of perception can play both the role that corresponds to the premise of the good ("Drink is good" – the evaluative cognition which gives rise to the appetite for drink) and the role that corresponds to the premise of the possible ("This is drink" – the instrumental cognition which shows how to satisfy the desire). For a pleasurable perception of some water is simultaneously a discerning of the water's ordinary perceptible qualities (coolness, wetness) and a discerning of its (apparent) goodness.

2.2 Pleasure as value-perception

We can begin with two uncontroversial points about Aristotle's account of the relation between the pleasant and the good. First, he holds that they coincide. People do of course take pleasure in things that are bad for them, but those things are not truly pleasant – not pleasant "without qualification," or "by nature."[14] Second, he holds that pleasure functions as a way of tracking the good: when all goes normally, animals and people can get what is good for them by going for what pleases them. This is the teleological role of pleasure, its function in furthering the survival and flourishing of the creatures who experience it. This holds for basic bodily pleasures:

> Taste [must belong to all animals] on account of nutrition, for by it one distinguishes the pleasant and the painful in food, in order to flee the one and pursue the other... When we are hungry the smells of [foods] are pleasant, but not pleasant to those who have been filled and need no more. (*de Sensu* 436b15-17; 443b22-23)

It also holds for complex, ethical pleasures, as we will see in detail in Chapter 8:

> One who is a human being is suited to and on the road for [virtue]... but the road is through pleasure: it is necessary for fine things to be pleasant [i.e. to become pleasant to the person]. (*EE* VII.2 1237a3-7)

Thus what is truly pleasant for an animal or person is good for it, and in pursuing the pleasant a creature tends to achieve its good. But Aristotle is sometimes taken to hold a stronger view. It is not simply that in pursuing the pleasant one thereby tends to hit on what is good, where this may be quite unwitting – may involve no awareness of the good as good. Instead, feeling pleasure in something *is* finding it good:

---

[14] See e.g. *EN* VII.12 1153a5-6, VII.14 1154b15-20, X.3 1173b20-25, X.5 1176a10-22.

[P]leasure is a way in which the goodness of the activity is experienced through its effects on our subjectivity in general, or our sensibility in particular. (Cooper 1996, 270)

[S]omething's being pleasant is a prereflective way of its seeming to be good... (Broadie 1991, 329)

This is an interpretation of a claim which, as we saw, Aristotle makes repeatedly: that the pleasant appears good (e.g. *EN* III.4 1113a33-b2, *EE* II.10 1227a39, *EE* VII.2 1235b26-29).[15] On the reading we are considering, Aristotle's claim is that in finding something pleasant we are struck by its value and worth. This is an idea captured by our use of phrases in English like 'tastes good' and 'feels good' to describe perceptually pleasant things. If we find chocolate pleasant, we say that it 'tastes good' – that is, that we perceive it as good through taste. Cognitively, this is an extremely simple and basic way of finding something good. It need not involve *thinking* that the thing is good; it is a purely sensory experience which may be independent of or even at odds with thoughts about goodness. (I will give some account of Aristotle's notion of thought, and of its differences from perception and *phantasia*, in Chapter 3; for now, the relevant points are that thought is beyond the capacity of non-human animals, and this because it involves a grasp of universals and also what we might call rational assent. To think something good is to bring it under an explicit concept of value, and to endorse it with the most authoritative faculty of one's soul; Aristotle can hold that pleasure is value-perception without holding that it involves anything like this.)

The claim that pleasure is a mode of value-cognition is controversial. (For a sustained attack on it see Corcilius 2011.) It is also opaque. The main aim of this chapter is to defend it in detail, largely by spelling out what we should take it to mean. I want to show that Aristotle does indeed construe pleasure as awareness of goodness; I also want to show that this claim, properly understood, yields an account of evaluative perception that meets the demands laid out at the end of Chapter 1: an account just deflationary enough to reconcile Aristotle's distinction between appetites and rational desires with his claims that even non-rational appetites are for what appears good.

2.3 Perceiving the good as such

There is some evidence for the view of pleasure as value-perception in Aristotle's most famous treatment of pleasure, in the *EN*. There Aristotle twice discusses the nature of pleasure, both times with reference to perceptual pleasures (among others). Most relevant is the characterization in Book X:

There is pleasure in accordance with each sense (κατὰ πᾶσαν αἴσθησιν), and likewise in accordance with thought and contemplation, but the most pleasant is the most complete, and the most complete is that of the thing in good condition relating to the best object in its domain. And pleasure completes the activity (τελειοῖ δὲ τὴν ἐνέργειαν ἡ ἡδονή). (*EN* X.4 1174b20-23)

---

[15] In Chapter 3 I will argue that the 'appears' here usually signals the involvement of *phantasia* (see Chapter 3); for now, however, we may join Broadie and others in reading the claim as a more general one.

Pleasure is the characteristic feeling of performing one's natural activities excellently: perceptual pleasure is what arises when, with senses in good condition, we perceive excellent objects; intellectual pleasure is what arises when, with intellect in good condition, we contemplate excellent objects. Thus pleasure is by its very nature connected with awareness of something good. It is not just that nature designs creatures to feel pleasure when they cognize something good for them (where nature could just as well have designed them to feel hot or go beep). It is that there is an essential link between the states of cognizing something good and of feeling pleasure, such that the latter cannot be understood or defined without reference to the former. (This is at the least compatible with the *EN*'s earlier definition of pleasure, in Book VII, as "unimpeded activity of a natural state" (ἐνέργειαν τῆς κατὰ φύσιν ἕξεως ... ἀνεμπόδιστον, 1153a14–15): pleasure – that is, unqualified pleasure – is the characteristic sign that all is going as it should.)

This is, however, too weak a claim for our purposes: it might be interpreted as meaning that pleasure is merely a response to awareness of something that is in fact good, rather than itself an awareness of something good, let alone awareness of it *as* good. We find a much stronger claim in a passage we saw briefly above, one that gives an explicit definition of pleasurable perception. The passage is from *de An.* III.7: it precedes the account of locomotion we examined in Chapter 1 but concerns a similar topic, namely cognition's role in generating action. (Here I quote only what Aristotle says about practical perception; in later chapters we will look at what he goes on to say about *phantasia* and thought in the lines that follow.)

3a. Perception, then, is analogous to simply stating or thinking. But whenever the perceptible thing is pleasant or painful, the soul, as if affirming or negating, pursues or avoids it.

b. In fact, to feel pleasure and pain is precisely to be active with the perceptual mean toward the good or bad as such (καὶ ἔστι τὸ ἥδεσθαι καὶ λυπεῖσθαι τὸ ἐνεργεῖν τῇ αἰσθητικῇ μεσότητι πρὸς τὸ ἀγαθὸν ἢ κακὸν ᾗ τοιαῦτα). (*de An.* 431a8–11)

The passage is much discussed, and although it is a difficult one there is a rough consensus among commentators ancient and modern as to its meaning. It is generally taken to say that feeling perceptual pleasure in something amounts to perceiving that thing as good:

In being pleased perception cleaves to its proper (οἰκεῖα) activity as good, while in being pained it rejects it as bad. (Simplicius, *Commentary on Aristotle's* de Anima)

When [perception] perceives something hot as hot, it perceives only its differentiating feature and fiery essence. But when it relates this sort of essence to the animal it then judges it not just as perceptible but as unpleasant or pleasant, that is, as preservative or destructive of the animal. (Philoponus, *Commentary on Aristotle's* de Anima)[16]

Sensation announces to us in the first place only the existence of an object, and towards this we place ourselves by the feelings of pleasure and pain in definite attitudes of acceptance or refusal.

---

[16] Translation based on W. Charlton's, from the Latin version of Philoponus' commentary on Book Three (1991).

We feel it to be good or bad, and there arises in us in consequence longing or abhorrence. (Zeller 1897, vol. 2, 108-9)

[Aristotle] defines pleasure and pain to consist in "the consciousness, by means of the discriminating faculty (τῇ αἰσθητικῇ μεσότητι) of the senses, of coming into contact with good or evil." (Grant 1874, vol. 1, 256)[17]

There is however an extensionalist alternative to this interpretation. 3b could be read as saying simply that one feels pleasure when one comes into perceptual contact with an object that is good for one, with the 'as such' indicating that the relevant perception is of the good-making quality of the object rather than of some other quality irrelevant to its goodness (e.g. of its taste rather than of its color); on this reading the perception need involve no awareness of the object *as* good.[18] I want to defend the widespread intensionalist reading of 'perceiving as good'; since the phrase is obscure, however, a full defense will require spelling out in some detail what precisely we should take it to mean.

The phenomenon at issue in the passage is clearly the same one discussed in the account of locomotion in the *MA*: perception of something pleasant or painful leads to action (pursuit or avoidance) (3a). Practical perception is identified with perception of the pleasant or painful, where this is to be understood (as in the *MA*) as perception that is itself pleasurable or painful: the discussion moves without comment or argument from talk of perceiving something pleasant (3a) to talk of experiencing pleasure in it (3b).[19]

What the passage adds to the *MA*'s account of pleasurable perception is an explicit definition, in 3b: feeling pleasure is "being active with the perceptual mean toward the good as such." 'The perceptual mean' (τῇ αἰσθητικῇ μεσότητι) is a reference to the faculty of perception itself, or perhaps to the "common sense," or to whatever organ of perception is involved in a given episode of perception.[20] The nearest and most natural antecedent for the 'as such' is 'the good or bad,' and this is how the passage is naturally and usually taken.[21] Thus 3b says that to feel pleasure in something is to be perceptually active toward it as good. But what does this mean?

"To be perceptually active toward something" means simply to perceive it: see e.g. *EN* 1174b14–15 ("every sense is active toward the perceptible (αἰσθήσεως δὲ πάσης πρὸς τὸ αἰσθητὸν ἐνεργούσης)"), and 1d from the *MA* ("whenever one is active with

---

[17] Grant refers here to *de An.* III.7. See also Broadie 1991, 329 (quoted above); Achtenberg 2002, 161; Whiting 2002; Charles 2006.

[18] Corcilius' (2011) "objective" reading of the passage fits this model; compare Irwin's (1990) extensionalist reading of the claim that appetites are for the apparent good, quoted in chapter 1.

[19] Thus Aristotle treats pleasantness and painfulness as response-dependent properties relativized to particular responses. My tasting chocolate on a particular occasion does not count as my perceiving something pleasant – and thus cannot be practical (action-inducing) – unless I am pleased by it on this particular occasion, even if chocolate is something that most people find pleasant, or that I find pleasant most of the time.

[20] Aquinas argues that it is the common sense; Hamlyn defends the other options (see their commentaries *ad loc.*).

[21] One might try to take the 'as such' to mean 'as perceptible' or 'as pleasant or painful' but these are grammatically unnatural enough that we should resort to them only if we cannot get a satisfactory account of what Aristotle might have meant by 'as good or bad'; I will argue that we can.

perception... toward the that-for-the-sake-of-which (ὅταν ἐνεργήσῃ... τῇ αἰσθήσει πρὸς τὸ οὗ ἕνεκα)" (*MA* 701a29-32)).[22] This implies that to be perceptually active toward the good as such is to perceive something good as good. What we need now is an account of what this means.

As I said in Chapter 1, what we are hoping to find is an account that is just deflationary enough. We do not want to saddle Aristotle with a view on which one can grasp that something is good through perception in the same way one could grasp that through thought: this would be to ignore the gulf between thought and perception, and the consequent differences between thought-based desires (rational desires) and perception-based ones (appetites). But neither do we want an interpretation which maintains that difference at the cost of a purely extensional reading of perceiving the good. Aristotle does clearly hold that creatures tend to feel pleasure in objects that are in fact good for them, but in this passage he seems to be saying something more: that pleasure is an awareness of the good object *as* good. Moreover, only if this is what he means can he be reasonable in claiming that we desire the pleasant *because* it appears good (*EE* VII.2 1235b27, *de An.* 433b9, quoted in Chapter 1).

What we must do then is to analyze 3b's claim; it will clarify things to begin with the meaning of 'good,' then proceed to 'being active toward something as good,' and finally to consider the role of perception.

First, the good at issue must be what Aristotle calls the "practical" (πρακτόν) good – the doable or to-be-done good – for it is only this which can be an object of pursuit (see especially *de An.* 433a27-30). Thus we need not worry about Aristotle's account of the good in general, but only about his account of the practical good. And here, fortunately, Aristotle is fairly clear. For throughout the corpus he identifies the practical good as the *telos* (end), i.e. the that-for-the-sake-of-which (οὗ ἕνεκα). Consider for example his explicit definition in the *EE*:

The good is said in many ways... and one kind is practical and another not. The practical is this kind of good: the that-for-the-sake-of-which (πρακτὸν δὲ τὸ τοιοῦτον ἀγαθόν, τὸ οὗ ἕνεκα). (*EE* I.8 1218b4-6)

He links good and *telos* also at *Phys.* 194a32-33, 195a23-25, *Pol.*1252b34-35, *Met.* 983a31-32, *Rhet.* 1362a21-23, the opening lines of the *EN*, and in both ethical works' function arguments: for everything that has a good, "its good resides in its function" (*EN* I.7 1097b26-27), where a thing's function (ἔργον) is identical with or closely linked to its end (see *EE* II.1 1219a8). Likewise in the biological works, 'the good' for an animal always refers to what contributes to and promotes its life: what is οἰκεῖον, familiar or proper to it, what benefits it in the sense of contributing to its actualizing its innate potentials, to realizing its form.[23] Thus the good in general for a thing is the

---

[22] In context the that-for-the-sake-of-which is drink, and to be active with perception toward it is for perception to "say 'This is drink'" (*MA* 701a32-33) – i.e. is for the agent to perceive that it is drink.

[23] See Gotthelf 1989, with many citations.

attaining of its overall end, and the good in a particular context is its particular end in that context.

There is a debate among scholars as to which is metaphysically basic: Gotthelf argues that good is defined in terms of *telos*, while Cooper and others argue that *telos* is defined in terms of good.[24] But our concern here is psychology, and whichever way the metaphysical grounding works (if either), Aristotle's equation between ends and practical goods entails that we can understand what sounds like a mysterious psychological state, being active toward something as good, in terms of one more readily intelligible: being active toward something as an end. This, surely, means aiming at the thing, striving for it, pursuing it or being disposed to do so. We are active toward something as a practical good, then, when we relate ourselves to it as to-be-pursued, to-be-done – when we have it as an end or goal. In the *Rhet.* Aristotle offers as a popular, uncontroversial definition of the good "whatever is chosen (αἱρετόν) for its own sake... and the things productive or preservative of such things" (*Rhet.* 1362a21-28; cf. 1363b13-17): the good is whatever one has as a *telos*, or what contributes to that *telos*.

Thus we can say that when a sapling draws water up through its roots, it is "being active toward the water as good." The water is good for it – contributes to its actualization and flourishing – and in drawing up the water the sapling is acting in the appropriate way toward the water, acting toward it *as* good. It is doing so with its only psychic capacity, its θρεπτικόν, faculty of nutrition and growth.

Now we are in a position to understand 3b's claim. Animals and people are active toward their food as good nutritively, in the same way that plants are, but they also have a more complex way to be active toward things as good. Through perception, they can become *aware* of something as good, not only having it as an end in the way that a plant can have an end, but being aware of it as an end, discerning (κρίνειν) it as an end. That is, there is a special state a perceptive agent can be in, a special kind of awareness such an agent can have, in which an object impacts her faculty of perception not simply as e.g. blue or sweet or in motion, but as to-be-gone-for.[25]

This interpretation of what it means to perceive something as good is supported by a comparison with Aristotle's characterization of intellectually cognizing things as good. In 2c from the *MA*, as well as in other discussions of practical syllogisms, he alternates between representing the major premise as being of the form "Φ-ing is good" and as being of the form "Φ-ing is to-be-done": compare for example "Every man should walk (βαδιστέον)" at *MA* 701a13 with "Walking is good (ἀγαθὸν) for man" at 701a27. More generally, 2c lists a number of premises in the to-be-done formulation (two with βαδιστέον, two with ποιητέον), and then categorizes these all as "premises of the

---

[24] See Gotthelf 1989; Cooper 1982.
[25] My analysis here is very similar to Tuozzo's analysis of evaluative cognition: "To think something good (in the focal sense) is to cognize it as an end of action, and thereby to have an impulse to pursue it" (1994, 544; cf. 543). For a modern equivalent, see Oddie: "the good just *is* that which needs to be pursued, or promoted, or embraced" (2005, 41). (He uses this analysis to argue for a very strong version of the link I find in Aristotle between cognizing something as good and desiring it: on his view the two are identical.)

good." Thus Aristotle equates thinking of something as good with thinking of it as to-be-done; I am arguing that the same equivalence holds in the realm of perception.

Moreover, we find this equation of cognizing-as-good with cognizing-as-end in Aristotle's famous ancient interpreter, Alexander of Aphrodisias. Alexander gives what he takes to be an Aristotelian account of motivation, in keeping with his general philosophical approach.[26] On his version, the appearances which induce desire are "appearances of things as to-be-chosen (φαντασιῶν περί τινων ὡς αἱρετῶν)" (de Fato 178.17-28), or "as to-be-done (φαντασίαν περί τινος ὡς πρακτέου)" (Mantissa 172.25-28; de Fato 184.3–11). Alexander thus evidently interprets Aristotle's "appears good" as "appears to-be-done"; I am arguing that he is right to do so.[27]

In fact, this is a fairly natural interpretation of what it is to find something good, even apart from Aristotle's teleological commitments. There is a clear use of phrases like "That mouse sure looks good to that cat" to mean that the cat is aware of the mouse as a goal, not merely in the sense of something it is in fact pursuing, but in the sense of something *worth* pursuing, something that is to-be-pursued or to-be-gone-for. The idea is something like: if you see, smell, hear, feel or taste something as good, you seem to represent it as having a special glow around it, or a special pull to it – something which marks it out as the thing to choose.

Returning now to the passage at hand, what 3b tells us is that this state of perceiving something as to-be-done – perceiving something as good – *is* the state of feeling pleasure. When someone perceives some water, she is "perceptually active toward" the water. When that perception is a pleasurable one, she is also perceptually active toward it as good.

This interpretation makes passage 3 fit very well with the *MA*'s account of practical cognition. On that account evaluative cognition – that is, the cognition which in a given episode of motivation "holds the same place as" a premise of the good, be it perception, *phantasia*, or intellect – is of a special kind. It is affectively charged – pleasurable – and it is essentially motivating, necessarily inducing desire for its object. In passage 3 we have an account of evaluative perception which fits this description perfectly. Such perception is obviously affectively charged, for it is itself the feeling of pleasure. It is also, as further attention to the passage will show, essentially motivating. "Being aware of something as to-be-pursued" certainly sounds like a state which naturally leads to desire: if the experience of tasting water simply strikes one as endlike, as to-be-gone-for, this presumably means that one thereby comes to desire it – or even that one thereby is desiring it. And indeed one or the other of these seems to be Aristotle's view in the passage, although it is not quite clear which. 3a repeats the claim

---

[26] "I am the principal exponent [of Aristotle's philosophy], having been publicly declared teacher of it by your testimonial" (*de Fato* 164.14).

[27] I am for now bracketing the difference between the perceived good and the apparent good; Chapter 3 will show that the basic notion of finding-good is the same in both cases, because the appearances derive their content from the perceptions.

we saw above that pleasurable perception necessarily entails desire: when the perceptible thing is pleasant, the soul pursues it. The lines following 3b are sometimes taken to make an even stronger claim:

3c. And actual avoidance and actual desire are this/are the same,[28] and the faculty of desire and the faculty of avoidance are not different either from one another nor from the perceptive faculty; but they are different in being.[29] (de An. 431a12-14)

On a widespread reading of these lines, pleasurable perception entails desire not because it generates desire, but because pleasurable perceptions *are* desires.[30] But the lines are infected by a textual difficulty and some philosophical obscurity.[31] Moreover, we have seen significant evidence that Aristotle elsewhere holds that perceptual pleasure causes rather than is identical with desire,[32] and the overall arguments of both *MA* 6-11 and *de An.* III.9-11, on which there are two movers, desire and cognition, certainly imply that Aristotle thinks of the two as distinct. What we can safely conclude is that, although he may have been unclear or even undecided about the precise details of the relation between pleasurable perception and desire, Aristotle consistently held that it is in the nature of pleasurable perception to be accompanied by desire.

Thus our interpretation of passage 3 confirms what we saw in the *MA*: evaluative perception is both pleasurable and essentially motivating.

The interpretation gains further support from Aristotle's teleology. Aristotle holds that there is a very close link between essence and function: for natural substances and many other things too, "what a thing is and what it is for are one and the same" (*Phys.* 198a25-26). Thus if we want to know what perceptual pleasure is, we should look to its function. Doing so will confirm that perceptual pleasure is discrimination of an object's goodness, understood as awareness of the object as to-be-pursued.

---

[28] The manuscripts are divided between τοῦτο and ταὐτόν or ταὐτό at 431a12: see discussion below.

[29] Οὐχ ἕτερον τὸ ὀρεκτικὸν καὶ τὸ φευκτικόν, οὔτ' ἀλλήλων οὔτε τοῦ αἰσθητικοῦ· ἀλλὰ τὸ εἶναι ἄλλο.

[30] See e.g. Philoponus' commentary; for extensive defense and discussion of the view see Charles 2006 and Tuozzo 1994.

[31] If we follow one group of manuscripts in reading τοῦτο at 431a12 the claim is clear. "Actual desire is *this*," i.e. is the subject of the previous sentence (3b) – pleasurable perception. There is just one psychic activity, with two aspects or descriptions. (This is consistent with the fact that we usually desire what we don't have, so that desire is overall a painful or at least non-pleasant experience: compare Plato's view of anticipatory desire as a mixture of pleasure and pain (*Philebus* 47c-d).) If we follow the other group and read ταὐτόν or ταὐτό instead, however, the passage simply underdetermines the relation between perception and desire: it says that "actual desire and actual avoidance are the same" (a claim not as absurd as it may sound: the point would be that both wanting and shunning are desires in a broad sense, goal-directed motivations). We get little help from the claim that the perceptive and desiderative capacities or parts are "the same although different in being": whatever precisely this relation involves, Aristotle's other mentions of it imply that for two capacities to stand in this relation is compatible with their exercises being distinct (e.g. seeing and tasting, in *de An.* III.2, or perceiving and exercising *phantasia*, at *Insomn.* 459a15-17).

[32] We desire things *because* they are pleasant or appear good (*EE* VII.2 1235b25-27, *de An.* 433b8-10, *Met.* 1072a27-28); cognition "prepares" desire (*MA* 702a15-19); and desire "comes to be" through perception or phantasia and thought" (703a34-36).

This emerges from consideration of Aristotle's view of the function of perception in general. Aristotle's theory of perception is thoroughly teleological. He asks himself why certain creatures should be endowed with perception, where this means asking in what way perception serves their good.[33] The answer is that perception furthers survival (σωτηρία) and well-being (τὸ εὖ) (*de Sensu* 436b15-437a2, *de An.* 434b22-27). Nature, which does nothing in vain, equips animals and people with a special faculty that increases their opportunities for survival and flourishing. How can perception – the most basic form of κρίσις (cognition or discrimination) – accomplish this task? Somehow it must be able to discriminate between objects that would benefit the perceiver and ones that would harm it.

That something is beneficial to a creature – that it contributes to her achieving her *telos*, i.e. that it is good for her – is on Aristotle's view an objective, although of course agent-relative, fact about that thing: goodness is a property of external objects out there to be discovered. More specifically, it is what the *Categories* would classify as a relation (πρός τι): for some food to be good for an animal (e.g.) is for that food to stand in a certain relation to the animal – the relation, as we saw above, of contributing to her *telos*.[34] But how can such a relation be discerned? Perception is a very unsophisticated faculty: it cannot reason that something is beneficial; on some interpretations, it cannot even recognize things as leaves or lions, food or threats, having access only to "proper" perceptible qualities (color, sound, etc.) and "common" perceptibles (size, shape, motion, number).[35] Aristotle scholars have wondered how such a limited faculty can possibly serve its teleological role in animals who lack the power of reasoning: how can it enable them to recognize things as food, or as threats? Some argue that Aristotle simply has no answer to this worry.[36] Others try to solve the problem by bringing in *phantasia*, ascribing to it powers or roles nowhere explicit in Aristotle's texts, on the grounds that some such filling-in is needed to make sense of his account (see my discussion of Nussbaum, Lorenz, and others in Chapter 3).

3a-b, however, suggests a simpler explanation: the perceptual faculty is designed so that when it comes in contact with beneficial and harmful objects, it normally responds

---

[33] This is ground well covered in the literature; see e.g. Irwin 1990, 303-5.

[34] For a detailed account along these lines, see Achtenberg, who argues that "perception of value is...perception of a certain kind of relatedness, namely, the internal relation [Aristotle] calls '*entelecheia*' or '*energeia*' and that we might call 'development', 'completion', 'or 'fulfillment'... 'Good', for Aristotle, simply means 'development', 'completion', or 'fulfillment'"; "Since good means *telos* or its variants, when we see something as good, then, we are seeing it as a *telos* or as *teleion* [complete/perfect] or a *teleiôsis* [completion/perfection], and so forth" (2002, 44 and 65).

[35] That is, "incidental" (κατὰ συμβεβηκός) perceptibles can only be recognized by perception in combination with the higher cognitive faculties that non-human animals lack: see e.g. Beare 1906, 286 ff., and Kahn 1992.

[36] "[There is] a major problem for the interpretation of animal perception. Clearly animals need to 'make sense' of their perceptions. Do they have something corresponding to sortal classifications like *man, dog* [which in humans are the province of *nous*]...? Aristotle has apparently nothing to say on this question except that, lacking *logos*, animals cannot have *our* way of understanding what they perceive" (Kahn 1992, 369, note); cf. S. Cashdollar 1973, 164.

with special feelings – pleasure and pain – and it is these feelings which guide the animal toward the beneficial and away from the harmful.[37] We get strong confirmation of this view from the passages quoted from the *de Sensu* at the start of section 2 above: creatures are designed to be pleased by the taste or smell of food when and only when the food will benefit them (*de Sensu* 436b16-18; 443b24-26). Moreover, creatures are also so designed as to experience appetites for whatever they find pleasant, as emerges from some passages on the connection between appetite and pleasure that we saw above:

> Wherever there is perception there is also pain and pleasure, and wherever these are there is of necessity appetite too... Whatever has the perceptive faculty also has the desiderative, for... whatever has perception also has pleasure and pain and the pleasant and painful, and whatever has these also has appetite. For appetite is desire for the pleasant. (*de An.* 413b23-24; 414b1-6)

> All animals have appetite for food because they have perception of the pleasure that arises from food. (*PA* 661a6-8)

Therefore, being pleased by beneficial things and pained by harmful ones is enough to ensure pursuit of the former and flight from the latter. An animal pursues her food not because she recognizes "this is food," or "this is a banana," and then reasons or intuits that she needs to eat such things in order to survive, but because when she smells or eats it, she gets a special feeling, pleasure. Another passage makes a similar point:

> Humans are poor at smelling, and perceive no smells without the painful and pleasant.... And it makes sense that hard-eyed creatures should perceive colors in the same way, and that none be manifest to them except the frightening and the non-frightening. (*de An.* 421a10-15)

Creatures who cannot recognize predators as such can experience fear (a species of pain)[38] at the sight of a proper perceptible, and thus will flee. Thus animals can discriminate the beneficial from the harmful without recourse to sophisticated forms of cognition: simple perception even of proper perceptibles can suffice, by being pleasurable or painful. (There will still be important questions as to how the animal associates the pleasant taste of her food with the mere sight of it, or what motivates her to set off in search of food when none is in view. Here *phantasia* must indeed play a crucial role, conjuring up a memory or anticipation of the pleasant taste; I will present an account of how it does so in Chapter 3. But I will argue that *phantasia*'s efficacy depends on its reproducing the pleasurable quality of perceptions, so that perceptual pleasure remains the basic mechanism of motivation.)

Thus the function of perceptual pleasure is to track the good – to discriminate the beneficial from the neutral and the harmful – in order to motivate pursuit. Of course

---

[37] Many have recognized that pleasure plays some crucial role here: see e.g. Freeland 1994, 49, Modrak 1986, 60, and Whiting 2002, 173. My interpretation differs from Modrak's and Freeland's by making the link between pleasure and perception more direct (not requiring the mediation of *phantasia*); it is in many ways close to Whiting's.

[38] See e.g. *Rhet.* 1382a21.

sometimes things go wrong: an animal might take pleasure in something actually harmful, and it is a crucial claim of Aristotle's ethical theory that people with bad ethical characters systematically take pleasure in base, harmful things (like overeating and adultery) that would not please the virtuous (*EN* III.11 1119a12, X.6 1176a13-22). It is notable, however, that Aristotle views taking pleasure in the bad not merely as a regrettable tendency, but as a kind of malfunctioning of the pleasure-taking apparatus, akin to ordinary perceptual error:

> The pleasures that bring reproach . . . are not pleasant: that they are pleasant for those in a bad condition does not mean that we should think them to *be* pleasant, except for this sort of person, any more than we should think things healthy or sweet or bitter that are so to people who are ill, or again think things to be white that appear so to those suffering from eye-disease. (*EN* X.3 1173b20-25)[39]

And since function is so closely related to essence, this confirms our interpretation of 3b. Perceptual pleasure is discrimination of the good, where this discrimination takes the form of awareness of something as to-be-pursued.[40]

I have argued that Aristotle construes perceptual pleasure as literal perception of goodness; before moving on to show that this account meets the demands raised in Chapter 1, we must consider one passage from the *Pol.* which may seem to undermine the account:

> Man alone of the animals has *logos*. For voice (φωνή) is a sign for the painful and the pleasant, wherefore it belongs to the other animals – for *their nature has come this far, to having perception* (αἴσθησιν) *of the painful and the pleasant* and to signifying these things to one another, but *logos* is for showing the advantageous and the harmful (τὸ συμφέρον καὶ τὸ βλαβερόν), and so also the unjust and the just. For *this is peculiar to man by contrast with the other animals, to have perception of the good and bad* and just and unjust and the others (τὸ μόνον ἀγαθοῦ καὶ κακοῦ καὶ δικαίου καὶ ἀδίκου καὶ τῶν ἄλλων αἴσθησιν ἔχειν). (*Pol.* 1253a9-18, emphasis mine)

The passage seems to show that pleasurable perception does not count as perception of the good in animals, for they perceive the pleasant but not the good. And if this is so, then either it does not count as such in humans either, or if it does, this must be for reasons more complex than the ones I have given above.

Such a reason could in principle be furnished: one might argue that humans can perceive what animals cannot because intellect expands our perceptual range, just as it does, on a widespread view, in perception of "incidental perceptibles" (substances – people, plants, tables and so on). There is a debate among interpreters about incidental

---

[39] Compare his claims that the things that please the base are not pleasant "without qualification" (ἁπλῶς), or not pleasant "by nature" (see e.g. *EN* 1153a5-6 and 1176a13-22).

[40] I am thus suggesting that Aristotle held something like Dretske's (1981) account of mental representation, on which a mental state represents an object just in case that mental state has the function of "carrying information" about that object (and also can misrepresent that object). Prinz uses this account to argue that emotions have representational content (2004, Chapter 3); I will show in Chapter 4 that Aristotle treats emotions as something like species of pleasure and pain.

perception: some think even animals have it, and others think that it is actually thought rather than perception, but many occupy a middle ground, as follows. Only humans can recognize things as roses (as opposed to merely as red, sweet-smelling, soft, roundish, etc.) because only humans have the intellectual capacities to understand what a rose is. But we nonetheless literally *perceive* things as roses: once we have attained an understanding of roses, we can non-inferentially recognize roses as such. We do not need to reason out, on the basis of things we can perceive, that a rose is present; instead, when we perceive a certain shape and color we simply see that the thing is a rose. The concepts we bring to bear on the world help to determine the contents of our perceptions.[41] Likewise, Aristotle might think that because we have the ability to reason out that something is good (e.g. by grasping that it is beneficial, or that it is fine), we can non-inferentially recognize good things as such – perceive them as good – while animals cannot.

This yields a much more demanding interpretation of perceiving the good than the one I have offered. Should we take the *Pol.* passage to outweigh the arguments I have given that perceiving something as good is instead simply a matter of being struck by it as to-be-gone-for, and thus accessible to non-rational animals as well as to humans? I think we should not. To begin with, I see no evidence that Aristotle distinguishes between human and non-human perceptual pleasure, or human and non-human appetite, in ways that imply that the human ones are more sophisticated cognitively. We share the pleasures of touch and taste, and thus also the appetites for them, with lower animals (*EN* III.10 1118a24-26). Aristotle does not explicitly say that there are no important differences between humans and animals in this respect, but it is notable that he draws much attention to the similarity and none to any differences.

In fact, however, the *Pol.* passage only makes trouble for my account if we take it to be using αἴσθησις in the narrow sense of sense-perception, and it is at least as likely that the word is here used more loosely. Certainly there is nothing technical about the context, and αἴσθησις is a standard word for cognition in general (see e.g. *Pol.* 1281b35-38, where Aristotle speaks of αἴσθησις of political matters, using the word interchangeably with τὸ κρίνειν). Meanwhile, in a passage from the *Rhet.* which we will consider in Chapter 4 – a passage where he is most likely using αἴσθησις in a narrow technical sense – Aristotle argues that justice and injustice are "least perceptible," in a context that seems to imply "imperceptible" (1382a10-12); if we want to avoid contradiction between this and the last line of the *Pol.* passage, it is most easily done by taking αἴσθησις in the *Pol.* passage in the non-technical sense.

In this case the passage is perfectly compatible with my account of pleasure: its point is that animals do not have the concept of goodness and so can only be aware of the

---

[41] This interpretation of incidental perception as non-inferential is widely accepted; it is defended in detail in Cashdollar 1973. For the more general point about intellect expanding our perceptual range, see e.g. Everson: "What content a perception has will depend... [in part] on the subject's own recognitional abilities – that is, on which concepts he is able to exercise in perception" (1997, 227).

good by feeling pleasure in it, while humans can recognize the good as something distinct from the pleasant, through thinking things good. The kind of "perception" that humans alone have of the good (and the just and "the others" – presumably other ethical qualities) would thus be perception in a broad or metaphorical sense, perception of the kind that Aristotle equates with *phronesis* (practical wisdom) at *EE* V/*EN* VI.11-12 1143b27-30 and 1143b5 – an intellectual grasp, not a sensory one. If this is right, this *Pol.* passage merely denies animals *phronesis*, leaving them with the kind of awareness of the good that I have here argued he elsewhere attributes to them – sensory perception of the good, which forms the basis for appetites, animal and human alike.

Of course if this is what Aristotle means in this passage one wishes he had not expressed himself just as he did. But his view of the relation between perception and goodness is, if my interpretation of it is correct, a very difficult one to articulate, and we should not be surprised to find him putting it in ways that seem at times contradictory. I return to this point at the end of the next section.

2.4 Just deflationary enough

I have been arguing for an interpretation of pleasurable perception as perceiving as good, where this means perceiving as to-be-gone-for, to-be-pursued. What I want now to show is that if this account is right, then perceptual pleasure counts as perception of the good in a way that is just deflationary enough to make sense of Aristotle's account of non-rational desire. That is, the account of perceptual pleasure developed above meets the demand raised in Chapter 1: it allows Aristotle to be saying something meaningful and substantive when he claims that we desire the pleasant because it appears good, without thereby collapsing the distinction between wishes for the good and appetites for the pleasant.

On the one hand, pleasurable perception is the most minimal, unsophisticated form of awareness of the good. As Tuozzo puts it in his analysis of passage 3, it is "the unconceptualized mental experience of the good" (1994, 536). Being aware of something as to-be-pursued need not involve being aware of *why* it is to-be-pursued. The possible reasons for this are various: that it contributes to one's survival or flourishing; that it is familiar or proper (οἰκεῖον) to one; in the case of distinctively human action that it is fine (καλόν), or more specifically just, courageous, generous, and so on. Arguably, grasping any of these requires thought. (I return to this subject in Chapter 4.) But, given Aristotle's view of perception, simply being aware *that* something is to be pursued does not.

The fact is that it is harder than one might expect to draw a principled line excluding value-properties from the range of Aristotelian perception. *De An.* II.6 divides objects of perception into proper, common, and incidental, and this might seem to rule out everything beyond material objects and their manifest physical properties (colors, motions, etc.). But Aristotle divides all the things that are into those that can be perceived and those that can be grasped by intellect (*de An.* 433b22), and when he offers a principle of division it leaves much more than we might expect on the perceptible side. "Particulars are necessarily perceived," while intellect grasps universals (*APo.* 87b37-39). In *Met.* I.1 – a text which lays out Aristotle's empiricist epistemology, and to which we will return in Chapters 7 and 8 – this difference is elaborated. Perception grasps *that* something is the case – a particular fact – while intellect grasps *why* it is the case – the underlying universal cause:

The senses do not tell us the *why* (τὸ διὰ τί) of anything, e.g. why fire is hot; they only say *that* (ὅτι) it is hot. (*Met.* 981b12–13)

This seems to leave a great deal to perception: perception suffices for grasping the "thats."[42] And thus it should suffice for grasping that something is to-be-gone-for – i.e. that it is good.

An analogy with perception of an uncontroversially perceptible property may be helpful. A baby or buffalo can feel the wetness of water: as Aristotle would put it in the language of the *Met.* passage quoted above, without presumably meaning to make a point about explicit predication, the baby's or buffalo's senses "say that the water is wet." These creatures of course lack the ability to use the word 'wet,' and also the ability to know what wetness *is*: to grasp the universal in the Aristotelian sense of being able to give an essence-revealing definition which supplies the underlying cause. They do not know what makes wet things wet; they do not understand that what they are in contact with is in a liquid state; they do not understand what it is for something to be wet. But none of this undermines the claim that they feel the wetness of the water, in a literal and non-metaphorical sense. The water has a property, being wet, and through the sense of touch the baby and buffalo are in perceptual contact with that property – "perceptually active toward the water as wet."

Likewise, I have been arguing, if the baby or buffalo is parched then the water has a certain relational property: being good for them. Through pleasurably tasting the water, they are in perceptual contact with that relational property – "perceptually active toward the water as good." That they cannot say that it is good, nor understand what goodness is, i.e. understand what makes the water count as good, in no way undermines the claim that they perceive its goodness. That they cannot say or understand the explanation for the fact that the water stands in a certain relation to themselves in no way undermines the claim that they perceive that it does.[43]

---

[42] For an extreme interpretation along these lines see M. Frede: "Hence perception and memory... suffice to account for our experience... To go by the account in *Metaph.* A1, one gets amazingly far without reason [νοῦς]. In fact... for all practical purposes one does quite well without reason altogether, just relying on experience" (1996, 162).

[43] Compare Achtenberg: "Since good means *telos* or its variants, when we see something as good, then, we are seeing it as a *telos* or as *teleion* or a *teleiôsis*, and so forth. We may not be articulately aware of what we are seeing, any more than a person who sees various items as circles may be articulately aware of the criterion on the basis of which he or she is selecting certain items out and collecting them together. Aristotle would say that the universal is in the perceptions, though we may have the perception more than once and still not know the universal (*Met* 1.1 980a27-981a7)" (2002, 65).

Thus our account of pleasure as value-perception is deflationary enough to avoid attributing to perception powers which Aristotle reserves for thought. But one might worry that in meeting this demand it has become too deflationary to respect Aristotle's claims that we desire the pleasant *because* it appears good. Our analysis of passage 3 equates perception of the good with an affective state, pleasure, and links it (either by identity or necessary causation) with a conative state, desire. Perceiving something as good is pleasurably perceiving it in a way that essentially entails desire. And this may seem to reduce perception of the good to a purely non-cognitive state. It may now seem, that is, that perceptual pleasure is not itself a way of perceiving the qualities of external objects, but rather a purely affective state, a feeling that arises from such perception as a separable result; 'perception of the good' might seem to be a mere metaphor, one we can cash out entirely in affective and conative terms.

But this is not so. Being aware of something as to-be-pursued is not simply a matter of being pleased by it, nor simply a matter of wanting it. Even if these are all ways of picking out the same state (I have argued that the first two are, and conceded some evidence for including the third), it is a state which cannot be understood simply in terms of how it *feels*, for it has an irreducibly cognitive aspect. It is a state by which one registers or discerns (κρίνει) a property of the object: the relational property of contributing to one's flourishing.

That this state is genuinely cognitive is confirmed by Aristotle's frequent implications that perceptual pleasure is an exercise of the perceptual faculty. This is strongly suggested by 3b, which calls pleasure an activity of the "perceptive mean." The simplest way to take this claim is as saying that pleasure is itself a form of perception, and this is how Aquinas takes it (construing pleasure as a form of "common perception" like perception of shape and motion).[44] There is moreover some evidence for this being precisely Aristotle's view:

The movements of *pleasures and pains and in general* (ὅλως) *of every perception* appear to begin from [the heart] and terminate there.[45] (*PA* 666a11-13, emphasis mine)

Aristotle nowhere else says that pleasures and pains *are* perceptions. But throughout the corpus he treats pleasures and pain as affections or states of the perceptual system, physiologically very similar to ordinary perception. Perception in general is a "kind of alteration" of the αἰσθητικόν, the perceptual system or perceptive capacity or part of the soul (*de An.* 415b24); in the *Phys.*, he defines pleasures and pains in just the same way, as "alterations of the αἰσθητικόν" (247a16-17). Some argue that this line from the *Phys.* must represent an Academic view that Aristotle later rejected, because it seems incompatible with *EN* VII's argument that pleasure is an activity (ἐνέργεια) rather than

---

[44] See his commentary *ad loc.*; Tuozzo (1994) argues for a similar view.
[45] Aristotle often uses 'x, y, and ὅλως z' when x and y are species of z: see e.g. *de Sensu* 436a9 ("spirit and appetite and in general desire (θυμὸς καὶ ἐπιθυμία καὶ ὅλως ὄρεξις)"), and *EN* II.5 1105b21–23 ("I mean by passions appetite, anger, fear... pity, in general (ὅλως) those things which pleasure and pain attend").

movement or process (κίνησις). If Aristotle changed his mind about whether pleasure is an activity or process, however, he remained constant about the capacity of which it is an activity or process: as we have just recalled, 3b from the *de An.* calls being pleased an activity (a way of ἐνέργειν) of the "perceptive mean."

When we turn to Aristotle's discussions of pleasure in the *EN*, we find confirmation that pleasure is at least intimately related to perception. *EN* VII defines pleasure as "unimpeded activity of a natural state" (ἐνέργειαν τῆς κατὰ φύσιν ἕξεως... ἀνεμπόδιστον, VII.12 1153a14-15). On a common way of understanding this claim, it identifies pleasure with pleasurable activities, and thus like the *PA* identifies perceptual pleasures with perceptions: pleasures are unimpeded activities, so when the activity of perceiving is unimpeded, it is not only pleasurable but is itself pleasure. *EN* X seems to offer a different view: as we saw above, it identifies pleasure as what "completes the activity" of perception (or thought) (*EN* X.4 1174b20-23). If pleasure is what completes the activity of perception then it is not identical with perception. This is at least a natural way to take Aristotle's point, in the above passage and later in the discussion:

Pleasures in activities... are so indivisible (ἀδιόριστοι) from them that it is disputed whether the pleasure is the same as the activity. Still, it does not seem likely that (οὐ μὴν ἔοικέ γε) pleasure is thought or perception – for that would be bizarre (ἄτοπον) – but on account of it being inseparable (τὸ μὴ χωρίζεσθαι) it appears to some to be the same. (*EN* X.5 1175b30-35)[46]

In fact, Aristotle may hold that pleasure is one species of perception – value-perception – while denying that it is identical with the perceptions of non-value properties from which it arises. (The pleasure of tasting water would thus be a perception of its value, distinct although "inseparable" from the perception of its taste.) Even if he means to be denying that pleasure is identical with any perception, however, *EN* X is compatible with 3b and with *Phys.* 247a16-17 (which calls pleasure an alteration of the αἰσθητικόν). If pleasure is an inseparable effect of activities, not identical with them but somehow "a supervening perfection like the bloom of youth on those in their prime" (*EN* X.4 1174b33),[47] then the pleasure proper to each activity is so closely bound up with the activity that the activity could not occur without it – would not be that very activity. And thus there is an intrinsic difference between the perceptual system on occasions when there is no pleasure and occasions when there is; pleasurable perceptions are different, *qua* perceptions, from non-pleasurable ones.

Thus on either view of pleasure, when one feels pleasure in the taste of food one's perceptual system is functioning differently from the way it functions when one feels no pleasure in the taste. And since the nature and function of the perceptual system is to discriminate (κρίνειν), this psychophysical difference makes for a cognitive difference as well. When one perceives the taste in an impeded or incomplete way, as for example

---

[46] Corcilius takes this as strong evidence against the view that pleasure is literal value-perception.
[47] Ἐπιγινόμενόν τι τέλος, οἷον τοῖς ἀκμαίοις ἡ ὥρα.

when one is ill, one merely registers (κρίνει) the taste. When one perceives it perfectly or completely – which is to say, perceives it pleasurably – that perfect exercise of the perceptual system registers the value of the food as well.

This is not to downplay the aspects of Aristotle's account of value-perception that make it sound at times non-cognitivist. Perceiving something as good is inseparable from having "pro-attitudes" toward it: being in favor of it, being disposed to pursue it, being pleased by it. But it does not reduce to these non-cognitive states. Even though it is an affective state (and on some interpretations of 3c a conative one as well), it is at the same time a genuinely cognitive state: perceptual discrimination of a perceptible feature of an external object.[48]

I submit, then, that we have in Aristotle's view of perceptual pleasure an account of evaluative perception that strikes the balance between too deflationary and too robust. This is not to say that the balance is easy to strike, nor that Aristotle has expressed himself as clearly as one could wish. If my analysis is correct, then the notion Aristotle is getting at is a difficult one, and it is understandable that in trying to express it one might wind up saying things that sound contradictory. Consider Themistius' attempt to explicate 3a-c:

> Perception is not able to grasp (ἀντιλαμβάνεσθαι) the good nor the bad, but only the pleasing or painful, while discerning (κρίνειν) the good and bad belongs only to intellect... But nonetheless perception supposes (οἴεται) the pleasant and the good to be one, and the painful and the bad. For (γοῦν) it draws one towards pleasant things and turns one away from painful things. (Themistius, *Commentary on Aristotle's de Anima*)

Perception cannot grasp or discern the good, and yet it "supposes" the good to be the same thing as the pleasant – which it could hardly do if it were not in some way aware of the good after all. Themistius here ties himself in a knot much like the one Aristotle ties himself in by saying both that pleasure is perception of the good as good (3b) and that animals perceive the pleasant but not the good (*Pol.* 1253a9-18), and by saying both that appetites are for the pleasant instead of the good and that appetite is for the pleasant because the pleasant appears good.

Although Themistius goes too far in saying that perception has no grasp of the good, we can see him as aiming toward the right idea. We will be most charitable to him, and to Aristotle as well, if we take them both to hold the view I have argued for above. In one sense feeling perceptual pleasure in something does not amount to cognizing the good (and thus desires based on such pleasure do not count as desires for things *qua* good): if one cannot distinguish the good from the pleasant, one has not really discerned or discriminated it – for κρίσις is a matter of separating something out from other things.[49] But in another sense feeling perceptual pleasure does amount

---

[48] For a similar view of perceptual pleasure as at once cognitive, affective and conative see Charles 2006 (although he argues that what is cognized is pleasantness rather than goodness); for a parallel view about decision (προαίρεσις) see Demos 1961-2.

[49] That is the original meaning of the word, still present in its other meanings (judge, distinguish, discriminate).

to cognizing the good: in being pleased by something, we are aware of it as to-be-gone-for, and thus (note Themistius' γοῦν) are aware of it as good. One upshot of this combination is that a creature who can recognize the good only through perceptual pleasure will not be aware that there is or could be any way in which things are good other than by affording pleasure: a dog does not recognize that water is to-be-gone-for because it is beneficial, for example, for it is aware that water is to-be-gone-for only insofar as its awareness of the water is pleasurable. And thus it is reasonable to say, as Themistius does here, that perception "supposes the pleasant and the good to be one"; it is also fairly natural to say, as Aristotle does at times, that perception-based desires are desires for the pleasant instead of for the good.[50]

Perhaps the clearest way to put the point is this: Those who deny that pleasure can count for Aristotle as genuine cognition of the good are thinking of cognizing the pleasant as alternative to cognizing the good. Sometimes Aristotle himself speaks that way. But I have been arguing that he in fact thinks, at least so far as perception is concerned, that cognizing the pleasant is a *way* of cognizing the good – a confused way, in that it fails to distinguish the good in any way from the pleasant, but a genuine way nonetheless.

2.5 Higher modes of cognition

In this chapter I have given an account of perceiving the good. But the notion which I want to establish as crucial to Aristotle's ethical views in Parts II and III is a somewhat different one: having an appearance of the good, where this is a function not directly of perception but of a more complex psychological capacity which derives from perception, *phantasia*. I turn to an account of the apparent good in the next chapter, but as we will see this account is much indebted to the account of the perceptible good we have seen here. For I will argue that Aristotle's understanding of perception's relation to the higher modes of cognition – *phantasia* and thought – entails that appearances and thoughts of the good must ultimately derive from perceptions of it.

This is a view I will call Aristotle's Practical Empiricism. Just as perception is on his account at the basis of theoretical cognition (see especially *Met.* I.1 and *APo.* II.19, discussed in Chapters 7 and 8), so practical perception is at the basis of all practical cognition. Pleasurable perceptions give rise to appearances (*phantasiai*) of goodness, which in turn form the basis for our thoughts about goodness – and hence for even our most rational desires.

---

[50] I argue that Plato holds a similar view of the appetitive part of the soul, in my 2006. Compare Price on Plato: "[I]t will fit the same phenomena to say that appetite aims only at pleasure and takes no interest in the good, or that it identifies the good with pleasure. Indeed, both may be true, according to different conceptions of the good: on a determinate conception [e.g. the good as the beneficial], to pursue only pleasure may be to turn one's back on the good...; on an indeterminate one, to pursue anything is to take it as a goal and so as part of the good" (1995, 50-51).

This will have important repercussions for Aristotle's moral psychology, which I discuss in what follows. But it also will provide another reason for counting perceptual pleasure as genuine cognition of value, in addition to the ones I have given above: according to Practical Empiricism, such perception forms the basis for our concept 'good.'

Given an epistemology like Aristotle's, the perceptual state one is in when all is going well and one looks at something square deserves to be called "perceiving as square" both because it is caused by squareness in an external object and because it is on the basis of such perceptions that one comes to have a concept of squareness. If pleasurable perception provides the inductive basis for the concept of goodness – and I argue in Chapter 8 that it does – then it deserves to be called "perceiving as good" for the same kinds of reasons.

3

Phantasia and the Apparent Good

We began in Chapter 1 with Aristotle's claim that all desire is for the apparent good. One might take this in a broad or loose sense: we only desire what seems good to us, i.e. what we find good through one mode of cognition or another. If this is right, then Aristotle uses 'apparent' (*phainomenon*) simply to indicate subjectivity and the possibility of error. We desire things not precisely in virtue of their being good, but in virtue of their goodness (or seeming goodness) being manifest to us – appearing to us. Moreover, as he says in passages like 2e from the *de An.* (desire can be "correct or not correct," and therefore the object of desire is "either the good or the apparent good"), we sometimes want things that are *merely* apparently good – that appear to be good but are not. As we have seen, Aristotle makes use of both these senses of 'apparent' in his discussion of wish in *EN* III.4: each person wishes for what appears good to her, but only to some people do things appear as they are.

It is sometimes suggested, however, that 'apparent good' in the passages on the object of desire should be taken in a narrower or more technical sense: as what we find good through one particular cognitive capacity, *phantasia*.[1]

We have already seen some evidence for this in the close connection Aristotle draws in several passages between *phantasia* and the apparent good. Recall the passage from the *EE* which we saw in the Introduction:

> The object of desire and of wish is either the good or the apparent good. And this is why the pleasant is an object of desire, for it is an apparent good; for some believe it is [good], and to some it appears [good] although they do not believe it so. For *phantasia* and belief are not in the same part of the soul. (*EE* VII.2 1235b26-29)

There are also two passages from the discussions of locomotion which make this connection. The *MA* implies that *phantasia* can "hold the place" of intellect in causing action precisely because the apparent good can "hold the place" of the good as an object of desire (1a-b); similarly, the *de An.* passage noted above (2e) implies that the object of desire is either the good or the apparent good precisely because we apprehend things as objects of desire either through intellect or through *phantasia*.

---

[1] See Segvic 2002, for an extended defense of this view; compare Charles 1984, 89, Hudson 1981, Richardson 1992, Freeland 1994, and Destrée 2007.

I have two aims in this chapter. First, I want to show that the discussions of locomotion also provide more comprehensive, systematic evidence for the connection between *phantasia* and the apparent good. They show that every locomotion-inducing desire is based, directly or indirectly, on an evaluative *phantasia* – a quasi-perceptual appearance of the desired object as good. Second, I want to show how the account of evaluative perception given in the previous chapter yields, in conjunction with an account of what precisely *phantasia* is, a detailed account of what it is for something to appear good through *phantasia* – an account of the notion of the apparent good. In the remainder of the book, I will argue that this very same notion of apparent goodness, the notion which this chapter shows to be crucial to Aristotle's account of locomotion, also plays a central role in his moral psychology and ethical views.

3.1 *Phantasia* in action

We have seen that Aristotle identifies two psychological causes of locomotion: desire and cognition. Neither the *MA* nor *de An.* discussions dwell much on which form of cognition plays which role in different cases of locomotion. Both strongly imply, however, that one particular form plays a role in every case: *phantasia*.

In the *MA*, the desires which cause locomotion are based only indirectly on thought or perception, but directly on *phantasia*:

The affections suitably prepare the organic parts, and desire the affections, and *phantasia* desire. This itself comes about either through thought or through perception. (*MA* 702a17-19)

A later passage characterizes movement as non-voluntary when neither *phantasia* nor desire controls it (*MA* 703b8-11), implying that these two are necessary conditions of voluntary movement. The *de An.* implies an equally crucial role for *phantasia*:

Locomotion is always for the sake of something, and is with *phantasia* or[2] desire. (*de An.* 432b15-16)

These passages seem to imply that *phantasia* is not merely one among several possible occupiers of the cognition-role in locomotion, but specially necessary for locomotion.[3] But why should this be so?

The question has received a fair amount of attention from scholars, and there is widespread agreement at a very general level (see citations below): locomotion is goal-directed movement ("always for the sake of something," *de An.* 432b15), and Aristotle must think that it is through *phantasia* that creatures apprehend objects as goals. Many have also recognized that in the case of animal action, apprehending objects as goals at least sometimes involves recognizing them as pleasant, and therefore that *phantasia* is

---

[2] Some emend the text to read 'and,' which would seem to capture Aristotle's view better (since he has been arguing that cognition and desire cause action together). In any case, it is significant that *phantasia* alone is mentioned, rather than perception or intellect.

[3] In fact, the *MA* seems to equivocate, sometimes arguably implying that perception can cause locomotion without the help of *phantasia*. See discussion below.

somehow responsible for associating objects with pleasure.[4] I accept both these claims, and offer arguments for them below. But why is *phantasia* necessary for these tasks – why cannot perception or intellect suffice? To answer this one must address the question discussed in Chapter 1, of what cognition as a genus contributes to locomotion; one must also address another and very vexed question, the question of what *phantasia* is and how it operates. Most accounts that have been offered of *phantasia*'s role in locomotion depend, I will argue, on mistaken answers to one or both of these questions.

As to the first question, we have already seen that Aristotle presents cognition in general as contributing to locomotion by cognizing things as good, as well as by identifying means to ends. Moreover, we have seen strong evidence for the evaluative role of *phantasia* in particular, in the passages that correlate practical *phantasia* with the apparent good (1a-b and 2e-f). Many commentators have recognized these implications, and argued (or assumed) that *phantasia* plays its crucial role in action precisely by receiving appearances of things as good, thereby rendering them objects of desire – goals.[5] (This is compatible with *phantasia* playing an instrumental role as well; the claim is simply that this is not what makes it necessary for locomotion, for the instrumental role could equally be played by perception or intellect, while for some reason, yet to be determined, the evaluative role must be played by *phantasia*.)

But what is it for something to appear good through *phantasia*, and why should such appearances be necessary for motivation? To answer this we need to turn to the second question, the question of what *phantasia* is.

A few things are clear. *Phantasia* is a close relative of perception, found in most animals as well as humans. It is more sophisticated than perception, in that the simplest animals lack it, but less sophisticated than reasoning or intellect, in that many non-rational animals have it. But beyond this, trouble lies: there is a marked lack of scholarly consensus about *phantasia*'s nature, scope, and role.[6] (There is even a difficulty about what it should be called: the word is standardly translated 'imagination,' but this is widely acknowledged to be misleading. It has its root in the verb φαντάζεσθαι, to appear or be made apparent, and thus to capture the literal force we should have to say something like 'being-appeared-to';[7] as this is awkward, I prefer to leave it untranslated.)[8]

The difficulty in giving a unified account of *phantasia* arises from the fact that Aristotle makes it responsible for a wide range of psychological phenomena, while

---

[4] See for example Irwin 1990, 318; Modrak 1986, 60; Lorenz 2006, Chapter 9.

[5] See those cited in footnote 1.

[6] Detailed and influential discussions are to be found in Nussbaum 1978; Schofield 1978; Modrak 1986 and 1987; Wedin 1988; Caston 1996 and 1998; Everson 1997; Lorenz 2006. I will not here take on a full discussion of these different views, but I refer to them where most relevant in what follows.

[7] As does White 1990, 7; cf. Everson 1997, 181.

[8] The situation is further complicated by the fact that Aristotle uses *phantasia* to refer variously to a capacity (as arguably at *de An.* 438a1-4), to the exercise of that capacity (as at *de An.* 428b11), and sometimes even to its contents or deliverances, apparently interchangeably with *phantasma* (as at *Insomn.* 460b20, quoted below). This is in fact very natural: compare a similar ambiguity in our 'perception.' For clarity's sake I will use the untranslated *phantasia* to refer only to the first two of these, translating the last use as 'appearance.'

defining it in such a way as to make this breadth mysterious. In the passages where he offers definitions of *phantasia*, he characterizes it as a close relative of perception (αἴσθησις), and emphasizes its role in nonstandard perception and perceptual error (see quotations below). This makes sense of its role in perceptual illusions (*de An.* III.3, *Insomn.*), and arguably also in dreams (*Insomn.*) and memory (*Mem.*). (I consider these subjects in Chapters 4 and 5.) The role Aristotle attributes to *phantasia* in other passages, however, is much broader: it is necessary for all thought (*de An.* 427b16, 431a14-17, 432a8-14; *Mem.* 449b31), and – as we have seen above – for all locomotion. This hodgepodge of roles has led to a notably wide variety of interpretations of *phantasia*, and some declare it futile to search for a unified account at all.[9] Why should the same capacity by which we experience dreams and after-images play a crucial role in all thinking, or – of most direct concern to us here – in moving from place to place?

I want to show that Aristotle does have a unified account of *phantasia*, one which adheres to the definitions he offers while also accounting for its role in motivation. (The necessity of *phantasia* for practical thought is the topic of Part III; I will there show briefly how my account explains *phantasia*'s necessity for theoretical thought as well, but the main concern of this book is with the practical sphere.)

3.2 *Phantasia*: the basic conception and beyond

Aristotle's most extended discussions of *phantasia* are in *de An.* III.3 and in the *Insomn.* The first discussion is concerned to distinguish *phantasia* from perception and thought, while the second aims to show how *phantasia* accounts for dreams and other perceptual illusions, but there is a good deal of consistency between the two. Here is a brief and I think largely uncontroversial account of the common claims, using the *Insomn.*'s more elaborate description of the psychophysical mechanisms of *phantasia*.

When in ordinary circumstances a perceiver, human or animal, comes into appropriate contact with a perceptible object (e.g. when her eyes are open and functioning well and a visible object is nearby and well lit), the object produces a change or movement in her perceptual system: what the *Insomn.* calls an *aisthêma*. To become aware of the *aisthêma* is to exercise perception – to perceive the external object.[10] Sometimes – arguably always, although Aristotle is not explicit on this point – the *aisthêma* gives rise to a further movement, more or less similar to itself: a *phantasma*. This further movement may go undetected, but if it reaches the central organ of perception,

---

[9] For example: *phantasia* always plays a role in actual perception as well as quasi-perception (Ross 1949); it is instead a capacity only for "non-paradigmatic sensory experiences" (Schofield 1978, 252); it instead interprets perceptions (Nussbaum 1978); it is instead a general representational capacity that plays a part in all cognitive functions (Wedin 1988); or, as Hamlyn concludes, "[T]here is clearly little consistency here" (comment *ad de An.* 427b27).

[10] I am following Everson's (1997) language here: to say that one is aware of the *aisthêma* is not to say that it is the object of one's perception; rather, one perceives the external perceptible object by being aware of the *aisthêma*.

the heart, one becomes aware of it. And to become aware of the *phantasma* is to exercise *phantasia*: "*phantasia* is that in virtue of which we say that some *phantasma* comes to be for us" (*de An.* 428a1-2).[11] Thus *phantasia* is "a movement arising from actual perception" (κίνησις ὑπὸ τῆς αἰσθήσεως τῆς κατ' ἐνέργειαν γιγνομένη, *de An.* 429a1-2; *Insomn.* 459a17-18).[12]

This account entails three central claims about *phantasia*:

(1) *Phantasia* always arises from perception – that is, every episode of *phantasia* is based in some way on an episode of perception:

Phantasia... belongs to perceivers and is of the objects of perception. (*de An.* 428b12-13)

Phantasia... does not arise without perception. (*de An.* 427b14-16)

The *phantasmata*, or residuary movements, which are based upon (συμβαίνουσαι ἀπό) the *aisthêmata*... (*Insomn.* 461a19)

Such movements arise in our souls from earlier perceiving (ἀπὸ τοῦ αἰσθέσθαι πρότερον)... (*Mem.* 451a3-4)[13]

Each [*phantasma*] is a remnant of an actual sense-impression (ὑπόλειμμα τοῦ ἐν τῇ ἐνεργείᾳ αἰσθήματος). (*Insomn.* 461b21-22)[14]

(2) *Phantasia* is independent of perceptible objects in a way that perception is not, for one can have a *phantasia* of something not present to perception:

Things perceptible by each sense-organ produce perception in us, and the affection (*pathos*) that they make come to be is present in the sense-organs not only when the perceptions are active, but also when they have departed. (*Insomn.* 459a24-28)

Even when the external perceptible has departed the *aisthêmata* remain and are perceptible. (*Insomn.* 460b2-3)[15]

(3) *Phantasmata* are similar to the *aisthêmata* from which they arise, and therefore have similar psychological effects – and thus a *phantasia* of an object is very like the actual perception of that object:[16]

---

[11] For this account see especially *Insomn.* 460b28 ff.: during the day, certain *phantasmata* are present in the blood but knocked aside and obscured by the stronger movements of perception and thought; at night, however, with no competition from perception, these *phantasmata* "are carried to the origin of perception, and become apparent" as dreams (ἐπὶ τὴν ἀρχὴν τῆς αἰσθήσεως καταφέρονται καὶ γίνονται φανεραί, 461a6-7).

[12] My account here follows Everson (1997, 175-177) and Caston (1998, 274).

[13] With reference only to the *phantasmata* that constitute memories.

[14] With reference only to the *phantasmata* that constitute dreams.

[15] ... ἐμμένει τὰ αἰσθήματα αἰσθητὰ ὄντα. Aristotle must here be using *aisthêmata* in a broad sense that includes *phantasmata* – i.e. as the genus of perceptible affections of the perceptual system as a whole, produced, directly or indirectly, by perceptible objects.

[16] This requires some clarification. To take an example from the *Insomn.* (460b7), if the sight of a person in the distance triggers a *phantasia* of one's enemy, the *aisthêma* from which this *phantasia* arises, and to which it is similar, is not the *aisthêma* directly produced in seeing the person in the distance but rather an *aisthêma* produced in the course of some previous perceiving of one's enemy.

Things appear in whatever way not only when a perceptible object moves a sense, but also when the sense by itself alone is moved, provided only it is moved in the same manner as it is by the perceptible object. (*Insomn.* 460b23-25)

Since... *phantasia* seems to be a movement and arises not without perception but for perceivers and of what perception is of, and since movement may arise from the activity of perception (ὑπὸ τῆς ἐνεργείας τῆς αἰσθήσεως), and this must necessarily be similar (ὁμοίαν) to the perception, this movement [i.e. *phantasia*] cannot happen without perception nor belong to nonperceivers, and the one who has it does and undergoes many things in accordance with it. (*de An.* 428b10-17)

One must think of this kind of thing that arises through perception [i.e. a *phantasma*]... as like a kind of painting (ζωγράφημα)... For the movement that arises imprints a kind of imprint (τύπον) of the *aisthêma*, just like those who seal things with signet-rings. (*Mem.* 450a27-32)

Because *phantasiai* remain [after the perceiving is over] and are similar to (ὁμοίας) the [original] perceptions, animals do many things in accordance with them. (*de An.* 429a4-6)

I submit that (1)-(3) exhaust the features that Aristotle consistently and explicitly attributes to *phantasia*. If that is right, then *phantasia* is essentially the capacity to have an experience very like the perception of some x but which is not directly caused by perceptual contact with any actual x (where x is a proper, common, or incidental perceptible – e.g. pinkness, roundness, a pig).[17] It is a capacity for making present to the mind something one has perceived before. Let us call this the basic conception of *phantasia*.

Now that we have an account of *phantasia*, our question is: how does this explain *phantasia*'s role in action? And here there seems to be a difficulty, for *phantasia* on the basic conception is most easily interpreted as a capacity for non-standard perceptual experiences like after-images, dreams, hallucinations and perceptual illusions. Indeed, several of Aristotle's most explicit and detailed characterizations of *phantasia* – including *Insomn.* 460b23-25, quoted under (3) above – come in the context of explanations of how illusions come about (see Chapter 5 for discussion).[18] But if *phantasia* is nothing but a capacity for experiencing illusions, then it can play a role only in a very small and strange set of actions: things like sleep-walking to get a dream-banana, barking at one's reflection in the mirror, or fleeing from someone who looks from far away like one's enemy.

One might think, then, that to explain *phantasia*'s role in locomotion – its ability to present objects as goals – we have to go beyond (1)-(3) and posit functions for it that are not explicit in Aristotle's texts. And indeed, recent literature has offered various versions of this claim.

---

[17] That there is *phantasia* of all three categories of perceptibles is strongly implied at *de An.* 428b25-30.

[18] Briefly, to have an illusion as of x is to have one's perceptual system affected as it would be by x itself; what directly causes the experience is not any perceptible object, but instead a *phantasma*, produced from an *aisthêma* of x which was produced in turn from past perception of x. When the stranger in the distance appears to be one's enemy the culprit is a *phantasma* of one's enemy, arising from past perception of him. When one appears to see Coriscus in a dream the culprit is a *phantasma* of Coriscus produced in the same way. And in keeping with this account, when the sun appears a foot wide (*Insomn.* 460b16-20, *de An.* 428b3-4) the culprit is – I would argue, although others have thought a more complicated explanation necessary – a *phantasma* of a foot-wide object, arising from past perception of one.

On the first, *phantasia* does not merely preserve or echo perceptions, but somehow interprets them. Through bare perception we can become aware of an object, but only through *phantasia* can we apprehend it as something we might want to pursue or avoid: *phantasia* "somehow presents the object of desire to the animal in such a way that it can be moved to action" (Nussbaum 1978, 240). On Nussbaum's account, this means interpreting proper perceptibles as aspects of incidental ones, i.e. of substances – lions or leaves, predators or prey:

> [P]*hantasia* is the faculty in virtue of which the animal sees his object as an object of a certain sort, so that we can say the perception has for him some potentially motivating content.... [W]hen we perceive a rose by sight, it is not the rose *qua* rose, but the rose *qua* white that acts upon our sight. But to be moved to action an animal has to become aware of something *qua* what-it-is-called; he has to see the man as a man, not just as pale. The forms said to be presented by *phantasia* were forms of the pleasant and the fearful, hence necessarily of the thing as a unitary object under some description, not just as an assortment of various perceptible characteristics. We are always passively receiving perceptual stimuli; but when we actively focus on some object in our environment, separating it out from its context and seeing it as a certain thing, the faculty of *phantasia*... is called into play. (Nussbaum 1978, 255-259)[19]

This certainly goes beyond the basic conception of *phantasia*: Nussbaum here attributes to *phantasia* a role nowhere explicit in the texts. But there are positive reasons to doubt the interpretation as well. First, whether or not he gives a clear account of how it is possible, Aristotle certainly speaks as if perception on its own, without the help of *phantasia* (or thought) can perceive all three classes of perceptibles.[20] We have seen this in 1d from the *MA*: "'This is drink' says perception *or phantasia* or thought" (701a32-33, emphasis mine). It is also (inconclusively) implied by a passage that seems to characterize *phantasia* as "movement arising from the activity of... these three [kinds of] perceptions," (*de An.* 428b25-429a2): if *phantasia* is what arises from the perception of common and incidental perceptibles (as well as of proper ones), then it is presumably not involved in that perception itself. In the same vein is what we have seen under points (1) and (3) above: if *phantasia* works by *simulating* perception, then there must be some content already contained in perception for *phantasia* to simulate – the content of perception on its own must be very similar to the content of *phantasia*.

Thus we should reject the idea that *phantasia* provides us with goals by interpreting the data of perception in the way Nussbaum describes. But others have also thought that practical *phantasia* works by somehow going beyond what perception can do on its own:

---

[19] Compare Schofield on *de An.* 428a14-15: "in *phantasia* we consciously or unconsciously interpret the data of our senses... [when we try to identify something in difficult conditions] we may have to exercise our imaginations, comparing and contrasting what we *can* see with the way familiar middle-sized things of our everyday acquaintance look, before we are able to conclude that it looks like a man; we may have to try seeing it under different aspects before we succeed in seeing it as a man" (Schofield 1978, 113). See also Richardson 1992, 385.

[20] Nussbaum is not alone in thinking that *phantasia* plays some role in ordinary perception: compare e.g. Caston 1996 (on the perception of common and incidental perceptibles) and Wedin 1988.

[Locomotion is produced by] a two-part cognitive process. *Aisthêsis* [perception] or *noêsis* [thought] presents an object, and *phantasia* elaborates on the object, reinterpreting it in the light of anticipated pleasures and pains. This description secures a place for *phantasia* even in cases where a different cognitive faculty presents the object. (Modrak, 1987, 97)[21]

I take Furley (1980) to be putting forth a related view: animals and people are moved by external objects because through *phantasia* we are able to see them *as* objects of desire, i.e. as good in some way.

On these views, *phantasia* is necessary for locomotion because it is only through *phantasia* that objects appear pleasant or good to us, thereby becoming objects of desire. These interpretations are right about something important: as I argue below, it is because *phantasia* is both pleasure-involving and evaluative that it plays its crucial role in action. But this is not enough to show why it should be necessary for locomotion. Perception on its own can be pleasurable or painful. And I argued in Chapter 2 that perception on its own can also be evaluative: one can perceive something as good. And thus perception on its own can be motivating: pleasurable perception, i.e. evaluative perception, essentially entails desire (see passage 3 – *de An.* 431a8-12). If this is right, then there is no special need for *phantasia* to interpret the data of perception as pleasant or good, nor to associate perceived objects with pleasure and goodness.[22]

There is a third strategy for explaining *phantasia*'s role in locomotion which also goes beyond the basic conception: on Lorenz's version, *phantasia* represents things as goals by letting creatures "envisage prospects." The idea is that what motivates a creature to locomote must be something much more complex than the mere representation of a (proper, common, or incidental) perceptible property that has been perceived at some point in the past. Rather, "the formation of purposes that motivate animals to engage in locomotion...always, or at least typically, involves accomplishing the cognitive

---

[21] See also: "Desire is always for the sake of something (433a15).... In the case of inarticulate desires, for instance, the desires of non-human animals, there must...be some representation of the object as desirable.... The association of pleasurable or painful sensations with certain objects as a result of past experience could play this part. Φαντασία would serve as the vehicle for these associations, by presenting the sensible qualities to which these sensations attach" (Modrak 1986, 60).

[22] One passage in *de An.* III.10 seems to imply that perception on its own cannot give rise to desire: "Insofar as the animal is capable of desiring (ὀρεκτικόν), this much is it capable of moving itself. But it is not capable of desiring unless it has *phantasia*" (*de An.* 433b27-29). If we take this to mean that perception never gives rise to desire without the help of *phantasia*, however, the passage is flatly contradicted by 1e from the *MA* (desire comes either through perception *or* through *phantasia* and thought – *MA* 701a35-36), and by the straightforward reading of passage 3 from the *de An.*, which either claims that pleasurable perception essentially gives rise to desire or even equates the two, with no mention of *phantasia*, and with a clear implication in the next lines that *phantasia* causes desire by simulating perception. It is also contradicted by another passage from the *de An.*: "All animals that have touch also have desire. About *phantasia* [whether they have it] is not clear..." (*de An.* 414b15-16) – for if we can know that an animal has desire, and therefore the ability to go for its good, without knowing whether or not it has *phantasia*, then *phantasia* cannot be a condition of desire. For a compelling argument that what Aristotle must mean at *de An.* 433b27-29 is merely that perception on its own cannot give rise to the desires that motivate locomotion – i.e., desires for absent or distant goals – see Lorenz 2006, Chapter 10.

task of envisaging a prospective situation" (2006, 131) – envisaging oneself drinking water, say, or taking shelter under a leaf. Therefore, *phantasia* plays a necessary role in locomotion because it is through *phantasia* that we envisage such situations.

This account is faced with the burden of showing two things which it is difficult to show: first, that Aristotle has in mind a crucial role for *phantasia* which he nowhere mentions, and second, that *phantasia* even in lower animals is capable of representing something as complex as "situations."[23]

One might reply that Aristotle's discussion of *phantasia*'s role in locomotion is cryptic enough that we are forced to go beyond the basic conception and offer speculative accounts. It is worth bearing in mind, however, that Aristotle not only consistently presents *phantasia* as exhausted by the basic conception, but also seems to claim that this conception suffices to account for *phantasia*'s role in locomotion. This comes out explicitly in the last passage quoted above under claim (3):

Because phantasiai remain and are similar to the perceptions (διὰ τὸ ἐμμένειν καὶ ὁμοίας εἶναι), animals do many things in accordance with them. (*de An.* 429a4-6, emphasis mine)

Through *phantasia* an agent can have an experience that is psychologically similar to the perception of some particular object, even when that particular object is not there to be perceived, and it is this very fact that explains why the agent "does things in accord with" *phantasiai* – acts on them. Aristotle's claim here is that *phantasia* contributes to animal action just by preserving and reproducing perceptions – not by interpreting them, or synthesizing them, or in other ways going beyond what perception on its own could do were it being actually exercised on the appropriate object at the moment. All the interpretations canvassed above hold that *phantasia* contributes to locomotion by

---

[23] Lorenz admits the first as a difficulty ("It should be acknowledged at once that, unfortunately, Aristotle does not say, in the *De Motu Animalium* or anywhere else, that animal locomotion always or typically involves envisaging prospects" (2006, 131), and gives compelling arguments to show how Aristotle could have extended his account of phantasia to address the second. I think, however, that interpretative charity dictates that if we can explain *phantasia*'s role in action without going beyond what Aristotle actually says about *phantasia* then that is just what we should do. The most explicit evidence Lorenz gives that animal motivation involves envisaging prospects is *EN* III.10 1118a23: the lion taking pleasure in the sight of the stag is pleased ὅτι βορὰν ἕξει, which Lorenz translates as "that he is going to get a meal," concluding that the lion takes pleasure "in the prospect of eating" (2006, 131). But the point of the passage is to show that animals take pleasure in sounds, sights, and smells only incidentally, i.e. because those are associated with other perceptions or experiences that provide pleasure in themselves: as the corresponding *EE* passage (III.2 1231a5-10) puts it – with no mention of anything as sophisticated as "that he is going to get a meal" – the smells animals enjoy are "the ones which we enjoy either in expecting or remembering, like those of foods and drinks, for we enjoy these on account of another pleasure." Thus arguably the ὅτι at *EN* 1118a23 should be taken as a 'because'; in that case the claim is just a variant on what we got at a19-20: "Dogs do not enjoy the scents of the hares but the eating." The point then is that the sight of the stag triggers in the lion a pleasurable anticipation of stag-taste; this fits perfectly with the account I go on to give below. (Malcolm Heath has pointed out to me another reason to doubt that animals do something so complex as envisage prospects: Aristotle at one point denies that they can "experience expectation and anticipation of the future (ἐν ἐλπίδι γίνεσθαι καὶ προσδοκίᾳ τοῦ μέλλοντος)" (*PA* 669a18-21) (although he elsewhere does attribute expectation to animals: see *HA* 612a12 on the panther who ἐλπίζουσα).)

adding some content to what we get from perception, and yet this is precisely what Aristotle's own account seems to deny.[24]

Now, the view that practical *phantasia* adds no content to perception is only mysterious if we assume that perception on its own cannot motivate – but I have argued in Chapter 2 that it can. To make sense of *phantasia*'s role, then, we need only two things. First, we need evidence that *phantasia*, by simulating perceptions, can motivate in the same way that perceptions do – that is, that *phantasia* can preserve and reproduce not just what we might call the narrowly representational content of perceptions (their representations of things as blue, sweet, round, and so on), but also their motivating character – the aspects of perception that make practical perceptions practical. Second, we need an explanation of why *phantasia* should be necessary for locomotion even if perception on its own can motivate.

In the next section, I show how to answer these demands. The argument will yield not only an explanation for *phantasia*'s role in locomotion that sticks to the basic conception, but also an account of the notion we have had in view all along, the notion of the apparent good.

3.3 Practical *phantasia*

We saw above that Aristotle presents *phantasia*'s ability to cause locomotion as a consequence of its similarity to perception: "*Because phantasiai remain and are similar to the perceptions, animals do many things in accordance with them*" (*de An.* 429a4-6, emphasis mine). I want now to show that one crucial similarity is affective similarity: *phantasiai* preserve the pleasurableness or painfulness of the perceptions from which they arise.

As I mentioned above, the idea that pleasure plays some central role in the explanation of how *phantasia* causes action is not a new one: several interpreters have given accounts on which *phantasia* at least sometimes renders something an object of desire by associating it with pleasure.[25] But most of these interpretations mention this as one among various functions of practical *phantasia*, rather than as the central feature which renders *phantasia* necessary for locomotion. One account does show that pleasure is central: Whiting's (2002) (which turns on a reading of passage 3 (*de An.* 431a8 ff.) similar to the one I offered in Chapter 2). I agree with much of Whiting's account, but there is one difference in our views which will be important for my analysis of the apparent good: she argues (as I interpret her) that *phantasia* motivates by representing objects as pleasant or painful.[26] I will argue that *phantasia* motivates by being *itself* pleasurable or painful, just like perception.

---

[24] I owe this last way of putting the point to Thomas Johansen (in conversation); Johansen gives an account of *phantasia*'s role in action which sticks to the basic conception, and with which I am mostly in agreement, in Johansen forthcoming.
[25] See e.g. Modrak 1986, 60, Lorenz 2006, 119, and Irwin 1990, 318.
[26] Animals "need to *move* in order to take in nourishment. So they need something to *motivate* them. This is the role played by pleasure and pain, which are essentially *motivational* states, states that simple animals are

58   THE APPARENT GOOD

As we have seen, on Aristotle's view the perception of any proper, common or incidental object of perception can give rise to a *phantasia* of that object: *phantasia* preserves and copies what we might call the narrowly representational component of perceptions.[27] But Aristotle also represents *phantasia* as preserving and copying the affective component of perception: its pleasurableness or painfulness. This emerges from two passages outside our main texts that are concerned with central functions of *phantasia*, memory and expectation:

Since to be pleased lies in perceiving a certain affection (ἐστὶν τὸ ἥδεσθαι ἐν τῷ αἰσθάνεσθαί τινος πάθους), and *phantasia* is a kind of weak perception (αἴσθησίς τις ἀσθενής), [and] some *phantasia* of what a person remembers or expects [or hopes – ἐλπίζει] would always attend in remembering or expecting – if this is the case, it is clear that pleasures come simultaneously to those who are remembering and expecting, since there is perception there, too.[28] Thus it is necessary that all pleasant things are either present in perceiving or past in remembering or future in expecting; for people perceive the present, remember the past, and expect the future. (*Rhet.* 1370a27-35)

[A]ll of ethical virtue is about bodily pleasures and pains,[29] and these are either in acting or in remembering or in expecting. The ones in action are on the basis of (κατὰ) perception, so that they are moved by some perceptible, while those in memory and in expectation are from this (ἀπὸ ταύτης) [i.e. are due to the perception]: for people are either pleased in remembering as they experienced, or in expecting as they will experience (οἷα ἔπαθον μεμνημένοι ἥδονται, ἢ ἐλπίζοντες οἷα μέλλουσιν). So that it's necessary for all such pleasure to arise from perceptibles (ὑπὸ τῶν αἰσθητῶν).... (*Phys.* 247a7-14)[30]

If the actual tasting of water was pleasurable, then so too will be the memory of tasting it, or the anticipation of tasting some more. Here Aristotle is following Plato's characterization of expectations (or 'hopes' – ἐλπίδες) in the *Philebus*: they are pleasures

---

moved either to sustain or to end and that complex animals – capable of representing them in imagination – are also moved either to bring about or to avoid" (Whiting 2002, 173).

[27] I use 'narrowly representational content' to contrast with evaluative content. Since on Aristotle's view evaluation is representational (as opposed to non-cognitive), we need something like 'narrowly' to mark the difference between representing something as e.g. blue or round and representing it as good.

[28] When Aristotle says that "there is perception" in remembering and hoping he is clearly using 'perception' in a broad sense on which *phantasia* is either a species of perception or quasi-perception (αἴσθησίς τις, as in the first line of the passage). Perception narrowly and strictly so called is only of things present (*Mem.* 449b13-15).

[29] 'Bodily' might seem to narrow things down too far to make the passage a basis for any general conclusions about pleasure, but the fact that the passage identifies bodily pleasures and pains as the domain of ethical virtue indicates that Aristotle must mean the category to include all pleasures and pains relevant to action; I defend this reading further, and give my own account of why the pleasures connected with virtue are perceptual, in Chapter 8.

[30] Compare *EN* X.3 1173b18-19, which includes among the pleasures of perception (κατὰ τὰς αἰσθήσεις) "memories and expectations." The *Rhet.* passage is explicit in attributing these preservations of perception in memory and expectation to *phantasia*; the *Phys.* passage is not, but Aristotle consistently attributes memory to *phantasia* elsewhere (see especially *Mem.* throughout), and attributes expectation to it as well in the *Rhet.* passage; moreover, the claim of the *Phys.* that the pleasures of memory and expectation are ἀπὸ ταύτης – from perception – and arise "from perceptibles" reminds us very much of *de An.* III.3's characterization of *phantasia* as being of perceptibles and arising from perception.

of the soul in which we "pre-enjoy" ($\pi \rho o \chi a i \rho \epsilon \iota \nu$) some future pleasure (*Phil.* 39d4 ff.; cf. "the expectation before the pleasures will be pleasant" (32c1)). Crucially, the idea is not – or not just – that we expect *that* something will be pleasant, or remember *that* it was pleasant. Rather, the expecting or remembering is in itself pleasurable. We get some of the enjoyment of an actual experience in anticipating or remembering it: we pre- or post-enjoy it.

Moreover, this is just what we should expect Aristotle to think, given that – as we saw in Chapter 2 – he construes the feeling of pleasure as an affection of the perceptual system itself (see especially *Phys.* 247a16-17, just following the lines quoted above: pleasure is an alteration of the $a\dot{\iota}\sigma\theta\eta\tau\iota\kappa\acute{o}\nu$). If perceiving something cool on a particular occasion is not a neutral but instead a pleasurable experience then the perception of the coolness is a special perception of the kind we discussed in Chapter 2: it heats or chills the area around the perceiver's heart, i.e. it is pleasurable. Because *phantasmata* are similar to the *aisthêmata* from which they derive, and thus affect the perceiver in similar ways, we might expect the *phantasmata* that result from that pleasurable perception of coolness – and which are active in the memory or expectation of the experience – to be heating or chilling and pleasurable as well.

We get direct confirmation of this view from some passages of the *MA*'s discussion of locomotion which we looked at in Chapter 2. Moreover these passages show, I will now argue, not only that *phantasia* preserves the affective component of perception, but also that this is precisely the feature of practical *phantasia* which renders it practical – desire-inducing. We saw in Chapter 2 that perceptions contribute to motivation insofar as they are pleasurable or painful; the *MA* shows that the same is true of *phantasiai*.

First, the *MA* confirms that the basic conception of *phantasia* is sufficient to account for its role in locomotion, by stating that *phantasia* contributes to action by simulating perception:

1f. ... *Phantasiai* and perceptions and thoughts alter the parts [thereby setting off a causal chain which leads to locomotion]. For perceptions are at once a kind of alteration, and *phantasia* and thinking have the power ($\delta \acute{v} \nu a \mu \iota s$) of the actual things ($\pi \rho \acute{a} \gamma \mu a \tau a$) ... (*MA* 701b13-19)

The appearance through *phantasia* of a thing (and also the thought of a thing) has the same capacity or power ($\delta \acute{v} \nu a \mu \iota s$) to affect us as the thing itself. Clearly Aristotle does not mean that the *phantasia* of a lion can bite, nor that imagining a meal can fill one's belly. 'The power of the things' must refer instead to the way things affect us through perception, and in particular to the locomotion-inducing effects he has referred to in the first lines of this excerpt: heating and chilling the area around the heart. As he puts it shortly afterwards:

1g. Now the origin of motion is, as has been said, the object of pursuit and avoidance in the practical sphere. Of necessity heating and chilling attend the thought and the *phantasia* of these things ... (*MA* 701b33-35)

Just having a *phantasia* of an object of pursuit or avoidance is in itself a heating or chilling experience. (So too is having a thought of such things, a point to which I return in Chapter 6.) Thus *phantasia* can stand in for perception in practical contexts because its physical effects are the same as perception's. But we saw in Chapter 2 that heating and chilling are the physical accompaniments of pleasure and pain, and thus to say that *phantasia* motivates by preserving and reproducing the heating and chilling effects of perception entails that it motivates by preserving its affective component. The next lines confirm this through a discussion of the same two functions of *phantasia* at issue in the *Rhet.* and *Phys.* passages, memory and expectation:

1h. This is clear from the *pathêmata* [passions, emotions]. For daring and fears and lusts and the other bodily painful and pleasant [passions?] are accompanied by heating or chilling, some of a part and some of the whole body. *Memories and expectations, using such things as images* (εἴδωλα), are sometimes less and sometimes more responsible (αἰτίαι) for the same things [i.e. heatings and chillings]. (*MA* 702a2-7, emphasis mine)

When *phantasia* reproduces a pleasurable or painful, heating and chilling experience in memory or expectation – when it "uses such things as an image" – the result is itself pleasurable or painful, heating and chilling. This is the material counterpart of the claim we saw above from the *Rhet.* and *Phys.*: that the memory or expectation of a pleasant or painful experience is in itself pleasurable or painful.

Our *MA* passages confirm, then, that a *phantasia* arising from a pleasurable or painful perception is itself pleasurable or painful. They also confirm that it is in virtue of this fact that *phantasia* is practical: the heating and chilling of the parts around the heart that are the material accompaniments of pleasurable or painful *phantasiai*, just like those that are the material accompaniments of pleasurable or painful perceptions, set off a chain of psychophysical events that gives rise to or focuses desire, and culminates in locomotion.

Thus we have answered the first demand I laid out at the end of section 2: the basic conception of *phantasia* can account for its role in locomotion because *phantasia* preserves and reproduces the affective component of perception as well as its narrowly representational component. We do not need to go beyond the basic conception to show how *phantasia* can cause action. What about the second demand, however? If all that practical *phantasia* does is simulate perceptions – rather than add content to them by interpreting them or otherwise going beyond them, as on accounts like Nussbaum's or Lorenz's – why should *phantasia* be *necessary* for locomotion, as Aristotle implies that it is? Why doesn't perception suffice?

First, a caveat: the *MA* seems to equivocate on this point. Passages like 1a, 1d-f, and *MA* 702b21-25 (quoted in Chapter 2) imply that perception can motivate on its own; moreover, given the view that perception heats and chill the area around the heart (see 1f and 702b21-25) it is very difficult to see why perception should not be able to initiate locomotion: as a physiological matter, why should not these heatings and chillings lead to expansions and contractions and thereby to large-scale bodily movement, just as they do when it is *phantasia* which induces them? Indeed, 1f seems to imply that they do. On the other hand, other passages of the *MA* imply that *phantasia* is necessary: when perception gives rise to locomotion, it does so only by first giving rise to *phantasia* (see 702a17-19, quoted in section 1). Moreover, in the *de An.* perception is not mentioned as a mover at all: locomotion is caused either by *phantasia* or intellect, and since intellect depends on the use of *phantasia* (see below), *phantasia* is necessary for all locomotion. I thus take Aristotle's considered view to be that *phantasia* plays a necessary role.

At any rate this *should* have been his considered view, for there is a compelling account to be given of why *phantasia* is necessary. This is an account which many have offered, and which I accept in broad outline. It goes as follows:

The phenomenon Aristotle wants to explain, in *de An.* III and in the *MA*, is locomotion, or more generally goal-directed action. (See note 14 in Chapter 1.) Such movement only takes place when an animal pursues something not immediately present: something at a distance, or not in view, which it has to move to get. For when the animal is in direct perceptual contact with something she likes (actually drinking water, for example), she has no need to move around. If *phantasia* is what enables us to represent perceptibles in their absence, then it is clear why it should be necessary for locomotion: only through *phantasia* can an animal or person be aware of something not present to perception, making that thing available as an object of her desire, a goal.[31] Moreover, because there is no thinking without a *phantasma* (see e.g. *de An.* 432a3-9) – and in particular because deliberation, the kind of thought particularly concerned with action, works through *phantasmata* (see *de An.* 431a14-17 and 434a7-10) – *phantasia* is involved even when the goal is apprehended by thought. Thus all locomotion requires *phantasia*, either on its own or as a medium for thought. (I will give more detailed arguments for the claim that practical thought requires *phantasia* in Chapter 6, but Aristotle is so explicit on this point that it should be uncontroversial.)[32]

It is clear how this account will work when we plug in the view of practical cognition I have argued for above. When an animal is in perceptual contact with something

---

[31] "Creatures that have appearances [i.e. *phantasiai*] have a point of view on their environment; they can respond to particular features of it without the normal sort of physical interaction with those features (as, e.g., animals respond to the presence of water before the water wets them)" (Irwin 1990, 305). "*Phantasia* is a capacity for sensory representation that enables the representation of features and objects of various kinds that are not currently perceived by way of the senses . . . Aristotle assigns to that capacity a prominent role in the production of behaviour, and in particular in the production of purposive locomotion, because he takes it to be able to do something that perception cannot do, which is to put an animal in cognitive contact with prospective situations" (Lorenz 2006, 114); cf. Modrak 1986, 59, D. Frede 1992, 289-90 (with reference to how practical thought makes use of *phantasia* to present situations for evaluation), and most recently Yurdin 2009.

[32] There may seem to be a problem in that, as we saw in Chapter 1, Aristotle sometimes contrasts acting on *phantasia* with acting on intellect: see *de An.* 429a5-8, 433a11, 433b12, and the passages that contrast the apparent good with the good as an object of desire. But we have seen evidence that *phantasia* is involved even in thought-based action (see *MA* 702a17-19 and the other quotations in section 1 of the present chapter); we should thus take the passages which contrast *phantasia*-based action with thought-based action to be contrasting actions that involve *only phantasia* with those that also involve thought, i.e. that involve *phantasia* as a tool for thought. I return to this subject in Chapter 6.

pleasing – actually tasting water, for example – she feels pleasure, and hence desire. (Perhaps Aristotle has in mind the desire to keep on going, or simply a positive disposition toward the activity.) When she merely sees some water, however – or when there is no water in view, but she remembers or anticipates or imagines getting some – there is no strictly perceptual pleasure to instigate desire and get her limbs moving in pursuit. *Phantasia* fills this gap: since a *phantasma* of something is similar to, and has similar causal powers to, the actual perception of that thing, *phantasia* can play the motivational role that perception just now cannot. In remembering or anticipating or imagining the pleasant taste of the water, the animal is having a pleasurable *phantasia* of it; this pleasurable *phantasia* induces desire and pursuit, just as would the actual pleasurable perception. *Phantasia*'s key contribution to action is its pleasurable representation of an object not presently perceived, which thereby becomes desired as a goal.

Thus we have an account of *phantasia*'s role in action which sticks to the basic conception: practical *phantasia* preserves and reproduces practical perception, rather than interpreting perceptions or adding content to them. I have argued that this account fits better with what Aristotle explicitly says about *phantasia* than its rivals do. Nonetheless, a few comments are in order on what the account might seem to be lacking.

First, I do not mean to imply that what I have described is the only role that *phantasia* ever plays in locomotion: as we have seen in the *MA*, *phantasia* can also supply the means to a given end – that is, can supply what corresponds to a "premise of the possible." But this cannot be what makes *phantasia* necessary for action, for that role can be played by perception or thought as well. (Recall 1d: any of the three forms of cognition can supply the information "This is drink.") Much of what Lorenz attributes to practical *phantasia* makes sense of its instrumental role, and shows why in many cases perception will not suffice for this role, while *phantasia* can fill the gap. Lorenz argues further, however, that *phantasia* is necessary for this role – that perception cannot guide animals in acting appropriately to achieve their goals.[33] If he is right, we should conclude that Aristotle *should* have had a theory about how animals figure out how to realize their goals, and moreover that had he had such a theory *phantasia* should have played a central role in it. Nonetheless, Aristotle may not have had any such theory at all, for he never gives one explicitly; and – to return to the crucial point – we can explain his claims that *phantasia* is necessary for locomotion without them.

Second, it is difficult to see how merely representing an object or action to oneself – even representing it in a pleasurable, desire-inducing way – can suffice to render it a goal. What makes the pleasurable *phantasiai* which count as representations of goals any different from pleasurable memories, or hallucinations? It seems that Aristotle needs the idea of different modes of presentation: presenting something as future and attainable, rather than as past, for example, or as a mere fantasy. This looks like a real gap in the account I have attributed to Aristotle. And this too may well be a gap that could in

---

[33] Lorenz 1996, 180–1 and Chapter 11.

principle be filled by a suitably expanded or fleshed-out conception of *phantasia*. But once again, the evidence seems to suggest that Aristotle neither noticed this gap nor intended to fill it with *phantasia*.

It is of course open to us to show how in his conception of *phantasia* Aristotle has the resources to present a fuller theory of action than he explicitly presents. My claim is simply that in what he does say Aristotle has done enough to show why *phantasia* should be essential for action. The key claim is that through *phantasia* we pleasurably or painfully represent objects not directly present to perception. I want now to show, at last, that in making that claim Aristotle is giving us an account of the notion that I have claimed is central to his theory of action: the apparent good.

I argued in section 1 that both the *MA* and *de An.* discussions imply that *phantasia* causes locomotion by producing appearances of things as good. What we have seen thus far is instead an account on which *phantasia* causes locomotion by reproducing the pleasurableness of the perceptions from which it arises. But we are now in a position to see that it follows from this chapter's account of the relation between *phantasia* and perception, in conjunction with the previous chapter's account of Aristotle's view of pleasurable perception, that the two claims amount to the same thing: a *phantasia* which is pleasurable and desire-inducing *is* an evaluative *phantasia* – a cognition of something as good.

When you touch something cool you perceive its coolness: you discern or become aware of (κρίνειν) its coolness through perception. Since *phantasia* preserves and reproduces perceptions, when you have a *phantasia* – e.g. a memory or anticipation – of something cool, you have an experience very similar to the perception of coolness. You do not in this case actually perceive coolness, but given the similarity of the experience it makes sense to say that you have an appearance (*phantasia*) of coolness.

Chapter 2 showed that when you touch something cool and the experience is pleasurable – e.g. when you dive into a cool lake on a hot day – you become aware through perception not only of coolness but also something else: goodness. Thus, when you have a pleasurable memory or anticipation of coolness (e.g. when you remember or anticipate diving into a cool lake on a hot day) you are having an experience very similar to the perception of good coolness. You do not in this case actually perceive good coolness: what you have is an appearance (*phantasia*) of good coolness. Thus we can say not only that you have an appearance as of coolness, but also that you have an appearance of it *as good*. Just as to have a pleasurable perception of something is to "be active toward it as good" with perception, to perceive it as good, so to have a pleasurable *phantasia* of something is to "be active toward it as good" with *phantasia* – to have an appearance of it as good.

The appearance of goodness is thus the representation through *phantasia* – the memory, anticipation, imagination, or other quasi-perceptual simulation – of perceptible goodness.

We now have an account of the apparent good as it functions in Aristotle's account of locomotion. An appearance of goodness is a pleasurable, essentially motivating *phantasia* of an object, a representation which ultimately derives from a pleasurable, essentially motivating perception of an object of (more or less) the same type.[34]

3.4 *Phantasia* and thought

My goal in the remainder of this book will be to show that the notion of apparent goodness explained above is the very same notion which plays a major role in Aristotle's moral psychology: in his theory of the passions, his account of *akrasia*, his theory of ethical character, and even his account of rational, deliberated action. Briefly, the explanation of why *phantasia* is necessary for locomotion will also entail that *phantasia* is necessary for a range of complex human motivations: any desire or aversion directed at something not present to perception – e.g. ambition for an unrealized goal, anger at a remembered slight, or the wish (βούλησις) to live a certain kind of life – must be based on an evaluative *phantasia*. I will establish these claims in detail, and examine their consequences for our understanding of Aristotle's ethical views.

In turning to consider Aristotle's moral psychology and ethics, however, we will be turning away from phenomena that are common to humans and animals toward phenomena that are distinctively human, and this will introduce important complications. In the first part of this book I have, following Aristotle's lead in the *de An.* and *MA* discussions, examined perception's and *phantasia*'s roles in motivation very generally, not drawing distinctions between animal and human motivation. But human motivation is at least sometimes very different from animal motivation, because human cognition is very different from animal cognition. In humans, perception and *phantasia* exist alongside, in various ways subserve, and sometimes come into conflict with a higher cognitive power: thought. (By 'thought' I mean to include all the species of cognition which Aristotle attributes to humans but denies to animals: reasoning or calculation (λογισμός), thinking (διάνοια), belief (δόξα), and *nous* in its various senses. I will have something to say about the differences and relations between these kinds of thought, but mainly only insofar as they differ in their relations to *phantasia*.) In order to understand human practical *phantasia*, and thus in order to understand the role of the apparent good in ethical character and action, we will therefore need to take into account the interactions between *phantasia* and thought.

One thing we will need to consider is whether and how the capacity for thought expands the possible content of perception, and thereby of *phantasia* (since *phantasia*, I have argued, derives its content from perception). Aristotle is often taken to hold that

---

[34] There are interesting questions as to how tightly *phantasia* must be tied to actual perceived objects: although Aristotle does not say as much, it is charitable to interpret him as holding that perception of a particular cool lake (for example) can give rise to a less specific *phantasia* of some cool lake or other – what Caston explains as a representation with "indefinite singular content," or Yurdin as a "non-specific" representation (Caston 1998, 290; Yurdin 2009, 81). Moreover, as Caston also argues, Aristotle might (and should) hold that we can have *phantasiai* of things we've never perceived (e.g. dreams of dragons), because *phantasiai* can be produced as distortions of actual perceptions (Caston 1996, 49).

a thinking creature can have perceptions that a non-thinking creature cannot: on a widespread interpretation, he holds that while humans can perceive incidental perceptibles like people and trees, lower animals can perceive only proper and common perceptibles. If this is right, it stands to reason that humans can also perceive value-properties that lower animals cannot. I will consider this idea in Chapter 4's discussion of the passions, using to it explain how humans can have *phantasiai* as of things like undeserved well-doing or unjustified insults, and in Chapter 8, to explain how we can have *phantasiai* of very general things like a certain way of life.

The other thing we will need to consider is the relation between *phantasiai* and thoughts concerned with the same objects. (This is a different point from the previous: once *phantasiai* are formed, whether or not they in some way depend on thought for their content, they can stand in a variety of relations to thought.) We have already seen evidence that *phantasiai* – and indeed perceptions – can have the same content as thoughts: for example, "'This is drink' says perception or *phantasia* or thought" (passage 1d). That is to say, *phantasia* and thought can be about the same things. And this entails that there are three relations in which they can stand.

First, *phantasia* can exist in the absence of any relevant thought, as it does in animals: we can have appearances of something about which we have no thoughts at all. I will argue that this happens in humans when our rational faculty is somehow impaired, as e.g. in sleep or a fit of intense passion.

Second, *phantasia* can conflict with thought: the two can contradict one another, as Aristotle puts it in the *Insomn*. (460b19–20). I discuss cases of this kind in Chapter 5, examining conflicts between thought and *phantasia* in non-evaluative cases (perceptual illusions) and in evaluative cases (*akrasia* and its opposite, *enkrateia*).

Finally, *phantasia* can agree with thought: the two can say the same thing. In fact, even though some thoughts conflict with some *phantasiai*, Aristotle must hold that for every thought there is a *phantasia* that agrees with or otherwise supports it, for on his view there is no thought without a *phantasma* (e.g. *de An.* 431a14-17, 432a8-9). Loosely and provisionally, we may interpret this as: there is no abstraction without a quasi-perceptual image of something particular and perceptible from which one abstracts. (We will consider how this works in more detail in Part III.) And this has a very significant repercussion for Aristotle's view of practical cognition: even practical thought – intellectual judgments that something is good or bad – will presuppose corresponding evaluative appearances through *phantasia*.

This last claim has two striking consequences, ones which I mentioned in the Introduction as the most radical aspects of the view I develop in this book.

First, it opens the way for *phantasia* to play a major role in phenomena that are traditionally thought to be purely intellectual. At various points in Parts II and III I will be arguing that Aristotle characterizes as *phantasiai* cognitions that others have thought must be intellectual; that is, I will be arguing that various instances of the phrase 'apparent good' are to be taken literally, along the lines developed above, where one might think that they are to be taken in a non-technical sense as references to what the agent thinks or believes. The standard objection to my reading will be as follows: "Aristotle can't mean that passions like envy (Chapter 4), let alone decisions and wishes (Chapters 6-8) are based on literal appearances through *phantasia*, because he thinks we envy, decide on and wish for what we *think* good." To which I reply: certainly Aristotle holds that we envy, decide on and wish for things we think good. But he holds that these evaluative thoughts presuppose – in very different ways, which I elaborate in those chapters – evaluative *phantasiai*: pleasurable or painful, essentially motivating appearances derived from previous perceptions of their objects. Moreover, it is the appearances that give the thoughts their content.[35] Recognizing this fact allows us, I will argue, to make sense of aspects of Aristotle's moral psychology that vex the standard, more intellectualist view.

Second, if Aristotle holds that all evaluative thoughts derive their content from evaluative *phantasia*, and thus ultimately from evaluative perception, then his theory of human motivation gives a strikingly central role to pleasure and pain – much more central than has been generally acknowledged. I have argued above that Aristotle characterizes *phantasia* as a necessary cause of *all* motivation. Given my analysis of how *phantasia* contributes to motivation, this entails that he thinks that the apparent good is the object of all desire: not just animal, but human as well, and moreover not just appetitive desire, but even distinctively rational desire, the kind that involves deliberation and other forms of thought. And this, given my analysis of the apparent good, entails that we only desire things of a type that we have previously experienced as pleasant. I will argue in Part III that this is just what Aristotle does mean: not only does practical thought, like all thought, make use of *phantasia*, but it derives its content from the *phantasiai*; therefore we think good only the kind of thing that has previously appeared to us as good, and thus only what we have at some point pleasurably perceived.

My account of practical *phantasia* thus makes pleasure and pain crucial to all motivation. Nonetheless, as I argue in more detail in Part III, it should not be taken to imply that Aristotle is a straightforward psychological hedonist who thinks that every action and desire aims at gaining pleasure or avoiding pain. The claim is not that desire is always desire *for* pleasure, but rather that desire is always based on a pleasurable cognition of the desired object. Pleasure is the efficient cause, but not necessarily the object, of all desire.[36]

---

[35] I will argue that wishes are based directly on thoughts which derive their content from *phantasiai*, while passions are based directly on the *phantasiai*, with the derived thoughts being epiphenomenal.

[36] On this point – as on many others – the view I am attributing to Aristotle is similar to that of the British empiricists. Consider Hume's view that impressions or ideas of pleasure and pain are "the chief spring and moving principles of all [the] actions" of the human mind (*A Treatise of Human Nature*, I.iii.x), which he accounts for as follows: "An impression first strikes upon the senses, and makes us perceive heat or cold, thirst or hunger, [i.e.] pleasure or pain of some kind or other. Of this impression there is a copy taken by the mind, which remains after the impression ceases; and this we call an idea. This idea of pleasure or pain, when it returns upon the soul, produces the new impressions of desire and aversion, hope and fear..." (ibid., I.i.ii). As in 1f-h from the *MA*, motivations are based on memories or similar reproductions of pleasurable perceptions.

PART II

The Apparent Good and Non-Rational Motivation

4

Passions and the Apparent Good

> Imagery is a powerful technique for coping with negative feelings. Mental pictures can sometimes connect directly with emotional experience in a way that words can't. (N.M. Elman and E. Kennedy-Moore, *The Unwritten Rules of Friendship*)
>
> People do not feel fear and distress when they have been persuaded through *logos* that something bad for them is present or approaching, but only when they get a *phantasia* of these things. For how could someone move the non-rational through *logos* unless he sets before it some kind of picture similar to a perception (τινα ἀναζωγράφησιν προσβάληται αἰσθητῇ παραπλησίαν)? (Posidonius, fragment 162)

We have seen that Aristotle gives evaluative *phantasia* a central place in animal locomotion by characterizing appetites – the desires for the pleasant which cause most animal motivation – as being for the apparent good. But appetites are not found only in animals: they play a crucial role in human motivation too. So too do the other members of the wider class in which Aristotle groups appetites: the passions (πάθη). My aim in this chapter is to show that Aristotle construes not just appetites but all human passions as involving appearances of things as good or bad, where these are appearances of precisely the kind discussed in Chapter 3. Fear, anger, shame, love, pity, jealousy and the like involve essentially motivating, pleasurable or painful, evaluative representations through *phantasia*, derived from previous pleasurable or painful perceptions. We feel fear when we have a quasi-perceptual appearance as of something dangerous, and anger when we have a quasi-perceptual appearance as of something insulting, where these are just the sort of appearances we might have in a vivid memory or a dream. Therefore evaluative *phantasia* plays a crucial role in human motivation – and thereby in human virtue.

Versions of this account have been presented in recent work on Aristotle, and some of what I say will repeat arguments others have made.[1] But the idea that passions involve *phantasia* remains controversial;[2] I aim to bolster it by showing crucial continuities between Aristotle's treatment of the passions in the *Rhetoric* and the theory of *phantasia*'s role in motivation that I derived from the psychological works in Chapter 3.

---

[1] See Achtenberg 2002; Cooper 1996a; Nehamas 1992; Nieuwenburg 2002; Sihvola 1996; R. Sorabji 1993, 56-58; and Striker 1996.

[2] For detractors see Fortenbaugh 2002; Leighton 1996; Nussbaum 1996; and most recently Dow 2009.

4.1 Doxastic vs. phantastic accounts of the passions

It is the *Rhetoric* that gives us Aristotle's fullest treatment of the passions, as well as the most striking evidence that he construes them as involving *phantasia*. Here is one example (we will see many others below):

Fear is a pain or disturbance arising from the *phantasia* of a destructive or painful future evil. (*Rhet.* 1382a21-22)

Noticing Aristotle's frequent use of the word *phantasia* and of variants on φαίνεσθαι ('to appear') in the *Rhetoric*'s definitions, some have concluded that Aristotle holds what we might call a phantastic account of the passions: passions are based on exercises of *phantasia*. But this argument is far too quick. No one would insist that Aristotle's every use of φαίνεσθαι and its variants is meant in the technical sense of quasi-perceptual appearance: sometimes he uses these words broadly, just as in English we often use 'it appears to S that p' to mean simply 'S believes that p.' Some interpreters – call them doxastists – argue that this is how we should take Aristotle's appearance-language in the *Rhetoric*'s definitions of the passions. For (the argument goes) people are afraid of what they *believe* dangerous, not of what merely appears dangerous. Indeed, Aristotle himself evidently recognizes this in his canonical discussion of *phantasia* in *de An.* III.3 (at 427b21-24, quoted below). Morever, even in the *Rhetoric* Aristotle often characterizes the passions using words like δοκεῖν (believe) and οἴεσθαι (think) as well as appearance-words. Therefore, he must hold that passions involve not quasi-perceptual *phantasia* but instead *doxa*, belief – a state he contrasts with *phantasia* as being distinctively human and distinctively rational, i.e. dependent on *logos* (see *de An.* 428a20-24, quoted below). And thus, the doxastists conclude, his use of appearance-language in the *Rhetoric* is non-technical: it is meant to emphasize the vividness of the beliefs in question, or their subjectivity.[3]

I have two aims in this chapter. First, I want to show against the doxastists that passions do indeed involve literal *phantasiai*, the very same kind of quasi-perceptual appearances that feature in memories and dreams. While the use of appearance-language in the *Rhetoric*'s definitions may be inadequate support for the claim, there is overwhelmingly strong evidence from elsewhere. In the ethical works Aristotle attributes the passions to a part of the human soul which exercises perception and *phantasia* but is not capable of belief (section 2), which entails that if they are based on cognition at all it must be non-rational cognition, perception or *phantasia*. In the *Rhetoric*, meanwhile, Aristotle characterizes the passions as essentially pleasurable and painful, and argues that all pleasure and pain are in perception or quasi-perception,

---

[3] "[N]o technical distinction between *phantasia* and believing is at issue in any of these analyses of emotion"; "In general, the account shows no awareness of the more technical psychological distinctions of the *De Anima*" (Nussbaum 1996, 307 and note 16); see also the others cited in the previous note, especially Dow. Although Dow now acknowledges that *phantasia* does play a crucial role in the passions (MS), I will take his 2009 paper as a target in much of what follows, since it presses the doxastic view forcefully, and gives a clear presentation of the challenges that face defenders of the *phantasia* view.

phantasia; this entails that – just as the ethical works lead us to expect – the passions must be functions of either perception or *phantasia*.[4] A close look at the *Rhetoric*'s characterizations of the passions shows that they involve *phantasia* in particular: they all depend on memory, expectation, or imaginative embellishment of a situation (e.g. visualization) – which are paradigm exercises of *phantasia* (section 3). Moreover, we find precedent for this view in Plato's characterization of the passions (section 4).

My second aim is to show – where previous defenders of the phantastic interpretation have not – how this interpretation can accommodate the textual evidence and the philosophical claims that have seemed to count against it (sections 5–6). Because experiencing a *phantasia* is a way of accepting or endorsing a representation, parallel to belief, the phantastic interpretation yields a view of the passions which is both consistent and compelling. And because *phantasiai* in normal cases track or trigger beliefs, the interpretation is compatible with Aristotle's implications that the passions correspond to evaluative beliefs.

I concede that although Aristotle gives us the resources to construct a good account of the relation between passions and beliefs, he is not at all as explicit as we might wish him to be, and thus the account I propose in the last section is somewhat speculative. But the main point I wish to make in this chapter is that any interpretation of Aristotelian passions must be constrained by decisive evidence that passions involve literal *phantasia*. Whatever relation passions bear to belief, it should be clear that they are based directly on *phantasia*. Chapter 5 will strengthen this claim by examining cases in which evaluative *phantasiai* and evaluative beliefs conflict (namely, cases of *akrasia*): when this happens, I will show, passions follow *phantasia*.

4.2 The passionate part of the soul

In the course of discussing virtue in both ethical works, Aristotle appeals to a claim familiar from the psychological works: that there is a division in the human soul (*EN* I.13, *EE* II.1). He distinguishes three parts of the soul, using as his criterion their relation to *logos* – reason or rational account. One part has or exercises *logos*: the rational (λόγον ἔχον) part. Another part is utterly non-rational (ἄλογον), in no way sharing in or responsive to *logos*: the vegetative part, responsible for nutrition and growth. Then there is a third part, not rational in the strict sense – not capable of exercising reason – but rational in an extended sense, for unlike the vegetative part it is able to listen to reason (or obey or be persuaded by it: πείθεσθαι or ἀκούειν) (*EE* 1219b30, *EN* 1102b31-33).

This third part is of particular significance in Aristotle's ethics – ethical virtue is at least in large part a matter of its being in good condition[5] – because it is the seat of what

---

[4] This point is the focus of Nieuwenburg 2002; he gives it a very good defense, and some of what I say in its support repeats his arguments.

[5] See *EE* 1221b28-31, *EE* 1220a8-11, and *EN* 1103a3-5. I discuss ethical virtue, and its relation to the passionate part of the soul, in detail in Chapter 7.

he calls the passions (πάθη): appetite (ἐπιθυμία), spirit (θυμός), fear, shame, anger, boldness, malice, joy, love, hate, longing, envy, pity and others (*EN* 1106b16-17, *EE* 1220b12-13). Hence his name for this part in the *Politics*, adopted by ancient commentaries on the ethical works: it is the παθητικὸν μόριον, the passionate part of the soul.[6]

The passionate part cannot exercise reason, as we have seen, but Aristotle strongly implies that it has its own forms of cognition: perception and *phantasia*. The ethical works call the seat of the passions the desiderative part (or faculty), τὸ ὀρεκτικόν (*EN* 1102a30, *EE* 1221b31); meanwhile, the *de An.* says that the desiderative part is the same as (although "different in being from") the perceptive part (αἰσθητικόν) (431a13-14 – passage 3c from Chapter 2), which the *Insomn.* declares to stand in this same relation to the *phantasia*-exercising part (φανταστικόν) (459a16-17). This identity is confirmed within the ethical works themselves: the *EE* refers to one part of the soul as "the perceptive and desiderative" (τὸ δ' αἰσθητικὸν καὶ ὀρεκτικόν, *EE* 1219b23).[7] Thus the passions belong to a part of the soul which lacks *logos* but can exercise perception and *phantasia*. The passionate part is, as Eustratius puts it, "the animal and desiderative part in man, which is both perceptive and phantastic (τὸ ἐν ἀνθρώπῳ ζωτικὸν καὶ ὀρεκτικόν, ὃ καὶ αἰσθητικὸν καὶ φανταστικόν ἐστι)" (119, 26-27, commentary on *EN* 1103a1 ff.).[8]

These identity-claims seem straightforward, but there are some passages which have been taken to count against them. After distinguishing the strictly rational part from the part that merely obeys reason (the passionate part), the *EE* says that both are "peculiar (ἴδια) to the human soul" (1219b37-38); the same is arguably implied by the corresponding passage of the *EN*'s function argument, in which the active exercise of these parts of the soul is said to be a distinctively human life (1097b33-1098a5). Drawing on these passages, Fortenbaugh (2002) has argued that the passionate part is a division of what the biological works call *nous*, intellect: it is an "alogical" intellectual part, but intellectual nonetheless, and should not be confused with the perceptive part we share with animals.[9]

The passages Fortenbaugh cites are not, however, decisive. First, given its interactions with the rational part, the human perceptive part is so different from the corresponding part in animals that one might well call it "peculiar" to us.[10] This is

---

[6] See *Pol.* 1254b8. Aristotle implies the same in the ethical works, both by naming this part after a paradigm passion, appetite (it is the "appetitive and in general desiderative part" (τὸ ἐπιθυμητικὸν καὶ ὅλως ὀρεκτικόν, *EN* 1102a30)), and by identifying it as the seat of character, where character is defined in part as a disposition to feel passions.

[7] Rackham inserts an extra τὸ before ὀρεκτικόν, translating "the sensory and appetitive parts"; Woods follows suit, without comment. In light of *de An.* 431a13-14, however, the emendation is wholly unnecessary.

[8] For an extended argument that the non-rational part is what one might call our animal soul, see Lorenz 2006.

[9] 2002, 26-27.

[10] This is Aspasius' account of the passionate part of the soul: "Presumably (ἴσως) the non-rational and passionate part of human beings differs also from that of animals, not to the extent that it seems to differ from the nutritive part (for their passionate part has something in common with ours, because it partakes of spirit

particularly plausible given Aristotle's views about the close relation between function and essence: a part whose function is limited to promoting the creature's survival is different in nature from a part whose tasks also include providing the material for thought and obeying the dictates of reason.

Moreover, it is important to note that the *EE* calls the two parts "peculiarly human" in the course of contrasting them with the nutritive part (θρεπτικόν): Aristotle's point in this passage is that the virtues of the nutritive part play no role in distinctively human virtue, and the passage notably omits any mention of the perceptive part. Only a few lines earlier, however, he has made this same point about the nutritive part in a passage that unambiguously assigns the perceptive part a crucial role in human virtue (and identifies it, as we saw above, with the passionate part itself (1219b23)). The context there is a claim that the virtuous are no better than the vicious when asleep: he offers as explanation the fact that the virtue of the nutritive part of the soul is irrelevant to human virtue, and that

> in sleep the nutritive part is more active, but the perceptive and desiderative is non-functioning in sleep. But insofar as they in some way share in motion, even the *phantasiai* of the virtuous are better. (*EE* II.1 1219b21-5)

Unlike the nutritive part, the perceptive part plays a crucial role in human virtue. Its near inactivity in sleep explains the similarity between sleeping heroes and sleeping villains; insofar as it is active – being, in its capacity as *phantastikon*, the source of the *phantasiai* (appearances) that constitute dreams – it explains the slight difference between the two. Thus in calling the parts relevant to human virtue "peculiarly human" in the later passage, Aristotle may well mean only to be contrasting them with the part we share with plants, the nutritive part; he is evidently ignoring animals altogether at this point and so we should not mean to deny that they have a passionate part. (Note in support that the other part described as "peculiarly human" at 1219b37-38 is also in fact shared with someone non-human – God.)

In any case, Aristotle clearly holds that animals feel at least some passions (a point the Stoics had to deny).[11] It would thus be natural for him to think that the part of the soul in virtue of which we feel passions is one we share with animals, although it may be quite different in our own souls.[12]

(θυμός) and appetite and in general of pleasure and pain), but it differs insofar as it is not obedient to *logos*" (comment *ad EN* 1102b13).

[11] See e.g. animal appetite and spirited passion (θυμός), at *EN* 1111b12-13 and *EE* 1225b26-7, anger, at *Rhet.* 1380a24-26; envy, at *HA* 608b10 and 619b27-31, and many passages on fear. (For further citations and discussion, see Sihvola 1996.) The doxastist has to say that what animals have is "only analogous" to human passions (see Fortenbaugh 2002, 69); this is not only at odds with Aristotle's many unqualified attributions of passions to animals but is also (as Sihvola argues) undermined by *HA* 588a18-26, which implies that animal passions differ from human ones only in degree.

[12] Fortenbaugh has another argument against equating the ethical works' ἄλογον part with the perceptive part: it makes nonsense of the *Politics*' claim that natural slaves wholly lack the rational, deliberative part (*Pol.* 1260a13) (2002, 53). For if what slaves are left with is what we share with animals, how can they be human

As to the other passage Fortenbaugh cites, from the *EN*'s function argument, Aristotle might hold that the life devoted to the exercise of the perceptive part is subhuman while still holding that the distinctively human function involves the (distinctively human) exercise of that part. Indeed, this is strongly implied by a later passage:

> To live is defined for animals by the capacity for perception, and for humans [by the capacities for] perception and thought.... To be [for humans] is to perceive or to think. (*EN* IX.9 1170a16–b1)

I conclude, then, that the ethical works attribute the passions to a part of the soul that exercises perception and *phantasia*. This fits very well with Aristotle's characterization of the passions in the *de An.*:

> The soul does not appear to undergo (πάσχειν) nor do most things without the body, such as to get angry, feel confidence, have an appetite, in general (ὅλως) perceive; thinking (τὸ νοεῖν) seems most like something peculiar to the soul... The passions (πάθη) of the soul all seem to be with the body: spirit, calmness, fear, pity, daring, and further both friendliness and hatred. (*de An.* 403a5–18)

On the *prima facie* reading of the 'in general' in 403a7, this passage outright identifies the passions as species of perception.[13] On any reading, it shows that the passions do not belong to the intellectual part of the soul, but have more in common with perception. Compare an argument from *EN* X.8: the life of ethically virtuous activity is more human than the quasi-divine life of excellent intellectual activity, because "some passions even seem to arise from the body, and character-virtue is much yoked to the passions" (1178a14-16). Intellect is in some sense separable from the body, but passions are not – and hence cannot be functions of intellect.

All this leads us to expect Aristotle to say that passions, insofar as they involve cognition of any kind, involve non-rational cognition – perception or *phantasia*. And when we turn to his more extensive discussion of passions, in the *Rhetoric*, this is just what we evidently find.

---

beings who use and understand language, and why should they "partake in *logos* to the extent of perceiving but not having it... whereas other animals do not perceive *logos* but obey passions" (*Pol.* 1254b22-24)? But Aristotle seems not to see a problem here: he says explicitly in the ethical works that barbarians, who are natural slaves are "by nature unreasoning and live only by perception (ἀλόγιστοι καὶ μόνον τῇ αἰσθήσει ζῶντες)" (*EE* VI/*EN* VII.5 1149a9-10). The notion of linguistically competent humans equipped only with a cognitive resource shared with animals may well be incoherent; all I can say is that if there is anywhere in Aristotle's works that we should positively expect incoherence, the discussion of natural slaves is it. (For an argument that Aristotle does in fact attribute some rational capacities to natural slaves, see Heath 2008.)

[13] So Nussbaum and Putnam 1992, 44. As they mention, Aristotle often uses ὅλως to indicate the species/genus relation: see e.g. *EN* II.5 1105b23, quoted in Chapter 3, note 45.

4.3 Passions in the *Rhetoric*

The *Rhetoric* instructs orators in the methods of persuasion, among them the art of playing on the audience's passions. In the service of that task it offers definitions and discussions of the passions much more elaborate than those we find in the ethical works – although consistent with the details the ethical works do provide.[14] What emerges, I will argue, is an account of the passions as having three essential features: they are pleasurable or painful; they involve evaluative representations; and these representations are the work of *phantasia*.

The *Rhetoric* offers one general definition of the passions as a class, which we will consider below, but we can begin with the more detailed definitions of the individual passions. Aristotle defines and discusses thirteen passions. Nine have much in common, so much that they seem to form a natural class. The other four are quite different, do not conform to the general definition of the passions, and are perhaps included only in deference to popular usage; I mostly ignore them in what follows. What I aim to offer is an account not of everything that Aristotle lists as a passion, but of a natural class which lines up roughly with that list: a group of psychologically similar states which are central to his notion of ethical character. If I can show that anger, pity, fear, confidence, shame and a few others are, like appetite, based on *phantasia*, I will have shown that evaluative *phantasia* plays a very important role in Aristotle's ethics.[15]

We have seen one above: fear is a pain arising from the *phantasia* of a future evil. Here are the others:[16]

Anger is desire, accompanied by pain, for revenge for an apparent (φαινομένην) slight. (*Rhet.* 1378a30-31)

Shame is a pain or disturbance concerning things appearing (φαινόμενα) to lead to loss of reputation; Shame is a *phantasia* of a loss of reputation. (*Rhet.* 1383b12–13; 1384a22)

Confidence (θάρσος) is the opposite [of fear] ... so that hope of safety is accompanied by the *phantasia* of it as being close, while frightening things are absent or far off. (1383a16-19)

---

[14] The avowedly practical intent and endoxic method of the *Rhetoric* does not preclude its being a source of a genuinely Aristotelian view of the passions: as Sihvola puts it, "A good orator has to be familiar with the emotions, because he must be able to *produce* them in his hearers. In order to do this in a reliable way it is not sufficient to know what people *think* the emotions are; he must also know what they really are" (1996, 53). For further defense see Fortenbaugh 1970.

[15] The passions I exclude are friendliness (φιλία), hatred or enmity (τὸ μισεῖν, ἐχθρά), kindness (χάρις), and unkindness (τὸ ἀχαριστεῖν). The last two I ignore completely, for although the *Rhetoric* catalogues them as passions they do not seem to belong to the same class as the others at all. (As Kennedy puts it, the discussion of these "differs from others on the emotions in that it primarily focuses on what *kharis* is, neglecting the state of mind of those who exhibit it" (1991, 149).) The definition of hatred explicitly excludes a feature common to the other passions and listed in the general definition of the passions (quoted below): it is without pleasure or pain. Thus it seems that neither it nor its opposite (friendliness) should really be classified as passions proper; for further discussion, see below.

[16] Calmness (πράυνσις) is defined as the opposite of anger, and so presumably shares anger's general features: it is pleasant where anger is painful, and involves appearances of good things (hope) where anger involves appearances of bad. I have not quoted its definition only because it is less explicit on these points than the others.

Pity is a pain taken in an apparent (φαινομένῳ) evil, destructive or painful, befalling one who does not deserve it, which one might anticipate oneself or someone close to one suffering, and this whenever it appears (φαίνηται) near. (1385b13-16)

To be indignant (νεμεσᾶν) is to be pained by someone apparently doing well undeservedly (ἐπὶ τῷ φαινομένῳ ἀναξίως εὐπράγειν). (1387a8)

Envy (φθόνος) is a pain taken in the apparent doing well (ἐπὶ εὐπραγίᾳ φαινομένῃ) of those like us. (1387b23-24)

Rivalry (ζῆλος) is a pain taken in the apparent presence of goods (ἐπὶ φαινομένῃ παρουσίᾳ ἀγαθῶν) possible for oneself to take, among others like oneself. (1388a32)

Also useful to us will be Aristotle's descriptions, in the context of a discussion of pleasure in *Rhet.* I.11, of states that he elsewhere characterizes as passions:

And victory is pleasurable ... for there is a *phantasia* of superiority, which all desire. (1370b32-34)

And honor and reputation are among the pleasantest things, through each person's *phantasia* that he has the qualities of an excellent person. (1371a8-9)

To be liked is pleasurable. There, too, the good, which all who perceive desire, is present to someone in his *phantasia*. (1371a18-20)

Despite some important differences, all these definitions and descriptions have enough in common to justify us in inferring several theses about the passions as a class.

First: all the passages characterize the passions as involving representations of value. Fear arises from the appearance of a future evil (μέλλοντος κακοῦ), pity is for an apparent undeserved evil (κακῷ), pride and ambition (at issue in the passages on victory and honor) involve representing oneself as superior to others, or excellent, or good. Anger is a response to an apparent slight (ὀλιγωρία) (being treated as less worthy than one is); indignation, envy and rivalry involve representations of others as doing well, or doing well undeservedly. There is a question as to what precise relation holds here: are passions themselves evaluations, or partly constituted by evaluations, or responses to them? Shame *is* a *phantasia* of something bad, while anger merely arises from such a *phantasia*; arguably Aristotle did not notice the tension here, having had no determinate view of the matter. What is clear, however – and what suffices for my purposes – is that passions essentially involve evaluations. To be afraid of death entails finding death bad; to be proud of a victory entails finding that victory good. Passions, then, are somehow dependent on evaluative cognition; Aristotle holds some version of what is now called a cognitivist account of the emotions. But what species of cognition does he have in mind?

Given my argument in section 2 that the ethical works attribute the passions to a non-rational part of the soul, we should expect it to be a non-rational form of cognition, and the passages quoted from the *Rhetoric* above certainly seem to confirm this: they characterize the passions as responses to how things appear.[17] If Aristotle is

---

[17] A few passages in the ethical works use similar language: see especially the discussion of the frightening at *EE* 1229b13-18.

here using *phantasia* and appearance-words in the same sense as he does in the psychological works, then his point is that passions involve quasi-perceptual representations, exercises of the psychological capacity for *phantasia* – which is, as I mentioned above, just what many interpreters take him to mean.

There is a controversy here, however, for as I mentioned above an influential line of interpretation denies that passions involve exercises of *phantasia* at all, arguing that they must instead involve beliefs. This doxastic interpretation draws apparent support from many passages in the *Rhetoric* itself, for Aristotle frequently characterizes the passions in ways that imply dependence on intellectual cognition. To take a striking example, only a few lines after characterizing fear as arising from a *phantasia*, Aristotle adds:

If fear is accompanied by the anticipation (προσδοκίας) of suffering some destructive thing, it's evident that no one who thinks (οἰομένων) that he will suffer nothing is fearful, nor [do people fear things] they do not think (οἴονται) they will suffer... Necessarily, then, those who think (οἰομένους) they will suffer something are fearful. (1382b29-33)

Likewise, the description of the object of pity as an apparent evil which appears close at hand (see above) is immediately explained by the claim that

it is clear that it is necessary for the one who is going to feel pity to think (οἴεσθαι) that some evil is present of the sort that he or one of his own might suffer. (1385b16-18)

In these passages Aristotle mixes talk of how things appear with talk of how people think things are.[18] Doxastists think there is a clear explanation: he does not mean to be marking any difference between the two. Aristotle's view is that the passions involve beliefs, and when he uses appearance-language he does so in a non-technical sense, to show that the passions are responses to things represented in a particularly vivid way, or to things *merely* apparent, or to things as one takes them to be.

I grant that we should never simply assume that Aristotle's use of the verb φαίνεσθαι or its participle φαινόμενον is technical; moreover, there are clearly passages in the *Rhetoric* which use such words in connection with the passions with the sense of 'manifest,' and arguably others which use them with the sense of 'dubious' or 'merely subjective.'[19] (The doxastists' point is much weaker as regards the noun *phantasia*, which occurs in six of the descriptions of passions: there is no established, widespread use of the word to mean 'vivid belief' or 'subjective belief,' nor does Aristotle himself frequently use it in a non-technical sense, as interchangeable with δόξα.[20]) But there is positive evidence that the *Rhetoric*'s appearance-language is technical, evidence that the doxastists ignore.

---

[18] See also 1387a24-25 (on indignation), which alternates between δοκεῖν and φαίνεσθαι.

[19] For 'manifest,' see especially the claim that we pity people most when "the suffering is apparent (φαινομένου) before our eyes" (1386b5-7).

[20] Dow 2009 cites *EN* 1114a32-b3, but I will argue in Chapter 7 that Aristotle has the quasi-perceptual sense in mind here too. Some passages in the *Met.* may count, but arguably even here there is a connection with perception.

Most unequivocal are some lines which follow closely on the first definition of a specific passion, the definition of anger:

And a kind of pleasure attends all anger, from the hope of getting retaliation...A kind of pleasure follows on account of this and also because people dwell in their minds on retaliating; the *phantasia* that then occurs produces pleasure, *just as does the phantasia that occurs in dreams* (ἡ οὖν τότε γινομένη φαντασία ἡδονὴν ἐμποιεῖ, ὥσπερ ἡ τῶν ἐνυπνίων). (1378b1-10, emphasis mine)

This is an explicit comparison between *phantasia*'s role in a paradigm passion and its role in one of the phenomena attributed to it by the psychological works, dreams (see *Insomn.*, throughout, and *de An.* 428a8). Anger and vengeful hope are pleasant for the same reason that sweet dreams are: they involve pleasure-inducing quasi-perceptual representations – *phantasiai*.

But we need not rely on a single passage. In what follows, I argue that the implication of the passage on anger is systematically borne out by Aristotle's discussion of passions in the *Rhetoric*, revealing his use of appearance-words to be narrow and technical throughout. (This will leave open a subtler doxastic interpretation, on which passions involve beliefs that are based on or accompanied by *phantasiai*; I consider and argue against this Stoicizing interpretation in section 4.)

We can begin with the *Rhetoric*'s very first mention of *phantasia*, in I.11's discussion of pleasure – a passage we saw in Chapter 3:

Since to be pleased lies in perceiving a certain affection (ἐστὶν τὸ ἥδεσθαι ἐν τῷ αἰσθάνεσθαί τινος πάθους), and *phantasia* is a kind of weak perception (αἴσθησίς τις ἀσθενής), [and] some *phantasia* of what a person remembers or expects [hopes – ἐλπίζει] would always attend in remembering or expecting – if this is the case, it is clear that pleasures come simultaneously to those who are remembering and expecting, since there is perception there, too. Thus it is necessary that all pleasant things are either present in perceiving or past in remembering or future in expecting; for people perceive the present, remember the past, and expect the future. (*Rhet.* 1370a28-35)[21]

We saw in Chapter 3 that *phantasia* as characterized in the psychological works is quasi-perceptual experience, derived from and similar to actual perceptual experience. This passage's definition of *phantasia* as "a kind of weak perception" is very naturally taken as a layman's formula, suitable for Aristotle's avowedly pragmatic purposes in the *Rhetoric*, of the psychological works' more technical "movement arising from actual perception." Meanwhile, its claim that "some *phantasia* of what a person remembers...would always attend in remembering" conforms to the *Mem.*'s

---

[21] In this passage and some others I translate ἐλπίζειν and ἐλπίς as 'to expect' and 'expectation,' but they also have the more specific sense of positive expectation, i.e. hope. 'Expectation' brings out that what Aristotle has in mind is the counterpart of memory: quasi-perception of the future. But we should also keep in mind the other sense, hope, to recall that ἐλπίς is pleasurable. Plato groups ἐλπίς with other passions, in the *Philebus* (see section 4 below); I suppose Aristotle excludes it because he thinks it a component or cause of other passions.

arguments that memory is itself an operation of *phantasia* (450a12-13 and throughout). Thus far, then, Aristotle is evidently using *phantasia* in its technical sense in the *Rhetoric*.

I want now to show that this "weak perception" passage entails that the passions as Aristotle characterizes them in the *Rhetoric* must involve literal *phantasia*. First I will establish that Aristotle holds the following:

(i) All pleasant and painful experiences involve perception or *phantasia*.
(ii) The passions are essentially pleasant or painful.

From this it follows that the passions must involve either perception or *phantasia*. Then I will argue that his specific characterizations of the passions show that he also holds:

(iii) The passions are directed at non-present objects,

from which it follows that they must involve not (just) perception but (also) *phantasia*.

The weak perception passage gives us half of claim (i): all pleasure lies in perceiving or in quasi-perceiving – remembering or anticipating something perceived, i.e. exercising *phantasia*. A later passage makes the same claim about pain: "the things which cause pain are all perceptible" (1382a10).[22] Thus insofar as something is pleasurable or painful, it must involve perception or *phantasia*. Another passage we saw in Chapter 3 makes the same point about the pleasures and pains relevant to ethical virtue, which certainly include passions:[23]

> they are either in acting or in remembering or in expecting. The ones in action are on the basis of (κατὰ) perception, so that they are moved by some perceptible, while those in memory and in expectation are from this (ἀπὸ ταύτης) [i.e. are due to the perception]: for people are either pleased in remembering as they experienced, or in expecting as they will experience (οἷα ἔπαθον

---

[22] The full sentence runs: "The things which cause pain are all perceptible, while things which are especially bad, injustice and folly, are least perceptible (τὰ μὲν λυπηρὰ αἰσθητὰ πάντα, τὰ δὲ μάλιστα κακὰ ἥκιστα αἰσθητά, ἀδικία καὶ ἀφροσύνη): for the presence of vice (κακίας) causes no pain" (*Rhet.* 1382a10-12). Aristotle's argument is hard to follow here: he is distinguishing between hatred and anger, and it is difficult to make sense of these lines in context. In particular it is difficult to know what to make of the claim that injustice, folly, and in general vice are "least perceptible": on what theory of perception is an insult or undeserved good fortune perceptible (and hence pain-inducing), but injustice not? Perhaps, in keeping with Aristotle's distinctions between perceptibles and intelligibles as discussed below, the idea is that insults, greed, and other manifestations of vice are observable, while vice itself is the underlying cause of such behavior, and as such merely intelligible. Alternatively, Aristotle might mean 'perceptible' in a looser sense here, intending the point that one's own injustice and folly tend to escape one's notice.

[23] The *Phys.* passage refers to these pleasures and pains as bodily (σωματικάς), which might seem to restrict (i) to a quite uncontroversial claim about the pleasures of food, drink, and sex, with little bearing on the passions. But given that the *Phys.* identifies these pleasures and pains as the ones relevant to virtue, this cannot be right: the pleasures and pains which virtue is 'about,' according to the ethical works, are not just the pleasures of touch and taste and the like but also fear, anger, envy, and the other passions (see note 25). Compare the *EN*'s claim that ethical virtue involves passions and is therefore, unlike intellectual virtue, connected to the body–soul compound, because passions "appear to be human [as opposed to divine]. Indeed, some even seem to arise from the body" (1178a14-16). The *de An.* shows that passions are bodily (μετὰ σώματος) in the sense of having physical aspects: anger, for example, involves the boiling of the blood (403a16-403b1).

μεμνημένοι ἥδονται, ἢ ἐλπίζοντες οἷα μέλλουσιν). So that it's necessary for all such pleasure to arise from perceptibles (ὑπὸ τῶν αἰσθητῶν).... (*Phys.* 247a7-14)

(In the *EN* Aristotle presents a different view: there are pleasures of thought distinct from pleasures of perception. But here it is clear that he does not think passions are pleasures of this kind: he explicitly contrasts passions with these intellectual pleasures of contemplation (see especially *EN* X.8 1178a14-16, quoted in section 2).)

Claim (ii) is explicit right from the start of Book II's discussion, where Aristotle offers a general definition of the passions as a class:

The passions are those things on account of which, by undergoing change, people come to differ in their judgments (κρίσεις), *and which pain and pleasure attend* (ἕπεται): for example, anger, pity, fear, and other such things and their opposites. (*Rhet.* 1378a19-22)

The definitions of individual passions, quoted above, bear this out: fear, shame, pity, indignation, envy and rivalry *are* pains, anger is accompanied by pain; confidence, being the opposite of fear, is presumably pleasant, as are the passions alluded to in I.11's discussion of pleasure (pride and ambition). Moreover, Aristotle makes the same claim in his general definitions of passions in both ethical works: passions are attended by pleasure and pain.[24] These works also assert an essential connection between passions and pleasure and pain in their frequent claim that virtue is "about pleasure and pain" (see e.g. *EN* 1104b8-9, 1172a20-25; *EE* 1220b37, 1221b39), for this feature of virtue turns out to be due in large part to its connection with the passions.[25]

Clearly, then, Aristotle holds that the passions stand in a very close relation to pleasure and pain (although it is far less clear that he has a consistent overall account of what precisely that relation is).[26] There is no feeling these passions without feeling

---

[24] "By passions I mean appetite, anger, fear, daring, malice, joy, love, hatred, longing, jealousy, pity – in general, those things which pleasure and pain attend (ἕπεται)" (*EN* II.5 105b21-23); "By passions I mean things like this: spirit (θυμός), fear, shame, appetite – in general those things which for the most part perceptual (αἰσθητική) pleasure and pain attend in themselves" (*EE* II.2 1220b12-14). (I comment on the significance of the *EE*'s "for the most part" and "perceptual" below.)

[25] Character-states like virtue and vice "are conditions of the passions, and the passions are defined (διωρίσται) by pain and pleasure; so that on account of this and on account of the earlier theses, it results that all ethical virtue has to do with pleasures and pains" (*EE* II.4 1221b36-39); "Virtue and vice are about excesses and deficiencies of pleasures and pains, and the pleasures and pains arise from the dispositions and passions (παθήματα)" (*EE* II.5 1222b10); cf. "One must take as a sign of people's characters the pleasure or pain that supervenes on their deeds" (*EN* II.3 1104b3-5), where the pleasures and pains in question are evidently states like calmness or fear, i.e. passions. To say that character is a state of being disposed to have certain passions (as at e.g. *EE* II.1 1220b7-10) is to say that character is a matter of being disposed to be pleased and pained in certain ways, pleasurably and painfully affected by things around one.

[26] Anger, shame, pity, indignation, envy and rivalry are all identified with pains, while fear is only "accompanied by" (μετά) pain; the I.11 passages might be read as identifying appetite, love and the others as species of pleasure, but they leave open the possibility that the relation is weaker, i.e. mere accompaniment. This is an indeterminacy we also see in the general definitions of the passions quoted above from the *Rhetoric* and from the ethical works: that pleasure and pain "attend" (ἕπεται) the passions might mean that they necessarily result from the passions, but (given Aristotle's use of "attend" elsewhere) might mean something stronger: Aspasius interprets the claim as meaning that pleasure and pain are the genera of which passions are species. I do not propose to argue that either of these views (or a related one, or hybrid)

pleasure and pain, and this is no contingent fact: part of what it is to feel these passions is to feel pleasure and pain.[27] And insofar as passions are essentially pleasurable or painful, they must, given claim (i), involve perception or *phantasia*.

Now we are ready to show that they involve *phantasia* in particular. *Rhet*. I.11's "weak perception" passage emphasizes that *phantasia* has the power to preserve not only the narrowly representational content of perception but also its affective component: in remembering or anticipating the taste of a delicious cake, one has a quasi-perception through which one re- or pre-experiences not only the taste but also the pleasure.[28] This power to preserve the affective component of perception is, we saw in Chapter 3, the very power that enables *phantasia* to play its crucial role in motivation. Directly following the weak perception passage, Aristotle shows how this same power explains the pleasurableness of various passions. He begins with anger:

Things remembered are thus pleasant.... And things expected... And in general, things that give delight when present [are pleasant], both when we expect them and when we remember them, for the most part. *Wherefore* (διό) even being angry is pleasant... (1370a35–b11, emphasis mine)

Memory and expectation (hope) are pleasant because in them *phantasia* preserves the pleasantness of pleasant perceptions. And from the fact that memories and expectations are pleasant, it follows (διό) that so too is a paradigm passion: anger. (Presumably

---

is, or should have been, Aristotle's underlying or all-things-considered view. What is crucial for my purposes is something that we can derive from these texts without speculation: that the passions are essentially connected with pleasure and pain.

[27] The *Rhetoric* does present one striking exception: hatred. Although it is listed as a paradigm passion at *EN* 1105b21-23 (cf. *de An*. 403a18), which characterizes the passions as pleasant and painful, the *Rhetoric* says very explicitly that hatred is *not* accompanied by pain (and does not in any way suggest that it is pleasant) (1382a12-13; cf. *Pol*. 1312b33-4). What are we to make of this apparent contradiction? A solution is suggested by *EE* 1220b14's qualified claim about the passions: that they are attended by pleasure or pain only "for the most part." This is sometimes interpreted as meaning that all passions are merely contingently related to pleasure and pain, but the way that Aristotle builds pleasure and pain into the definitions of the individual passions in the *Rhetoric* belies this, and the characterization of hatred suggests a different interpretation: while most species of passion are essentially pleasurable or painful, hatred – possibly along with some others, although Aristotle gives no further examples – is not. Even this admission will seem to weaken the claim that pleasure and pain are essential to the other passions, or essential to them *qua* passions, but it is worth noting that Aristotle's characterization of hatred makes it look very different indeed from the other passions, so much so that we might reasonably conclude that he includes it with the others in conformity with popular opinion but conceives of it in such a way that it really belongs in a different and more rational class (perhaps along with its opposite, friendliness (φιλία)). (Notably, the *Politics*' discussion of hatred says that unlike anger it does not interfere with reasoning (λογίζεσθαι), perhaps suggesting that it is not even a state of the non-rational soul.) Thus Aristotle's treatment of hatred need not undermine the claim that nearly all the states he calls passions, and certainly all those which conform to his general definition of passions, are *essentially* pleasurable or painful. As I said above, my aim is to give an account of a group of states which Aristotle characterizes as forming a natural class, and which play a central role in his notion of ethical character, although this means ignoring a few of the states which he calls passions.

[28] See also *Physics* 247a, quoted above. In both passages Aristotle is following Plato's analysis of hopes as anticipatory pleasures in the *Philebus*: hopes are pleasures of the soul, in which we "pre-enjoy" (προχαίρειν) some future pleasure (*Philebus* 39d4 ff.; cf. "the hope before the pleasures will be pleasant" (32c1)).

Aristotle's idea is that anger involves the hopeful expectation of revenge, although the lines that follow do not make his thought particularly clear.)[29]

Next Aristotle makes the same claim about another paradigm passion, appetite (ἐπιθυμία): appetites are pleasant "*for* (γὰρ) people enjoy a certain pleasure as they remember how they got something or as they expect they will get it" (1370b16-17). The pleasantness of appetites, like that of anger, is explained by *phantasia*'s power to preserve the affective component of an experience in memory or expectation. Then Aristotle turns to love (ἔρως) (a species of appetite) and mournful nostalgia, making precisely the same point, this time emphasizing the quasi-perceptual nature of the cognitions involved. Lovers get pleasure from talking about or otherwise referring to their beloved, "for in all such things they suppose that *in remembering the beloved they are as if perceiving him* (μεμνημένοι οἷον αἰσθάνεσθαι οἴονται τοῦ ἐρομένου)"; mourners feel "pleasure in *remembering and, in a way, seeing* (ἡδονὴ δ' ἐν τῷ μεμνῆσθαι καὶ ὁρᾶν πως) [the departed] and what he used to do and what he was like" (1370b21-22; 26-28, emphasis mine). These passions are pleasant insofar as they involve memories that reproduce the experience of perceiving – that is, insofar as they involve *phantasia*.

Thus when in the lines that follow Aristotle explicitly attributes the pleasures of victory, honor, and being liked to *phantasia* (1370b23-1371a20, quoted above), we have every reason to take the word literally: the *phantasia* mentioned in *Rhetoric* I.11's descriptions of passions is the self-same *phantasia* at issue in the psychological works. And thus these passions, just like the appetites we discussed in Chapter 3, are based on evaluative appearances: on *phantasiai* which preserve the affective and motivating character of the pleasurable or painful perceptions from which they derive.

But can we extend this interpretation to cover all of Aristotle's passions? Can we use it to show that even in Book II's definitions (quoted at the start of this section) he means his appearance-talk technically? Let us return now to those, and see how we fare.

In two cases it is very easy to see a necessary role for literal *phantasia*: fear, which arises from the *phantasia* of a future evil (1382a21-22), and confidence, which is accompanied by the *phantasia* of safety being close and frightening things far off (1383a17-19). We are afraid of future things (Aristotle must mean that even when one fears the presently advancing enemy, the fear is of the future experience of being pierced by their swords), but future things are not present to perception. Essential to fear, then, is the ability to represent perceptibles in their absence – the defining feature of *phantasia*. Likewise for fear's opposite, confidence, for this too is future-directed: we are confident about future safety.

---

[29] Being angry is pleasant "for no one gets angry at those apparently unable to get revenge, and people don't get angry, or get less angry, at those who are above them in power" (1370b13-15). Presumably the second point shows that anger depends on hope of revenge (as at 1378b1, quoted above), but I am not sure what the first is meant to show. In any case, however, the "wherefore" at 1370b10 makes clear that anger is pleasant insofar as it involves memory and expectation – and therefore, as the weak perception passage shows, insofar as it involves *phantasia*.

PASSIONS AND THE APPARENT GOOD 83

In other cases it is at first less obvious that there is a role for *phantasia*. Consider anger (painful desire for revenge for an apparent (φαινομένην) slight (1378a30-31)) and pity (pain taken in an apparent (φαινομένῳ) evil (1385b13-16)). It is of course possible to feel anger or pity toward something past, or in prospect toward something future, but these passions can just as well be directed toward something present – I can be angry at the thing you are doing right now, or pity you the pain you are undergoing before my eyes – and it might thus seem that mere perception would suffice for these passions. We have already seen, however, that on Aristotle's account anger involves memory and expectation (1370b1-11), and he says just the same about pity. What we pity people for are things that we might anticipate (προσδοκήσειεν) befalling ourselves or our loved ones (1385b14); one feels pity

> .... in general whenever one is so disposed as to *remember* such things happening to himself or to one of his loved ones, or to *expect* such things to occur to him or to one of his loved ones. (1386a1-3, emphasis mine)

Thus both pity and anger turn out to involve representations of things past and future, just like confidence and fear, and we should take the variants on φαντασία and φαίνεσθαι in their definitions literally.

But is Aristotle's view that *every* species of passion involves memory or expectation? I see no evidence that it is. The way he characterizes the other passions suggests, however, that they involve visualization – and thus *phantasia* – in other roles: not now in remembering or expecting non-present events, but in imaginatively embellishing one's present situation – picturing things not present to perception even when the bare facts are thus present.

This comes out particularly clearly in Aristotle's advice to the orator on how to induce pity:

> Since sufferings are pitiable when they *appear* near at hand, while people either do not feel pity for what is ten thousand years in the past or future or not in the same way, because they do not *expect or remember* it, it is necessary that those who contribute to the effect by gestures and cries and displays of feeling and generally by acting (ὑποκρίσει) are more pitiable, for they make the evil *appear* near at hand, by *putting it before one's eyes* (πρὸ ὀμμάτων ποιοῦντες), as about to be or having been ... And most pitiable of all is the virtuous person being in such situations. For all such things better induce pity on account of making [the suffering] *appear* near, both since he is unworthy [of suffering] and since the suffering is *apparent to our eyes* (ἐν ὀφθαλμοῖς φαινομένου). (1386a29-b7, emphases mine)

Pity here is characterized as a response not to the mere awareness that someone is undergoing something bad, but to a vivid, quasi-perceptual representation, a picturing of the bad scenario as near at hand. Emulating the workings of memory and expectation, the speaker "puts something before the eyes" of the audience. Clearly the operative faculty here is *phantasia*: *de An.* III.3's canonical discussion of *phantasia* describes the exercise of *phantasia* as "to put something before one's eyes" (πρὸ ὀμμάτων τι ποιήσασθαι, 427b18-19), and in both the *Mem.* and *Insomn.*, *phantasia* "places something before one's eyes" (τίθεται πρὸ ὀμμάτων) (*Mem.* 450a5, *Insomn.* 458b20 ff.). In vividly imagining what a speaker describes, as in remembering, hoping, and dreaming, we quasi-perceptually represent absent perceptibles.

An earlier passage has implied a similar account of another passion, shame. People feel shame when they are being observed by others,

> as Cydias said to the people in the debate about the allotment of land in Samos; for he thought the Athenians *should suppose* (ὑπολάβειν) *the Greeks standing around them in a circle*, actually seeing and not only later hearing about what they might vote. (1384b32-35, emphasis mine)

Shame was defined as a response to something that apparently (φαινομένην) damages one's representation, or as being itself a *phantasia* of loss of reputation (1383b13; 1384a22). Here Cydias induces shame by making people vividly imagine the loss of their reputation – by having them entertain a shameful scenario, which is to say by engendering in them a literal *phantasia*, a quasi-perceptual representation.

In these passages it is an orator who puts something before the audience's eyes. Although Aristotle is not explicit on the point, there is a good case to be made that he thinks that we often induce passions in ourselves by putting things before our own eyes. Consider I.11's claim that winning is pleasurable on account of a *phantasia* of superiority, or that honor and reputation are pleasant on account of a *phantasia* of being like the excellent person (1370b32-4, 1371a8-9). In both these cases, someone's passion (pride or ambition) is a response not merely to publicly available facts (that she has won a victory or received some honor), but also to her imaginatively embellished representation of herself: as being superior to others, or as being like the excellent person. Something similar occurs with indignation, envy and rivalry, which are described as responses to the apparent (φαινόμενον) success of others (1387a8, b23, 1388a32): these passions are plausibly construed as depending on representations that go beyond the straightforwardly perceptible facts of the situation. One sees an enemy finely dressed and paints oneself a mental picture of his past bad deeds contrasted with his present and future indulgences; one sees a friend receive an honor and pictures it being bestowed on oneself instead.

If this is correct, it may still be the case that in every one of these passages the appearance-words connote vividness or manifestness, as some doxastic interpreters would have it. But the reason the impressions at issue are so vivid will be that they are exercises of *phantasia* – instances of picturing things to oneself, putting scenarios "before one's eyes" just as the orator does when he wants to arouse emotions. To represent absent perceptibles to oneself, combining them in new ways to create imagined scenarios, is to exercise *phantasia* in the technical sense. It may, however, often involve making the represented things particularly vivid – apparent (φαινόμενον) in a looser sense.

4.4 Platonic precedent

Given Aristotle's tendency to take on ideas from his teacher, making explicit and systematic what Plato leaves at the level of suggestion and metaphor, it should count strongly in favor of the above interpretation of Aristotle's passions that there is clear precedent for it in Plato. In two of his most detailed discussions of states which Aristotle calls passions, Plato describes these states as dependent on vivid, quasi-perceptual images. I discuss these texts in more detail elsewhere, and explore the question of whether or not Platonic passions involve rational cognition (I argue that they do not);[30] a brief look here will suffice to show that Plato makes quasi-perceptual imaginative embellishment a *necessary* condition of the passions, and thus add support to my reading of Aristotle's *Rhet.* above.[31]

Plato never offers a definition or classification of the passions as explicit or systematic as what we find in the *Rhetoric*. In many dialogues, however, he groups together anger, fear, pleasure, pain, appetites, *erôs*, and similar states, and at various points refers to them all as πάθη or παθήματα. Two dialogues offer detailed characterizations of these states: the *Timaeus* and *Philebus*.

The *Philebus* offers an implicit definition of the passions as a class: "anger and fear and longing and sorrow and *erôs* and jealousy and malice and however many other such things there are" (47e1-2) are mixtures of pleasure and pain which the soul experiences without the body (47d5-9). An earlier passage gives an extensive discussion of one psychic pleasure, hope (ἐλπίς – the same word I have translated as 'expectation' in passages from the *Rhet.* above). The passage has received a great deal of attention as a discussion of false pleasures; it is notable, however, that at the end of the discussion Socrates takes himself to have established that not only hopes but also "fears, spirited passions (θυμῶν), and all things of that sort" can be false (40e2-4) – thus implying that the passage's analysis of hope applies to the states mentioned at 47e as well, i.e. that here Plato offers an account of the passions.

What is crucial for our purposes in this account is that it presents hope as a response not only to a representation of a state of affairs, but to a vivid, quasi-perceptual representation. A scribe writes words (*logoi*) on our souls, and then a painter comes along, illustrating those words with pictures (39a-b). It is in beholding these painted *phantasmata* in our souls (φαντάσματα ἐζωγραφημένα, 40a9) – that is, in imagining certain scenarios – that we feel passions like hope. Plato gives one example:

Someone often sees (ὁρᾷ) himself in the possession of an enormous amount of gold and a lot of pleasures as a consequence. And in addition he also beholds (καθορᾷ) an inner picture of himself (ἐνεζωγραφημένον), beside himself with delight. (40a10-12)

---

[30] Moss 2012; much of this section is excerpted from that piece.
[31] Hackforth notes that the *Philebus* passage provides an antecedent for Aristotle's *phantasia* (1945, 72), and Lorenz 2006 finds precedent for Aristotelian *phantasia* in both the *Philebus* passage and the *Timaeus* one, although neither Hackforth nor Lorenz relates these passages to Aristotle's discussion of the passions.

The mere belief that one might acquire a fortune, the passage implies, will not inspire the kind of psychic pleasure that constitutes hope; but the vivid, quasi-perceptual imagination of one's future wealth will. Furthermore, the "beside himself with delight" clause shows that hope is a response to imagining the future scenario *as pleasant*: as in Aristotle, what inspires passions is not merely a quasi-perceptual image, but one representing an object as in some way good.

The other passage which suggests a similar account is from the *Timaeus*. (The passage offers an account of only one class of what Aristotle will call passions; for an argument that Plato means key features of the account to cover all the states which the dialogue calls παθήματα (a close cousin of πάθη – see *Tim*. 69c-d), see my 2012.) Timaeus has distinguished the rational part of the soul from the non-rational; now he is discussing how the latter can be controlled:

> [The gods knew that the appetitive part] was not going to understand *logos*, and even if it were in one way or another to have some perception (αἴσθησις) of some *logoi*, it would not have an innate regard for any of them, but would be much more persuaded by images and *phantasmata* night and day. The god conspired with this very tendency by constructing a liver, a structure which he situated in the dwelling place of [the appetitive] part of the soul. He made it into something dense, smooth, bright and sweet, though also having a bitter quality, so that the force of the thoughts sent down from the mind might be imprinted upon it as upon a mirror that receives the imprints and returns images. So whenever the force of the mind's thoughts could avail itself of a congenial portion of the liver's bitterness and threaten it with severe command, it could then frighten this part of the soul. And by infusing the bitterness all over the liver, it could project bilious colors onto it and shrink the whole liver ... causing pains and bouts of nausea. And again, whenever thought's gentle inspiration should paint quite opposite *phantasmata* its force would bring respite from the bitterness by refusing to stir up or to make contact with a nature opposite to its own. It would instead use the liver's own natural sweetness on it and restore the whole extent of it to be straight and smooth and free, and make that portion of the soul that inhabits the region around the liver gracious and agreeable, conducting itself with moderation during the night when, seeing that it has no share in reason and understanding, it practices divination by dreams. (*Tim*. 71a3-d4)

The passage is difficult, but we can extract from it the following account.[32] The appetitive part of our souls often experiences passions like lust and fear. As creatures equipped with a higher, rational part, we can disapprove of these passions and try to counteract them; one way for the rational part to counter existing appetitive passions is to induce new ones. If appetite is craving some base pleasure, the rational part can frighten it with the threat of painful consequences; if appetite is shrinking in fear from some noble duty, the rational part can embolden it with talk of rewards. There is, however, a difficulty about communication. The rational part has rational cognitions – thoughts – which it would naturally communicate as *logoi* (arguments, rational

---

[32] My reading of this passage has much in common with that of Lorenz 2006; it differs mainly in emphasizing the evaluative nature of the images in question.

accounts). The appetitive part of the soul, however, is not responsive to *logoi*: perhaps it has no awareness of them whatsoever; certainly it will not be persuaded by them (71a). So the good gods devised a solution: they designed our bodies in such a way that the rational part's thoughts reflect off the shiny surface of the liver, yielding images (*phantasmata*). These images, unlike *logoi*, can directly influence the appetitive part. The responses they induce are pleasurable or painful. In fact, the passage strongly implies, they are paradigm passions: fear, calm, and presumably others as well.

Thus the passage characterizes rationally induced appetitive passions as based on images. And Plato, like Aristotle, characterizes the images as quasi-perceptual. The constitution of the liver – smooth and dense – is just like that of the eyes, as described at 45b-c, which encourages us to take it that the images at issue here are very similar to those that play a role in sight; moreover, Timaeus goes on to say that these liver-images also play a crucial role in dreaming (71d-72b), which he has earlier described as a kind of quasi-perception involving the same inner processes as perception (45d-46a). Here the parallel with Aristotle is striking: *phantasia*, as we saw in the passage on anger above (1378b1-10), plays a role both in passions and in dreams.

Moreover, the content of these passion-inducing images is evaluative. The images are, as we have seen, reflections of thoughts which the rational part wants to communicate to the appetitive. These are thoughts about what to do or avoid; in particular, they are thoughts about what is beneficial to do or avoid (see 71a1-2). If these thoughts were expressed as *logoi*, the *logoi* would be exhortations, threats, warnings, or reassurances. In claiming that thoughts can be reflected as images, Plato implies that the images capture this aspect – that the images are themselves threatening or reassuring, presenting things as good or bad, to be done or to be avoided. It is this fact that lets images stand in for *logoi* in influencing the appetitive part of the soul: the rational part cannot explain to the appetitive part why it is best to pursue or refrain from some course of action, but the liver-images make the course of action simply *look* good or bad, the way something can look good or bad in a picture.

In these two dialogues, then, Plato characterizes certain states which Aristotle will call passions as non-rational, pleasurable or painful responses to quasi-perceptual evaluative appearances. And thus we should take very seriously the implications that Plato's student works with just this same view.

4.5 First doxastic objection: the contents of perception

I have given textual, philosophical, and historical arguments that Aristotelian passions are based on literal *phantasiai* – quasi-perceptual appearances. Despite all this, however, some will still protest that this cannot have been, or should not have been, Aristotle's view. They will make two objections: first, these representations have complex and sophisticated contents inaccessible to *phantasia*; second, Aristotle's use of words like δοκεῖν and οἴεσθαι in the *Rhetoric* shows that passions are for things we *believe* good or bad, rather than for things that merely appear so.[33] In the remainder of this chapter I argue that both objections are based on inadequate accounts of human perception and *phantasia*, and in particular of their interactions with intellect in the human soul.

According to the first objection, because *phantasia* inherits its representational content from perception and thus can only represent what can be literally perceived, one simply cannot have *phantasiai* of imminent danger as bad, one's neighbor as doing well undeservedly, revenge as sweet, and so on. Perception is of perceptibles, proper, common, or incidental (*de An.* II.6), but the representations involved in passions go beyond things like the white, the round, and the son of Diares. They are propositional in structure: in them one thing is predicated of another. Moreover, what is predicated are value-properties like being a slight, or doing well undeservedly, which cannot be literally perceived.

But what we saw in Chapter 2 shows that this simply does not do justice to Aristotle's view of perception. As to the worry about propositional structure, Aristotle standardly characterizes the perception of both common and incidental perceptibles as propositional: we perceive *that* (ὅτι) the white thing is round, or *that* it is a man (*de An.* 418a21-22, 430b29-30).[34] However literal or elaborate a theory of predication we take this to entail, it means there is no special problem for a theory of the passions which attributes complex representations to *phantasia*. And as to the claim that the value-properties which incite passions are beyond perception's range, we have already seen in Chapter 2 that Aristotle thinks value literally perceptible.

Perhaps this last point is not so simple: one might protest that even if we can literally perceive the pleasant and painful, or even the beneficial and harmful – the values most plausibly at issue in passage 3 from *de An.* III.7 – this does not show that we can perceive the more abstruse qualities at issue in many passions: qualities like the insulting or the undeserved. That is, even if Aristotle thinks perception can form the basis for a simple passion like appetite, he cannot think that it forms the basis for a sophisticated one like anger or envy.

Is this objection warranted? The simple response is that it cannot be. Whether or not Aristotle has an account of *how* things like insults or undeserved well-doing are perceptible, he clearly thinks that they are. As we have seen, he holds both (i) and (ii): all painful and pleasant things are perceptible, and the passions are essentially pleasurable and painful responses; therefore the things to which they are responses must be perceptible. Moreover, in assigning passions to a part of the soul which is equipped with perception but not reason, the ethical works assume the same. Additional confirmation that *phantasia* in particular can represent sophisticated, passion-inducing value-properties comes from a passage from the ethical works on anger:

---

[33] Both objections are developed in Dow 2009.

[34] For more citations and an extended argument in favor of a robust reading of these 'that's, see Sorabji 1996, which argues that having denied animals reasoning and belief, Aristotle had to build predication and propositions into their perceptions; see also Tuozzo 1994.

Logos or *phantasia* has shown that something was hubris or a slight, and spirit (ὁ θυμός), as if having reasoned that one must fight against such a thing, is distressed right away. (*EN* VII.6 1149a32-34)

Here Aristotle is clearly at pains to distinguish different forms of cognition: the contrast he draws between *phantasia* and *logos* belies a doxastic interpretation on which *phantasia* is being used in a loose sense. The clear implication is that one can have a *phantasia* of something as an outrage or an insult, and that such a *phantasia* will induce anger. With this in mind, when we read the *Rhet.*'s definition of anger as a response to an apparent (φαινομένην) slight we have good reason to take the 'apparent' in the narrow and technical sense. (Notably, the *EN* passage says that anger can also be a response to a report from *logos*; I consider this point in addressing the second doxastic objection below.)

Thus there is a simple response to the doxastist's objection: Aristotle evidently thinks that slights, undeserved good fortune, and the other passion-inducing properties are literally perceptible.[35] Perhaps this is because, as I suggested in Chapter 2, he thinks that *all* particulars are objects of perception, while only universal underlying causes are beyond perception's range.[36] Or perhaps he thinks that the perception of complicated value-properties works in a way similar to incidental perception (on a widespread interpretation thereof, mentioned in Chapter 2): intellect expands our perceptual range, so that we can literally perceive things that animals cannot (as opposed to inferentially grasping those things on the basis of what we perceive). Just as our intellectual grasp of what a rose is gives us the ability to perceive roses as roses, so too might an intellectual grasp of what an insult is give us the ability to perceive insults as insults – to perceive that someone's sneering tone is insulting just as directly as we perceive that it is loud.

At any rate, Aristotle clearly does think that such things are perceptible, and it is worth noting that he is followed, both in this view and in the assumption that it needs no defense, by his philosophical successors: the Stoics and Epicureans characterize value-impressions (*phantasiai*) as perceptual, apparently without offering any explanation or justification.[37]

---

[35] Two other considerations may seem to confirm that Aristotle thinks sophisticated value-properties literally perceptible, but we should approach them with caution. First is the *Pol.* passage we considered in Chapter 2 which says that humans "have perception (αἴσθησις) of the good and bad, just and unjust, and the others" (*Pol.* 1253a10-18). This may show that we literally perceive things like justice, but (as I urged in Chapter 2) Aristotle may instead mean 'perception' here in the loose sense of awareness: certainly there is nothing technical about the context, and taken literally the passage conflicts with a literal reading of the *Rhet.*'s claim that injustice is imperceptible (1328a10-12, discussed above). I argued in Chapter 2 that we should perhaps take the *Pol.* passage to have in mind metaphorically perceptual intellectual cognition instead, and this bring us to the second consideration: one might think that the ethical works' characterization of *phronesis* as something like perception provides further evidence that sophisticated value-properties can be literally perceived, but this would be a mistake. *Phronesis* is an intellectual virtue, i.e. a state of the rational part of the soul, and thus even though Aristotle compares it to perception in various ways those comparisons cannot support claims about the kind of cognition available to the non-rational part.

[36] See Chapter 2.4, and in particular the discussion of Michael Frede's view of rationality.

[37] Chrysippus "says that goods and bads are perceptible... '... it is possible to perceive theft and adultery and similar things, and in general, folly and cowardice and many other vices, and not only joy and benefactions and many other right actions but also prudence and courage and the remaining virtues'" (Plutarch, *On Stoic self-contradictions*, 1042e-f, trans. Long and Sedley); Epicurus "denies that any reason or

4.6 Second doxastic objection: accepting vs. believing

Doxastists also raise another objection: passions are responses to how we take things to be, rather than to how things merely appear to us, and therefore passions must be based on thoughts or beliefs rather than *phantasia*.[38] There are really two claims here, which I shall take in turn. One is based on a simple mischaracterization of *phantasia*. The other is more complex, and explaining how it goes wrong will involve a careful consideration of the relations between *phantasia* and belief.

The first claim is that *phantasia* gives us mere appearances and hence cannot induce passions. There does indeed seem to be good textual evidence for this claim, in a passage from *de An.* III.3. Aristotle is arguing that *phantasia* is not identical with supposition (ὑπόληψις, a genus whose species include belief (δόξα)). One mark of distinction, he claims, is that *phantasia*

is up to us (ἐφ' ἡμῖν) whenever we want, for it is putting something before one's eyes. ... but believing (δοξάζειν) is not up to us. (*de An.* 427b17-20)

Next comes another distinction:

Further, whenever we believe (δοξάσωμεν) something terrible or frightening, we are affected (συμπάσχομεν) straight away, and likewise for something reassuring. But with respect to *phantasia*, we are in the same condition as when we observe something terrible or reassuring in a picture. (*de An.* 427b21-24)

These lines imply that *phantasia* is motivationally and affectively inert, or at least weak: a *phantasia* of something frightening will induce a shiver, but not real fear. *If* this is meant as a general claim about *phantasia*, it is decisive support for the doxastic interpretation of the passions. But the context strongly suggests that it is not. Aristotle has just said that *phantasia* is "up to us," and while this is true of one type of exercise of *phantasia* – active imagination, in which we conjure up an image, voluntarily "put something before our eyes" – it is clearly false as a general claim: the appearances we experience in dreams and illusions are not "up to us" in that way at all. Thus the "up to us" claim should be taken to apply only to one species of *phantasia*. Moreover, it is just this voluntary kind of *phantasia* that would seem to be at issue in the second part of the passage: actively imagining something terrible

---

argument is necessary to show why pleasure is to be pursued, pain to be avoided. He holds that we perceive these things, as we perceive that fire is hot, snow white, honey sweet" (Cicero, *De Finibus* I.30).

[38] See especially Nussbaum 1996 and Dow 2009. Dow characterizes the phantastic interpretation as the view that passions involve "things merely *appearing* to the subject to be as they are represented, rather than the subject's actually taking them to be so" (2009, 143). As he points out, this is the way that some proponents of the phantastic interpretation characterize their view. See especially Cooper: "It seems likely that Aristotle is using *phantasia* [in the *Rhetoric*] to indicate the sort of nonepistemic appearance to which he draws attention once in *De Anima* 3.3 (428b2-4), according to which something may appear to, or strike one, in some way (say, as being insulting or belittling) even if one knows there is no good reason for one to take it so. If so, Aristotle is alert to the crucial fact about the emotions, that one can experience them simply on the basis of how, despite what one knows or believes to be the case, things strike one – how things look to one when, for one reason or another, one is disposed to feel the emotion" (1996a, 417).

is no more frightening than seeing it in a picture, but dreaming or hallucinating something terrible can surely induce fear. Thus we should conclude that the passage is not making a general claim about *phantasia* at all. Despite his lack of explicit qualification, Aristotle means to be arguing that one type of exercise of *phantasia* does not induce passions, while leaving it open that others do.[39]

In fact, we should be surprised to see him making even this weaker claim. A major premise of the *Poetics* is that when we watch tragedies we experience pity and fear, genuine passions; if we can feel fear at a representation of something terrible on stage, we can presumably also feel fear at a representation of something terrible "in a picture," or in active imagination. Arguably Aristotle is working with a view about the suspension of disbelief: if we remind ourselves that it is just a picture, or just a mental image, or just a play, we experience the passions to a much lesser extent, or possibly even not at all. I return to this point below.

At any rate we cannot read the passage as making the blanket claim that *phantasia* cannot induce passions without rendering Aristotle's overall treatment of *phantasia* badly inconsistent. For we have seen ample evidence that elsewhere in the corpus – including in the same chapter of the *de An*. itself (429a4-8) – Aristotle unequivocally characterizes *phantasia* as able to cause action, by inducing emotions and desires. A quick glance back at some excerpts from passages 1 and 2 should suffice here to confirm the point:

Phantasiai and perceptions and thoughts alter the parts [thereby initiating the changes which lead to locomotion]. For perceptions are at once a kind of alteration, and *phantasia* and thinking have the power of the actual things. (*MA* 701b16-19)

The origin of motion, as has been said, is the object of pursuit and avoidance in the practical sphere. Of necessity heating and chilling follow the thought and the *phantasia* of these things. (*MA* 701b33-35)

The affections suitably prepare the organic parts, and desire the affections, and *phantasia* desire. (*MA* 702a17-19, cf. 700b17-21, 701a29-36)

The object of desire... moves, itself unmoved, by being thought or represented by *phantasia* (φαντασθῆναι). (*de An*. 433b11–12)

At this point, the doxastist might throw up her hands. Surely, she will say, the point of the passage from *de An*. III.3 is that to have a *phantasia* as of a terrible dragon before one (for instance) is merely to be subject to the appearance, and not yet to believe it – and for that reason not yet to be moved by it. Moreover, she will add, that is surely the right thing for Aristotle to say: if one merely entertains such an appearance without actually believing that there is a terrible dragon present, one will not be afraid. So when Aristotle does say in various places that we can moved by *phantasia* without the help of belief he must simply be confused.

---

[39] For arguments that Aristotle's use of '*phantasia*' in these passages is precisely the kind that he dismisses a few lines below as merely metaphorical (κατὰ μεταφοράν, 428a1-5), see D. Frede 1992, and an unpublished paper by Anders Dahl Sorensen, "*Phantasia* and Emotional Response in *De Anima* 3.3," to which I am indebted for my understanding of these passages.

In order to state this objection most clearly, and also in order to show how it is to be answered, I want to rephrase the point in Stoic terminology. This may seem an odd thing to do in a discussion of Aristotelian passions: not only anachronistic but also potentially misleading, because Stoic psychology is so obviously different from Aristotle's. In fact, however, not only is Aristotle's view of *phantasia* more similar to the Stoics than has been generally recognized, but examining the differences will help us clarify how the doxastic objections mentioned above go wrong.

4.7 Aristotle and the Stoics on *phantasia*, assent, and passion

Two concepts are central to the Stoic view of both belief and passion: *phantasia* and assent (συγκατάθεσις). On the Stoic view, all sentient creatures (animals and people) are subject to *phantasiai*, appearances.[40] Rational creatures have an ability which non-rational ones lack: we can criticize and question these appearances. If we decide an appearance is false we reject it; if we decide it is true we assent to it. Only once we have assented do we have belief (δόξα).[41] This entails that animals cannot have beliefs – precisely as Aristotle holds (*de An.* 428a20-22). But does it entail that they have no functional counterpart of belief – that they are always in the state of merely entertaining appearances? Not at all: since animals lack the ability to question appearances, they can no more withhold assent from an appearance than they can give it. This means that they simply go with the appearances, by default.[42] Let's introduce the term 'acceptance' to name a genus which includes both active assent to appearances and passive failure to question them. We can then say that while for people experiencing an appearance does not yet amount to accepting it, for animals the distinction between experiencing and accepting simply does not arise.

Phantasia and assent are also crucial concepts in the Stoic theory of motivation, including their theory of the passions. Some *phantasiai* are "impulsive" (ὁρμητικαί): they have it in their nature to give rise to motivation. These obviously play a similar role in Stoic theory to the role I have attributed to evaluative appearances in Aristotle's, and indeed the Stoics construe impulsive appearances as evaluative (although the details are complicated, and we need not explore them here).[43] Just as rational creatures can assent to or reject ordinary *phantasiai* so we can assent to or reject

---

[40] It is standard to translate *phantasia* as 'impression' in the context of Stoic philosophy, but I think 'appearance' does as well here as it does in Aristotle.

[41] For the Stoics δόξα is a lowly cognitive achievement, "weak and false," by contrast with knowledge and apprehension (ἐπιστήμη, κατάληψις): see e.g. Sextus Empiricus, *Adversus Mathematicos* 7.151. And since Stoics construe passions as a species of belief (as I go on to show), this entails that passions are all false. But this aspect of the Stoic view need not concern us here: the crucial distinction for our purposes is between merely being subject to an appearance and assenting to it.

[42] For citations and discussion of the Stoic view see Sorabji 1993, 41.

[43] Here is a simple version with clear affinities to Aristotle: "Once the good appears it straight away moves the soul towards itself, while the bad moves the soul away from itself. A soul will never refuse a clear *phantasia*

impulsive ones. Assent yields motivation of one type or another; assent to *phantasiai* with the appropriate kind of content yields passions.

From these claims follows what is most notable about the Stoic theory of passions: because passions result from assents to appearances, passions are a species of a belief, and only rational creatures can have them. But does this mean that animals have no functional equivalent to passions? Again, clearly not. Animals have impulses (ὁρμαί) which are at least very similar to fear and appetite, aversion and desire. And the explanation is the same as the one we saw above: since they cannot actively assent or withhold assent to appearances, for them, experiencing an appearance is tantamount to accepting it – and thus experiencing an impulsive appearance is tantamount to being moved by it.[44]

Now we are ready to consider the most striking difference between the Stoic and Aristotelian theories of the passions. Stoic passions are rational: they are the result of rational assent, and thus belong only to rational creatures.[45] On the Aristotelian account, I have been arguing, they are non-rational: they are exercises of a non-rational part of the soul common to humans and non-rational animals alike. This means that what Aristotle calls passions are the kind of thing the Stoics attribute to animals, and refuse that name: default, passive acceptances of appearances rather than active, rational assents.

How does this help us with the doxastic objection at hand? The objection was that passions must involve belief because they depend not on the mere awareness of an appearance but on the acceptance of it: we are not afraid of things that merely look scary, but of things we really take to be scary. But we have seen now that this distinction only makes sense with reference to a rational being: someone who can distinguish between how things appear and how they really are, and thus can be subject to an appearance as of *p* without accepting that *p*. For a non-rational part of the soul, as for a non-rational animal, there is no meaningful distinction between being subject to an appearance and accepting it. Of course this acceptance will not be *rational* acceptance – not reflective acceptance on the basis of reasons grasped as reasons, as we might put it: it will be a default, automatic, unreflective acceptance. But it makes sense to view it as a kind of acceptance: just as the rational soul takes it that *p* in believing that *p*, so the non-rational soul takes it that *p* in being appeared to as if *p*. And when the appearance is an evaluative one, this acceptance will be or cause a feeling of fear or shame or pity or the like – a feeling which the Stoics would call a mere protopassion (since it is not the product of rational assent) but which Aristotle calls a passion.

Therefore we can answer the doxastist's objection as follows: on Aristotle's view, being subject to an appearance of something as terrible will not always entail *rational*

---

of good ... This is the source of every movement both of men and of God" (Epictetus, *Discourses* 3.3.4). For discussion of the more complex versions of the Stoic view see M. Frede 1986.

[44] See especially Origen, *On Principles* 3.1.2, which emphasizes that creatures like spiders and bees are moved simply by *phantasia*.

[45] They are also, confusingly enough, irrational – i.e. false. But this need not concern us here.

acceptance, i.e. belief that the thing is terrible, but it will always entail *non*-rational acceptance – i.e. fear.[46] (This still leaves us in difficulties about the *de An.* III.3 passage, which implies that one can be subject to the appearance without feeling fear. I propose two possible ways to reconcile this passage with all the evidence we have seen that evaluative appearances are essentially passion-inducing. Possibly Aristotle's point in the passage is that we do feel *some* fear, as he arguably thinks we do when we look at a frightening picture (or when we remember something terrible). Alternatively, the idea might be that when we actively, deliberately entertain appearances (when the exercise of *phantasia* is "up to us"), we are not subject to them in the same way as we are when they simply strike us. I return to this question in Chapter 6's discussion of deliberative *phantasia*.)

It is, as previous advocates of the *phantasia* view of the passions have noted, a strong advantage of this interpretation that it renders passions independent of beliefs. One can in certain circumstances (although given my arguments about belief below one normally will not) have a passion in the absence of a corresponding evaluative belief. This is a point that doxastist interpreters of Aristotle – and Stoics – have to deny, but that common sense upholds and many philosophers have emphasized. Here, for example, is Hume:

> ...let us consider the case of a man, who being hung out from a high tower in a cage of iron cannot forbear trembling, when he surveys the precipice below him, tho' he knows himself to be perfectly secure from falling.... His imagination runs away with its object, and excites a passion proportion'd to it. (Hume, *A Treatise of Human Nature*, I.iii.xiii)

Our beliefs can fail to influence our passions, because passions are the province of a different form of cognition: according to Hume, "imagination;" according to Aristotle, I have argued, imagination's Greek ancestor, *phantasia*. The *Rhetoric* does not discuss the possibility of dissonance between passions and evaluative beliefs – not surprisingly, since inducing such dissonance would be of no use to the orator. But Aristotle certainly recognized its occurrence, for in the ethical works he devotes a good deal of attention to a paradigmatic species of such dissonance: *akrasia*. I take up this subject in the next chapter, arguing that Aristotle's characterization of *akrasia* confirms that passions are based on *phantasia*, and are therefore independent of evaluative beliefs.

4.8 Aristotle and the Stoics on passions, *phantasia*, and belief

Thus we should lay to rest the doxastist's claim that *phantasia* cannot give rise to passions. But a serious complication remains: we have not accounted for the substantial textual evidence that passions *do* correlate with evaluative beliefs. We see this in the

---

[46] For a compelling contemporary account of non-rational motivation along these lines see Gendler 2008.

de An. III.3 passage: "when we believe something terrible or frightening, we are affected straightaway." We also see it in the passage on spirited passion quoted above from *EN* VII.6: the awareness of a slight which induces anger can come from *phantasia*, but it can also come from *logos*. And there is plenty of evidence in the *Rhet.* too: when Aristotle says, for example, that "those who think (οἰομένους) they will suffer something are necessarily fearful" (1382b33), or that "if people think (οἴωνται) that they have done wrong and suffered justly anger does not arise" (1380b16-17), or uses variants on νομίζεσθαι and δοκεῖν (1385b24, 1387a24), it is extremely natural to take him as saying that passions depend on thoughts. Moreover, as some doxastists point out, this seems crucial to Aristotle's whole purpose in discussing passions in the *Rhetoric*: his claim is that an appeal to passions can help persuade an audience, and this would seem to entail that passions involve beliefs rather than mere *phantasia*.

This objection goes deeper than the others the doxastist raises: it is true that Aristotle often speaks as if passions depend on thoughts or beliefs, although he elsewhere clearly attributes them to *phantasia*. Indeed, I can see some appeal to concluding that he simply contradicts himself on this topic, or does not have a fully determinate view, or (as Sihvola concludes) thinks that some passions require belief while others do not. In fact, however, his texts do give us the resources for a consistent view – and it is one on which passions depend only on *phantasia*.

The key is to take account of the interactions between *phantasia* and thought, which I mentioned briefly at the end of Chapter 3. Aristotle holds, we will see, that (a) all thought requires an exercise of *phantasia* – i.e. *phantasia* is a necessary condition for belief; and (b) in standard cases a *phantasia* as of *p* automatically triggers the belief that *p* – i.e. *phantasia* is in standard circumstances sufficient for belief (in creatures with the capacity for belief). Thesis (a) entails that even if passions normally track beliefs *phantasia* is necessary for passions; thesis (b) entails that even if passions normally track beliefs *phantasia* is sufficient for them.

The evidence for (a) is explicit:

Since nothing exists, as it seems, separated and apart from the perceptible magnitudes, it is in the perceptible forms that the intelligible forms exist ... And on account of this, no one would learn or understand anything without perceiving, and also whenever one contemplates (θεωρῇ), it is necessary that he contemplate some *phantasma* at the same time. (*de An.* 432a3-9)

To the thinking soul the *phantasmata* serve like *aisthêmata*.[47] And whenever it affirms or denies good or bad, it flees or pursues. Wherefore the soul never thinks (νοεῖ) without a *phantasma*. (*de An.* 431a14-17)

Phantasia is a necessary precondition and indeed accompaniment of all (mortal) thinking. Thought requires visualizing or other sensory equivalents: it employs universal concepts, but we think by imagining particular instances. We think about triangles in general, for example, but do so by way of inspecting a mental image

---

[47] *Aisthêmata* are perceptual states: see Chapter 3.2.

(*phantasma*) of a particular triangle (*Mem.* 449b30-450a9). The second passage shows that this applies in the practical sphere as well as in the theoretical: in deliberating about what to do, thought makes use of mental images; as a passage that follows shortly afterwards puts it, thought "thinks the forms in *phantasmata*" (*de An.* 431b2). I discuss *phantasia*'s role in deliberation in more detail in Chapter 6, but we can already see an important consequence: thinking about what good or bad things will happen in the future entails having *phantasmata* of those possible events. Thus when someone "thinks that he will suffer something," for example (1382b33), he will in so doing have before his mind a *phantasma* of such suffering. (Compare again the painter and scribe in Plato's *Philebus*.)

Thus *phantasia* is – just as my arguments in sections 2-3 entail – a *necessary* condition of the passions. Even when a passion depends on an intellectual evaluation – e.g. when it is *logos* which declares a slight, as in *EN* VII.6, or when one believes (δοξάζειν) that something is terrible or frightening, as in *de An.* III.3 – evaluative *phantasia* is necessarily present too.[48]

This *might* suggest a modified doxastic position, on which passions are based on beliefs which are supplemented, like all beliefs, by *phantasmata*. This is certainly a more promising position than the pure doxastic one, for it accommodates all the evidence we have seen that *phantasia* is at least a necessary condition of passions. But because it makes belief a necessary component as well, it cannot do justice to the evidence we saw in section 1 that passions belong to the non-rational part of the soul. Is that evidence simply irreconcilable with the passages which suggest that passions track thoughts and beliefs?

It is not: we can make sense of these passages even while holding that *phantasia* is sufficient for passion. Once again, it will help to use the Stoic view to illuminate Aristotle's: I want to show that he holds a proto-Stoic view of the relation between *phantasia* and belief – and thus holds that the *phantasiai* which give rise to passions normally also trigger corresponding evaluative beliefs.

Various commentators on the *de An.* have taken Aristotle's claims that *phantasia* is necessary for thought in a way different from that discussed above: as a version of the Stoic view on which forming a rational judgment is a matter of assenting to or contradicting a *phantasia*. Consider two passages from early in the discussion of *phantasia* which lend themselves fairly naturally to this interpretation:

Phantasia does not arise without perception, and without it there is no supposition (ὑπόληψις)... And these are the different kinds of supposition: knowledge (ἐπιστήμη) and belief (δόξα) and practical wisdom (φρόνησις) and their opposites. (*de An.* 427b14-16; b24-26)

Of thinking (τὸ νοεῖν)... the one part seems to be *phantasia*, the other supposition (ὑπόληψις). (*de An.* 427b27-28)

---

[48] Lorenz argues that this is the basic mechanism whereby the rational part's commands influence the non-rational part's desires (2006, 118).

Themistius, Alexander, and more recently Hicks (1907) take these passages as advancing a proto-Stoic view: when Aristotle says that thinking is part *phantasia* and part supposition (ὑπόληψις), 'supposition' is playing the role of the Stoic's 'assent' (συγκατάθεσις); when he says that non-rational animals lack belief because they lack the conviction (πίστις) which follows from *logos* (428a20-24), 'conviction' is playing this same role.

Aristotle certainly says nothing to confirm this explicitly, and in fact (as I argue in Chapter 6) the commentators are over-Stoicizing his view: unlike the Stoics, Aristotle does not take *all* "supposition" nor all thinking to rely on *phantasia* in this particular way (although he clearly does think it all relies on *phantasia* in some way or other – again, see discussion in Chapter 6). But this leaves open the possibility that *some* of our suppositions – e.g. beliefs, or one type of beliefs – are products of assent to appearance.[49] We find strong evidence for that view from a different source: the discussion of illusions in the *Insomn.*[50]

If it escaped someone's notice that a finger was pressed under his eye, one thing would not only appear (φανεῖται) to be two but he would believe that it was (δόξει), while if it did not escape his notice it would appear but he would not believe. (*Insomn.* 461b31-462a2)

The perceiver in this case begins with a *phantasia* as of two objects before him; if he rejects the *phantasia* he does not form the belief that there are two objects there, but otherwise he does. In other words, unless the perceiver has reason to doubt the *phantasia*, he forms a belief in accord with it. And this suggests that Aristotle did indeed hold thesis (b): in standard cases, a *phantasia* as of *p* automatically triggers a belief that *p*.[51]

The *Insomn.* passage thus offers an implicit proto-Stoic account of what we might call appearance-based beliefs, beliefs which have their causal basis in how things appear. This will be a wide class, including all quasi-perception-based beliefs (e.g. the belief one has, on the basis of seeming to see a red rose in the vase, that there is a red rose in the vase). Such beliefs, the passage implies, are to be construed as what the Stoics would call assents – most of them automatic or unreflective – to appearances.

My proposal is that Aristotle construes the evaluative beliefs relevant to passions – e.g. the thought that one will suffer something frightening (1382b29-33), or that an evil of the sort one might suffer is present (1385b13-17) – as belonging to this class. If it

---

[49] On Sextus' interpretation, this is true of all beliefs: "[According to the Peripatetics] whenever the soul yields to the *phantasia* arisen from perception and agrees and assents to what appears, it is called *doxa*" (*Adversus Mathematicos* 7.225-6). I will argue for a more restricted claim below.

[50] My interpretation here agrees with Gallop 1991 and Everson 1997, 214-15.

[51] It is not immediately clear how Aristotle might have reconciled this thesis about belief with *de An.* III.3's claim that belief presupposes conviction (πίστις), which in turn presupposes having been persuaded (τὸ πεπεῖσθαι), which in turn presupposes *logos*. Perhaps the idea is that even when a belief follows an appearance automatically, what makes it count as a belief is that were one to be asked "why do you believe there are two things there?" one can answer by giving a reason: "*because* it appears to me so." One recognizes the appearance as evidence in retrospect, even though one performed no explicit, conscious inference at the time.

appears to you that the spear in your enemy's hand is both long (a visual appearance) and terrible (an evaluative one), you will normally on that basis acquire both the belief that the spear is long (a vision-based belief) and the belief that it is terrible (an evaluative one). I have argued that the evaluative appearance will trigger a passion, fear; therefore it follows that fear is normally accompanied by a belief that the feared object is frightening.

Note that I am not attributing to Aristotle a Stoic account of the passions, according to which the passions are based not on the appearances but on the beliefs.[52] This would be a version of the doxastic view: when one is merely subject to an appearance of the spear as terrible one does not feel fear; fear only results when one accepts or assents to that appearance, thus coming to believe that the spear is terrible.[53] But this strongly Stoicizing interpretation of Aristotelian passions will not do. It does accommodate all the evidence we saw above that *phantasia* is necessary for the passions (section 3), but it clashes with the evidence that passions are non-rational, the province of a part of the soul not itself capable of belief (section 2). And thus we should conclude that Aristotle held a subtly different view: the passions themselves are based on *phantasiai* alone, but those *phantasiai* normally prompt corresponding beliefs.

It is true that Aristotle is nowhere explicit about this view; it may also be true that in writing the *Rhet.*, where his purposes are practical, he did not have or keep it clearly in view. But I submit that it is the only view consistent with all our evidence, and thus that charity dictates attributing it to Aristotle as what either was or would have been (had he developed one) his underlying view. For only this view lets us respect both the non-rationality of the passions and their alignment with evaluative beliefs. It accommodates on the one hand claims like "those who think they will suffer something are fearful" (*Rhet.* 1382b33) and "whenever we believe something frightening we are affected" (*de An.* 427b21-22), and on the other hand evidence that passions are exercises of a non-rational part of the soul incapable of belief.

For on this view, even though it is *phantasia* that gives rise to passions – which is why passions can be the province of the non-rational soul, and why they can in some cases conflict with evaluative beliefs – evaluative beliefs are their normal, default accompaniments: unless the agent actively withholds assent, the evaluative *phantasia* which gives rise to a passion will also give rise to a corresponding evaluative belief. Fear is a response to a *phantasia* of a future evil, but those subject to such a *phantasia* will normally also *believe* that there is a future evil. Therefore one can for the most part characterize the passions by way of corresponding beliefs, as Aristotle often does in the

---

[52] Or on which the passions simply *are* beliefs, as on the Stoic view; I am not convinced that Aristotle had a determinate view about the relation between passions and cognitions, and so have intended to leave that question open throughout, although for convenience I sometimes speak of cognitions as giving rise to passions.

[53] Arguably Andronicus interpreted Aristotle this way. He claimed that the passions involve supposition, ὑπόληψις; Aspasius took this to mean that they require rational assent, and argued to the contrary that *phantasia* is sufficient (Aspasius, in *EN* 44,33-45,10). For discussion see Sorabji 1993, 57.

Rhetoric. And – to turn to Aristotle's specific concerns in that work – one can predict that a person's passions will usually influence her beliefs in a way that makes appeal to passion a useful device for influencing juridical opinions.[54] In fact, this interpretation accords much better with Aristotle's discussion of the role of passions in persuasion than does the doxastic one: he speaks of passions as affecting judgments (κρίσεις) made in lawcourts or assemblies – by which he plausibly means a species of belief – rather than as themselves being (or being entailed by) those judgments.[55]

Passions can result from beliefs, because the thinking which leads to belief is supplemented by visualizing or other exercises of *phantasia*; passions normally entail beliefs, because the *phantasiai* on which they are based normally trigger beliefs. But passions are not themselves a function of belief. Just as seeing something as round can result from, and will normally entail, and yet is essentially independent of, the belief that it is round, so feeling anger at someone can result from, and will normally entail, and yet is essentially independent of, the belief that they have done you wrong.

In the next chapter I give further evidence that this must have been Aristotle's view – and at the same time give further evidence that evaluative *phantasiai* play a crucial role in his ethical theory – by examining cases in which passions and evaluative beliefs diverge: cases of *akrasia*.

---

[54] Or: the appearances on which her passions are based will influence her beliefs. Given my argument above that for a non-rational soul-part being subject to an appearance amounts to accepting it, and therefore being subject to an evaluative appearance amounts to feeling a passion, we can put the point either way.

[55] "One should not warp the jury by leading them into anger or envy or pity, for that is the same as if someone made crooked the ruler he was going to use" (1354a24-26); "[There is persuasion] through the audience when they are led to passion by the speech. For we do not render judgments in the same way when we are pained as when we are enjoying, or loving and hating" (1356a14-16); inducing a passion is a means of "preparing the judge" (τὸν κρίτην κατασκευάζειν) (1377b24). The point emerges also from the general definition of passions which we saw above: the passions are "those things *on account of which* (δι' ὅσα), by undergoing change, people come to differ in their judgments" (1378a19-20). An angry person is more likely to judge a wrongdoing voluntary, but her anger does not already entail a judgment (a κρίσις in the legal sense).

5

Akrasia and the Apparent Good

5.1 A puzzle about *akrasia*

In Chapter 3 I argued that *phantasia* owes its crucial role in motivation to its independence from perceptibles: because it can represent absent objects, it can furnish us with goals. But this same independence from perceptibles also opens up a serious danger: *phantasia* can misrepresent things, leading us astray. The capacity to preserve and reproduce perceptual experience in the absence of appropriate contact with the perceptibles is most readily understood as a faculty for experiencing perceptual illusions, and this is a role that Aristotle clearly and consistently attributes to *phantasia*. Moreover, various passages present *phantasia* as playing a similar role in practical contexts, misrepresenting things as good (see quotations below). Not all appetites are for things that will in fact contribute to our survival or well-being; not all passions are appropriate responses to the actual value of their objects. When someone craves a base pleasure because it appears good, or is excessively afraid of performing a noble deed because doing so appears overall bad, or excessively angry at a mild insult because it appears outrageous, *phantasia* is misrepresenting facts about value, just as in ordinary perceptual illusions it misrepresents facts about shape or size. Thus Aristotle uses the phrase 'the apparent good' not only to refer to the genuinely good apprehended as a goal through *phantasia*, but also and indeed more frequently to refer to the *merely* apparent good – to things in fact harmful which *phantasia* nonetheless apprehends as good.

The aim of this chapter is to use the parallels Aristotle draws between *phantasia*'s roles in ethical error and ordinary perceptual illusion in order to give an account of one way that *phantasia* leads us astray in ethical matters. I will use the parallel to show that the psychological works contain a neglected account of a phenomenon of which the ethical works' account is famous but famously confusing, and to show that the psychological works' account can illuminate that of the ethical works. The phenomenon I have in mind is one particular species of ethical error: *akrasia* (incontinence, weakness of will, lack of self-control). (I consider *phantasia*'s role in other kinds of ethical error in Chapters 6-8.) I will argue that Aristotle construes *akrasia* as based on a conflict between the belief that something is bad and the *phantasia* that it is good.

Discussions of Aristotle's view of *akrasia* usually center on Book VII of the *EN* (= Book VI of the *EE*), and in particular on the notoriously difficult third chapter of that book. Here Aristotle argues that Socrates was in some sense right to maintain that *akrasia* involves ignorance. This much is clear. As to the details, however, the text is so dense and so thorny as to leave little of Aristotle's view beyond doubt. What is the akratic agent ignorant of: the minor premise of the practical syllogism forbidding her action, or only the conclusion?[1] And what is the nature of her ignorance? Does she lack the relevant knowledge altogether, or merely neglect to combine it with her other beliefs? Or does she know it in some sense but not in the crucial sense of having integrated it into her character?[2]

Underlying these questions is a much broader worry: How does an account of *akrasia* as involving ignorance of any kind fit with the more straightforward account we find elsewhere in the corpus, on which *akrasia* involves a struggle between opposing desires? The starkest statement of that account is in *de Anima* III.11 – in *akrasia*, desire conquers desire (434a12-14) – but it is clearly present in the ethical works too. Consider how Aristotle first describes *akrasia* in the *EN*:

We praise the reason (λόγον) and the reasoning part of the soul of enkratic and akratic agents: for this exhorts them correctly and toward what is best. But there seems to be something else in them too, by nature contrary to reason, which fights and resists it. For exactly as with paralytic limbs which when their owners decide to move them to the right take off in the wrong direction, moving to the left, so it is in the case of the soul. For the impulses of the akratic agent lead in opposite directions (ἐπὶ τἀναντία γὰρ αἱ ὁρμαί)... [T]here is something in the soul besides reason, opposing it and going against it. (*EN* I.13 1102b14-25)[3]

This picture of *akrasia* as a struggle between the opposing "impulses" of the rational and non-rational parts of the soul – a close descendant of Plato's account of motivational conflict in *Republic* IV – is clear enough. The *EE* gives it even more emphasis: in *akrasia* (and *enkrateia* – continence, strength of will, self-control), so separate and opposed are the rational faculty and the appetitive that we could even speak of one being forced and compelled by the other (*EE* II.8 1224b24 ff.). Does Aristotle simply ignore this picture

---

[1] The former view has been predominant. For the latter, see Kenny 1966, Santas 1969 (attributing the view to Gregory Vlastos), and Charles 1984 and 2009; the view dates back to the medieval commentator Walter Burleigh.

[2] For the view that the akratic agent knows the relevant information but fails to combine it with her other beliefs see Joachim 1951, 224-29, and Irwin 1999, 261. Dahl defends the view that the akratic agent has the relevant knowledge but has failed to "integrate it into her character" (1984: see especially 188 and 213); I think McDowell's and Wiggins' views (discussed below) can be understood as versions of this one (see McDowell, e.g. 1998, and Wiggins 1975); compare also Charles 2009.

[3] Some propose an alternative reading of these lines on which there is no conflict between impulses: "the impulses of the akratic agent lead in the opposite direction [sc. to what reason commands]." Two considerations support the conflicting-impulses reading, however. First, later passages in the *EN* make clear that the akratic agent acts on appetite against a contrary motivation: in Book VII akratic agents act against their decisions (προαιρέσεις – for discussion and citations see below); in Book IX they "have appetites for some things and rationally wish (βούλονται) for different things" (IX.4 1166b7-8). Second, Aristotle attributes ἐναντίας ὁρμάς to the akratic and the enkratic agent at *EE* II.8 1224a33, where the context makes it very clear that this means impulses opposite to one another.

later in both works (at *EN* VII.3/*EE* VI.3)[4] when he characterizes the akratic agent as ignorant?

There are two problems here. First, why, given his resources for a "Platonic" account of *akrasia* as the victory of non-rational over rational desire, did Aristotle see the need for a "Socratic" account of *akrasia* as involving ignorance at all?[5] Second, and more gravely, how can the account of *akrasia* as involving a struggle between opposing desires even be compatible with an account on which the agent is unaware that she is doing something wrong?

Ross puts this second worry sharply in his criticism of *EN* VII.3. He, along with a majority of scholars, interprets the chapter as saying that the agent lacks the minor premise of the syllogism forbidding her action. The problem with this explanation, he argues, is this:

> It says nothing of a moral struggle; the minor premise of the moral syllogism (and with it the conclusion 'I ought not to do this') has never been present, or it has already been suppressed by the appetite. And the account which explains how the wrong act can be done in the absence of this knowledge cannot explain how the knowledge has come to be absent. But Aristotle elsewhere shows himself alive to the existence of a moral struggle, a conflict between rational wish and appetite... We must suppose that interest in his favourite distinctions of potential and actual, of major and minor premise, has betrayed him into a formal theory which is inadequate to his own real view of the problem. (Ross 1949, 140)

Other responses are more radical. Perhaps the chapter was written by some other author and smuggled into Aristotle's text (Cook Wilson 1879). Or perhaps, despite appearances, VII.3 does not explain *akrasia* in terms of ignorance at all: Aristotle proposes ignorance not as an explanation, but rather as a special description, of failure to do what one judges best (Broadie 1991; cf. Dahl 1984).

In what follows I will argue that we can reconcile the struggle account of *akrasia* with the ignorance account, and can do so without downplaying the ignorance at issue in *EN* VII.3. Properly understood, that chapter's explanation of *akrasia* in terms of ignorance is not only compatible with the picture of *akrasia* as involving a struggle between opposing desires, but also supplements it by offering an explanation of how the non-rational desires win out over the rational ones. To see why Aristotle thought the victory of non-rational desire in need of special explanation, however, and to settle the question of just what explanation VII.3 provides, we will have to look outside the ethical works altogether.

I wish to show that Aristotle provides the resources for another account of *akrasia*, one that has not been properly appreciated, in our passage 2, from *de An.* III.10.[6] This

---

[4] In the remainder of this chapter I use only the *EN* numbering.

[5] The so-called Platonic account is that of *Republic* IV, the so-called Socratic that of the *Protagoras*. Many of those who discuss *EN* VII.3 address the relation between the two accounts, although not always in these terms.

[6] The account has received surprisingly little attention. It receives brief mention from Cook Wilson (1879, 50) and Walsh (1963, 124-27), and is otherwise generally neglected. (What Walsh does say suggests an understanding of the relation between the two accounts very much in line with what I propose here.) Many

account is philosophically interesting in its own right, and also proves very useful in illuminating the discussions of *akrasia* in the ethical works. It presents *akrasia* as involving a conflict in the agent between rational judgment on one side, and on the other side *phantasia*. This entails that *akrasia* is the practical equivalent of (certain cases of) being taken in by perceptual illusion.

By following the parallels between *akrasia* and perceptual illusion through the psychological works, we will uncover an account which fleshes out *EN* VII.3's comparison of the akratic agent with the person mad, drunk, or asleep (1147a12-15), and thereby guides our interpretation of Aristotle's account of akratic ignorance in that chapter, dictating answers to its main interpretative puzzles. The view that results will reconcile the account of *akrasia* as ignorance with the account of *akrasia* as a struggle between desires, for it will show that non-rational desire wins out not by overpowering rational desire in a direct battle of strength, but rather by undermining the cognitive basis of that desire. That is, the non-rational desire wins by driving out the agent's knowledge of what is to be done or avoided, and with it the rational motivation dependent on that knowledge.[7]

Finally, the parallels between *akrasia* and perceptual illusion will indicate why Aristotle may have thought such an explanation of *akrasia* necessary in the first place – why he may have thought it impossible for appetite to overpower rational desire directly, and thus have sought to explain *akrasia* in terms of ignorance instead.

5.2 *Akrasia* in *de An*. III.9-10

The passage that will be our main focus here is one we have seen already in Chapter 1: passage 2, from *de An.* III.10. But first we must back up to the lines which directly precede that passage: the last lines of *de An.* III.9. Aristotle's investigation of the psychological causes of locomotion is already underway, and he has narrowed down the candidates to intellect and desire. In these lines he argues that neither of these is authoritative or decisive (κυρίον) for locomotion, by appeal to the phenomena of *akrasia* and its opposite, *enkrateia* (continence, strength of will, self-control):

Neither can the reasoning faculty (τὸ λογιστικόν) and what is called intellect (νοῦς) be the mover. For... even when intellect does give an order (ἐπιτάττοντος) and thought (διανοίας) says to avoid or pursue something, [the agent] isn't moved, but acts in accordance with appetite (ἐπιθυμίαν), as for instance does the akratic... But neither is desire (ὄρεξις) decisive (κυρία) for movement: for enkratics, although desiring and having an appetite, do not do what they have a desire to do, but follow intellect. (*de An.* 432b26-433a8)

---

have argued that *de An*. III.10's general theory of action is relevant to an understanding of *akrasia*, but without attention to what I see as that chapter's distinctive account of *akrasia*: see e.g. Santas 1969 and Destrée 2007.

[7] This same view is defended, on different grounds, by Charles 1984 (see especially 163-64).

104   THE APPARENT GOOD AND NON-RATIONAL MOTIVATION

This passage characterizes *akrasia* and *enkrateia* as conflicts between intellect and desire: in *enkrateia* the former wins out, in *akrasia* the latter. But the discussion that follows shows the fuller picture to be more complex. It will be convenient to repeat most of passage 2 here:

2a. It is apparent then, at any rate, that there are two movers, desire or intellect, if one classifies *phantasia* as a sort of thinking (νόησιν) ...

d. And when *phantasia* moves it doesn't move without desire ... [And] intellect doesn't appear to move without desire. For wish (βούλησις) is desire, and whenever one is moved in accordance with reasoning, one is moved in accordance with wish.

e. But desire moves contrary to reasoning [too]: for appetite is a kind of desire. While intellect is always correct, however, desire and *phantasia* can be correct or not correct. Wherefore while the object of desire always moves, this is either the good or the apparent good ...

f. Since desires arise that are opposed to one another, and this happens when the *logos* and the appetites are opposed, and this occurs in those who have perception of time – for intellect orders one to hold back on account of the future, but appetite [orders? moves?] on account of the now; for the presently pleasant appears both without qualification (ἁπλῶς) pleasant and good without qualification, from a failure to look to the future ...

g. the mover will be one in form, the desiderative faculty, insofar as it is desiderative, but before everything the object of desire, for this moves, itself unmoved, by being thought or represented by *phantasia* (φαντασθῆναι) ... (*de An.* 433a9-b12)

As I argued in Chapter 1, these lines present practical cognition as evaluative: intellect moves us by judging things good or bad, and *phantasia* moves us by presenting appearances of things as good or bad. To turn to the subject at hand, how do these lines characterize motivational conflict, *akrasia* or *enkrateia*? The last lines of III.9 characterized such conflict as a conflict between something cognitive on one side and something conative on the other, but here, in 2d-g, we find that the full picture is more complex: the agent is torn between two desires, each based on a different form of evaluative cognition. On one side is her wish, the desire that moves her "in accordance with reasoning" (2d), i.e. that follows intellect's command (2f). To be moved by wish is to be moved by intellect: one has a wish for something because intellect thinks that thing good. (Thus it is true but incomplete to say, as in the preceding passage, that the enkratic follows intellect: more precisely, she acts on a desire – a wish – for what intellect declares good.) On the other side is an appetite for what appears good, the present pleasure (2f) – that is, a desire in accordance not with intellect but with *phantasia*.

One way to describe this conflict, which fits well with Aristotle's account of *akrasia* and *enkrateia* elsewhere (see e.g. the passage from *EN* I.13 quoted above), is as a conflict between rational and non-rational desire. Wish is based on reasoning or intellect, and thus counts as rational desire. (Thus Aristotle speaks indifferently, in 2 and other passages, of desire in accordance with intellect, desire in accordance with thought (διάνοια), desire that follows reasoning, and wish (βούλησις), distinctively rational desire (e.g. 432b5).)[8] Appetite, meanwhile, is based on *phantasia*, a non-rational form of cognition possessed by animals as well as humans, and thus counts as non-rational desire.[9]

Thus *de An.* III.10 attributes conflict between rival desires – the kind of conflict at issue in the brief mention of *akrasia* later in the *de Anima* ("desire conquers desire," (434a12-14)) – to a conflict between rival cognitions, each of which represents something as good: an appearance through *phantasia* on one side, and a rational judgment by intellect on the other. In the case described in 2f it is obviously better to follow intellect than *phantasia*. 2e provides a general explanation as to why this should be so: when we engage in rational thought about what is good, we hit on what is genuinely good, but when we have a *phantasia* of something as good the appearance may be false. Intellect is always correct (or rather, rational thought is naturally such as to hit on the truth).[10] *Phantasia*, however, is not, and thus "the object of desire always moves, but this is either the good or the apparent good." Therefore, although the passage does not make the distinction explicit, *akrasia* will be a matter of going with *phantasia* against intellect, and *enkrateia* the opposite.

---

[8] It will be important for what follows that Aristotle also ascribes belief (δόξα), to rational animals alone – see the argument distinguishing belief from *phantasia* on just these grounds at *de An.* 428a22 ff., and the *EN*'s equation of the δοξαστικόν, faculty of belief, with the λογιστικόν, faculty of practical reasoning or deliberating (*EN* VI.5 1140b25-28) – so that when he speaks of desire in accordance with belief he is again referring to desire specially linked to reasoning.

[9] I am here restricting my discussion to what Aristotle later calls perceptual *phantasia*, in contrast with rational or deliberative *phantasia*, which he introduces only after our passage (III.10 433a29, III.11 434a5-7). It is clear from context that the former kind, the kind we share with non-rational animals, is the kind at issue when we act against reason, as in *akrasia*. We have seen evidence in Chapter 3 that all desire and all action involve *phantasia* (432b15-16, 433b27-29; cf. *MA* 702a17-19); if this is right, then strictly speaking when we act against perceptual *phantasia* by following intellect, we will be acting in accordance with *phantasia* of a different kind, the rational (λογιστική) *phantasia* involved in deliberation. I return to this subject in Chapter 6 but ignore it in what follows (although see my comment on Destrée in note 48 below).

[10] 2e seems to overstate its case: we do, as Aristotle is well aware, sometimes make mistakes in our practical thinking. (For a telling example, see the discussion of Neoptolemus at *EN* VII.2 1146a16 ff.: like one who acts akratically, he goes with passion against rational judgment, but in his case his rational judgment is wrong, and it is passion that leads him to do what is good. Here is a case where (on the account of *akrasia* I offer below) it is better to go with *phantasia* and appetite than with rational thought and rational desire.) This might suggest that in 2e Aristotle is using *nous* in the restricted sense he often employs on which it is a "success term": if one makes an error, one turns out not to have been exercising intellect, but mere thinking. But this restricted use will not fit Aristotle's purposes here, where he has been using *nous* to cover rational cognition more generally (note that the contrast between *nous* and *phantasia* in 2e looks as if it is meant to be exhaustive). We can, however, generalize the point about the correctness of *nous* to other forms of rational cognition by comparing the present argument with that of *EN* III.4. There Aristotle argues that the object of wish is "without qualification" (ἁπλῶς) the (genuine) good, although for each person the object of wish is what appears good to them, and thus vicious people wish for things in fact bad. If wish (βούλησις) is, as I have argued, desire for what one rationally judges good, then by *EN* III.4's logic rational cognition "without qualification" is correct, although in particular cases it will get things wrong. Vicious people will have false rational judgments about the good, and corresponding wishes for what is not in fact good, but it is still somehow in the nature of rational cognition (and therefore of wish) to hit on the genuine good, while this is not in the nature of *phantasia* (nor therefore of appetite).

5.3 Ethical error and perceptual illusion

This account has a striking consequence: it entails a very close parallel between motivational conflict and something on the face of it quite different, the experience of perceptual illusion.[11] Just like someone who believes that the lines in the Müller-Lyer illusion are of equal length but cannot help seeing one as bigger than the other, akratic and enkratic agents experience conflict between how things quasi-perceptually appear to them and how they rationally judge things to be. Indeed, earlier in the *de An.* Aristotle has explained the experience of perceptual illusions as involving precisely the same kind of conflict that explains *akrasia* in III.10: a conflict between *phantasia* and rational thought. He has appealed to the fact that

False things appear (φαίνεται) concerning which one at the same time has true supposition (ὑπόληψιν): for example, the sun appears a foot wide although it is believed (πιστεύεται) to be larger than the inhabited earth. (*de An.* 428b2-4)

to argue that *phantasia* cannot be identical with belief (δόξα): in one who believes the truth but experiences the illusion, *phantasia* and rational cognition are opposed.

The same argument appears in a passage from the *Insomn.* which we saw in the Introduction and in Chapter 3:

The cause of all these things happening is that the faculty (δύναμιν) in virtue of which the ruling part (τὸ κυρίον) judges (κρίνειν) is not identical with that in virtue of which *phantasmata* arise [i.e. the faculty of *phantasia*]. A proof of this is that the sun appears (φαίνεται) only a foot wide, though often something else contradicts (ἀντίφησι) the *phantasia*. (*Insomn.* 460b16-20)

As we have seen, this passage closely echoes one from the *EE* on the object of desire:

The object of desire and of wish is either the good or the apparent good. And this is why the pleasant is desired, for it is an apparent good; for some believe it is [good], and to some it appears [good] although they do not believe it so. For *phantasia* and belief are not in the same part of the soul. (*EE* VII.2 1235b26-29)

Aristotle is explaining both the motivational conflict one experiences when tempted by a pleasure one judges bad, and the cognitive dissonance one experiences when subject to a perceptual appearance one recognizes as illusory, as conflicts between the rational faculty and *phantasia* – between what one believes and how things appear. In perceptual illusion the appearances in question are straightforward perceptual appearances such as the appearance of the sun as a foot wide; in *akrasia* and *enkrateia* they are appearances of things as good.

For confirmation of this parallel, consider Aristotle's odd remarks about melancholics. In the psychological works he describes melancholics as being particularly sensitive to *phantasmata* (appearances through *phantasia*), or experiencing particularly

---

[11] Here Aristotle is following Plato, who draws this parallel in the *Protagoras* and in *Republic* X. For discussion of Plato's use of the parallel, see my 2008.

lively ones (*Mem.* 453a21, *Div. Somn.* 463b17). When we look to the ethical works, we find that these same people are particularly prone to ethical error: they tend toward impetuous *akrasia* (*EN* VII.7 1150b25-26) and are "constantly in a strong state of desire ... intemperate and base" (*EN* VII.14 1154b11-15). People in whom *phantasia* is strong are prone not only to nonveridical perceptions but also to the desires that prompt vicious and akratic behavior; this encourages us to accept that such desires are based on literal *phantasiai*.[12]

In Chapter 3, I argued that value-appearances are pleasurable appearances through *phantasia*, derived from pleasurable perceptions, which are perceptions of value. Just as we can anticipate or imagine or remember something as blue by having a *phantasia* that preserves and reproduces the perception of blueness, so we can anticipate (etc.) something as good by having a *phantasia* that preserves and reproduces the perception of goodness – that is, that preserves and reproduces the affective component of a pleasurable perception. Aristotle's parallels between ethical error and perceptual illusion further suggest that just as we can *mis*perceive something as a foot wide by having a false appearance of it as such through *phantasia*, so we can misperceive something as good by having a false appearance of it as such through *phantasia*. How does this work?

Let us begin with *phantasia*'s role in ordinary perceptual illusion. We get our fullest account from Aristotle's work on dreams, the *Insomn.*, where he characterizes dreams as a species of perceptual illusion, and attributes all such illusions to the workings of *phantasia*. After detailing various illusions, he concludes:

> The cause of the illusion (τοῦ διεψεῦσθαι) is that things appear in whatever way not only when the perceptible moves [the faculty of perception], but also when perception itself is moved, so long as it is moved in the same manner as it is by the perceptible. (*Insomn.* 460b22-25)[13]

An illusion is caused when one's perceptual system is affected as it would be by direct perceptual contact with some type of perceptible, in the absence of such contact. And this kind of affection is, as we know from Chapter 3, the work of *phantasia*. Illusions can occur because "the condition (*pathos*) produced by perceptibles [i.e. movement in the blood] does not only persist in the sensory organs when the perceptions are actual, but also after they have departed" (459a26-27; cf. 459b6-7); "even when the external perceptible has departed, the *aisthêmata* persist and are perceptible" (460b2-3). In creatures with *phantasia*, the perceptual system can be indirectly affected by objects perceived in the past, as if actually perceiving them in the present.

---

[12] Here as at various points modern psychology shows Aristotle to be on to something: psychiatric conditions like depression and anxiety disorders seem to be correlated with excessive or abnormal mental imagery (see the review in Holmes and Mathews 2010).

[13] One might read "the illusion" in the first line as referring only to the immediately preceding example, the finger illusion, but the explanation can cover all the cases Aristotle has given in the preceding discussion; I think Gallop is right to describe this as "a general explanation of illusions by a principle that will later be applied to dreams" (note *ad loc.*).

Thus one component of having an illusion as of x is having one's perceptual system affected as it would be in normal circumstances by x – that is, having a *phantasma* of x in the absence of appropriate perceptual contact with any x.[14] This on its own is not enough to differentiate illusions from other operations of *phantasia* – memories, anticipations or imaginations. Presumably one difference is that in illusions the experience of the *phantasia* is similar enough to the experience of actual perception that it can be mistaken for one. But there is also another factor: in many cases of illusion – perhaps on Aristotle's account all – it is not just that one has an appearance of x, but that some particular y falsely appears as x.[15] Many of the *Insomn.*'s examples fit this pattern: a man in the distance appears to be one's enemy, some lines on the wall appear to be animals, one object appears to be two (460b20-21). In these cases the perceiver is affected by a y as she would be in normal circumstances by an x: the perception of the y somehow triggers a *phantasma* of an x.[16]

One might protest that this cannot be Aristotle's comprehensive account of misperception, as it does not seem to fit one of his favorite examples: the sun appearing a foot wide (used both in the *de An.* and *Insomn.*; in both cases the claim is that the appearance of the sun as being a foot wide is a false appearance through *phantasia*). Indeed some commentators have argued that this is best understood as an ordinary perception rather than an illusory *phantasia*.[17] But the context in the *Insomn.* shows that he thought it fit his general account of illusions – he gives the sun example just before the finger example, which is followed by the general explanation of illusions – and it is not difficult to see how: the idea must be that the sun affects our visual system as a foot-wide object at some optimal distance would. Insofar as this sounds implausible, I plead that the fault lies not with my analysis of the example but with the example itself: as others have noted, it is far from clear in what sense the sun "looks to be a foot wide" at all.

With this account of *phantasia*'s role in ordinary perceptual illusion in mind, let us now turn to its role in what we might call evaluative illusion. I want to show that roughly the same phenomenon is at issue. In evaluative illusion, the agent is perceptually affected by a y as she would be in normal circumstances by an x: the cognition (sight, thought, etc.) of the y somehow triggers a *phantasma* of an x. Specifically, the cognition of something that is pleasant only in a qualified way triggers a *phantasma* of something good and pleasant without qualification – and thus induces desire.

---

[14] Where x is any proper, common, or incidental perceptible – redness, roundness, a man. Aristotle does not say "in normal circumstances" at *Insomn.* 460b25, but clearly intends some such qualification.

[15] The simplest cases of illusion are after-images (see 459b7-23), but even these fit the pattern: a white wall appears green, a stationary object appears to be moving, a blank wall appears to have something shaped like the sun on it.

[16] Aristotle emphasizes that similarity (ὁμοιότης) plays the crucial role in such mistakes: "the stronger the *pathos* [the emotion or illness that increases our susceptibility to illusions – see discussion below], the less similarity is needed for these things to appear" (460b7-8). I am not sure that similarity plays a parallel role in the ethical case; see discussion below.

[17] See for example Everson, who uses the sun example to argue that Aristotle sometimes uses *phantasia* in a broad sense which includes ordinary perception (1997, 179).

These terms require some explaining. We have seen two descriptions of false value-appearances attributed to *phantasia*: an elaborate one from the *de An.* – the presently pleasant appears without qualification (ἁπλῶς) pleasant and good without qualification (2f) – and a simpler one from the *EE*: the pleasant appears good (1235b27). The latter, simpler claim is repeated in various passages:

> In the many the deception seems to occur on account of pleasure. For it appears good while not being so. Thus they choose the pleasant as good, and flee pain as bad. (*EN* III.4 1113a33-b2)

> The *telos* is always something good by nature... but against nature and by perversion not the good but the apparent good... And the cause [of error] is the pleasant and the painful. For things are such that the pleasant appears good to the soul and the more pleasant better, and the painful bad and the more painful worse. (*EE* II.10 1227a18-b1)

This simpler claim, that the appearance of the pleasant as good is false, is surprising, for both common sense and the teleological view of pleasure we saw in Chapter 2 hold that very often pleasant things *are* good, and even that their pleasantness is a sign of their goodness. Indeed, I argued in Chapter 2 that perceiving something pleasurably amounts to perceiving it as good. Is Aristotle now telling us that all such perceptions are false? Surely not. Instead, he is implicitly appealing to a distinction he draws explicitly elsewhere:

> The pleasant is on the one hand what is without qualification (ἁπλῶς) pleasant and without qualification good, and on the other hand what is [pleasant] to somebody and apparently good. (*EE* VII.2 1236a9-10)

The without qualification pleasant is genuinely good.[18] What is merely apparently good, according to this passage, is what is pleasant with some qualification (more on the nature of the qualification below). Thus the simpler claim should be read as equivalent to the more elaborate one: when Aristotle talks of the pleasant falsely appearing good, 'pleasant' should always be read as an abbreviation for 'pleasant but not without qualification.'

Does this tell us what it is to have a cognition of the qualified pleasant trigger a *phantasma* of the without qualification good and pleasant? There are several thorny issues to be worked out here.

First, we need not take the *phantasma* at issue to consist of two distinct representations – one of the object as without qualification pleasant, and the other of it as without qualification good. I argued in Chapter 2 that for the non-rational part of the soul, to desire something as pleasant *is* for it to desire that thing as good: this part of the soul cognizes the good only through pleasure, being unable to discriminate the two. Thus we should read the καί ('and') in 2f as epexegetical – as an 'i.e.'.

Second, we need to be careful in interpreting the 'without qualification.' The word is ἁπλῶς – *simpliciter*, in Latin; it may also be translated 'absolutely' or 'simply.' 2f

---

[18] Cf. *EE* 1235b32-33, *EE* 1236b27, and *EN* 1156b22-23.

contrasts the pleasant without qualification with the presently pleasant, suggesting that 'without qualification' means "in the long run, overall." Other passages, like *EE* 1236a9-10 (quoted just above), contrast the pleasant without qualification with what is pleasant "to somebody," where this turns out to mean "somebody not virtuous": different things appear pleasant and good to different types of people, but only those things that please and appear good to the virtuous person are without qualification pleasant and good (*EN* III.4 1113a23-31).[19] But do these uses help us understand what it is to have a *phantasma* of something as pleasant and good without qualification? If Aristotle's point is that the akratic imagines the present pleasure to be the kind of thing that would please the virtuous, or to be the kind of thing that is pleasant all-things-considered and taking into account all the consequences, he will be saying something absurd.[20] Thus we should not read the 'without qualification' in 2f's description of the appearance intensionally. Instead, we should take the point to be that the akratic's *phantasma* of the pleasant object contains no qualifications, no caveats about the pleasantness that might weaken her appetite for it. The present pleasure *simply* appears pleasant and good (that is, "pleasant, i.e., good") – it appears so without any qualifications. Indeed, that Aristotle means to be giving a characterization of the kind of appearance which lies at the basis of all appetites – that is, simply an appearance of an object as good – is strongly implied by 2f. The claim that appetite urges us toward the temptation *because* it appears pleasant and good without qualification suggests that to find something pleasant only in a qualified way – to recognize it merely as presently pleasant, for example – induces no desire.

Consider how this might work in a particular case. An agent is presented with a base pleasure: a third helping of cake, for example. The cake is pleasant, but only in a qualified way: it will be pleasant now but have painful consequences, and/or it would please a non-virtuous person but not a virtuous one. If our agent is non-virtuous – intemperate, or with akratic or enkratic tendencies – the sight or mention of the cake will induce an appetite for it; if she is temperate, it will not. (This seems a hard doctrine, but it is indeed Aristotle's: the temperate person takes no pleasure in the base things which please the intemperate (*EN* 1102b27-28, 1119b15-18, 1152a2-3), or is even

---

[19] Other passages contrast the merely apparently good and pleasant with what is truly good and pleasant along the same lines: see *EN* 1176a15-19 and 1144a33-36.

[20] A *prima facie* more plausible interpretation is that she has a *phantasma* of it as "pleasant overall, pleasant in the long run," but this too is problematic. Such a *phantasma* could only be the product of deliberation (albeit bad deliberation): she would have to have considered the consequences and weighed them against the present pleasure. But in *akrasia* the appetite is opposed to the deliberated desire (προαίρεσις): it is not that the akratic deliberates twice about the benefits of eating the cake, reaching two different conclusions which ground two opposing desires, but rather that she has one desire which follows her deliberation and another, the appetite, which disregards it. It is not that the non-rational soul makes an all-things-considered judgment, taking into account (although miscalculating) the future consequences of the desired action, along with other relevant concerns; instead, the problem is that it engages in no such deliberation at all, and cannot, for it lacks the ability to exercise *logos*. (This is not to say that appetites cannot be *indirectly* influenced by deliberation: surely they can. I return to this point in Chapter 6.)

disgusted by them (1176a15-22); she has no appetite for the kind of thing the intemperate person goes for, or only a moderate one (1119a14).)

What Aristotle implies in 2f is an explanation of this desiderative difference by way of a cognitive difference: the non-virtuous person is, while the virtuous person is not, subject to a *phantasma* of the cake as pleasant, i.e. good. We know from Chapter 3 what such an appearance is: it is a pleasurable, motivating appearance, derived from previous pleasurable perceptions of objects of a similar type. So when the non-virtuous agent sees or thinks of the cake she calls to mind a representation derived from some pleasurable perception in her past – a representation of the delicious taste of chocolate. But the virtuous agent does not: for her, the sight or thought of the cake triggers no pleasurable memories or anticipations. Perhaps for her the cake calls to mind a *phantasma* of bad consequences, or perhaps it simply does not excite her imagination at all. At any rate, she is not pleasurably affected by the cake; it does not appear good to her, and so she has no appetite for it. This need not mean that she cannot recognize the cake as presently pleasant: it is not that her tastebuds are different from other people's, but rather that for her the fact that something affords immediate pleasure is no more appealing – no more prone to conjure up pleasurable *phantasmata* – than e.g. the fact that it is square.

This is perhaps easier to imagine in the case of something we recognize as morally forbidden. It is not that the temperate man, on seeing the gorgeous but married woman next door, pleasurably imagines smooching her but overcomes the resulting desire; it is rather that he is simply not the sort of person to whom such an image – such a fantasy (from *phantasia*) – would occur. And therefore he can look at her without feeling any desire. That, at any rate, is how Aristotle sees it.

Thus part of what virtue entails is an immunity to a certain sort of false appearance: the appearance of qualified pleasures as good. The virtuous person has correct non-rational cognition of a kind that all others lack (except perhaps the person with "natural" virtue – see *EN* VI.13, and discussion in Chapter 7). I will say much more about this in Chapter 6, but it is worth noting, especially in the context of a discussion of *akrasia*, that this is importantly different from a similar-sounding claim that McDowell and Wiggins express by saying that the virtuous person "perceives" things differently from the enkratic: what they have in mind is a point about the intellectual cognition central to *phronesis*, a kind of cognition Aristotle sometimes compares to perception. (For citations and brief discussion see below.) It is certainly right that on Aristotle's account only the virtuous excel at perception in this metaphorical sense, for only they have *phronesis*; what I wish to emphasize is that the virtuous also excel at something psychologically closer to literal sense-perception, namely evaluative *phantasia*.[21]

---

[21] In Chapter 7 I will argue that this is what we should expect, given that character-virtue is the excellent condition of the *non*-rational part of the soul, the part that exercises not intellect but perception and *phantasia*.

Thus *phantasia* plays a role in evaluative illusion at least loosely parallel to its role in ordinary perceptual illusion: through *phantasia*, a thing of one kind affects the perceptual system the way that, in ideal circumstances, something of a different kind would. Cognition of a *y* – a merely qualified pleasure – triggers a *phantasma* of an *x*: something pleasant and good without qualification. My aim in the remainder of the chapter is to use this parallel between perceptual and evaluative illusions to answer the questions about *akrasia* with which we began. The parallel explains, I will argue, why Aristotle thought it necessary to explain akratic action as the result of ignorance, how the ignorance account can be compatible with the motivational-struggle account, and what sort of ignorance he must have in mind.

5.4 Following appearances against knowledge

It would be puzzling indeed for someone who recognizes an ordinary visual appearance as illusory to let her actions be guided by it. To use an example from the *Insomn.* mentioned briefly above, could we take seriously the claim of someone who says "I know those cracks in the wall are just cracks, but they look like animals, and that's why I'm swatting them"? (Or: "I know the sun is larger than the inhabited portion of the earth, but it looks a foot wide, and that's why I'm going to try to catch it with my net"?) The most we could say of such a person is that she is able to say the same words as someone who really knows that the appearance is false; so long as she continues to act as she does, however, we must assume that she does not really believe, or perhaps even understand, what she is saying, for if she really knew that the appearance was false she would not act on it.

On the account we have derived from *de An.* III.10, the akratic agent is just like the swatter of illusory animals. Both the akratic and the enkratic agent experience a false appearance (of the present pleasure as good), and both – as we will see from *EN* VII.3 – may be able to say words that contradict it. If one of them nonetheless acts as if the appearance were true – eats a third piece of cake, for example – it is natural to think that although she can say the same words as the other, she does not really believe or does not really understand them: that she is in some sense ignorant of the fact that what she is doing is bad.

One might protest that if the appearance is affectively charged, i.e. is a value-appearance of the kind at issue in cases of *akrasia* (the cake looks delicious, the high bridge dangerous), the mystery dissolves: the resulting passion simply motivates one, rational objections notwithstanding.[22] I will return to this view in the final section, but my point in this section is to show that whatever the philosophical merits of the view, it cannot have been Aristotle's: he thought it impossible to act on an appearance one actively recognizes as false. For he held, I want to show, that (a) it is the proper function

---

[22] For interesting treatment of the roles of affect and belief in such cases, with discussion of historical background and recent experimental psychology, see Gendler 2008.

of the rational part to scrutinize appearances and reject the false ones, and that (b) one only ever acts on false appearances in cases where the rational faculty has failed to perform this function.

We can begin by noting that Aristotle does acknowledge that in some sense people act on appearances that conflict with how they know things to be: earlier in *de An.* III.10's account he has claimed that "many [people] follow *phantasiai* contrary to knowledge" (433a10-11 – passage 2b). But a passage from his extended discussion of *phantasia* earlier in the *de An.* (III.3) qualifies this claim:

> Animals do many things in accord with *phantasiai*, some because they have no intellect, i.e. beasts, some because intellect is sometimes covered over by *pathos* or diseases or sleep, i.e. humans. (*de An.* 429a5-8)

If a person "follows *phantasiai* contrary to knowledge" she does so, this passage implies, only because her intellect is impaired, "covered over" by something like an eye that is shut.[23] Thus 'contrary to knowledge' must mean contrary to what she usually or dispositionally knows, rather than to what she is actively contemplating just now – precisely the distinction Aristotle exploits to explain acting against knowledge in his discussion of *akrasia* in *EN* VII.3, discussed below. Furthermore, the passage adds, the cause of the impairment is some psychophysical affection: disease, sleep, or a *pathos*.[24] *Pathos* – literally 'suffering' or 'undergoing' something that happens to one as opposed to something one does – refers in some contexts to a broad range of conditions and experiences, but the juxtaposition with sickness and sleep here shows that Aristotle has in mind the narrower sense we saw in Chapter 4: emotions and appetites, like those involved in *akrasia*.

We get a more fleshed-out account of how such conditions can "cover over" intellect and leave us to follow *phantasia* in Aristotle's most extensive discussion of perceptual illusions, in the *Insomn.* Although that discussion is not directly concerned with *akrasia*, the parallels we have seen above suggest that we can use it to fill out the account of *akrasia* we have derived from the *de An.* I will lay out the *Insomn.*'s account of following *phantasia* against intellect in this section, apply it to *de An.* III.10's account

---

[23] For this reading, with helpful citations for ἐπικάλυμμα (cover or lid), see Lorenz 2006, 199, note. Aristotle calls *nous* the eye of the soul at *EN* I.6 1096b28-29, and implies the same analogy at VI.13 1144b10-12.

[24] A passage in the *de Sensu* might suggest another explanation: when there are conflicting motions in the soul, "the greater motion always knocks out (ἐκκρούει) the lesser, wherefore people do not perceive things held right before their eyes if they happen to be intensely thinking about something, or feeling fear, or hearing a loud noise" (447a14-17). If thinking can knock out perceiving, then perhaps perceiving (or misperceiving) can knock out thinking (although it is perhaps significant that Aristotle does not mention this converse as a possibility). Given the emphasis in *EN* VII on the causal role of the agent's appetite in *akrasia*, however – and given that our analysis of *de An.* III.10 shows that experiencing a *phantasia* of something as pleasant and good entails having an appetite for it – we can safely take *de An.* III.3's explanation of going with *phantasia* against intellect as most relevant to cases of *akrasia*. See also the passages I cite below in which it is *appetites* rather than perception that "knock out" (ἐκκρούειν) reasoning: *EN* III.12 1119b10 and *EE* II.8 1224b24.

of *akrasia* in section 5, and then consider how the resulting account of *akrasia* fits with *EN* VII.3's discussion in section 6.

In the *Insomn.*, as in *de An.* III.3, Aristotle is concerned to distinguish between being subject to an appearance and actually accepting it – the distinction which underlies what I called his proto-Stoic account of belief in Chapter 4 (section 6). In Chapter 4 we considered this account only in relation to straightforward cases, when the rational part assents to appearances and forms a corresponding belief. But the *Insomn.*'s subject is false appearances (dreams and others like them), appearances which one ought not to accept. On the Stoic view, humans can experience a false appearance without thereby coming to have a false belief, because it is one function of the rational faculty to scrutinize appearances and, when necessary, reject them; the *Insomn.* shows that this is Aristotle's view too. Recall the sun illusion passage:

the faculty in virtue of which the ruling part (τὸ κύριον) judges (κρίνειν) is not identical with that in virtue of which *phantasmata* arise. A proof of this is that the sun appears only a foot wide, though often something else contradicts (ἀντίφησι) the *phantasia*. (*Insomn.* 460b16-20)

The "ruling" or authoritative element in us judges the appearance, and if it finds it false "contradicts" it (cf. 462a8, quoted below): it may for example say of a dream-image (one species of *phantasma*), "This appears to be Coriscus but is not Coriscus" (462a5). The natural interpretation is that this judging and contradicting element is the rational faculty, and this is confirmed by an earlier passage:

Sometimes [when one is dreaming] belief (δόξα) says that [the appearance] is false, as it does for those who are awake. (*Insomn.* 459a6-7)[25]

We should take 'belief' here as shorthand for the part or capacity of the soul responsible for belief – the δοξαστικόν or λογιστικόν, i.e. the rational part.[26] As we saw in the discussion of perceptual illusions above, to be subject to an appearance one rationally judges false is to be subject to cognitive conflict between *phantasia* and belief, i.e. between the non-rational and rational parts of the soul.

Now we come to an important complication: sometimes the rational faculty does not perform its proper function. The very next lines of the *Insomn.* open up this possibility, for here is the sentence we saw above in full:

Sometimes belief says that [the appearance] is false, as it does for those who are awake, while at other times it is held in check (κατέχεται), and follows the *phantasma*. (*Insomn.* 459a6-8)

---

[25] At 461b26-29 Aristotle seems to imply that the "common sense" (the central faculty of perception) is responsible for noticing and contradicting false appearances, but this (*pace* Modrak 1987, 94 and 137-38) cannot be his considered view, for he explicitly contrasts the appearance-contradicting part with the appearance-receiving part at 460b16-18, while elsewhere he identifies the common sense as itself the organ of appearance-reception (the organ of *phantasia*) (*Mem.* 450a1-11).

[26] For this equation see *EN* VI.5 1140b25-28, quoted in footnote 8 above.

If the rational part is "held in check," it fails to contradict the false appearance. This idea is illuminated by a later passage on illusions, which we saw in part in Chapter 4. When one is asleep,

> ... that which is similar to something seems to be the real thing (δοκεῖ τὸ ὅμοιον αὐτὸ εἶναι τὸ ἀληθές). And so great is the power (δύναμις) of sleep that it makes this escape one's notice (ποιεῖν τοῦτο λανθάνειν). For just as if it escaped someone's notice that a finger was pressed under his eye, one thing would not only appear to be two but he would believe that it was (δόξει), while if it did not escape his notice it would appear but he would not believe, so it is in sleep: if one is aware (αἰσθάνηται)[27] that one is sleeping, i.e. [aware of] the sleeping condition (*pathos*) that one's perception is in, something will appear, but something in the person says that this appears to be Coriscus but is not Coriscus. For often something in the soul of the sleeper says that what appears is a dream. But if it escapes his notice (λανθάνῃ) that he is sleeping, nothing contradicts the *phantasia*. (*Insomn.* 461b29-462a8)

In the finger-on-eyeball example, the agent's rational faculty is functioning normally: she simply happens not to know that there is something non-standard in her viewing conditions, and thus fails to notice that what appears to her is a mere appearance. Here there is no systematic psychological or physiological explanation for why her rational faculty fails to contradict the false appearance. The dreamer example, however, is importantly different: here a *pathos* – sleep – inhibits the agent's ability to notice the difference between real things and mere appearances, and thus prevents anything within her from "contradicting the appearances."[28] Other *pathē* – sickness, emotions, and desires – can have the same effect:

> We are easily deceived in our perceptions when we are undergoing *pathē*, and different people according to their different *pathē*; for example, the coward when excited by fear, the person in love by *erōs*; so that from a slight similarity the first seems (δοκεῖν) to see his enemies, the second his beloved. And the stronger the *pathos*, the less similarity is needed for these things to appear. In the same way all people become more prone to deception when they are angry or undergoing any appetite, and the more so the more strongly they are undergoing the *pathos*. This is also why lines on the walls sometimes appear to feverish people to be animals, from a slight similarity in how the lines are put together. And sometimes these things increase along with (συνεπιτείνει) the *pathē* so that, if the people are not severely ill, it doesn't escape their notice (λανθάνειν) that the appearance is false, but if the *pathos* is greater, they even move themselves in accordance with the appearances. (*Insomn.* 460b3-16)

---

[27] We could translate 'perceives,' but Aristotle clearly means to contrast this with λανθάνει: hence 'notices' or 'is aware' seems better. (See note 25 above on the problems with taking the perceptual faculty as the subject of these verbs.)

[28] Aristotle acknowledges that sleep does not always have this effect: sometimes we are aware that we are asleep, and in these cases we can experience the dream-appearances without mistaking them for real things ("Sometimes belief says that the appearance is false" (459a6).) He does not say what accounts for the difference between the two kinds of case, but a natural suggestion is that it is a matter of how deeply one is asleep, i.e. how powerful the *pathos* is. The passage quoted next in the main text confirms this suggestion.

Someone slightly angry or fevered, the passage suggests, may be subject to a false appearance but will notice that it is false. If the *pathos* is stronger, however, the fact that it is a mere appearance will "escape her notice" (λανθάνει again), and thus nothing in her will contradict it.

I take these passages from the *Insomn.* to illustrate the *de An.*'s claim that we follow *phantasia* against intellect when the latter is "covered over" by a *pathos*, and also to elucidate what this "covering over" consists in. For the rational faculty to be covered over – or, as the *Insomn.* puts it, to be "held in check, or not move with its proper motion" (461b5-7; cf. 459a6-8) – is for it to be unable to perform its proper and crucial function of noticing and contradicting false appearances.

Moreover, the last lines quoted above confirm that if the agent does notice that the appearance is false, she will not act on it – will not "move herself [or 'be moved,' κινεῖσθαι] in accordance with it." Someone with a slight fever may see the cracks on the wall as animals, but so long as her rational faculty remains unimpaired she will not get out of bed to swat at them. Strong *pathê* lead us to act on appearances, then, because they impair the rational faculty, preventing it from detecting false appearances. (The earlier lines of the fever passage suggest that *pathê* can also be responsible for generating false appearances in the first place. I will comment on the possible application of this fact to the explanation of *akrasia* below.)

There remains a question about the *Insomn.*'s view of the dreamer's or fevered person's rational attitude toward the appearances she follows. Does her rational faculty actively assent to the appearances, as 459a6-8 arguably implies (belief "follows" the appearance), or is it simply silent on the matter? The latter seems a more plausible view: to say that the dreamer outright believes the appearances is to ignore the difference between cases in which the rational faculty is impaired by a *pathos* and cases (like the finger-on-eyeball illusion) when it is functioning normally. (This is Gallop's interpretation of Aristotle's view: in dreams, belief "simply fails to oppose" the appearances, so that they "gain acceptance by default" (1991, 25). Pickavé and Whiting (2008, 342) offer compelling arguments for a similarly nondoxastic interpretation of the fever example.) Passages like 459a6-8 seem to count against this interpretation, but Gallop points out that Aristotle's use of δοκεῖν and variants is looser here than in the *de An.*, where Aristotle criticizes Plato for conflating seeming (δοκεῖν) with mere appearing (φαίνεσθαι). (See e.g. *Insomn.* 458b29, a clear case of Aristotle using δοκεῖ to mean φαίνεται and, arguably, the use of δοκεῖν in the passage just quoted above, at 460b6.) Given this loose and inconsistent usage, I think it most likely that Aristotle did not have a clearly worked out position on the question in the *Insomn.*; I will argue below that he has a decisive answer to a parallel question that arises in the *Ethics* regarding *akrasia*.

I have been arguing in this section that Aristotle holds a proto-Stoic view of rationality: it is one of reason's proper functions to scrutinize and judge appearances, and this function is crucial not merely for the regulation of belief but also for the regulation of action. (The view can be traced back to Plato (which further supports the claim that Aristotle holds it): see my 2008. But the Stoics are most explicit, and so their terminology is most useful in explaining Aristotle's view.)

The appearances we have considered in this section are all value-neutral appearances: appearances of things as a foot wide, or as an animal, and so on. Such appearances do often play a role in action, but only contingently: if one happens to want something a foot wide, or happens to fear animals, they become potentially motivating. But the Stoics's view of reason also applies to what we might call practical appearances: appearances with an essential tendency to motivate – what the Stoics call 'impulsive' appearances, which clearly correspond to Aristotle's evaluative appearances:

> Ensouled things are moved by themselves when a *phantasia* occurs within them which calls forth an impulse... A rational animal, however, in addition to its phantastic (φανταστικῇ) nature, has *logos* which judges (κρίνοντα) *phantasiai*, rejecting some of these and accepting others, in order that the animal may be guided accordingly. (Origen, *On Principles* 3.1.2-3 (SVF 2.988))[29]

Reason is the judge of the impulsive appearances to which the agent is subject. If it accepts such an appearance, the agent acts on it, but if it rejects the appearance she does not.

Aristotle surely likewise intends his view of reason's role to apply to practical appearances as well as value-neutral ones. For when he says that humans follow *phantasia* against knowledge (2b), or that we act on *phantasia* when intellect is covered over (*de An.* 429a5-8), the context both times is a discussion of *phantasia* in its practical role – and practical *phantasia* is, I have argued in the first part of this book, first and foremost evaluative. Notably, the view that when reason rejects evaluative appearances we do not act on them is explicitly championed by a philosopher who was not only Aristotle's devoted follower but also influenced by Stoic terminology, Alexander of Aphrodisias. Here is a passage we saw excerpted in Chapter 2:

> It is agreed by everyone that man has this advantage from nature over the other living creatures, that he does not follow *phantasiai* in the same way as them, but has *logos* from her as a judge (κριτὴν) of the appearances that impinge on him about certain things as deserving to be chosen (τῶν προσπιπτουσῶν φαντασιῶν περί τινων ὡς αἱρετῶν). Using this, if, when they are examined, the things that appeared *are* indeed as they initially appeared, he assents to the appearances and so goes in pursuit of them; but if they appear different or something else [appears] more deserving to be chosen, he chooses that, leaving behind what initially appeared to him as deserving of choice.[30] (*de Fato* 178.17-28, trans. Sharples)

Alexander here uses Stoic terminology to express what he takes to be an Aristotelian view; I have been arguing that his interpretation is correct and illuminating. On Aristotle's view, as on the Stoics', humans can be subject to practical appearances

---

[29] Translation based on Long and Sedley 1987.
[30] Compare: "For man alone of the other living creatures is able, after an appearance has impinged on him that something is to-be-done (φαντασίαν περί τινος ὡς πρακτέου), to enquire about it and deliberate whether he should assent to what appeared or not" (*Mantissa* 172.25-28).

without acting on them, because reason acts as the judge and censor. So long as reason is performing its proper function, then, we do not act on false appearances. If someone does act on a false appearance – that is, if she does act on an appetite or passion which reason *should* oppose – we can conclude that reason is not doing its job.

There is of course a major difference between the Stoic view and the Aristotelian one: the Stoics hold that without rational assent to an impulsive appearance there is no genuine appetite (or other passion), while Aristotle holds, as I argued in Chapter 4, that there is: the non-rational soul's passive acceptance of the appearance suffices to generate an appetite (or other passion). Thus on Aristotle's view when reason plays its proper role, rejecting false value-appearances and thereby preventing us from acting on them, we act not only against an appearance but also against the passion resulting from that appearance. Alexander brings this out clearly in another passage which describes a conflict between appearance and appetite on one side and reason on the other, much like 2f:

> Man has *logos* as a judge of the *phantasiai* which impinge on him from outside about things that are to be done (περὶ τῶν πρακτέων), and using this he examines whether each of these things not only appears the way it appears, but also is that way.... In this way then he often holds back from certain things that appear pleasant, *although he has a desire (ὄρεξιν) for them, because the logos is not in harmony with what appears* (μὴ τὸν λόγον ἔχεν τῷ φαινομένῳ συνᾴδοντα).... (de Fato 184.3-10, emphasis mine)

Refraining from a desired pleasure because one rationally rejects it is, in Aristotle's terminology, acting continently. What we have seen in this section and the previous one entails that Aristotle must think continence the norm when there is motivational conflict. Conflicts between rational and non-rational desires are based on conflicts between evaluative beliefs and evaluative appearances, and when reason contradicts appearances we do not act on them. Unless, that is, intellect is somehow covered over or held in check by sleep, sickness or a *pathos*. This suggests an account of how *akrasia* comes about; in the next section I develop that account.

5.5 The illusion account of *akrasia*

The *Insomn.* explains the cognitive effects of *pathê* in physiological terms: sleep and other conditions involve changes in the blood which affect cognition. We do not need to go into the details of Aristotle's physiology here; what is crucial for our purposes is that he treats appetites and emotions as involving similar bodily conditions (see especially *de An.* I.1 (403a7 ff.), which explains why *erôs* or anger can have the same effects as fever or sleep, as at *Insomn.* 460b4 ff.). Indeed, Aristotle reminds us of the physical aspects of emotions and desires in *EN* VII.3 itself, in a passage that compares the cognitive effects of such *pathê* to those of more straightforwardly physical ones: the famous comparison of the akratic agent to one mad, asleep, or drunk (1147a10-18, quoted below).

This gives us strong encouragement to use the account of following *phantasia* against intellect that we derived from the *Insomn.* to fill out the account of *akrasia* implied by *de An.* III.10. The result will be as follows:

Sometimes an agent reasons that some temptation – e.g. a third helping of cake – is to be avoided (intellect "orders her to hold back" (2f)). Nonetheless, the cake appears to her "without qualification pleasant and good without qualification." This is a *phantasia*, and it is a false one: a temperate person would not even be subject to it.

Thus our agent, like someone knowingly experiencing a perceptual illusion, has conflicting rational and non-rational cognitions. Her case is special, however, because the cognitions in question are evaluative ones, and we have seen that these have motivational consequences. The rational judgment that the cake is to be avoided brings with it a rational desire to abstain from it (what *de An.* III calls wish (βούλησις), and *EN* VII decision (προαίρεσις)). The appearance of the cake as good, meanwhile, brings with it an appetite to eat the cake.[31] Thus just as the temperate person is not subject to false evaluative appearances, neither is she subject to appetites that conflict with what her rational faculty commands (see *EN* 1102b27-28, 1119b15-18). And thus our ethically inferior agent has conflicting desires as well as conflicting cognitions: she undergoes motivational struggle.

For some time, these conflicting motivations wage war; then a crucial change occurs. The appetite for sweets is a bodily *pathos*, and it can affect cognition in much the same way as *pathê* do in the *Insomn.*'s examples: it can impair the rational faculty's crucial function of noticing and contradicting false appearances. If the agent's appetite were milder, or her rational faculty more resilient, she would continue to recognize the appearance as false, but she is like those "who become drunk quickly, on a little wine, and on less than most people" (*EN* VII.8 1151a4-5): the *pathos* "covers over" her intellect.

Now there is no longer anything to contradict the *phantasia*, and so she follows it. I have argued that even in the perceptual illusion case such following is best understood as default yielding rather than as active rational assent (whether or not Aristotle was clear on this point in the *Insomn.*); in the case of akratic action, this is certainly so. Someone who acts akratically, unlike someone who is self-indulgent (ἀκόλαστος), pursues harmful pleasures without believing that they are good (see *EN* 1146b22-24, 1151a20-24, and 1166b8-9). She does not actively assent to the appearance as true, but with her rational faculty impaired neither does she reject it as false: there is simply nothing active in her to resist the appearance. Likewise, she does not acquire a rational desire to eat the cake, but with her intellect silent she temporarily loses her rational motivation to avoid it, and so there is nothing active in her to resist the appetite.

---

[31] This may seem to clash with Aristotle's assertion in *EN* VII.3 that the appetite that causes akratic behavior "happens to be present" (see below). If we appeal to the distinction between general and specific appetites that I mention below, however, we can say that the agent just happens to be in a state of general craving, but only after the false appearance focuses that craving on the cake does she have the appetite that causes her action.

120   THE APPARENT GOOD AND NON-RATIONAL MOTIVATION

Appetite can (as we will see Aristotle emphasize in *EN* VII.3) move the agent all on its own, and with nothing left now to counter its force, it does: she eats the cake.

There remains a complication. We saw above that *pathê* can cause false appearances: an emotion, desire, or fever can exaggerate similarities so that a stranger appears to be one's enemy or some lines on the wall an animal. (If one were not afraid one would not even be subject to the appearance of the stranger as one's enemy; if one were not fevered one would not even be subject to the appearance of the lines on the wall as animals.) Is the agent's appetite, like the fever in that passage, responsible not only for rendering intellect unable to contradict a false appearance but also for generating that appearance in the first place? Aristotle does say elsewhere that an appetite can *cause* something to appear good.[32] When we try to apply this idea to the case of *akrasia*, we get an account which may seem worrisomely circular: earlier (in 2f from *de An.* III.10), we saw that the false appearance of something as pleasant and good without qualification gives rise to an appetite, while now we see this kind of false appearance itself generated by an appetite. We can, however, construe this not as a vicious circle but rather as a causal chain, if we distinguish general states of intense desire from specific desires for particular objects that can directly cause action.[33] First the general craving for sweets distorts appearances to make the cake appear pleasant and good without qualification; then, because the appetitive part of the soul goes for what appears pleasant and good without qualification, that general craving gets focused on the cake. (Or perhaps the right thing to say is: a new appetite arises, a specific one for this particular piece of cake.) There will be a further question as to whether the general appetite has arisen in its turn from a general *phantasia* of pleasures as good: I will argue briefly in Chapter 8 that it has.

We have now developed a full account of *akrasia* based on Aristotle's psychological works; let us call it 'the illusion account.' We have also seen some reasons – beyond the general but highly defeasible principle of wishing to find consistency in Aristotle's thought – to expect this account to be compatible with the account of *akrasia* in *EN* VII.3. First, because it is hard to understand how someone could act in accordance with appearances that she recognizes as illusory, construing motivational conflict as a species of perceptual illusion naturally invites an account on which acting akratically involves some kind of ignorance – just the kind of account we find in VII.3. Second, the fact that VII.3 appeals to the body-altering and knowledge-impairing effects of appetites and emotions in a passage that compares these with more straightforwardly physical

---

[32] "Things do not appear the same to people insofar as they are friendly or hostile, nor to the angry and the calm...but either altogether different or different in importance. To one who is friendly [i.e. favorably disposed], the person about whom he makes a judgment seems not to do wrong or only slightly; to one who is hostile, the opposite; and *to a person appetitively desiring something* (ἐπιθυμοῦντι) *and full of good hopes, if something in the future is a source of pleasure, it appears that it will come to pass and will be good*; but to an unemotional person and one in a disagreeable state of mind, the opposite [appears]" (*Rhet.* 1377b31–1378a5, translation based on Kennedy 1991, emphasis mine).

[33] For another account of Aristotle's view of *akrasia* that makes use of this distinction, see Destrée 2007.

conditions like sleep (quoted below) suggests that the chapter's account of *akrasia* is meant to be compatible with – and indeed naturally supplemented by – a physiological account of how such conditions affect cognition, an account of the kind Aristotle himself supplies in the *Insomn*.[34] A remark later in VII.3 bolsters this suggestion:

> As to how the ignorance is resolved and the akratic agent becomes a knower again, the same account [holds] as about the drunkard and the sleeper, and is not particular to this *pathos*; this account we must hear from the students of nature (φυσιολόγων). (*EN* VII.3 1147b6-9)

Let us turn, then, to the text of *EN* VII.3, to see if we can provide an interpretation that bears out these suggestions by rendering the chapter compatible with the illusion account of *akrasia*. I will not pretend that the fit is easy or obvious: VII.3 makes no mention of false appearances, and hardly any mention of *phantasia* at all. But I hope to show that we can read Aristotle as presupposing the illusion account as the background for VII.3. This will prove that chapter compatible with the struggle picture, and help illuminate the other questions that plague its interpretation.

5.6 *Nicomachean Ethics* VII.3

The discussion opens with the question of whether akratic agents act "knowing (εἰδότες) or not, and in what way knowing" (1146b8-9). The preceding discussion has made clear that this is a version of the question Socrates famously answered in the negative in the *Protagoras*: Does anyone willingly do what she knows is not best? (See especially 1145b26-27.)

Beginning at 1146b31, Aristotle introduces several distinctions between ways of knowing, with the aim of showing that while in some senses of 'knows' it would be very strange for someone to do what she knows she should not, in others it would not be strange at all: one may act against the dictates of knowledge one is not presently exercising (1146b31-35), and, as a particular case of this phenomenon, one may act against one's general maxims if one does not notice that they apply in a particular situation (1146b35-1147a10). Someone might know, for example, that all dry food is good for people, and that he is a person and that some type of food is dry, but if he "either does not have or is not exercising" the knowledge that some particular morsel of food is of this type (1147a8), there will be nothing strange in his failing to eat it.

Many have taken this "dry food" case to be an example of *akrasia*.[35] But if we are to fit VII.3 to the illusion account, this cannot be right. As Ross points out in the passage quoted in the introductory section, the person who fails to eat something dry because he simply does not know that it is dry, or is not "exercising" that knowledge (where the contrast with the condition Aristotle immediately goes on to describe (quoted

---

[34] For this same approach, with rather different results, see Pickavé and Whiting 2008.
[35] Translators often beg the question by making "the incontinent man" the subject at 1147a8 (thus Ross), although in fact there has been no mention of the ἀκρατής within the discussion of ways of knowing at all.

below) shows that this means something like: he happens not to be attending to the fact), undergoes no inner struggle. He has no *logos* commanding him to eat the food, and thus no corresponding rational desire (decision – προαίρεσις) to eat it. Perhaps we are meant to assume that he has some appetitive aversion to it, but this is not enough to make his avoidance of it akratic. Thus we should conclude that, as Kenny puts it, in this passage "Aristotle is simply explaining *one* sense in which a man can εἰδὼς ἃ μὴ δεῖ πράττειν [knowingly do things he should not]" (1966, 173).

This reading is confirmed by the next passage, the passage I mentioned above on the body-altering and knowledge-impairing effects of appetites and emotions. For its opening lines strongly indicate that only here does the explanation proper of *akrasia* begin:

> Furthermore, there is *another way besides those just mentioned* in which having knowledge belongs to human beings. For within 'having but not using' we observe *a different condition*,[36] such that one both has it in a way and doesn't have it, like the one sleeping or mad or drunk. But those who are in the grip of *pathê* are in this kind of condition: for spirited passions (θυμοί) and appetites for sex and some other things of this sort clearly alter (μεθιστᾶσιν) the body too, and in some cases even cause madness. It's clear, then, that we should say that akratic agents are in a condition similar to these people [the sleeping, mad and drunk]. (*EN* VII.3 1147a10-18, emphasis mine)

The akratic agent's ignorance, like that of those mad, drunk, or asleep, is to be explained by the presence of a body-altering *pathos*, and this is "another way" (ἄλλον τρόπον) of being disposed with regard to knowledge, different from "those just mentioned" (1147a11-12). People affected by *pathê* do not merely fail to exercise knowledge that is at their disposal, as do those who inadvertently neglect to eat nutritiously because they do not recognize a particular piece of food as being of a particular kind; instead, they "both have it in a way and don't have it" (1147a12-13). While under the influence of the *pathos* they are literally unable to exercise their knowledge, as Aristotle says in a related passage from the *Physics*:

> Whenever someone has passed from being drunk (μεθύειν) or asleep or diseased to the opposite state... he was earlier [while affected] *incapable of using his knowledge* (ἀδύνατος ἦν τῇ ἐπιστήμῃ χρῆσθαι)... [The change back to] using and activity occurs through the alteration of something in the body. (*Phys.* 247b13-248a6, emphasis mine)[37]

This can serve as a preliminary answer to our interpretative question about the nature of akratic ignorance; I return to the point below.

This reading entails that (contrary to e.g. Dahl 1984, 209) both the young students and the actors mentioned in the next lines (1147a21-23) are brought in only as illustrations of the fact that one can say "words that come from knowledge" without possessing that knowledge, and the one undergoing *akrasia* is like them only in this

---

[36] Διαφέρουσαν τὴν ἕξιν: possibly "an extreme condition"?
[37] Compare also the sleeping geometer often cited in this context (*GA* 735a9-11), who must undergo a bodily change before he can exercise his knowledge.

respect. She speaks in the same way as them insofar as she says something she does not really know, but in her case – like that of the drunkard who recites proofs or verses of Empedocles (1147a20), but unlike that of the students or the actors – the ignorance results from a strong bodily *pathos*.

Next we must face one of the most difficult passages of the chapter, Aristotle's attempt to explain *akrasia* in terms of the beliefs the agent holds and the way they combine to influence action (1147a24-b5). The passage is very hard to understand on its own terms; there is also a serious *prima facie* obstacle to reconciling it with the illusion account of *akrasia*. I want to show that we can in fact reconcile the two, and also that we can use the illusion account to go some way toward illuminating the passage itself.

Aristotle begins by laying out his theory of the syllogism: when universal and particular premises combine, they yield either assent to a conclusion, or an action (1147a25-28). Then he applies the theory to cases of *akrasia*:

Whenever one universal [belief? proposition? premise?] is present forbidding tasting, and another, that all sweets things are pleasant, and this is sweet, and this [belief/proposition/premise] is active, and appetite happens to be present, then the one [belief/proposition] says to avoid this, but the appetite leads: for it is capable of moving each of the parts.[38] (*EN* VII.3 147a31-35)

Most commentators interpret this passage as describing two syllogisms. The first one is a practical syllogism forbidding tasting. Remaining fairly neutral on the details underdetermined by the text, we can represent it as follows (using 'U' for universal premise, 'P' for particular, and 'C' for conclusion):

(U1) Avoid all F things
(P1) This [piece of cake] is F
(C1) Avoid this[39]

(I mean to leave it open for now whether the middle term is 'sweet' or something else (e.g. 'unwholesome'); we will return to this point below.)

The syllogism passage tells us that the agent reasons that she should avoid the cake, which is to say that her rational faculty generates a rational command, a *logos*, to hold back (compare 2f above). But there is something else that "happens to be present" in her, an appetite, and as we find out a few lines below, "the appetite is opposed (ἐναντία) . . . to the correct *logos*" (1147b2-3). I will return to the intervening lines shortly. For now we can note that this description is strikingly similar to the picture we saw in *de An.* III.10, where "desires arise that are opposed (ἐναντίαι) to one another, and this happens when *the logos and the appetites are opposed*" (2f). This encourages us to read *EN* VII.3 as employing the

---

[38] Or "each of the parts [of soul: rational and non-rational] is capable of moving [the body]" – a less common reading, but one which fits well with the *de An.* III.10 account of *akrasia*.

[39] Some, wishing to deny that the agent ever reaches the conclusion of the syllogism forbidding tasting, insist that 'Avoid this' must be a universal premise, not a conclusion. But this is so plainly out of keeping with the idea that a universal premise contains no reference to particulars (like 'this') that I think we should rule it out.

same shorthand we found at the end of *de An.* III.9.[40] That passage characterized *akrasia* as a conflict between a motivational state on one side and a cognitive one on the other, but the ensuing discussion made clear that on a fuller description it is a conflict between two pairs of states: a rational evaluative cognition with its corresponding rational motivation on one side, and a non-rational evaluative cognition (an appearance through *phantasia* of the cake as good) with its corresponding non-rational motivation (an appetite) on the other. The syllogism passage, like *de An.* III.9, mentions only a rational cognition and a non-rational motivation. Elsewhere in *EN* VII, however, Aristotle mentions the rational motivation that depends on the *logos* forbidding action: he says that the akratic agent acts against her decision (προαίρεσις) (see e.g. 1148a9), where a decision is a (partly) desiderative state.[41] Thus, *contra* Ross and others, VII.3 does imply the struggle picture: in *akrasia* a rational motivation conflicts with an appetite.

As to how the appetite wins out, this passage says nothing explicit, but a remark Aristotle makes a few lines below strongly suggests that the explanation is the same as on the illusion account. On that account, after the appetite and the rational desire vie against one another for some time, the physical alterations involved in the appetitive state impair the agent's rational faculty so that it no longer "contradicts the appearance," i.e. no longer orders her to hold back. But to say that appetite wins out when the agent is intellectually impaired is to say that it wins out when she becomes in some way ignorant. And in keeping with this explanation, after some more comments on the syllogistic explanation to which we will return, Aristotle concludes the discussion with a comment we have seen above: "As to how the ignorance is resolved and the akratic agent becomes a knower again, the same account [holds] as about the drunkard and the sleeper..." (1147b6-8). Commentators have sometimes argued that these lines must be misplaced (see e.g. Irwin (1999)), but on our reading they are just where they should be: they serve to remind us that appetite was able to "lead" the agent in the syllogism only by way of inducing the kind of ignorance we saw it capable of inducing in the comparison with madmen, drunkards, and sleepers.

This, however, brings us to a serious worry about applying the illusion account to VII.3, concerning the cognition that grounds the agent's appetite. I have argued that in the *de An.* this cognition is a non-rational one, a *phantasia* of the cake as pleasant and good. But Aristotle's syllogistic explanation in VII.3 does not merely neglect to mention explicitly that the agent's appetite is grounded in *phantasia*; it strongly implies that it is grounded in rational cognition instead. This comes out in the lines immediately following the syllogistic account:

---

[40] For this same strategy see Santas 1969.
[41] Decision is described as deliberative or intellectual desire at *EN* VI.2 1139a23 (ὄρεξις βουλευτική) and 1139b5 (ὄρεξις διανοητική). In *de An.* III.10-11 the rational motivation is called a wish (βούλησις) rather than a decision (there is only one mention of decision in the *de An.*, at 406b25), but the description of wish as desire in accordance with reasoning (2d) applies well to the *EN*'s notion of decision. It seems that in the *de An.* Aristotle uses βούλησις to cover all forms of rational desire, not employing the ethical works' distinction between desire for an end (βούλησις) and desire for something within one's power that contributes to an end (προαίρεσις); I return to this subject in Chapters 6 and 7.

Thus it happens that the agent acts akratically in a way by the agency of *logos* and belief (ὑπὸ λόγου πως καὶ δόξης ἀκρατεύεσθαι), but not [belief] that is opposed in itself, but only accidentally: for the appetite, but not the belief, is opposed to the correct *logos*. (*EN* VII.3 1147a35-b3)

The appetite for the cake is guided by the belief that it is pleasant, and this belief is the product of a piece of full-blown reasoning, the second syllogism implied in the syllogism passage:

(U2) All sweet things are pleasant
(P2) This [the cake] is sweet
(C2) This is pleasant[42]

This is compatible with the view that the agent acts on *phantasia*: as we saw in Chapter 4 a belief (like "This is pleasant") can give rise to an appearance (of the thing as pleasant and good without qualification) and thereby an appetite. But if appetite is dependent on a syllogism and belief, even indirectly dependent, how can it win out by "covering over" intellect? Once intellect is impaired, the worry goes, won't the agent lose access to the beliefs that guide appetite, in addition to those that sustain her decision? If so, then appetite can no longer motivate action, for it will revert to the status of objectless craving.

Before we respond directly to the worry, it is worth noting that the characterization of akratic action as dependent on reasoning is in apparent tension not only with the illusion account, but also with common sense, and even with Aristotle's claims later in *EN* VII. One might on occasion become aware that some cake is pleasant by beginning with a universal belief about sweet things and going through the steps of a syllogism, but surely this is not the standard case. And Aristotle himself, in a later passage contrasting those who are led to act akratically by appetite with those who are so led by spirit, recognizes that a much simpler form of cognition can do the job:

Appetite, if *logos or perception* only says that something is pleasant, impels one to enjoy it... (*EN* VII.6 1149a34-b1, emphasis mine)

This passage tells us that while the akratic agent's appetite can be guided toward an object by *logos*, it can also be guided by mere perception.[43] This means that the syllogistic account describes at best one species of akratic action, and the claim that the agent acts "in a way by the agency of *logos* and belief" (1147b1) picks out at best a contingent feature of *akrasia*; perhaps Aristotle got carried away in those passages by

---

[42] Contrast the pseudo-syllogism in our passage 1d from the *MA* ("'I must drink,' says appetite..."), which involves no universals and no calculation (no reasoning – μὴ λογισάμενοι, *MA* 701a28), and can thus represent the psychology of non-rational animals as well as humans.

[43] Aristotle must have in mind not only the direct perception of some pleasant quality (e.g. tasting something sweet), but also cases like the one he mentions in *EN* III.10, where the sight, sound, or smell of food alerts an animal that pleasure is near. (On the account he gives in the psychological works this will probably involve *phantasia*, but he does not mention that here, and indeed contrasts such perception with *phantasia* at 1149a32-35.)

his zeal for the explanatory power of syllogisms. If the illusion account can accommodate cases of the kind described in VII.3, therefore, we should not worry too much if it does not emphasize them. And there are, I think, two plausible ways to reconcile the syllogistic account with the illusion account.

The first is to suppose that even if *phantasia* is first alerted to the fact that the cake is pleasant by a belief to that effect, it can continue to apprehend the cake as pleasant – and thus continue to guide appetite toward it – even when the rational faculty is silent and the agent loses her grasp on her beliefs. To use one of Aristotle's metaphors for communications between the rational and non-rational parts of the soul, if a father's offhand remark that there is cake in the cupboard excites his child, the child can on his own cognitive steam set off to find it after the father has fallen asleep (or passed out drunk).

The second possibility is to suppose that even when intellect is impaired to the extent that it cannot command "Avoid this," it is still able to function in other ways. Our worry stems from the assumption that on the psychological works' view, we follow *phantasia* against intellect only when intellect is completely disabled by a *pathos*. This may be a natural reading of the *de An.*'s claim that we act on *phantasia* when intellect is "covered over," but the *Insomn.* implies a less radical account. Even someone asleep or mad with fever can exercise intellect and reason to some degree: his rational faculty is "held in check or not moving with its proper motion," but not totally inert, as evidenced by the fact that – as the text seems to imply – he still has beliefs and thoughts.[44] The account I gave in section 4 of what it is for the rational faculty to be "held in check" gives us a non-arbitrary way to demarcate these intellectual abilities and disabilites. Aristotle is interested, both in the *Insomn.* and in VII.3, in a kind of intellectual impairment that is drastic but nonetheless localized.[45] When affected by the *pathos* intellect cannot perform its crucial function of noticing and contradicting false appearances, the function essential to it on the proto-Stoic account of rationality I attributed to Aristotle above. It may however be able to perform other

---

[44] On a plausible reading of the *Insomn.*, Aristotle holds that even while we are being taken in by dreams we can still have thoughts (see 458b15-26, 462a28-29) and beliefs (recall for example the claim that belief, when held in check, is not utterly inert but rather "follows the *phantasma*" (459a6-8); the same point is made at 461b6-8). None of these passages provide indisputable evidence that the rational faculty is active even when "held in check," however. For doubts about the strictness of Aristotle's use of δόξα and δοκεῖν in the *Insomn.*, see the discussion in section 4 above. As to the thoughts we have when dreaming, what Aristotle says is that "when we are sleeping we sometimes think other things παρά the appearances" (458b17-18; cf. 462a28-29 which also uses παρά. I have (following Gallop 1991, 138) taken him to mean that we sometimes think about other things, "over and above" the dreams. We might, however (following Modrak 1987, 101), translate παρά as 'contrary to,' in which case Aristotle has in mind thoughts like "I'm asleep right now, and this is just a dream" – in other words, the thoughts that constitute the noticing and contradicting of false appearances; if this is right, then these passages provide no evidence that intellect can be active even when "held in check," for these are thoughts we only have when it is *not* held in check. I find Gallop's reading more natural, especially given the emphasis on what is thought being something "other" than the appearances (ἀλλά, 458b18), but this is inconclusive. (The passage on mnemonics in dreams (458b18-25) might settle the point in Gallop's favor, if only we knew how to interpret it, but I do not.)

[45] Charles 2009 argues that it is important that VII.3 compares akratic agents to those who are οἰνωμένοι, "tipsy-drunk," rather than μεθύοντες, "dead-drunk," unable to think at all.

functions. Thus the agent's appetite, in "covering over" intellect, might leave intact her belief that "This is sweet," and even her belief that "Everything sweet is pleasant"; what it knocks out is her ability to recognize that "This appears to be good but is not." (I will consider which element of the syllogism this corresponds to below.)

We might even suppose that the effect on intellect is so localized as to be surgical: the *pathos* knocks out the agent's awareness that the cake is bad but leaves everything else intact. On this interpretation, even when in the grips of passion our agent is aware of the difference between how things appear and how they really are in general (she will, for instance, reach for the cake on the counter instead of its reflection in the mirror); all she loses is her ability to notice and contradict one crucial false appearance, the appearance of the cake as good. This may be a more philosophically plausible picture than the one I have suggested. I do not, however, see any principled way to extract it from the psychological works' characterizaton of *pathos*-induced ignorance. What physiological fact could explain so specific an effect?

A final note on this subject: while there is certainly no explicit claim in *EN* VII that the akratic agent's appetite is grounded in a *phantasia* of the cake as pleasant and good, there are two mentions of *phantasia* that fit well with that account. The first of these immediately follows the claim that in *akrasia* an appetite is opposed to a *logos*:

Beasts are not akratic, because they have no universal supposition, but only *phantasia* and memory of particulars. (*EN* VII.3 1147b3-5)

Beasts lack the rational faculties that yield universal knowledge, so in their case acting on (an appetite for what appears good to) *phantasia* cannot be acting as their knowledge would forbid if it were active. We do not fault dogs for pursuing the present pleasure any more than we fault them for barking at their own reflections: where *phantasia* is the highest form of cognition, there can be no blame for following its lead.[46]

The second is an otherwise puzzling remark in *EN* VII.7. Here Aristotle is distinguishing weak akratic agents, who deliberate but then act against their decisions, from impetuous ones, who "are led by the *pathos* on account of not having deliberated": the latter, he says, "don't wait for the *logos*, because they tend to follow the *phantasia*" (1150b27-28). Our account makes sense of the remark: the impetuous akratic agent goes with his *phantasia*-based desire, i.e. appetite, without ever thinking through the *logos* that would oppose it. The weak one, by contrast, follows a *phantasia*-based desire in opposition to a *logos*-based one. (Thus the impetuous akratic does not undergo active motivational conflict. On my understanding, most of what Aristotle has to say about *akrasia* – including in passage 2f from the *de An.*, and in *EN* VII.3 – applies only to the weak variety, and what Aristotle does in *EN* VII.7 is to indicate a similar

---

[46] Compare 2f: *logos* and appetites can be opposed only "in those who have perception of time" – i.e. in rational creatures (see Hicks' note *ad loc.*). 1147b3-5 is often taken to concern the role of rational cognition in generating the "bad" syllogism, but given Aristotle's claim later in book VII that akratic appetites can depend on perception alone (1149b1-3, quoted above), this would be very misleading.

phenomenon. The illusion account gives us a good explanation of why impetuous *akrasia* is similar enough to weak *akrasia* to deserve the same name: in both, one follows a *phantasia*-based desire against what reason *would* say were it doing its job.)

In sum, *EN* VII.3's syllogistic account of *akrasia* is in obvious tension with the illusion account's focus on *phantasia* as the cognition that grounds appetite, but I have tried to show that this plausibly represents a difference of emphasis rather than a substantial change of view.

We are nearing the end of VII.3, but the last lines are among the most disputed. Giving an interpretation of them will mean addressing head-on one of the main points of interpretative dispute that I mentioned in the introduction: what is the proper object of akratic ignorance? When appetite impairs intellect, does the agent lose her grasp on (P1), the minor premise of the syllogism that forbids tasting, or does she retain her grasp on that premise but lose her grasp of (C1), the conclusion? That is, what is "the last *protasis*" in the following lines?:

> Since the last *protasis* [premise or proposition] is a belief about something perceptible, and is decisive (κυρία) for actions, it is this that the one undergoing the *pathos* either does not have or "has" in the way that we saw is not [really] having knowledge but [merely] speaking, like the drunk with the verses of Empedocles. (*EN* VII.3 1147b9-12)

The first thing to be said is that our account of the chapter renders this question much less pressing than it would otherwise be. The most common reading of the passage takes "last *protasis*" to refer to the minor premise, and makes this very significant by in effect taking the passage as confirmation that the "dry food" syllogism discussed above is a paradigm of akratic reasoning: the agent never notices that the cake falls into the category of things forbidden by the major premise, and thus never reaches the conclusion "Avoid this." I have argued, however – as have all those who want to make VII.3 compatible with some version of the struggle picture of *akrasia* – that at some stage before her action the agent grasps both premises of the syllogism forbidding tasting, and thus reaches the conclusion; it is only after this that her ignorance sets in. (More precisely, this is what occurs in the cases Aristotle later calls "weak" *akrasia*, in which "people who have deliberated do not stick with the results of their deliberation on account of the *pathos*"; impetuous akratic agents "are led by the *pathos* on account of not having deliberated" (VII.7 1150b19-22), and thus, it would seem, never undergo struggle. As many have pointed out, if the standard version of the minor-premise reading is correct – if *akrasia* is to be understood on the model of the dry food syllogism – all *akrasia* reduces to the impetuous kind.) This view is in principle compatible with either reading: perhaps under the influence of appetite the agent loses her grip on the minor premise, and thereby also on the conclusion which depends on it, or perhaps the appetite leaves the minor premise intact and robs her only of the conclusion. So long as she has earlier grasped both, we can account for her having undergone struggle before appetite won out.

One would still like to know which account Aristotle has in mind, and while our interpretation does not rule decisively in either direction it does put important constraints on the answer. First, the knowledge the akratic lacks must be the product of, and dependent on, the proper functioning of her rational faculty. This follows from the picture of *akrasia* as a conflict between *phantasia* on one side and intellect on the other (see 2f and *de An.* 429a5-8). Second, more specifically, the knowledge she lacks must be the product of, and dependent on, her rational faculty's capacity to notice and contradict the falsity of the appearance on which she acts – the appearance of the cake as pleasant and good without qualification, i.e. as to-be-gone-for. This follows from the characterization of being taken in by perceptual illusions in the *Insomn.*: she acts as she does because she is temporarily unaware of something analogous to "The sun is in fact larger than the inhabited portion of the earth," or "Those things on the wall are really just lines."

The reading on which 'last *protasis*' refers to the conclusion meets both constraints very naturally. "This is to-be-avoided" is a direct contradiction of "This is to-be-gone-for," and as the conclusion of a piece of reasoning (syllogizing), it is produced by and depends on that reasoning.

What about the much more common reading, on which the agent lacks the minor premise? As to the first constraint – that the knowledge she loses be dependent on the proper functioning of her intellect – things might look bad, for on the standard interpretation the minor premise is the province not of reasoning but rather of perception. Perception is a close cousin of *phantasia*, and both are activities of what is in some sense the same faculty of the soul, the perceptual faculty (*Insomn.* 459a15). If grasping (P1) simply amounts to being aware of some perceptible fact (e.g. "This is sweet" or "This is cake"), then the minor premise reading construes *akrasia* as a conflict between contradictory perceptions rather than, as the illusion account has it, a conflict between a perceptual cognition (*phantasia*) on one side and a rational cognition on the other. (Furthermore, this reading offers no explanation of why the *pathos* knocks out one perception while leaving the other intact.)

There is, however, a version of the minor premise reading on which it meets the constraint. In several passages Aristotle describes *phronesis* (the excellent condition of practical intellect) as a quasi-perceptual capacity primarily concerned with particulars (1142a23-30, 1143a25-b5). McDowell and Wiggins have applied these claims to VII.3's analysis of *akrasia*, arguing that the agent's grasp of the minor premise – or more precisely her "selection [of it] *as* minor premise: as what matters about the situation"[47] – is itself an exercise of practical intellect. If this is right then the "covering over" of intellect will after all entail the loss of the minor premise.[48]

---

[47] McDowell 1998, 29; cf. Wiggins 1975.
[48] There are other readings which make the grasp of the minor premise intellectual. Greenwood argues that recognizing something as belonging to a certain class (e.g. recognizing some cake as falling into the category of unhealthy things) must be an act of intellect (1909, 55). Destrée gives an account on which (P1) is grasped by rational or calculative (λογιστική) *phantasia* (2007, 152-54). This would fit our constraint, but I do not think it is right: as I understand Aristotle's brief description of calculative *phantasia* (*de An.* 434a7-10), what it yields are decisions about what to do – conclusions, rather than particular premises, of practical syllogisms.

As to the second constraint – that the missing piece of knowledge be an exercise of the rational faculty's capacity for contradicting false appearances – the commonest version of the minor premise reading, on which (P1) is "This is sweet," clearly fails to meet it: there is no conflict at all between the belief that the cake is sweet and the appearance of it as good. Here too, however, there is a version of the minor premise reading which may work, one in fact presupposed by the McDowell/Wiggins reading. We might take it that (U1) (the universal forbidding tasting) is not "Avoid sweets," but instead something like "Avoid excessive numbers of sweets" or "Avoid unwholesome foods" – that is, that the middle term of the syllogism is evaluative or prescriptive in nature – and thus that (P1) is something like "This is one too many," or "This is unwholesome."[49] If this is right, then (P1) is arguably a contradiction of the appearance on which the agent acts. To recognize something as unwholesome or excessive is precisely to notice qualifications about it that render it not pleasant and good "without qualification."

This version of the minor premise reading has its supporters on other grounds, and is perhaps a philosophically attractive view of *akrasia*. It is worth noting, however, that it is a particularly hard fit with the text of VII.3: it would be strange for Aristotle, having spelled out both premises of the second syllogism, never to name the crucial middle term of the first, nor to draw any attention to the fact that it must be something different from 'sweet.' Insofar as our account makes this the only viable version of the minor premise reading, therefore, it may count in favor of rejecting the minor premise reading altogether.

Both the minor premise reading and the conclusion reading struggle with the lines that follow, and the illusion account gives us little help here:

And since the last term (ὅρον) seems to be neither universal nor scientific (ἐπιστημόνικον) in the same way as the universal, what Socrates sought also seems to happen. For it is not what seems to be knowledge in the strict sense that is present (παρούσης) when the *pathos* occurs, nor is this dragged around on account of the *pathos*, but instead the perceptual kind [of knowledge]. (*EN* VII.3 1147b13-17)

These lines seem to say that what the agent lacks is knowledge of the universal premise forbidding tasting. This is formally compatible with the conclusion reading: if one loses one's grasp of (U1) there is no syllogism, and so one loses one's grasp of (C1) as well. It also fits the constraints we derived from the illusion account: "Avoid all sweets" (or "Avoid all unwholesome foods") plausibly contradicts the appearance of the cake as to-be-gone-for, and, being a universal claim, it is clearly a product of intellect. On the other hand, this reading is a bad fit with the preceding lines (1147b9-17), in which we are told that the knowledge the agent lacks is knowledge of something perceptible – with the strong implication that this is the *only* knowledge she lacks, not that she lacks it as a consequence of lacking universal knowledge – and thus most interpreters reject the

---

[49] For variations on this reading see Aquinas' commentary and Grant's.

implication that the agent lacks knowledge of the universal premise, often resorting to *ad hoc* emendation of the text.⁵⁰ If we do take the passage at face value it lends support to the conclusion reading and counts strongly against the minor premise reading; I can, however, see no argument based on the illusion account for choosing this reading over the straightforward reading of the preceding lines.

In sum, the illusion account rules out the standard versions of the reading on which *akrasia* involves ignorance of the minor premise, leaving admissible some philosophically intriguing but textually thin interpretations. It fits very well with the reading on which it involves ignorance of the conclusion. I will not claim, however, that these arguments are decisive.

As to the nature of the agent's ignorance, our account has yielded a much firmer answer. She is at the time of action literally unable to access the knowledge that would prevent tasting. She does not merely fail to combine it with other propositions (Joachim, Irwin), nor does she merely fail to use her knowledge in the sense that she fails to act on it (Broadie), nor is her lacking it a matter of her having failed to integrate it fully with her character or with her conception of the good life (Dahl, McDowell, Wiggins). And certainly she does not merely fail to use it the way that an absent-minded person might fail to notice that the piece of cake she is about to eat is her third. Instead, she is literally prevented by her physical condition from exercising some knowledge that would otherwise be at her disposal. That is why Aristotle compares her not to those who simply fail to use their knowledge, but instead to those who, like the madman, sleeper, and drunkard "both have knowledge in a way and don't have it," and that is why he says we must go to the φυσιολόγοι to discover how her ignorance is resolved.⁵¹

---

⁵⁰ Supporters of the minor premise reading often follow Stewart's proposal, reading περιγίνεται for παρούσης γίνεται in 1147b16, to yield "It is not in what seems to be knowledge in the strict sense that the *pathos* overcomes... but the perceptual kind." Kenny 1966 and Charles 2009 offer plausible readings of the unemended text in support of the conclusion reading: *akrasia* does not occur in the "immediate presence" (παρούσης) of the universal knowledge (Charles), or "it is not the mental utterance of the major premiss" which gives rise to the appetite (Kenny); instead, trouble sets in when one comes to the level of the particular. A version of this strategy should be available to supporters of the minor premise reading as well: *akrasia* occurs not when we are merely contemplating universal truths, but rather when we are faced with the task of applying such truths to tasty particulars. For an extended defense of the face-value reading of this passage, the view that the akratic lacks knowledge of the universal (that is, fails to actualize her universal knowledge by applying it to the relevant particular), see Pickavé and Whiting 2008.

⁵¹ For this reading see also Charles 1984, Pickavé and Whiting 2008, and Lorenz 2006, 197. It gains support not only from the *Physics* passage cited above on drunkards (247b13-248a6) but also from a passage from the *EN*'s discussion of temperance: "if the appetites are large and intense they even drive out (ἐκκρούουσιν) reasoning" (1119b10; cf. *EE* 1224b24). It is worth noting too that there is strong precedent for this view in Plato. See *Timaeus* 86b-c (when undergoing intense pleasures, pains, or appetites a person "*is incapable of seeing or hearing anything right*. He goes raving mad, and is at the moment *least capable of reasoning*"), and especially *Laws* 645d-e and 649d-e, a discussion to which Aristotle is surely indebted in *EN* VII.3: strong passions, just like excessive wine, make all forms of cognition "abandon" us (ἀπολείπει – *Laws* 645e2). If I am right then Aristotle's view is a modification of Plato's in the *Timaeus* and *Laws*: passion drives out reasoning, but leaves perception and *phantasia* operative.

This interpretation leaves Aristotle vulnerable to an objection which has often been leveled against his account of *akrasia*: surely not every instance of acting against one's knowledge of what is best involves a strong passion, let alone any bodily affect. The present suggestion makes the complaint even sharper: surely not every instance of failing to act on one's rational judgment about what is best involves a passion so strong that it shuts down one's ability to think. To this I reply simply that while there may be cases of "clear-eyed" irrational action, they are not among those Aristotle is concerned to explain under the rubric of *akrasia*. As the passage on drunkards, madmen, and sleepers so strongly suggests, Aristotle's akratic has little in common with Austin's cool bombe-hogger, let alone Davidson's bedtime tooth-brusher:[52] she is someone in the grip of strong passion. The account I have developed here indicates that it is a mistake to expect Aristotle's account of *akrasia* to apply even in an extended way to cases that do not involve powerful passions. This might arguably be a defect of Aristotle's account of *akrasia*, but it is not a quirk of my interpretation.

Thus Aristotle's akratic agent is closer to Socrates' than many have thought. She is far from "clear-eyed": her intellect, the eye of her soul, is not merely clouded but actually covered over. In the grips of the *pathos* she loses the ability to distinguish how things appear from how they are, and – what amounts, on our account, to the same thing – to distinguish what is good for her from what is presently pleasant.

5.7 Ignorance and struggle revisited

I began the chapter with two questions about the relation between *EN* VII.3's account of *akrasia* and the struggle picture that we find elsewhere in the corpus. Why, given his resources in the struggle picture for a common-sense account on which non-rational appetite overpowers rational motivation and leads us to do what we know full well is wrong, would Aristotle want to make the radical Socratic claim that *akrasia* must in some way involve ignorance? And is the ignorance account a stark rejection of the struggle account, as it has seemed to many, or is there some way to reconcile the two? I have tried to answer these questions by fleshing out an account of *akrasia* implicit in the psychological works and applying this account to the interpretation of *EN* VII.3.

First, because Aristotle construes motivational conflict as involving a variety of perceptual illusion, and because he holds the plausible view that no one who recognizes an appearance as illusory will let it guide her behavior, he has strong reason to deny that one can act on an appetite in direct defiance of a rational desire. If *akrasia* involves a choice between what quasi-perceptually appears good and what reason declares to be good in direct opposition to that appearance, then a clear-eyed akratic will be no more possible than a clear-eyed swatter of illusory animals. One might object that because the illusions involved in *akrasia* are evaluative ones, and so

---

[52] Austin 1961, 146; Davidson 1970.

necessarily have motivational force, here, unlike in ordinary perceptual illusion cases, it becomes possible for appearances to overpower knowledge in a battle of brute strength. Perhaps Aristotle overlooked this possibility, or perhaps he had reasons to reject it; in any case on the interpretation I have argued for he has susbstantive and compelling reasons, if not decisive ones, to hold that *akrasia* must involve temporary ignorance.

Second, the account of *akrasia* as ignorance is not merely compatible with the more straightforward account of *akrasia* as the victory of non-rational over rational desire, but forms a crucial part of that account. Appetite wins out over rational desire precisely by knocking out the rational cognition on which that desire depends – by rendering the agent temporarily ignorant of the fact that her action is bad.

If the arguments of this chapter have been successful, they show that attention to the psychological works can illuminate the ethical works. In particular, recognizing *phantasia* as the cognitive basis of non-rational motivation allows us to use what we know about the nature of evaluative appearances, and of the interactions between *phantasia* and intellect, to make sense of what the ethical works say about non-rational desire and its interactions with reason. In Chapters 7 and 8 I will argue that this same recognition helps us solve another vexing set of problems in the interpretation of the ethical works, the contribution of non-rational character to our conception of happiness. But to get to this point we will need to lay some groundwork. In Part II, we have seen how evaluative *phantasia* serves as the direct basis for non-rational passions. In the last part of the book I turn to show that it plays an equally important role, although a less direct one, in the desires we have here seen contrasted with and sometimes opposed to passions: distinctively human, distinctively rational desires – wishes and decisions.

PART III

The Apparent Good and Rational Motivation

6

Phantasia and Deliberation

6.1 Rational desire

Thus far I have argued that the very same "apparent good" that the psychological works characterize as the object of animal motivation is also the object of non-rational human passions: emotions and appetites are based on quasi-perceptual appearances, exercises of *phantasia*.

Despite the various complications and objections I have considered along the way, this conclusion should be in a sense unsurprising. Non-rational passions are, in a word, non-rational. Given my arguments in Chapter 1 that all motivation is based on evaluative cognition of some kind, we should thus expect them to be based on non-rational cognition. And therefore when we find Aristotle saying that appetites, envy and the like are responses to what *appears* good, it stands to reason that, as I argued in Chapters 4 and 5, he has in mind literal appearances through *phantasia*.

In the remainder of the book, however, I will argue for a more radical thesis: that *phantasia* underlies *all* human motivation. Even our most rational and distinctively human desires are based in one way or another on *phantasia*. Therefore even these desires are in some sense for what quasi-perceptually appears good. And therefore – given my account of the apparent good in Chapter 3 – even these desires are ultimately based in pleasurable perceptions.

If this thesis seems surprising, or plain wrong, that is because it apparently ignores the enormous importance Aristotle assigns to the distinction between the rational and the non-rational in both his psychology and his ethics. Humans are different from animals – and thus capable of achieving virtue and happiness – precisely in that we possess *logos*. We share the cognitive powers animals have – perception and *phantasia* – but on top of these we also have rational cognition: thought (διάνοια), intellect (νοῦς), and reasoning (λογισμός).[1] Moreover, rational cognition can be practical as well as theoretical, and hence our cognitive difference from animals entails a motivational difference: we have distinctively human, distinctively rational desires.

---

[1] I will have some occasion to discuss the differences between these in what follows, but it should be clear that Aristotle thinks them all distinctively rational: they are all activities of the part of the soul that has *logos*, and therefore all unavailable to lower animals.

More precisely, there are two species of motivation that Aristotle assigns to humans alone, each of which plays a crucial role in virtue and hence happiness: wish (βούλησις), and decision (προαίρεσις). Each is denied to non-rational animals (EN III.2 1111b11-13); moreover, each is explicitly called rational or noetic at some point in the corpus (see *Rhet.* 1369a1-4 on wish, and *EE* V/*EN* VI 1139b4-5 on decision). The natural and nearly universal interpretation is that each is based on rational cognition. Indeed, this distinction between species of rational desire clearly corresponds to the distinction we saw in the *MA* between two roles for practical intellect: identifying an end (supplying the "premise of the good" in a practical syllogism) and working out the means to it (supplying the "premise of the possible"). In the ethical works Aristotle distinguishes (as he does not systematically in the *MA* or *de An.*) between wish, as desire for ends, and decision, as desire for the particular doable things that realize ends.[2] A very natural inference is that wish is based on practical intellect in its first role, decision in its second. Let us accept this characterization for now (the arguments I go on to give in the rest of the book will support it). The question I want to raise is: does this entail that these kinds of desire are therefore not based on *phantasia,* and therefore not for the apparent good in the technical sense developed in Part I of this book?

Certainly one might suppose so, and Aristotle himself seems to say as much in the discussions of locomotion we examined in Chapter 1. For at many points in both the *de An.* and *MA* passages he speaks of *phantasia* and intellect as mutually exclusive alternatives, one or the other of which – but not both – plays the cognition-role in each episode of motivation. For example:

2a-b. [T]here are two movers, desire or intellect, if one classifies *phantasia* as a sort of thinking. For many follow *phantasiai* contrary to knowledge, and in the other animals there is neither thinking nor reasoning, but *phantasia.* (*de An.* 433a9-12)

g. [T]he object of desire ... moves, itself unmoved, by being thought or represented by *phantasia* (φαντασθῆναι). (*de An.* 433b11-12)

See also the *MA*'s claim that *phantasia* (as well as perception) can "hold the same place" as intellect in causing action (1a – *MA* 700b18-20). Correspondingly, these texts imply that intellect-based desire is for the good *by contrast with* the apparent good: see the *MA*'s claim that the apparent good, and therefore the pleasant, can "hold the same place" as the good (1b – 700b28-29), along with two other passages we saw in Chapter 1:

The apparent fine (καλόν) is the object of appetite (ἐπιθυμητόν), whereas the really fine is the primary object of wish (βουλητόν). (*Met.* 1072a27–28)

---

[2] The *de An.* mentions decision once (406b25), the *MA* several times, but neither explains a difference between it and wish; I will argue below that the *de An.* uses 'wish' to refer to what the ethical works call decision.

2e. While intellect is always correct, however, desire and *phantasia* can be correct or not correct. Wherefore (διό) while the object of desire always moves, this is either the good or the apparent good. (*de An.* 433a26-29)

Rational desire, these passages imply, is based on intellect rather than on *phantasia*, and thus is for the good rather than for the apparent good. Moreover, given Aristotle's frequent equation of the apparent good with the pleasant, this is in keeping with another distinction we saw in Chapter 1: rational desire is for the good rather than for the pleasant (see *EN* III.2 1111b17 on decision, and *Top.* 146b37-a8 on wish).

If this is right, it entails that rational motivation is psychologically entirely different from non-rational. In particular, while non-rational motivation is ultimately based on perception of the pleasant, we can in no way infer that the same is true of rational motivation. Rational desire is for the good rather than for the pleasant – another way of saying that it is for the good rather than for the apparent good – and therefore does not depend on pleasure for its motivational power. Thus, for example, Aquinas' comment on a passage from *de An.* III.7 (3h below):

[In the case of perception], from the apprehension of what is good or what is bad, appetite or avoidance did not follow immediately as it does here, in connection with intellect. Instead, pleasure or pain followed, and on that basis, appetite and avoidance followed subsequently... [T]he desire of the intellective part is moved immediately by the apprehended good or bad. (Aquinas, Commentary on *de An.* 431a14-17, trans. based on Foster and Humphries)

Appetites are based on perception, and so can only motivate by way of pleasure and pain; rational desires, by contrast, are based directly on cognition of the good, and therefore have no basis in pleasure and pain.

I want to show that this view of practical intellect, and thus of rational motivation, is wrong. Thoughts about what is good presuppose evaluative *phantasiai*, and thus desires based on such thoughts are in some robust sense desires for the apparent good – and thus even our most rational desires are ultimately based on pleasurable perception.

In fact, we have already seen strong evidence that *phantasia* plays a role in distinctively rational motivation. For as we saw in Chapter 3, despite the passages quoted above both the *MA* and *de An.* seem to say at other points that *phantasia* is involved in *every* episode of motivation:

[Locomotion occurs when] the affections suitably prepare the organic parts, and desire the affections, and *phantasia* desire. (*MA* 702a17-19)

Locomotion is always for the sake of something, and is with *phantasia* or[3] desire. (*de An.* 432b15-16)

How then are we to reconcile the evidence above that Aristotle contrasts acting on *phantasia* with acting on intellect (and see especially the cases of *akrasia* and *enkrateia*

---

[3] See note 2 in Chapter 3: some read 'and,' but in either case my point here is that *phantasia* alone is mentioned, rather than perception or intellect.

discussed in Chapter 5) with the present passages' widely accepted implication that all motivation involves *phantasia*?

A very simple answer is suggested by a claim about the relation between *phantasia* and thought which we encountered in Chapter 4: "The soul never thinks without a *phantasma*" (*de An.* 431a14-17). All thought involves *phantasia*. Moreover, Aristotle makes clear that this holds in the practical sphere as much as in the theoretical: the claim just quoted comes in the course of a discussion of practical intellect (see 3d-h below). And therefore thought-based motivation, although it is to be contrasted with motivation based exclusively on *phantasia*, will itself involve *phantasia* in some way. I want to show in the remainder of the book that this simple answer is right.

It looks to be immediately confirmed by a surprising comment Aristotle makes in summing up *de An.* III.10's discussion of locomotion:

And in general, as we have said, insofar as the animal is desiderative, thus far is it able to move itself. But it cannot be desiderative without *phantasia* (ὀρεκτικὸν δὲ οὐκ ἄνευ φαντασίας). And all *phantasia* is either rational or perceptual (λογιστικὴ ἢ αἰσθητική); of the latter, the other animals too have a share. (*de An.* 433b27-30)

This looks to be saying that non-rational motivation is based on perceptual *phantasia* and rational motivation on rational (or 'calculative') *phantasia*.[4] In fact the details turn out to be more complicated: I will argue that while rational *phantasia* is at the basis of decision, wish relies instead on perceptual *phantasia*. But the broad outlines of the simple answer are right: all thought relies on *phantasia*, and thus even thought-based desire is based in some way on *phantasia* as well. Moreover, the *phantasia* presupposed by practical thought is, just as one might expect, practical *phantasia*: pleasurable, evaluative *phantasia*, derived in its turn from pleasurable, evaluative perception. Therefore even our most rational desires are in some sense – a very substantial sense, I will argue below – for what appears good through *phantasia*, the apparent good.

The argument of Part III of this book will thus be an argument that Aristotle holds a view that we can call Practical Empiricism. Just as theoretical thought depends on *phantasia*, and thus ultimately on perception, so practical thought – thought about what is good, to-be-done – depends on practical *phantasia*, and thus ultimately on practical perception. Spelling out the details and the ramifications will take some work. In this chapter I argue that deliberation, the process that yields the premise (or premises) of the possible, involves evaluative *phantasia*, and thus that decisions are in some sense for the apparent good. In Chapters 7 and 8 I argue that our intellectual grasp of ends – premises of the good – also presupposes evaluative *phantasia*, and thus that wishes too are for the apparent good.

As I mentioned at the end of Part I, Practical Empiricism will have two major consequences for our understanding of Aristotle's ethics. First, practical intellect does

---

[4] This reading is for instance implied by Charles 1984, 89.

quite a bit less on Aristotle's view than is widely thought. We are indeed able, in virtue of our rationality, to have cognitions about the good, and corresponding motivations, that are unavailable to lower creatures. But this is not so much a matter of grasping distinctive content as a matter of manipulating and conceptualizing content in sophisticated ways. The content of our thoughts about the good – that is, the kind of actions, lives, goals, and objects we think good – is determined by non-rational cognition: by evaluative perception and *phantasia*, the cognitive capacities of the non-rational soul.

Second, Aristotle is more of a thoroughgoing psychological hedonist than is widely thought. Even though the pleasant is not the object of rational desire, pleasure plays a crucial causal role in determining the content of our thoughts about the good, and therefore in generating even our most rational desires.

6.2 Starting-points vs. calculations

My strategy in what follows will be to use Aristotle's fairly detailed discussion of how theoretical thought depends on *phantasia* to shed light on his much briefer claims about how this works in the practical sphere.

In using an account of theoretical thought as a guide to understanding practical thought I am following Aristotle himself, who explains practical reasoning (syllogisms) by analogy with theoretical reasoning (see *EE* VI/*EN* VII.3, and passage 1c from the *MA*), and explains practical wisdom, *phronesis*, by comparing it with the virtues of theoretical intellect (*EE* V/*EN* VI). In both contexts Aristotle's analogies between theoretical and practical thought rely on a distinction that he evidently thinks central for an understanding of thought in either domain, and that will be crucial for my arguments in what follows: the distinction between starting-points (ἀρχαί) and the reasoning or calculation (λογισμός) done from them. Here is how he puts it in a passage to which we will return in Chapters 7 and 8:

For just as in theoretical sciences the hypotheses are our starting-points, so in the productive ones the end (τέλος) is a starting-point and hypothesis. 'Since that person needs to be healthy, it's necessary for this thing to be, if that is to come about,' just as there [in the theoretical realm] 'If the triangle is [equal in degrees to] two right angles, it's necessary for this thing to be.' (*EE* II.11 1227b28-32)

In both the practical and theoretical spheres, reasoning involves two components. First, we must have a grasp of the starting-points: in the theoretical sphere, these are universal, necessary truths, which take the form of axioms, postulates, or definitions; in the practical sphere, as this passage tells us, they are the goals for the sake of which we plan to act. Second, we calculate what follows from these starting-points: we reason from them to a conclusion. In the theoretical sphere this reasoning takes the form of demonstration; in the practical, it is deliberation. (I provide more textual evidence for these claims in Chapter 7.)

Given that grasping starting-points and reasoning from them are both exercises of thought, we should expect them both to involve *phantasia*: as we have seen, Aristotle states very explicitly that "The soul never thinks without a *phantasma*" (*de An.* 431a14-17) (and see various different formulations quoted below). But although he makes clear that thought relies on *phantasia*, he does rather less to clarify precisely what the relation is. I will show below that if we systematize some scattered discussions of theoretical thought, we will find that there are in fact several different relations here.[5]

In the passages where Aristotle makes his explicit claims to the effect that thought requires *phantasia*, I will argue, he has in mind the second component of thought, calculation, in both the theoretical and practical sphere. Most of this chapter is devoted to showing how calculation makes use of *phantasia*; I will argue that the roles *phantasia* plays in theoretical and practical calculations are closely analogous, and I will use the former to illuminate the latter.

As to our grasp of starting-points, Aristotle makes clear that in the theoretical sphere this too owes a great deal to *phantasia*, although the role *phantasia* plays here is very different from the one it plays in deductive thought. In Chapter 7 I show how *phantasia* aids our grasp of the starting-points of theoretical reasoning; in Chapter 8 I use this account to argue that it plays a similar and perhaps even more substantial role in our grasp of the starting-points of practical reasoning – in our grasp of ends.

6.3 *Phantasia* and Calculations

When Aristotle says that there is no thought without a *phantasma*, what does he mean? First, we need to set aside an answer that may seem to be implied by my arguments about *phantasia* and belief in Part II, but that turns out to be insufficiently general.

In Chapter 4 I discussed a way in which some rational cognitions depend on *phantasia*: some beliefs (δόξαι) are, as on the Stoic view, the result of accepting the content of an appearance. If the person in the distance appears to be my enemy and I see no reason to question the appearance, I will thereby come to believe that it is my enemy. But this cannot explain why *all* thought should depend on *phantasia*: unless we are determined to assimilate Aristotle's view to the Stoics' (as some of his interpreters have been), there is no evidence for attributing to him the view that all beliefs come about this way. Some are based directly on perception: if I see red in front of me I will normally come to believe that there is red in front of me, and on the minimalist "basic conception" of *phantasia* which I defended in Chapter 3 there is no role for *phantasia* in this process. Moreover, many beliefs are not directly derived from perception or perceptual appearance at all. My belief that 3 is a prime number seems entirely unlike my belief that there is a stranger in the distance: in the latter case I begin by passively

---

[5] Much of what I say below is loosely in line with D. Frede's (1992) discussion of this topic (although my arguments in Chapter 3 for accepting only the basic conception of *phantasia* count against her view that one of its roles is to synthesize something like a "field of vision").

experiencing a *phantasma*, and then assent to its content, but nothing we have seen in Aristotle's discussion of *phantasia* suggests that this is so in the former case as well.

Thus while the *Insomn.* gave us evidence that Aristotle construes some beliefs as assents to appearances we have no positive evidence that he construed all beliefs that way. We do, however, have very explicit evidence that he thinks *phantasia* necessary for thought in a quite different way (which I mentioned briefly in Chapter 4): as an actively conjured aid to reasoning. Here *phantasia* is required not as a necessary precursor to one's present intellectual state, but as a simultaneous aid. Suppose one is thinking about some aspect of triangles, e.g. whether a given triangle can be inscribed within a given circle. While this is happening, Aristotle holds, one is not merely thinking about triangles but also representing them through *phantasia*:

And since there is no thing (πρᾶγμα) that exists in separation from perceptible magnitudes, as it seems, the intelligibles are in the perceptible forms – both those which are called abstractions, and all the states and qualities of perceptible things. And on account of this, without perceiving one would not learn or understand anything. And whenever one contemplates (θεωρῇ), one necessarily at the same time contemplates by means of *phantasmata*.[6] For *phantasmata* are just like sense-perceptions (*aisthêmata*), except without the matter. (*de An.* 432a3-10)

The proper objects of thought (νοητά) are universal, imperceptible essences, but just as such objects only exist in enmattered form, so we can only think about them as such: as abstractions from particular, material, perceptible objects. And this means that thought of the thinkables cannot be exercised without simultaneous perception of the perceptibles. More precisely, thought requires quasi-perception, *phantasia* – presumably because we need to think about more variations and examples than we could perceive all at once (we mentally compare many different triangles by putting them before the mind's eye, for example). We get a fuller statement of this account in a passage from the *Mem.*:

It is not possible to think (νοεῖν) without a *phantasma*. For the same affection occurs in thinking as in drawing diagrams. For in the latter case, though we do not make any use of the fact that the quantity in the triangle is determinate, we nevertheless draw it as determinate in quantity. And the thinker works in the same way: even if one thinks something that has no quantity one puts a quantity before one's eyes, but thinks about it not *qua* a quantity... So that it is clear that the recognition (γνῶσις) of these objects is through the primary faculty of perception. And memory, even of intelligibles, is not without a *phantasma*. (*Mem.* 449b31-450a13)

The mathematician reasoning about triangles needs perceptible triangles as examples from which to draw her abstractions; *phantasia* provides them.[7]

---

[6] Reading φαντασματι at a8; alternatively, "one at the same time contemplates some *phantasma*," or "one at the same time contemplates *phantasmata*."

[7] Arguably this is also what Aristotle has in mind in the passages we saw in Chapter 4, passages which Hicks and some ancient commentators take as evidence for the proto-Stoic view: "*Phantasia* does not arise without perception, and without it there is no supposition (ὑπόληψις)" (*de An.* 427b14-16); "Of thinking (τοῦ νοεῖν)... the one part seems to be *phantasia*, the other supposition (ὑπόληψις)" (*de An.* 427b27-28). These passages occur so early in the *de An.* discussion of *phantasia* that we have very little to go on in determining

Returning now to the characterization of theoretical reasoning with which we began, we can see that theoretical intellect will use *phantasia* in this way when performing its second task, deducing conclusions from given starting-points. (We may leave open for now the question of whether *phantasia* plays the very same role in the grasping of starting-points; I will argue below that it does not.) Thinking about triangles in the ways described above is clearly something one does when performing calculations. A geometer deducing theorems from her postulates will be thinking about triangles, lines, angles and the like; while doing so, we have now learned, she will be conjuring up *phantasmata* of all of these.

What about the practical analogue of demonstration, namely deliberation? Here Aristotle is very explicit that a parallel phenomenon takes place. Although his extensive discussions of deliberation in the ethical works make no mention of *phantasia*, the *de An.*, which of course focuses more than the *Ethics* on the psychological underpinnings of action, twice argues that deliberation depends on *phantasia*. In deliberation, just as in theoretical deduction, we use *phantasmata* as aids, envisaging or otherwise imagining possible options.

The first argument to this effect comes in *de An.* III.7's discussion of practical thought. It follows immediately on 3a-c, the lines that were our focus in Chapter 2, where Aristotle claims that pleasurable and painful perceptions are perceptions of the good and bad, and trigger pursuit and avoidance. Now he turns to thought:

3d. But to the thinking soul (τῇ διανοητικῇ ψυχῇ),[8] *phantasmata* serve just like *aisthêmata*, and whenever it states or denies good or bad, it avoids or pursues. This is why the soul never thinks without a *phantasma*...[9]

e. Thus the faculty of thought thinks the forms in *phantasmata* (τὰ μὲν οὖν εἴδη τὸ νοητικὸν ἐν τοῖς φαντάσμασι νοεῖ), and as in these cases [when one is actually perceiving the objects] the objects of pursuit and avoidance have been determined for it, so also outside perception, whenever it is engaged with *phantasmata* (ὅταν ἐπὶ τῶν φαντασμάτων ᾖ), it is moved.

---

their meaning, but if we read them with the later passage quoted above (432a3-11; cf. 431a13-17 and context) we get the following account: to make a rational judgment to the effect that e.g. this triangle can be inscribed in this circle presupposes having first conjured up an image of a triangle inscribed in a circle, and then assenting to it. In this case these passages do not give evidence of the proto-Stoic view of appearance-based belief that I discussed in Chapter 4; nonetheless we have sufficient evidence for that view in the *Insomn*.

[8] 'The thinking soul' could be another name for the faculty of thought (νοητικόν) we find in 3e; one might instead argue that it refers to the soul which has such a faculty, on the grounds that it is the whole soul rather than the faculty of thought which avoids and pursues: see Hicks' note *ad* 431b3-5 on the difficulties of finding a consistent subject throughout the passage. It makes no difference to our understanding of the workings of practical thought, however: even if Aristotle here has in mind the whole soul, the activities he attributes to it in these lines are ones it performs in virtue of its thinking part.

[9] The lines that follow seem to be an interpolation or digression; I omit them here.

f. For example, perceiving the beacon [the person/faculty of thought judges] that it is fire,[10] and seeing it move with the common sense (τῇ κοινῇ), one recognizes that it is the enemy.

g. But sometimes it calculates and deliberates about future things in relation to present things, using the *phantasmata* and thoughts (νοήμασιν) in the soul, as if seeing.

h. And whenever it says that there is something pleasant or painful, then it flees or pursues (ὅταν εἴπῃ ὡς ἐκεῖ τὸ ἡδὺ ἢ λυπηρόν, ἐνταῦθα φεύγει ἢ διώκει)[11] – and in general does one thing. (*de An.* 431a14-b10)

Like perception, thought is practical by being evaluative: when we think something good we are thereby motivated to pursue it. But there is a complication: "to the thinking soul, *phantasmata* serve just like sense-perceptions" (3d). Just as in theorizing about triangles one conjures up a *phantasma* of triangles, so in deliberating about what to do one is somehow "engaged with *phantasmata*" (3e).

What does Aristotle have in mind? We find more details in 3g, where he tells us that *phantasmata* are needed for cognition about the future.[12] This fits well with our account of *phantasia*'s role in action from Chapter 3: when the goal is not present to perception, *phantasia* puts us in touch with it. What 3g adds to this account is that this will be the case even when thought is involved. When we deliberate about future options, we actively call up and inspect *phantasmata* of them (alongside thoughts about them), so that we can, "as if seeing" them actually occurring, judge whether or not to pursue them.

We get somewhat more detail from the *de An.*'s second discussion of *phantasia*'s role in deliberation. As we saw in section 1, toward the end of the *de An.*'s discussion of locomotion Aristotle mentions that in addition to perceptual (αἰσθητική) *phantasia*, which belongs to most animals, there is another kind, exclusively human: calculative (or 'rational' – λογιστική) or deliberative (βουλευτική) *phantasia* (*de An.* 433a29, 434a5-7). He goes on in III.11 to describe this as follows:

Deliberative *phantasia* is present in rational animals. For whether to do this or this is already the task of reasoning (λογισμοῦ), and it is necessary to measure by one thing, for one pursues the greater; so that they [rational animals] are able to make one out of many *phantasmata*. And this is the reason why [the other animals] do not seem to have belief (δόξαν), because they don't have the kind [of *phantasia*][13] that comes from syllogism... (*de An.* 434a7-11)

---

[10] My translation here loosely follows Hicks 1907.
[11] I discuss alternative translations of this line below.
[12] 3f is widely and I think correctly taken to give a case in which thought works with actual perception (we see the fire in motion, and thereby infer that the enemy is advancing). It thus provides a contrast with 3g, which describes the kind of case that 3e referred to as "outside perception": now we are concerned with future objects, and thus no longer seeing an object of pursuit or avoidance, as in 3f, but only "*as if* seeing" it, through *phantasia*. Does 3f thus describe a case in which practical thought *doesn't* require a *phantasma*, contrary to 3d? No. First, in inferring the presence of one's enemy a *phantasma* of him will come into play (see 432a3-10). Second, inferring that the enemy is present does not yet count as having decided what to do: one will also need premises of the good and possible, and *phantasia* will play its role here.
[13] So Hicks 1907. Ross 1961, Hamlyn 1968 and others take the implied noun here to be 'belief,' but this makes the claim a *non sequitur*.

The passage is very compressed, and has been subject to various quite different interpretations, but we need not go into all the details here. What is clear is that the claim that deliberation involves "making one out of many *phantasmata*" describes the active use of *phantasmata* in the aid of practical thought. In other words, this is another characterization of the phenomenon described in 3d-h: in deliberating, one makes use of *phantasmata*. Notably, then, this does *not* imply that what Aristotle describes here is (as sometimes thought) a different species of *phantasia*, the exercise of a *phantasma*-producing capacity which people have over and above perceptual *phantasia*; instead, 'calculative or deliberative *phantasia*' refers to a use to which rational creatures can put the products of perceptual *phantasia*. (Compare the theoretical case: in conjuring up images of triangles the geometer is activating the same capacity, perceptual *phantasia*, that is operative when he is subject to an illusion or memory of a triangle.)

What the passage says is that in reasoning about what course of action to take, one conjures up various images – presumably of the various options and their possible consequences – and somehow synthesizes them into 'one.' Here there is a debate: some take 'one' to mean 'one *phantasma*,' while others take it to mean something like 'one plan.' Grammatically the first interpretation is most natural. Moreover, it gets strong confirmation from a passage we have seen from the *MA*: the *phantasia* which "prepares" desire and thereby gives rise to action "itself comes about either through thought or through perception" (*MA* 702a17-19). This implies that when we make use of *phantasia* to aid us in deliberation, the result is itself an exercise of *phantasia*: the representation that emerges from deliberation, synthesized from the various *phantasmata* of different options, is not one that could be had by a lower animal, but it is nonetheless a literal *phantasma*.

Thus these passages from the *de An.* show that deliberation relies on *phantasia* just as much as theoretical demonstration does.[14] Just as we cannot deduce theorems about triangles without envisaging triangles, so we cannot deliberate about possible courses of action or objects of desire without envisaging them. What we have not yet determined is the nature of the *phantasmata* that play a role in practical reasoning. I want now to show that they too are practical: pleasurable and evaluative.

This is a very natural interpretation. It is suggested by my arguments in Chapter 3 that *phantasia* plays a necessary role in action because it is through *phantasia* that we can represent absent things as good; it is embraced by various interpreters, e.g. Frede:

All activities, whether based on non-rational or on rational desire, presuppose that I envisage something as good or bad for me, to be pursued or avoided. The necessary condition of my thinking that something is good or bad, according to Aristotle, is that the soul shall have certain

---

[14] Note that this is so even on the interpretation on which the one thing synthesized from the *phantasmata* is not itself a *phantasma*. Aristotle's claim would still be that deliberation is an activity of the rational soul, but one which makes use of the non-rational soul's capacity to represent absent perceptibles. In reasoning about whether to do x or y (*de An.* 434a7-8), one imagines – actively calls up *phantasmata* as of – x and y, and uses these imagined representations to decide.

phantasmata (431a14-17); I have to have the image of a future good or bad... (D. Frede 1992, 288-89)[15]

What I want now to show is that this interpretation is in fact entailed by the account of practical *phantasia* I developed in Chapter 3.

Consider an episode of deliberation: with a view to the end of enjoying herself moderately, someone is deliberating about whether to eat one more piece of cake or call it a night. Since there is no thought without a *phantasma* – since one cannot reason abstractly about non-present perceptibles without quasi-perceiving them – she will in so deliberating have to imagine eating, and imagine abstaining. Suppose, then, that she first imagines the actual eating. This is an act of *phantasia*, which preserves and reproduces previous perceptions – previous experiences of actually eating cake. Now for the crucial point: as we saw in Chapter 3, if these perceptions were pleasurable ones – if eating cake is the sort of thing she has enjoyed in the past – then the imagining will be pleasurable too. That is, it will be the kind of representation we discussed in Chapter 3: a pleasurable, evaluative *phantasia* which has it in its nature to generate appetite for its object – an appearance of an option as to-be-done, to-be-pursued.

But our agent is a deliberator, and she is not done: the rational part of her soul does not make the non-rational error of automatically conflating the presently pleasant with the pleasant and good without qualification (see *de An.* 433b8-10, passage 2f), but instead considers possible qualifications. She now imagines the possible consequences of eating the cake: perhaps a tummy-ache, or a feeling of regret. The perceptions these imaginings preserve and reproduce (remembered aches and regrets) were painful ones, and so the imaginings will be painful too: they will be appearances of their objects as bad which have it in their nature to generate aversion – appearances of things as to-be-avoided. (Now she may go on to imagine what it will be like to walk away from the cake, and also the consequences of doing so.)

One question to consider about this process, before we consider its culmination: do these pleasurable and painful imaginings actually induce appetites, aversions, and other passions, as they would outside the deliberative context? Arguably yes. This much at any rate is implied by a passage from the *EE* on the deliberations (not explicitly so-called) of akratics and enkratics:

The person who is being continent both feels pains in finally acting against his appetite and also enjoys the pleasure that comes from the expectation (ἐλπίδος) that he will later be benefited and

---

[15] The continuation of the passage is also helpful: "The intellect by itself can only think what is non-sensible, the intelligible forms; but the intellect needs sensible images to decide whether something is desirable or not; it has to envisage concrete situations containing material objects to decide that something is worthwhile or should be avoided. Sense-perception, on the other hand, is strictly limited to what is before the sense at the time when it is.... There can, of course, be no sense-perceptions of future goods and evils. All sensible projections are due to imagination... 'to the rational soul images serve as perceptions'" (D. Frede 1992, 289).

even now is being benefited by being healthy; and the acratic enjoys acratically obtaining what he has an appetite for but is pained by the pain that comes from expectation, for he supposes that he is doing something bad. (*EE* II.8 1224b16-21)

Here we learn that – as my discussion in Chapter 4 predicted[16] – in the course of considering the future consequences of their actions the enkratic feels the pleasure of hope, and the akratic the pain of expecting something bad. These passions accompany their deliberations, as products, we now see, of the *phantasmata* of the future scenarios which deliberation necessarily involves.[17]

On the other hand, Aristotle does have the resources to argue that the *phantasmata* which we actively conjure up in deliberation either induce no passions at all, or at least induce far weakers ones than do those *phantasmata* which simply assail us. Recall a passage from *de An*. III.3, discussed in Chapter 4.6:

Phantasia is up to us whenever we want, for it is putting something before one's eyes.... Further, whenever we believe (δοξάσωμεν) something terrible or frightening, we are affected (συμπάσχομεν) straight away, and likewise for something reassuring. But with respect to *phantasia*, we are in the same condition as when we observe something terrible or reassuring in a picture. (*de An*. 427b17-24)

I argued in Chapter 4 that this passage's claims apply only to active imagination – but that is precisely the use of *phantasia* at issue in deliberation. When in the course of deliberation we actively put an image of some suffering or reward before our eyes, and contemplate it as a mere possibility, we feel at least less fear or hope than we do when we believe that it will come to pass.

At any rate, we can conclude that in the process of deliberation our agent conjures up various *phantasmata* which are pleasurable or painful – and are therefore, as we learned from Chapter 3, *phantasmata* of the options as good or bad, to-be-pursued or to-be-avoided – and in consequence feels various passions to some degree or other. Then, finally, she reaches a conclusion. In the words of the *de An*. III.11 passage, she somehow "makes one out of these many *phantasmata*": synthesizes a single image which represents one option as overall best. Now she has settled on one course of action: she makes her decision, and acts upon it.

Thus when one decides on an option one will necessarily have a pleasurable, evaluative, motivating *phantasia* of it at the same time. One might think Aristotle's point here is that decisions carry with them a way of influencing the non-rational soul,

---

[16] See the brief discussion of deliberation in Chapter 4.6.

[17] Note that this does not entail the undesirable consequence that the virtuous person will experience inappropriate passions in the course of deliberation. If the situation is such that eating the extra piece of cake would in fact count as intemperate, then either it will not even occur to her to consider eating it (the possibility is not one that is salient to her, to use McDowell's language) or, if it does occur to her, the *phantasma* of cake-eating which she conjures up will not be a pleasurable one, since she takes only moderate pleasure in things like cake, and would not enjoy an extra piece.

for the *phantasia* which results from deliberation will influence non-rational motivation just as much as do ordinary perceptual *phantasiai*.[18] But if this were so, then the akratic – who has after all deliberated, and decided on a good course of action – would have some non-rational passion supporting her decisions, alongside those that oppose it; Aristotle implies that she does not. Moreover, if the synthesized *phantasma* is a sophisticated synthesis, one that represents comparisons and calculations – a representation of something as "overall best" – then it will not be intelligible to the non-rational soul. (It will be like a visual picture which is too abstract or complex to be intelligible to a non-reasoning creature: a blue-print or graph, or – to return directly to the theoretical parallel – the diagram the geometer produces in proving the Pythagorean theorem.)

I think Aristotle's point is quite different. The synthesized *phantasma* is described not merely as a by-product or accompaniment of deliberation, brought along to keep the non-rational soul in line; instead, it seems to be a necessary part of the process of deliberation, an indispensable aid for reaching a decision. Particularly if we read the last lines of the passage as I have done above – lower animals lack belief because they lack syllogistic, i.e. deliberative, *phantasia*[19] – Aristotle's claim here is a very strong one. The belief that one particular thing is to be done, the belief that is the conclusion of the practical syllogism, and the cognitive basis or component of a decision, is something like an assent to an evaluative appearance – an assent to the single *phantasma* generated through deliberation. Deliberation yields an appearance of one option as best, and one therefore rationally judges it best. Thus the thought arises *from* the *phantasma*. Decisions – paradigm exercises of practical thought – derive their content from evaluative *phantasia*.

If this is right then one can decide only on options one has pleasurably imagined. Two passages on practical thought strongly support this conclusion, by associating practical thought with pleasure. First consider 3h, from *de An.* III.7. When the thinking soul deliberates about the future it uses *phantasmata* (and thoughts) "as if seeing" (3g). On the translation of 3h which I gave above (following e.g. Ross), "whenever it says that there is something pleasant or painful, then it flees or pursues." That is, one of the *phantasmata* representing future options represents an option as pleasant, and it is this option which thought selects, and rational desire pursues. We can make this fit with III.11's account of deliberative *phantasia* as follows: the one *phantasma* synthesized through deliberation represents an option as best, which is to say that it represents it pleasurably; noticing this feature of the option, thought selects it. (More precisely, the

---

[18] I think this is what Lorenz implies, although he is not specifically referring to deliberative *phantasia* here: "Perhaps taking his cue from the *Philebus*' simile of the illustrated book, [Aristotle] sees intellect and sense as integrated so that all acts of the intellect are accompanied by exercises of the sensory imagination in and through which the subject envisages the objects of thought in a sensory mode. As a result, his psychological theory can easily explain how it is that thoughts of, say, prospective pains or pleasures can get a grip on the non-rational part or aspect of a person's action-producing apparatus" (2006, 118).

[19] For deliberation as a kind of syllogism see especially *Mem.* 453a13.

phantasma represents this option pleasurably without any qualifications, or at least with the fewest qualifications of the available options.)[20]

Precisely in order to avoid this hedonistic interpretation of 3h, however, alternative translations have been proposed of the crucial line, ὅταν εἴπῃ ὡς ἐκεῖ τὸ ἡδὺ ἢ λυπηρόν, ἐνταῦθα φεύγει ἢ διώκει. Taking the ἐκεῖ and ἐνταῦθα as antithetical, Hicks, for example, translates "And when you pronounce, just as there in sensation you affirm the pleasant or the painful, here in thought you pursue or avoid." This is admissible, but strained.[21] But many will prefer this reading because it avoids the implication that we think things good *because* we find them pleasant. (See again Aquinas' commentary on passage 3, quoted above: intellect, unlike perception, is motivated directly by the good without needing to represent it as pleasant.)[22] We need confirmation from elsewhere, then, that pleasure and pain play a crucial role in practical thought. We find it from passages we have already seen in Chapter 2: the *MA*'s discussion of practical intellect.

Recall from Chapter 1 that the *MA* groups together all three forms of cognition as playing roughly the same role in locomotion. In Chapter 2 we examined perception, and saw that it is practical insofar as it is pleasurable. When a creature perceives something pleasant (e.g. tastes something sweet), the perception involves heating and chilling of the area around its heart – the physiological aspects of pleasure and pain – and these lead to other bodily changes and thereby to locomotion. In Chapter 3 I argued that the *MA* attributes just the same workings to practical *phantasia*, and I noted in passing that it extends these claims to practical thought. Let us look at those passages again:

1f. . . . *Phantasiai* and perceptions and thoughts (ἔννοιαι) alter the parts. For perceptions are at once a kind of alteration, and *phantasia* and thinking have the power of the actual things. (*MA* 701b16-19)

---

[20] This is not necessarily to say that Aristotle subscribes to a maximizing version of psychological hedonism. There is a fairly natural interpretation of the *de An.* III.11 passage on which he does: the references to "measuring by one thing" and "pursuing the greater" remind us of the art of hedonic measurement in Plato's *Protagoras*, and suggest that what Aristotle has in mind here is some kind of hedonic calculus. But the passage is far too compressed for us to be able to endorse this reading with confidence, and arguably the fact that he says "measuring by one thing" without naming pleasure as that one thing counts against it: perhaps he is being deliberately vague, or perhaps he thinks we use different criteria in different situations. My claim is simply that the pleasure and pain we feel in imagining various options guide our choices.

[21] "In sensation" and "in thought" are not explicit in the text, and even if one wants to take the ἐκεῖ and ἐνταῦθα as antithetical ("in these cases/in those cases"), the nearest antecedent antithesis is between cases where thought is accompanied by perception of the desired or avoided objects, and cases where that object is absent to perception – which would imply that in the former cases, thought does after all go for things because they are pleasant.

[22] Likewise, "Torstrik objects that A. of all men would be least likely to make rational action depend solely upon pleasure and pain" (Hicks' note *ad loc.*).

1g. For in a certain way the thought form of the pleasant or frightening is like the actual thing itself. That is why we shudder and are frightened just thinking of something. All these are affections (πάθη) and alterations; and when bodily parts are altered some become larger, some smaller.... Now the origin of motion is, as has been said, the object of pursuit and avoidance in the practical sphere. Of necessity heating and chilling attend the thought and the *phantasia* of these things. For the painful is avoided, and the pleasant pursued, and the painful and pleasant are nearly all accompanied by some chilling and heating (but we don't notice this happening concerning very small things). (701b19-702a1)

Thought leads to action in the same way that perception and *phantasia* do: the thought of something pleasant or painful is accompanied by heating and chilling – i.e. is pleasurable or painful – and thereby generates or guides desire. Thus practical thought, just like practical perception and *phantasia*, has as its object the pleasant and painful. This does not entail that the content of one's thought will always or even often be "This option is pleasant": only the decisions of someone whose goal is to obtain pleasure will reliably have that content. The most general form will be "This option is best," where, depending on one's general ends, this might mean most pleasant, most healthful, most lucrative, most virtuous, etc. But we learn from these passages that the option declared best is the option that one finds pleasure in, and therefore that the thought "This option is best" will be a pleasurable one.

We saw in Chapter 3 that the aspects of practical perception which make it practical – its affective and evaluative components – are preserved in practical *phantasia*. What 1f-g suggest is that they are also preserved in practical thought. And while unlike the *de An.* and *Mem.* the *MA* does not explicitly say that practical thought depends on *phantasia*, it does imply that view by saying that thought preserves something of perception (1f). Thus we can reconcile Aristotle's view here with that of the *de An.* if we take him to have in mind a progression as follows:

1) In the cognitively simplest cases, practical (pleasurable, evaluative) perception directly conditions desire.
2) In more complex cases, practical perception gives rise to practical *phantasia*, which then conditions desire.
3) In the most complex cases, practical perception gives rise to practical *phantasia*, which is then used by practical thought (deliberation), which then conditions desire.

At each stage the higher mode of cognition derives its character – affective as well as narrowly representational – from the stage which precedes it. Thus if the thought of x is pleasurable, and hence motivating (heating and chilling, and hence leading to locomotion), this is because at some point in the past one pleasurably perceived something like x, and recalled that perception through *phantasia* in the process of deliberation.

Thus Aristotle's account of deliberation winds up giving an enormous importance to pleasurable perception. In deliberating we use *phantasmata* as we go along, conjuring up images of the various options; the option which is pleasurable to imagine is the one we choose. But the nature of the *phantasmata* relies on previous perception, for the things we imagine pleasurably will always be the type of things we have previously perceived pleasurably. Thus only someone who has experienced pleasure in doing virtuous things – and I will argue in Chapter 8 that such pleasure is indeed properly construed as perceptual – will reliably be able to conjure up pleasurable *phantasmata* of the right option, and therefore only she will reliably be able to recognize that option as best, and thus to decide on it.[23] This is one reason why one cannot have *phronesis*, which consists at least in large part in excellence in deliberation, without having the right non-rational character. (More on this topic in the next chapter.)

This characterization of deliberation may sound plainly wrong, for it may seem to impute to Aristotle straightforward psychological hedonism: all people, including the virtuous person, always pursue what they judge pleasant, and do so because they judge it pleasant. In a sense this is precisely right. But in a sense it is wrong: nothing I have said entails that practical thought takes the form "*x* is good because it is pleasant." Rather, because *x* is represented pleasurably, practical thought concludes "*x* is good." Pleasure in the representation of an object causally explains the thought that the object is good, and thereby the rational desire for it, but it can do all this without pleasantness being the desired feature of the object. As I said at the end of Part I, Aristotle's view is that pleasure is the efficient cause, but not necessarily the object, of all desire.[24]

I have argued in this chapter that calculation – reasoning from given starting-points – relies on *phantasia* in the practical sphere just as much as in the theoretical. This then is one aspect of Aristotle's Practical Empiricism. Practical calculations have their basis in perception, because the *phantasmata* they depend on derive from perception. And because the relevant perceptions are pleasurable or painful ones, every practical thought – every motivating thought to the effect that something is good or bad – has its ultimate basis in feelings of pleasure or pain. Even decisions, our most indubitably rational desires, are based, albeit indirectly, on pleasurable, evaluative *phantasia*.

In the next chapter I turn to the other aspect of practical thought: our grasp of the starting-points of practical reasoning.

---

[23] Of course a non-virtuous person may accidentally hit on the right action: perhaps she has experienced pleasure in helping old ladies across the street because they have paid her, or flattered her, and so can pleasurably imagine helping this old lady across the street now. But what she pleasurably imagines, and therefore decides on, will be the wrong aspect of the action: she will not be "deciding on the virtuous action for itself" (*EN* II.4 1105a32) and therefore will not really be acting virtuously.

[24] Compare Broadie: "pleasure and pain are the matter from which the formation of rational choice takes its start" (1991, 331). See also Zeller, who has no qualms about casting Aristotle as a hedonist in the sense I advocate here: "Moral virtue is concerned with pleasure and pain, since it has to do with actions and emotions which cause these feelings: pleasure and pain are the primary source of desire, and the criterion of all our actions, to which we refer in a certain sense even the motives of utility and right... The thought of the good operates upon the will through the medium of feeling, the good presenting itself as something desirable and affording pleasure and satisfaction" (1897, vol II, 157-58, with note).

7

Happiness, Virtue, and the Apparent Good

7.1 *Phantasia* and the starting-points of reasoning

In the previous chapter I argued that *phantasia* plays a crucial role in the process of reasoning out conclusions from starting-points, both in the theoretical realm and in the practical. But what about the grasping of the starting-points themselves? We can begin by looking at the theoretical realm: here Aristotle's discussion makes clear that *phantasia* is a necessary condition of this component of thought as well.

Aristotle discusses our grasp of theoretical starting-points in *Met.* I.1 and *APo.* II.19. He outlines a process by which we come to grasp the universal, necessary truths which form the assumptions from which we reason – e.g. definitions of mathematical entities like triangles – as follows:

i) One perceives triangles many times.
ii) The perceptions are preserved in memory, via *phantasia* (*APo.* 100a3; cf. *Met.* 980a28-29).
iii) From many memories of triangles arises one experience (ἐμπειρία) (*APo.* 100a5-6; *Met.* 980b29-981a1), which implicitly contains a universal (*APo.* 100a6-7), which is a cause explaining why triangles have the properties they do (*Met.* 981a28-30).
iv) One achieves explicit grasp of this explanatory universal, which will then serve as the starting-point for demonstrations (*APo.* 100a6-9;[1] cf. *Met.* 981a5-7); the state one is now in is called *nous*[2] (*APo.* 100b12).

Universals are present in particulars, and hence although perception is of particulars it implicitly contains an awareness of universals.[3] Thus it is from perception that we

---

[1] "From experience, or [i.e.?] from the whole universal that has come to rest in the soul (... the thing that is one and the same in all those things), arises the starting-point (ἀρχή) of craft (τέχνη) or science (ἐπιστήμη)." (Craft is productive knowledge rather than theoretical knowledge; I discuss it in section 5.)
[2] This is a narrow and technical sense of *nous*; I argued that in the *MA* and *de An.* III.9-10 Aristotle uses the word in a broader sense in which it covers all rational cognition. One passage of the *EE/EN* introduces a technical sense for *nous* in the practical realm; I discuss this below.
[3] "One perceives the individual, but perception is of the universal – for example, of man rather than of the man Callias" (*APo.* 100a17-b1).

come to have contact with the universal (perception "instills the universal in our souls" (100b5)). Through the process described above, induction (ἐπαγωγή) (100b4), the universals are made explicit: repeated perceptions give rise, via memory, to a generalized but not yet explicitly universal representation – an "experience" – which in turn forms the basis for a direct intellectual grasp: *nous* in a special sense, sometimes translated "intellectual intuition." Thus perception is at the base of all knowledge: one cannot come to have knowledge of triangles without having first had perceptions and *phantasiai* of triangles. One way to put the idea is in terms of content: thought can only grasp content which is implicitly, inarticulately contained within previous perceptions. And this makes observation extremely important: one simply cannot come to grasp the first principles of geometry if one's senses are so deficient, or one's environment so impoverished, that one has never had adequate perceptual contact with triangles, squares, lines and so forth.

Aristotle does not emphasize *phantasia* in his discussions of this process, but what he does say is enough to show that it plays a necessary role. Experiences (ἐμπειρίαι) arise directly from memory, which is, as we know from the *Mem.*, a function of *phantasia*; the *APo.* alludes to *phantasia*'s role in the process by speaking of the "resting of the sense-perception (μονὴ τοῦ αἰσθήματος)" which enables memory and thereby experience (99b36-37). Arguably experience itself is also at least mainly a function of *phantasia*, for Aristotle implies that an experience simply *is* a collection of memories, and also says that animals have a little of it, although only a little.[4]

Thus it is *phantasia* which forms the bridge between the particular objects of perception and the universal implicit in them. And this is what the account of *phantasia* given in Chapter 3 leads us to expect: retaining and eventually synthesizing the contents of many episodes of perception must be the function of a capacity with the same independence from direct contact with perceptibles, and ability to preserve and reproduce perceptions, which explained *phantasia*'s role in animal motivation and human passions.[5]

---

[4] "From frequent memory of the same thing arises experience: for the memories, many in number, are one experience (αἱ γὰρ πολλαὶ μνῆμαι τῷ ἀριθμῷ ἐμπειρία μία ἐστίν)" (*APo.* 100a4-6); animals have a little experience according to *Met.* 980b26-27. I return to this topic in Chapter 8.

[5] As D. Frede puts it, "sense-perception is not only confined to the moment of actual perception, it is also always narrowly limited to the *particular* object directly under inspection ([*de An.*] 417b22-28). The scientist, however, has to have not just a view of this or that leopard in front of him...; he has to form a picture of 'leopards'... before he can go into the more abstract business of his science. It seems that *phantasia* is supposed to render us that service as well... *Phantasmata* are often depicted as inaccurate impressions... But it is that less detailed but more general picture that we need for our generalizations" (1992, 291). She goes on to argue that although *phantasia* is not mentioned in *APo.* II.19 it must be doing most of the work in induction: "only the collected *phantasiai* of [i.e. derived from] many sense-perceptions can lead to the sight of the universal feature in the particular" (1992, 292). Johansen puts it well: "Because *phantasia*, unlike perception, does not rely on the presence of a perceptible object, *phantasia* allows us to accumulate perceptual information serviceable for comparison and generalisation of the sort that Aristotle thinks leads to the articulation of the most fundamental concepts" (Johansen, forthcoming).

In the remainder of the book I will argue that Aristotle holds a loosely parallel view about the starting-points for practical reasoning: judgments as to what is good *qua* end, i.e. of what goals to pursue. Just as our grasp of theoretical starting-points emerges from ordinary perception and *phantasia*, so our grasp of practical starting-points is dependent on practical – i.e. pleasurable and evaluative – perception and *phantasia*. Therefore one cannot grasp the true starting-points of action – cannot know what is worth pursuing – without having had appropriate perceptions and *phantasiai* of the good. Moreover, it is these perceptions and *phantasiai* which determine the content of one's thoughts about the good. In fact, I will argue, *phantasia* plays an even more important role in the practical case: it supplies the entire content of practical starting-points, although not their status as such.

The main idea, which I argue for in detail in Chapter 8, is that habituation, the process which according to Aristotle molds ethical character, is the practical analogue of induction. Being habituated into virtuous activity entails having repeated practical perceptions of such activity: pleasurable perceptions, i.e. perceptions of such activity as good. This corresponds to stage i of theoretical induction. At the next stages, corresponding to stages ii and iii, these perceptions are preserved and generalized via *phantasia*, to yield a generalized appearance of virtuous activity as the goal of life, i.e. as *eudaimonia*. It is this appearance – once assented to and thereby conceptualized by intellect (stage iv) – which forms the starting-point of practical reasoning, deliberation about what to do. Intellect merely makes explicit what is already contained in the appearance, and thus in no way affects what goal we pursue (although it makes all the difference to how we pursue it).

If my arguments succeed, then evaluative *phantasia* plays an absolutely central role in human virtue and happiness. Aristotle opens both versions of the *Ethics* with an argument that it is of paramount importance in life to have in view the correct end. We all by nature aim at one highest good, and all agree on calling it happiness (*eudaimonia*), but different people have different views about what happiness is. Most people think it is "something obvious and manifest, like pleasure or wealth or honor" (*EN* I.4 1095a22-23); only the few and refined know that it is the life of virtuous activity or of contemplation. Without the right view of the end, one cannot be virtuous, and cannot be happy. What I will argue in what follows is that this view is a product of perception and *phantasia*.

This account of *phantasia*'s role in practical reasoning is certainly not explicit in Aristotle's texts. Nonetheless, I will argue, it is required to make sense of what he does say about how we come to grasp the starting-points of practical reasoning – how we come to have the right ends for our actions, i.e. the right objects of the special sort of desire he calls wish.

7.2 Virtue makes the goal right

Theoretical reasoning has starting-points: the hypotheses, axioms, postulates, and definitions which form the premises for demonstrations. So too does practical reasoning, and Aristotle draws explicit parallels between the two:

For just as in theoretical sciences the hypotheses are our starting-points (ἀρχαί), so in the productive ones the end (τέλος) is a starting-point and hypothesis. 'Since that person needs to be healthy, it's necessary for this thing to be, if that is to come about,' just as there [in the theoretical realm] 'If the triangle is [equal in degree to] two right angles, it's necessary for this thing to be.' (*EE* II.11 1227b28-32)[6]

Both kinds of reasoning begin from accepted premises on which the rest depends; in the practical case, these are statements (or cognitions) of the goal or end of action, that for the sake of which one is acting.

In the theoretical case, as we saw above, Aristotle holds that the starting-points are grasped by *nous* (in the narrow sense), as the result of a process of induction. In asserting this, Aristotle is emphatically contrasting our grasp of starting-points with our grasp of what follows from them: the starting-points of reasoning cannot themselves be the product of reasoning (see especially *APo*. I.3 and II.19). As he sums it up in the *Ethics*'s discussion of theoretical knowledge,

Demonstration is from universals. There are therefore starting-points from which demonstration proceeds, which are not themselves reached through demonstration. Therefore, [they are reached through] induction. (V/VI[7].3 1139b29-31)

Demonstrations must proceed from premises which are not themselves deduced from anything else. Thus *nous*, although it is the highest intellectual state, is not strictly speaking a form of λογισμός, reasoning.

In the practical case, Aristotle makes precisely the parallel claim. Just as the starting-points of demonstration (theoretical reasoning) are secured by something other than deduction, so the starting-points of deliberation (practical reasoning) are secured by something other than deliberation, for as Aristotle repeatedly claims, there is no deliberation of ends:

We do not deliberate about the ends, but about the things toward the ends (τῶν πρὸς τὰ τέλη).[8] For the doctor does not deliberate about whether to heal, nor the orator about whether to persuade, nor the politician about whether to make good laws, nor do any of the others [deliberate] about the end. Instead, having laid down (θέμενοι) the end, they investigate how and through what to achieve it. (*EN* III.3 1112b11-16; cf. 1112b33-34, *EE* II.10 1226b9-10, 1227a7-8)

In both forms of reasoning, then, the starting-points must be secured through something other than reasoning. One might think that the analogy suggests that in the practical case as well as the theoretical starting-points are grasped through *nous*, on

---

[6] The present passage is concerned with "productive" (ποιητική) reasoning, but the context makes very clear that its conclusions apply to strictly practical reasoning as well; moreover this is in keeping with what Aristotle says elsewhere, for example "Practical syllogisms (οἱ συλλογισμοὶ τῶν πρακτῶν) are equipped with a starting-point: Since the end and the best is of such a sort..." (V/VI.12 1144a31-33).

[7] Hereafter I will use only the book numbers, omitting the titles, for the common books *EE* IV-VI = *EN* V-VII.

[8] I join many modern translators in rendering τὰ πρός as "things toward" ends, in order to avoid the (as I will argue in section 6) overly narrow implication of "means."

the basis of induction: indeed, some have made just this claim.[9] But this is not what Aristotle says. Instead, in the few passages where he makes explicit claims about how we get our grasp of practical starting-points, he makes a strikingly different claim:

> Virtue and vice respectively keep healthy, and corrupt, the starting-point, and in actions the that-for-the-sake-of-which is the starting-point, just as in mathematics the hypotheses are. Neither indeed in that case is the *logos* instructive of the starting-points, nor in this case, but virtue either natural or habituated [is instructive] of right belief about the starting-point. (VI/VII.8 1151a15-19)

> Does virtue make the goal right or the things toward the goal? We suppose the goal, because there is no syllogizing or *logos* about this. Instead, this must just like a starting-point (ἀρχή) be laid down (ὑποκείσθω). (*EE* II.11 1227b22-25)

> *Phronesis* is yoked to virtue of character, and this to *phronesis*, since the starting-points of *phronesis* are in accordance with (κατά) the character-virtues, and the correctness (τὸ δ' ὀρθόν) of the character-virtues are in accordance with *phronesis*. (*EN* X.8 1178a16-19)

The role played by intellectual intuition in the theoretical case – laying down the starting-points for reasoning – is played in the practical case by ethical character. So Aristotle says, and he confirms the claim in passages which evidently restrict practical reasoning to working out how to achieve ends, while assigning the setting of the ends themselves to character:

> Virtue makes the goal right, *phronesis* [practical wisdom] the things toward the goal. (V/VI.12 1144a7-9)

> Decision (προαίρεσις) won't be right without *phronesis* nor without virtue: for the one makes us do the end and the other the things toward it. (V/VI.13 1145a4-6; cf. *EE* II.11 *passim*)

Excellence in practical reasoning – *phronesis* – shows us the right ways to achieve our ends, but never tells us what ends to pursue. Having the right ends is instead a function of having the right character; and character is (as is widely and, I will argue, rightly held) not an intellectual state at all, but a state of the non-rational part of soul.

That at least is the face-value reading of the five passages just quoted (let us call them the Goal passages). Nonetheless, a formidable array of interpreters have refused to accept it. Aristotle's claim that virtue makes the goal right is "misleading" (Cooper, Hardie); on the *prima facie* reading "absurd" (Broadie); it "risks obscuring" Aristotle's genuine view (McDowell); it "must be modified" (Greenwood), or "must be treated as a lapse on Aristotle's part" (Joachim); given his other commitments, Aristotle "is wrong to claim that there is no reasoning about ethical first principles" (Irwin).[10] For despite what Aristotle seems to say in these passages, these interpreters insist, he must in fact hold that intellect plays a crucial role in identifying our ends: either (despite his

---

[9] See Cooper 1975, Dahl 1984, Reeve 1992 and others, discussed below.

[10] Cooper 1975, 64; Hardie 1968, 213; Broadie and Rowe 2002, 49; McDowell 1998, 30; Joachim 1951, 218; Greenwood 1909, 51; Irwin 1975, 578. Other influential opponents of the face-value reading of the claim include Allan 1953, Gauthier and Jolif 1958-9, and Wiggins 1980.

apparent denials) we do after all reason about ends, or (despite his apparent silence on the point) we grasp them through some function of intellect distinct from reasoning – perhaps dialectic, or perhaps as in the theoretical case "intellectual intuition" (*nous*).[11]

Why does the face-value reading of the Goal passages meet so much resistance? First, it seems to conflict with various statements Aristotle makes about virtue and *phronesis* in other places. I address those passages below, and argue that they can and should be accommodated by a straightforward reading of the Goal passages. But there is a second and deeper motive for resistance as well, which opponents of the face-value reading make perfectly clear. They think that if Aristotle assigns non-rational character responsibility for determining our ends, he is turned, in effect, into Hume (or rather, into a crude Humean of the kind that Hume himself may not have been): if reason plays no role in setting our ends, the job must fall to mere desire.[12] And indeed, most of the face-value reading's few defenders have attributed to Aristotle just this view.[13]

Certainly Aristotle holds the very un-Humean view that we want our ends *because* we find them good. This emerges most clearly from his characterization of the special, distinctively human desire we have for things *qua* ends – wish (βούλησις) – as being for what we find good (see the passages quoted in Chapter 1.1 and especially those from *EN* III.4-5 quoted below). But does that mean that wish is for what we *rationally* judge good? In assuming that it does, we saddle Aristotle with a stark dichotomy between the rational on one side and the purely conative on the other. If intellect does not supply our goals, the thought goes, then only desire and passion are left to do the job. But this interpretation turns on an equation of the non-rational with the non-cognitive: the rational part is made the sole source of all cognition, including all judgments of value, while the non-rational part is reduced to a purely conative force, its only role being to provide motivational force in support of or against such judgments.[14]

But, as we have seen at length in earlier chapters of this book, this is simply not how Aristotle carves up the soul. Intellect is one species of discrimination or cognition (κρίσις or γνῶσις) – one mode of receiving information about the world. But there are non-rational forms of cognition too: perception and *phantasia*. If Aristotle does hold that character has the power to set our ends, he will not be attributing that role to a

---

[11] For the first kind of view see Irwin and Wiggins; for versions of the latter see Cooper, Dahl, and Reeve (cited below). Some take 1143a35-b5 as evidence that ends are grasped by *nous*, but I will argue that this is a misreading.

[12] For clear expression of this worry as a motive for the intellectualizing reading, see for example Sorabji: if we deny intellect a role in choosing goals, "Aristotle is assimilated to Hume and the emotivists" (1973-4, 209). See also Allen 1953, and Cooper 1975, 62-63. Compare Irwin's discussion of the tension between Humean and non-Humean elements in Aristotle's ethics (1975, 568 and throughout).

[13] See especially Walter 1874 and Zeller 1897, vol II, 159-60 with 182-88.

[14] See for example Sorabji's argument that habituation must involve intellect because it is "not a mindless process" (1973-4, 216), Taylor's claim that the non-rational soul cannot supply first principles because its activities are "not cognitive at all, but rather affective" (2008, 211), and Cooper's argument that if habituation is non-rational it amounts to "mechanical" training (1975, 8). For compelling arguments against equating the non-rational with the non-cognitive, however, see Cooper 1998, 244-45.

purely conative force. Instead, he will be attributing it to a part of the soul which has its own forms of cognition, including evaluative cognition – perception and *phantasia*.[15]

Here, then, is a proposal rather naturally suggested by the parallels Aristotle draws between practical and theoretical starting-points: perhaps in claiming that character supplies our practical starting-points he means that we grasp these through *phantasia*, as the culmination of a process which roughly parallels theoretical induction. Virtue makes the goal right because in order to become virtuous one must have had the correct practical perceptions of virtuous activity and thereby come to have a correct practical *phantasia* of virtuous activity – a generalized appearance of it as the good.

In fact, we find a striking implication that Aristotle does think *phantasia* the cognitive basis of the desire for virtuous activity as the end, in his most detailed discussion of the way in which wish is for the good:

Should we say that what is wished for (βουλητόν) without qualification is the good, but for each person the apparent good (τὸ φαινόμενον)? For the virtuous person, then, what is wished will be what really is [good/to-be-wished-for], while for the base person what is wished for is some chance thing... For the virtuous person discerns (κρίνει) each thing rightly, and in each case the truth appears (φαίνεται) to him. (*EN* III.4 1113a23-31)

And suppose someone said that everyone longs for the apparent good, but they are not in control of the *phantasia*: whatever sort of person one is, in that way the end appears (φαίνεται) to one? (*EN* III.5 1114a31-b1)[16]

See also a passage on starting-points:

Practical syllogisms are equipped with a starting-point: "Since the end and the best is of such a sort..." And this does not *appear* (φαίνεται) except to the good man. For vice perverts, and makes us be deceived about the practical starting-points. (V/VI.12 1144a31-36, emphasis mine)

In Chapters 4 and 5 I argued that when Aristotle talks of someone having an appetite or other passion for something because it appears good, we should take this in the narrow and technical sense: the cognitive basis of our appetites, anger, pity, and fear is evaluative *phantasia*. Might the same be true here? If so – if Aristotle does mean these words for appearance and *phantasia* in the technical sense – then these passages resolve the dilemma we saw above. Aristotle can hold a Humean view of practical reasoning as restricted to working out "things towards ends," while still holding the very

---

[15] In making this claim I am in large part agreeing with, and hoping to revive, the interpretation of Burnet (1900, 64-68) (although for doubts about the role he assigns to *nous* see Chapter 8). Others have given related interpretations: see Achtenberg 2002 and Fortenbaugh 1964. My aim is to give the face-value reading of "virtue makes the goal right" a more thorough and sustained defense than it has hitherto received, both by showing that it is the natural reading of the texts and by explaining how it can accommodate what its opponents have considered powerful textual and philosophical arguments against it.

[16] This is a complicated argument for the conclusion that we should be held responsible for our moral characters. For my purposes, what is crucial is the correlation of the way the end appears with the kind of ethical character one has, and it is clear that Aristotle takes this as established: what is up for debate in the passage is whether or not we have control over our characters, which would give us indirect control over the appearance of the end.

un-Humean view that we want our ends because we find them good, for his claim is that we find them good through *phantasia*.

The objections to reading Aristotle this way will be obvious. Wishes, unlike appetites and other passions, are distinctively human desires; at some points Aristotle says that they are for what we *think* good, and at some points he even outright calls them rational (see citations below). Therefore the object of wish must be what is judged good by intellect rather than what merely appears good through *phantasia*. Moreover, many will add, this is what we should expect given the importance and the difficulty of grasping the correct end: Aristotle can hardly leave this most important of tasks to capacities we share with animals. Even granting that *phantasia* can cognize particular objects or scenarios as good in the perceptual way I laid out in Chapters 2-3, it is simply unsuited to represent the very general goods that form the ultimate starting-points of deliberation – the life of virtuous activity, to take a salient example. How can *phantasia*, which preserves and reproduces particular perceptions, represent such a general, abstract goal? Thus (many will argue), despite the face-value reading of the Goal passages Aristotle must in fact think that getting ends right is a function of practical intellect. Wishes are based not on quasi-perceptual appearances, but instead on practical thought – and arguably even on its highest deliverances.[17]

Therefore, our objector will conclude, it would be perverse to take these occurrences of *phantasia* and φαίνεσθαι in the technical sense of the psychological works. Aristotle's point in these passages is that we wish for what we *think* good (the doxastic use of 'appears,' discussed in Chapter 4), and he uses the language of appearance only to emphasize the subjectivity of these thoughts.[18] Note that this strategy is parallel to one we saw in Chapter 1: when Aristotle says that the apparent good is the object of appetite he is met with a deflationist reading of 'good'; when he says it is the object of wish he is met with a deflationist reading of 'apparent.'

When we look closely at the passages connecting wishes and ends with appearance, however, we find that they characterize these appearances in ways that make them look much less doxastic than perceptual. Consider expanded versions of the first two passages:

Should we say that what is wished for without qualification is the good, but for each person the apparent good? For the virtuous person, then, what is wished will be what really is [good/to-be-wished-for], while for the base person what is wished for is some chance thing, just as for those in good bodily condition what is healthy is what is so in truth, while for the sickly things other than these, and *likewise for what is bitter and sweet and hot and heavy and so on*. For the virtuous person discerns (κρίνει) each thing rightly, and in each case the truth appears (φαίνεται) to him. For *distinctive things are fine and pleasant in accordance with each character-state, and the virtuous person*

---

[17] I discuss the evidence for all these claims below.
[18] Cooper, for example, argues that when Aristotle speaks of the apparent good as the object of wish he is using the phrase in "a different sense" from that in which the pleasant is an apparent good, for now he is using the phrase to mean "what one takes or holds actually to be good" (1996b, 270).

presumably excels the most at seeing (ὁρᾶν) the truth in each case, being like a standard and measure of these things. (*EN* III.4 1113a23-33, emphases mine)

And suppose someone said that everyone longs for the apparent good, but they are not in control of the *phantasia*: whatever sort of person one is, in that way the end appears to one. If then each person is somehow responsible for his character, he will be responsible for the *phantasia* as well. If not... one needs a sort of natural, inborn *sense of sight* (φῦναι δεῖ ὥσπερ ὄψιν ἔχοντα), by which one will discern (κρίνει) finely and choose what is really good... Whether then the end does not appear (φαίνεται) in whatever way to each person by nature, but is partly due to himself, or whether the end is natural... vice will be no less voluntary [than virtue]. (*EN* III.5 1114a31-b20, emphasis mine)

Both passages use perceptual metaphors: the virtuous person "sees" the truth; we grasp the end as if through a "sense of sight," inborn or otherwise. Moreover, the first passage compares virtuous and vicious discernments of value with healthy and unhealthy discernments of the bitter, sweet, hot, and heavy. Sick people may well *believe* (on the basis of memory or testimony, for example) that the wine which tastes bitter to them is sweet, or the air which feels hot to them cool; what they are lacking is the ability to perceive things properly, and if their beliefs about the bitter etc. do come to differ from those of healthy people, this is *because* their perceptions do. Thus Aristotle's analogies strongly suggest that the kind of cognition or discernment (κρίσις) which virtue enhances and vice perverts is perceptual rather than rational. Note also that this passage explains the claim that "the virtuous person discerns each thing rightly, and in each case the truth appears to him" by referring to affective or aesthetic reactions: "For (γὰρ) distinctive things are fine (καλά) and pleasant in accordance with each character-state." If the virtuous person's ability to discern facts about value is a matter of being pleased and pained in the right ways, or admiring and being disgusted by the right things, then this discernment is an operation of non-rational cognition.[19] This is further supported by a passage from the *EE*:

The virtue concerned with each thing discerns (κρίνει) rightly the greater and the lesser – just the things which the *phronimos* would command virtue also [performs? commands?], so that all the virtues follow *phronesis*, or it follows all of them. (*EE* III.5 1232a35-38)

The κρίσις due to virtue is in accord with the commands of *phronesis* but not a function of *phronesis* itself, the passage implies; it is instead something distinctive to character by contrast with intellect – and hence non-rational.

These passages more than casually suggest, then, that one desires something as an end because it quasi-perceptually appears good. Should we nonetheless dismiss this implication on the grounds that wishes are rational desires?

It turns out that there are several different claims one might be making about wish in insisting that it is rational, and it is important to distinguish them. One question is whether or not they belong to the rational part of the soul; on this point, it seems fairly

---

[19] I defend this aesthetic reading of 'fine' in Chapter 8.

safe to say that Aristotle's considered opinion is no.[20] But this is arguably consistent with their being rational in a second sense: being based on rational cognition.[21] Here we seem to have better evidence: in the *de An.* when one is moved by wish one is moved "in accordance with reasoning (λογισμόν)" (433a23-25), and in the *Rhet.* it is rational (λογιστική) desire (1369a3). But it is notable that nowhere in the *EN* or *EE* does Aristotle repeat those claims. He does strongly imply that wish is distinctively human (*EN* III.2 1111b12-13, *EE* II.10 1225b25-26), but this is as far as he goes. Meanwhile the *Pol.* – which Aristotle presents as a continuation of the *EN* – not only places wish in the non-rational part of the soul but also groups it with appetite and spirited desire as being present in children straight from birth, "while reasoning (λογισμός) and *nous* arise in them as they grow older" (1334b17-25).

Turning now directly to the ethical works, we find that they strongly support at least one part of this last claim from the *Pol.*: namely that wish is not based on reasoning (λογισμός). For they explicitly distinguish wish from another form of motivation, decision (προαίρεσις), and characterize the latter as the outcome of deliberation, which they equate with practical reasoning (V/VI.1 1139a12-13). Thus it seems that what was called wish at *de An.* 432a23-25 – desire which accords with reasoning – is now called decision.[22] Wish, by contrast, is characterized as being not for the particular things one decides on as the result of deliberation, but rather as for goals or ends – and, as we have seen above, Aristotle says that these starting-points of deliberation are not themselves the product of deliberation. This looks then like support both for the face-value reading of the Goal passages and for the technical reading of the claims that wish is for the apparent good. Wishes are for ends, which are grasped not through reasoning but rather by the non-rational part of the soul, through *phantasia*.

But there is one final claim people have in mind when they say that wish is rational desire: that it is for what we *think* good, even if those thoughts are not the product of practical reasoning in the strict sense. The *Pol.* passage we saw above denies that wish is based on *nous* (as well as reasoning), but the ethical works twice seem to say that the object of wish is what is thought good. In between characterizations of the object of wish as what appears good the *EN* also once characterizes it as what seems or is thought good (τὸ δοκοῦν, 1113a21), and while this may be a loose use of δοκοῦν as equivalent to φαινόμενον (cf. *Insomn.* 458b29, discussed in Chapter 5.4), it may be strictly doxastic; the *EE*, meanwhile, says that no one wishes for what they think (οἴεται) bad (*EE* II.7 1223b6). Moreover, it is very hard to make sense of the implications that wish is

---

[20] He only assigns them to the rational part (λογιστικόν) in the *Topics* (126a13); on a common and I think correct view this is an Academic holdover, while *de An.* 432b5, which says that it would be absurd to "tear apart" desire by placing wish in the rational part (λογιστικόν) with appetite and spirited desire in the non-rational, along with *Pol.* 1334b17-25, which places wish in the non-rational (ἄλογον) part, give Aristotle's considered view: all desire belongs to one and the same part of the soul.

[21] For defense of this view see for example Alexander, and Gauthier and Jolif 1958-9.

[22] The *de An.* mentions προαίρεσις only once, at 406b25. It seems not to work with the *EN/EE*'s distinction between wish and decision, using 'wish' as a generic term for distinctively human desire.

distinctively human (see above) without taking it to involve some sort of cognition beyond what is available to lower animals.

In Chapter 8 I will argue that we can respect both this evidence that wishes are based on some form of thought and the countervailing evidence that they are based on *phantasia*: Aristotle's idea is that they are based on beliefs which are mere assents to *phantasia*, adding no content to what the appearances already contain (see 8.5). Thus wish is rational in one sense, but this in no way conflicts with the face-value reading of the Goal passages: it is the non-rational soul rather than the rational, *phantasia* rather than thought, that provides our view of the end.

What I have presented in this section is a way to give Aristotle a coherent account of how we come to have the goals we do. There are three conditions for the argument to work: we must accept the face-value reading of the Goal passages, a technical reading of the claim that wish is for the apparent good (understood as: wishes are based on beliefs which are mere assents to appearances), and the idea that habituation is a practical analogue of induction. All three will be met with objections; the aim of the rest of the book is to defend them.

I begin in the present chapter with a defense of the face-value reading of the Goal passages: a thorough examination of Aristotle's views on virtue and *phronesis* shows that he indeed attributes our view of ends to the non-rational part of the soul. This entails that it must be *phantasia* rather than thought which is responsible for their content. This has the very strong advantage of absolving Aristotle of the charge of incoherence about practical reasoning: he can hold his Humean view of practical reasoning without embracing the (sub-) Humean view that our ends are set by brute desire. Thus we need not conclude (as many have) that on the question of how we get our goals Aristotle is simply confused, inconsistent, or prone to making badly misleading statements at crucial points. In Chapter 8 I show that this non-rationalist account of the starting-points of practical reasoning is well grounded in Aristotle's overall view, through an argument that secures the second and third conditions: wishes are for what appears good through *phantasia*, because habituation is a form of practical induction.

7.3 Virtue is non-rational

My aim in the remainder of this chapter, then, is to demonstrate that Aristotle means in the Goal passages just what he seems to say. The ultimate goal each person pursues is happiness (*eudaimonia*) as he or she views it, and we each reach our view about what happiness consists in – virtuous activity, for example, or the life of pleasure or of honor – not by any intellectual process, but instead through the non-rational habituation of the non-rational part of the soul.

Let us use the label 'Intellectualists' for those who resist this interpretation, arguing that Aristotle grants the task of setting ends not to character but to intellect. There are two Intellectualist strategies for accommodating the Goal passages. One is to allow that virtue plays a crucial role in giving us our goals, while insisting that it can do so only because it is in part an intellectual state.[23] The other is to accept that virtue is non-rational, while denying that it literally supplies our goals.

I begin in this section by arguing against the first Intellectualist strategy: textual evidence overwhelmingly supports the view that virtue – or at the very least the kind of virtue which "makes the goal right" – is exclusively a state of the non-rational, passionate part of the soul.[24] In section 4 I argue against the second and more common Intellectualist strategy: textual evidence shows clearly that Aristotle characterizes virtue not as merely making us want our goals, but as literally supplying their contents. Thus the straightforward reading of Aristotle's texts is one on which a non-rational character state determines our goals.

Then I will argue that there are no good reasons to reject this straightforward interpretation: the burden of proof lies on those who oppose it. Contrary to widespread opinion, Aristotle does not characterize *phronesis* in such a way that it must include a grasp of ends (sections 5-6). Moreover, because ethical character involves non-rational cognition of ends, Aristotle can restrict practical intellect to reasoning about "things toward the end" without embracing a Humean view of motivation or moral judgment – that is, without abandoning his view that we desire our ends because we find them good (section 7; this argument is completed in Chapter 8).

Let us begin, then, by examining the evidence that virtue is a non-rational state of the soul. To many this will seem obvious: on the standard reading of the ethical works, virtue – that is character-virtue (ἠθική ἀρετή), by contrast with intellectual virtue[25] – is the excellent condition of the non-rational part of the soul. That is how Aristotle introduces virtue in both ethical works:

There are two parts of the soul, and the virtues are divided in accordance with (διῄρηνται κατὰ) these, and the intellectual virtues belong to the rational part (αἱ μὲν τοῦ λόγου ἔχοντος διανοητικαί), while the others [i.e. the character-virtues] belong to the part that is non-rational but has desire (αἱ δὲ τοῦ ἀλόγου ἔχοντος δ' ὄρεξιν). (*EE* II.4 1221b28-31; cf. 1220a8-11)

[There is a distinction between the part that exercises reason and the part that obeys it], and virtue is also defined in accordance with (διορίζεται κατὰ) this same difference: for we call some of the virtues intellectual and others ethical. (*EN* I.13 1103a3-5)

---

[23] Irwin 1975; Engberg-Pedersen 1983, 126-27. See also a recent paper by Lorenz (2009), which argues that this is Aristotle's view of virtue in the *EN*, although not in the *EE*; while I agree that the *EE* is more explicit in its characterization of virtue as non-rational, I do not see sufficient evidence for attributing to Aristotle a change of mind on this point, for, as I argue below, the apparently intellectualist passages from the common books (*EN* V-VII/*EE* IV-VI) can be read as consistent with the clearly non-intellectualist earlier books of the *EE*.

[24] This is the standard interpretation, held by the ancient commentators and most modern ones. In light of the difficulties in accommodating the passages cited below, however – difficulties forcefully urged in Irwin 1975 and Lorenz 2009 – it is worth defending at some length.

[25] Here and throughout the chapter I follow Aristotle in using the unqualified term 'virtue' (ἀρετή) as short-hand for 'character-virtue' (ἠθική ἀρετή).

The *EE* passage is unambiguous in its claim: intellectual virtues belong to the rational part of the soul, character-virtues to the non-rational.²⁶ The corresponding passage in the *EN* says only that the virtues are "defined in accordance with (διορίζεται κατά)" the distinction between the two parts of the soul; especially given the similarity to the *EE*'s language, however (virtues are "divided in accordance with (διῄρηνται κατά)" the parts), it is very natural to read this passage as making the same point, and this is how it is taken by the vast majority of commentators. That character-virtue is a state of the non-rational soul is also very strongly implied by many other passages: the argument that virtue is the product of habituation in actions and passions (see discussion below), and the descriptions of character-states as dispositions to feel passions in particular ways.²⁷ Moreover, if Aristotle in fact thinks character-virtue in part intellectual then the ethical works' whole project of contrasting intellectual virtues, acquired through teaching, with ethical ones, acquired through habituation, is awkward, misleading, and incomplete. Indeed, the interpretation on which virtue is wholly a state of the non-rational soul is so straightforward that we should only abandon it if there is clear textual evidence against it.²⁸

According to the first species of Intellectualist, there is. The virtues "are decisions (προαιρέσεις), or not without decisions" (*EN* II.5 1106a3-4), for an act to be done virtuously it must be "decided on" (*EN* II.4 1105a31-32), and virtue is a "prohairetic state" (ἕξις προαιρετική, most naturally translated as 'a state issuing in decisions' – *EN* II.6 1106b36, V/VI.2 1139a22-23, *EE* II.10 1227b9; cf. *EE* III.1 1228a24 and III.1 1230a27) – while decisions are the result of rational deliberation (e.g. *EN* III.3 1113a9-12). Virtue is a state not merely κατὰ τὸν ὀρθὸν λόγον, in accordance with the right *logos* (reason or rational account), but μετὰ τοῦ ὀρθοῦ λόγου, *with* the right *logos* (V/VI.13 1144b26-27). And therefore it does not occur without *phronesis*, the excellence of practical intellect (V/VI.13 1144b8-17, 31-33). Moreover, *logoi*, while not sufficient to instill virtue, seem to play some role (*EN* X.9 1179b20 ff.). All this has been taken to show that virtue is in part intellectual, in which case it must belong not exclusively to the non-rational part of the soul, but also to practical intellect (just as e.g. the virtue of being harmonious belongs jointly to more than one note).²⁹

---

²⁶ See also *MM* 1185b5-12 for an equally explicit claim using ἐν. 'Unambiguous' is perhaps too strong a term: Irwin (in conversation) urges that the virtue which perfects one part may be partly a state of another part. This may be a possible reading, but it is certainly an oblique one, and if we can show that there is no strong evidence from elsewhere which pressures us to adopt it then we should avoid it.

²⁷ See especially *EE* II.2 1220b18-19: "Character-states (ἕξεις) are those things which are responsible for these things (the passions) being present either in accordance with (κατά) *logos* or in the opposite way." Lorenz thinks that the *EN*'s revision of this definition to include actions alongside passions signals a change in Aristotle's view: now virtue must be responsible for everything that goes into action, which includes deliberation and decision. But the *EE* clearly holds that virtues influence how we act, and it seems natural to take the *EN*'s revised definition as simply making that point explicit.

²⁸ This is of course compatible with virtue being rational in an extended sense: in a virtuous person, the non-rational part not only obeys reason but is in harmony with it and follows it in everything.

²⁹ "Aristotle's allocation of the virtues of character to the non-rational part of the soul, and of the virtues of intellect to the rational part, is at least misleading... he ought to have said that virtue of character involves

Is Aristotle simply contradicting himself? Or does he consistently hold one of these views about virtue, in which case the passages implying the other view are in need of careful reinterpretation? I will argue that the case for this Intellectualist interpretation is in fact quite weak: the passages its proponents cite are all either inconclusive or in fact best read as evidence for the non-Intellectualist account.

Let us begin with what has seemed one of the strongest pieces of evidence for the Intellectualist account: Aristotle's definition of virtue as a prohairetic state (ἕξις προαιρετική). This is, as I mentioned above, naturally and standardly read as implying that virtue is a state which itself issues in decisions (προαιρέσεις).[30] But there is only one passage in which Aristotle himself explains the phrase, and what he says there belies this reading:

Since all virtue is prohairetic – and what we mean by this (τοῦτο δὲ πῶς λέγομεν) has been said earlier: that *it makes one choose everything for the sake of something* (ἕνεκά τινος πάντα αἱρεῖσθαι ποιεῖ), *and this is the that-for-the-sake-of-which, the fine* (τὸ καλόν) – it's clear that courage, being a virtue, makes one endure fearful things for the sake of something... [i.e.] because [the action] is fine. (*EE* III.1 1230a27-32)

Aristotle has defined virtue as a prohairetic state at *EE* II.10 1227b8; what "has been said earlier" (a27) is thus a reference to the discussion which follows that definition: a discussion which argues that virtue "makes decision right" by making its goal right, i.e. by aiming at the mean (II.11 1227b12-1228a3, which includes one of the Goal passages quoted above). The present passage explicitly reiterates this claim in telling us what it means for virtue to be prohairetic: it means that virtue gives one the right goal for one's decisions – "makes one choose everything for the sake of... the fine." And this shows that the claim that virtue is prohairetic is, properly understood, simply a reiteration of the Goal passages. Virtue is a prohairetic state in that its function is to make decisions correct (cf. 1144a86-89), although because it controls only one component of decisions it needs the help of something else – *phronesis* – to fulfill its function. (Compare "the eyes are for seeing," which is plausibly essence-giving despite the fact that seeing also requires the cooperation of the brain.)[31]

---

both parts of the soul" (Irwin 1975, 576); "Aristotle in the *Nicomachean Ethics* conceives of the virtues of character as rational states, states partly constituted by a... quickness to grasp suitable reasons for acting..." (Lorenz 2009, 178).

[30] Compare for example the description of knowledge (ἐπιστήμη) as a ἕξις ἀποδεικτική (V/VI.3 1139b31-32), and *phronesis* as a ἕξις πρακτική (V/VI.5 1140b4-6). (One might try to get a non-Intellectualist reading by insisting that *prohairesis* does not have its technical meaning at all in *EN* II.5, but this conflicts with the beginning of III.2, which introduces the technical discussion of *prohairesis* by saying that we have already seen the importance of *prohairesis* for virtue.)

[31] This is further confirmed by the previous pages of the *EE*. At II.10 1227a18-23 Aristotle argues that pleasure appears good and bad, where this means that pleasure appears good as an *end* of action (τέλος, a25), i.e. as an object of wish (1227a27-31). Immediately following, at 1227b1-5 we get: "It is clear from these things that virtue and vice are about pleasures and pains, for they are about objects of decision (προαιρετά), and decision is about the good and bad and what seem such, and these are by nature pleasure and pain." That

This understanding of the relation between virtue and decision also undermines the Intellectualists' interpretation of Aristotle's claim that for an action to be done virtuously it must be decided on (*EN* II.4 1105a31-32). This will mean not that the reasoning which culminates in the decision is itself an exercise of virtue (as on the Intellectualist reading), but that virtue has not been manifested unless its function has been fulfilled, i.e. unless it has set a goal toward the realization of which a decision has been made. This is strongly supported by the claim that follows: that it is habituation which ensures that we decide on virtuous actions for themselves (*EN* II.4 1105b4-5, noted above). I will argue below that habituation is non-rational; if it can ensure that we decide on virtuous actions for themselves, this can only mean that it ensures that our decisions have the right ends.[32]

The other text that has seemed most strongly to support the Intellectualist account is one in which Aristotle distinguishes mere "natural" (φυσική) virtue from "strict" (κυρία) virtue. The former is found in non-rational creatures (children and beasts) as well as adults, but:

The strict kind does not occur (γίνεται) without *phronesis*... For virtue is not merely the state which is in accordance with the right *logos*, but that which is with the right *logos* (οὐ μόνον ἡ κατὰ τὸν ὀρθὸν λόγον, ἀλλ' ἡ μετὰ τοῦ ὀρθοῦ λόγου ἕξις ἀρετή ἐστιν). (V/VI.13 1144b16-27)

The Intellectualist takes this to mean that virtue includes an excellent rational state as a component: it does not arise without *phronesis* because it includes *phronesis*, and it is "with *logos*" because it is itself in part a rational state. But immediately preceding this passage, Aristotle has given what is evidently a reiteration of our strongest evidence for the non-Intellectualist account, namely the distinction between character-virtues and intellectual virtues made in *EE* II.1 and *EN* I.13 (quoted at the start of this section):

So that just as there are two species [of good condition] in the case of the believing part of the soul (ἐπὶ τοῦ δοξαστικοῦ δύο ἐστὶν εἴδη), *phronesis* and cleverness, so too there are two in the case of the character-part (ἐπὶ τοῦ ἠθικοῦ): natural virtue on the one hand and strict virtue on the other. (V/VI.13 1144b14-16)[33]

Phronesis belongs to practical intellect, here identified as the part of the soul that has beliefs.[34] Virtue, by contrast – even strict virtue – belongs to the "character" part of the soul; given that Aristotle also describes this part here as the seat of natural virtue, a state

---

virtue is concerned with decision, then, means that it is concerned with the *goals* of decision – the ends, the objects of wish.

[32] As to the claim that the virtues "are decisions, or not without decisions," it is clear that Aristotle accepts only the latter option, which we can now explain along the same lines as the claim that they are prohairetic states.

[33] I have translated ἐπί with the genitive as 'in the case of'; we get even more direct support for my reading if we take it as 'in' (following for example Irwin 1999).

[34] This part is δοξαστικόν, believing (V/VI.5 1140b26-27) (by contrast with ἐπιστημονικόν, knowing – V/VI.1 1139a12) because it is about things that could be otherwise; earlier Aristotle has called it the calculating part (λογιστικόν) on the grounds that it is the part which deliberates (βουλεύεσθαι) (1139a12-13).

found in non-rational creatures, he evidently has in mind the non-rational, passionate part.[35] And thus the ensuing claims that virtue cannot exist without *phronesis* and is "with *logos*" should be taken – as they often are – to mean simply that genuine virtue is dependent on *phronesis*. "Strict" virtue is, like natural virtue, an excellent condition of the non-rational capacities for passions, in which they tend to be in a mean between extremes, but strict virtue belongs only to souls that also possess *phronesis*, and natural virtue only to souls that do not. On one version of this reading, this difference is merely extrinsic: we do not dignify someone whose non-rational soul is in good condition with the unqualified label 'virtuous' unless he is overall excellent, i.e. also possesses *phronesis*.[36] But there is a more compelling version, which makes the difference substantive rather than merely terminological: the passions and actions of a strictly virtuous person do not merely happen to coincide with what well-functioning practical intellect *would* prescribe, but they are such as to wait upon the right prescription (the ὀρθὸς λόγος) before becoming active. As the *EE* puts it with regard to one particular virtue, courage, virtue is "attendance on the *logos*" (ἀκολούθησις τῷ λόγῳ) (*EE* III.1 1229a1–2). And therefore strict virtue, unlike natural (or merely habituated) virtue, cannot exist without *phronesis*.[37] We can make the point clearer by way of one of Aristotle's own analogies for the relation between the rational and non-rational parts of the soul: a servant who receives no instructions, or no good instructions, from his master, might nonetheless tend to do the right thing, but will be in a state very different from that of a servant practiced in obedience to an excellent master. The former acts on his own impulses; the latter takes the lead from his superior. And it would be reasonable enough, if somewhat odd to our ears, to say that only in the latter case is the servant truly (or 'strictly') an excellent one.

It is true that Aristotle uses the phrase 'with *logos*' (μετὰ λόγου) elsewhere in the ethical works to mean something like "intrinsically rational."[38] But this is not decisive. Aristotle first introduces the non-rational part of the soul as μετέχουσα πῃ λόγου (partaking in a way in *logos*) (*EN* I.13 1102b14, cf. *EE* II.1 1219b27); the phrase μετὰ λόγου may be meant as a reference back to this. Moreover, the *Rhetoric* characterizes as μετὰ λόγου certain appetites (ἐπιθυμίαι) which result from "having listened or been persuaded (ἀκούσαντες καὶ πεισθέντες)" (*Rhet.* 1370a18–27), a description

---

[35] The Intellectualist must claim that τὸ ἠθικόν refers to a compound of the non-rational part with some aspect of the intellectual part; this seems to me too strained a reading of the sentence to be credible.

[36] See Greenwood: "combination with" cleverness (δεινότης) – the quality of being good at deliberating toward any given end, regardless of its value (V/VI.11 1144a24–27) – makes natural virtue into strict virtue (1909, 56).

[37] This is, I think, what Aquinas has in mind when he says that "when we act repeatedly according to reason, a modification is impressed in the appetite [the non-rational part of the soul] by the power of reason. This impression is nothing else but moral virtue" (commentary on *EN* 1103a18–26, trans. Litzinger). This view of virtue is compellingly defended in Smith 1996, which aims to reconcile the Goal passages with the evidence that virtue "seems to be a matter of following the dictates of wisdom" (1996, 58).

[38] See for example V/VI.4 1140a6–8, 5 1140b20–22, 6 1140b33, and especially *EE* II.1 1220a4–12, which characterizes the intellectual virtues as "with *logos*" and argues on that basis that they belong to the rational part of the soul; Lorenz rests much on these passages.

which strongly recalls the virtuous non-rational soul's obedience to the rational in *EN* I.13 and *EE* II.1. If an appetite counts as "with *logos*" insofar as it is influenced by listening and being persuaded, then so too should a non-rational character-state. Aristotle's point in V/VI.13 will thus be that character-states that are κατὰ λόγον merely happen to coincide with what *logos* would command, while those that are μετὰ λόγου actually result from obedience to *logos* – just the contrast the non-Intellectualist finds here.

Thus the passages which have most seemed to cast doubt on the non-Intellectualist account of character-virtue can be accommodated.[39] Moreover, this is, as I argued above, the most straightforward reading of the ethical works. Finally, the view is a philosophically defensible one. Lorenz resists attributing it to Aristotle on the grounds that it would be "repellent for a theory of virtue to deny that having an outstandingly good character in important part actually consists in being disposed to grasp reasons" (2009, 178). But in excluding an intellectual element from what *he* calls character (ἠθικὴ ἕξις), Aristotle is in no way denying that the grasp of suitable reasons for actions is part of the condition that Lorenz is evidently thinking of as character (plausibly in keeping with modern usage): overall excellence in matters to do with action. It is simply that Aristotle construes that overall excellence as a composite state made up of two excellences: excellence in practical reasoning, and excellence of non-rational character. As he puts it in the *EE*, after distinguishing the rational and non-rational parts, "just as good [bodily] condition (εὐεξία) is composed of the virtues of the parts, so also is the excellence of the soul (ἡ τῆς ψυχῆς ἀρετή)" (*EE* II.1 1220a3-4).[40]

---

[39] Lorenz also cites the claim that temperance and courage "seem (δοκοῦσι) to be the virtues of the non-rational parts" (*EN* III.10 1117b23-24), which arguably implies that the other character-virtues are not. The 'seem,' however, is often taken as a significant rather than a casual one, indicating an *endoxon* which Aristotle rejects. See Burnet's note *ad loc.*, drawing attention to the plural "non-rational parts" (ἀλόγων μερῶν): "sc. θυμοῦ καὶ ἐπιθυμίας. Aristotle starts as usual from τὰ δοκοῦντα, in this case the Platonic view. Aristotle did not himself believe in 'parts of the soul.'" (For this strategy see also the commentaries by Taylor 2006, Gauthier and Jolif 1958-9, and the Anonymous commentator.) Alternatively, Aristotle may be saying that everyone recognizes that courage and temperance are concerned with passions, while in the cases of the other virtues (for example justice) this is far less obvious; thus only courage and temperance "seem" non-rational.

[40] Lorenz also objects that separating virtue from *phronesis* "seems to introduce a gap between virtue and action. It seems to remove, say, courage from the courageous person's thoughtful and intelligent activity in the course of which they implement a suitable way of achieving the goal of, say, rescuing the children left behind in the burning building. That activity itself turns out to be, it seems, not an exercise of courage, but of cleverness [i.e. δεινότης] or *phronesis*" (2009, 203). But this, I take it, far from being an objection to the non-Intellectualist interpretation, is precisely Aristotle's point in distinguishing virtue from *phronesis*. The idea is that it is one thing to have the right goal, the proper feelings about it, and the proper responsiveness to reasoning about how to achieve it, and another thing to be good at the actual reasoning. Courage will still be manifested during the implementation of the goal – the courageous person persists in his determination to save the kids even if reasoning reveals it to be harder or more dangerous than he first thought – so it is not that character-virtue simply lies dormant after the goal is set. But figuring out how to achieve the goal is not itself an expression of courage; it is an expression of *phronesis*. Courage is manifested in having the right goal, caring about it, and feeling the right feelings throughout the process of implementing it, but not in the reasoning that goes into figuring out how to do so.

In sum, then, the burden of proof is squarely on the Intellectualists: on a straightforward, textually and philosophically defensible reading of both ethical works, virtue is solely a non-rational state.

Now I come to the second main argument of this section, which shifts attention from what Aristotle means by 'virtue' in general to what he is doing in the Goal passages. I want to show that even if someone is willing to shoulder the burden of proof – even if someone insists that there remain reasons for thinking Aristotelian character-virtue a partly intellectual state – she should nonetheless concede that what does the work of making the goal right is a state of the non-rational soul.

The evidence for this claim comes from the last of the Goal passages, from the discussion of *akrasia* in VI/VII.8. What instructs us in right opinion about the goal, according to this passage, is "virtue, either natural or habituated (φυσικὴ ἢ ἐθιστή)" (1151a18-19). There are two ways to read this qualification: either Aristotle is explaining more fully than he does in the other Goal passages what he means by 'virtue' – all virtue is either natural or habituated, and either type can make the goal right – or he is restricting the work of making the goal right to two species of virtue among several. Leaving open for now which he intends, the claim is that the state which makes the goal right is either one acquired by nature or one acquired through habituation. What sort of states might these be?

The case of natural virtue is straightforward: all the other passages which mention it explicitly characterize it as non-rational. As we saw above, natural virtue is a condition which resembles but falls short of genuine or "strict" (κυρία) virtue (V/VI.13 1144b14-16); at least one reason that it falls short is that it is neither "with" nor even "in accordance with" *logos*:

Each virtue exists both by nature and in another way, with *phronesis* (ἑκάστη πως ἀρετὴ καὶ φύσει καὶ ἄλλως μετὰ φρονήσεως). (*EE* III.7 1234a29-30)

The courage on account of spirited passion (θυμὸν) seems most natural (φυσικωτάτη), and when decision and the that-for-the-sake-of-which are added, [seems really] to be courage. (*EN* III.8 1117a4-5; cf. *EE* III.1 1229a20-28)

Natural virtue bears this same relation – not identical, but similar – to strict virtue (τὴν κυρίαν). For our characters seem to belong to all of us by nature in a way, for we are just and temperate and brave and have other states straight from birth.... The natural states belong also to children and beasts, but are manifestly harmful without *nous*[41] ... But if one acquires *nous*, it makes a difference in action.[42] And this state which is similar [to natural virtue] is virtue strictly. So ... there are two [species of good condition] in the case of the character-part: natural virtue on the one hand and strict virtue on the other, and of these the strict does not come to be without *phronesis*. (V/VI.13 1144b2-17)

---

[41] We can leave it open for now whether this is meant as practical *nous* in a technical sense, or simply some input from intellect in the broad sense of rational cognition.

[42] Or possibly "one does very well in action" (ἐν τῷ πράττειν διαφέρει).

Naturally virtuous agents fall short of full virtue, either because they lack intellect and reasoning altogether (as with children and beasts), or because they fail to exercise it in the proper way: fail to make decisions at all, or fail to decide on the fine, or fail to be practically wise (*phronimos*). I have argued above that the contrasting state of strict or genuine virtue itself merely depends on, rather than includes, intellectual excellence; in any case, however, the status of *natural* virtue is clear: it is solely a state of the non-rational part of the soul, a condition of the passions without any intellectual component at all.

What about habituated virtue, the other state mentioned as "making the goal right" at 1151a19? Here the story is somewhat more complicated, but I will argue that on any viable interpretation this too is a state of the non-rational soul alone.

Both ethical works introduce character-virtue as a state acquired through habituation:

Intellectual virtue for the most part has its origin and growth from teaching... while character-virtue arises from habit... By doing just actions we become just, by doing temperate ones temperate, by doing brave ones brave ... (*EN* II.1 1103a14-17; b1-2)

Moreover, Aristotle seems to hold not merely that habituation is necessary for virtue, but that it is sufficient:

By nature we are able to receive the virtues, and we are completed (τελειουμένοις) through habit. (*EN* II.1 1103a25-26)

The lawgivers make the citizens good by habituating them. (*EN* II.1 1103b3-4)[43]

Intellectualist interpreters who accept the clear implication of these passages that habituation is sufficient for virtue must therefore argue that habituation has an intellectual component: it involves learning explanations of why certain actions and reactions are appropriate, why they are good.[44] But this fits poorly with the distinction we have just seen between acquiring states through habituation and acquiring them through teaching or *logos* (*EN* II.1, cf. *Pol.* 1334b8 ff.). Moreover, Aristotle's extensive discussions of habituation not only make no mention of any intellectual aspects, but explicitly present the repetition of actions and passions as what does the work:

By acting in dangerous situations and by becoming habituated to fearing or feeling bold (ἐθιζόμενοι φοβεῖσθαι ἢ θαρρεῖν), some become brave and others cowardly – and it is similar

---

[43] Lest one think that habituation is only part of the lawgiver's tactic, supplemented by some kind of intellectual teaching here unmentioned, consider a passage from the *Politics*: "the law has no force for persuading other than habit (ἔθος)" (1269a20-21). And as I pointed out above, even with regard to what has seemed the most intellectual component of virtue – that for an act to be done for example justly or temperately it must be "decided on, and decided on for itself" – Aristotle says that this "arises (περιγίνεται) out of frequently doing just and temperate things," i.e. from correct habituation (*EN* II.4 1105a31-b5).

[44] See for example Cooper: "Now, though he is not careful to say so, this process of training is not the purely mechanical thing it may at first glance seem ... the habituation must involve also (though Aristotle does not explain how it does so) the training of the mind. As the trainee becomes gradually used to acting in certain ways, he comes gradually to understand what he is doing and why he is doing it" (1975, 8). I have already argued that this presents a false dichotomy: between intellectual and "mechanical" training there is a middle ground, the shaping of non-rational cognition.

for things concerning appetites and angers.... And in one word, the character-states (ἕξεις) come to be from the similar activities (ἐνεργειῶν).⁴⁵ (*EN* II.1 1103b16-22; cf. II.2 1104a33-b2).

It is by doing the actions and feeling the passions that one attains the corresponding state. The same is implied by the passages which describe habituation as working mainly by means of pleasure and pain: see e.g. *EE* VII.2 1237a1-7 and *EN* II.3 1104b8-12. Thus habituation is a non-intellectual process (although not at all a non-cognitive one, I will argue in Chapter 8). But it is very difficult to see how non-intellectual training on its own can yield an excellent intellectual state; therefore we should conclude that the virtue which results solely from habituation is itself non-intellectual, a disposition to feel the right passions and motivations in the right ways – which is precisely how Aristotle seems to be describing virtue at many points in *EN* II and *EE* II. If habituation is sufficient for virtue, virtue must be a state of the non-rational soul alone.

A more promising strategy for Intellectualists, then, is to argue that despite the implications of *EN* II.1 and *EE* II.1-2, habituation is not in fact sufficient for virtue.⁴⁶ If this is right, then habituated virtue, the state paired with natural virtue in our Goal passage (VI/VII.8 1151a15-19), is not itself full or "strict" virtue, but instead is a species of the same genus as natural virtue: a state of the non-rational soul which resembles full virtue but falls short of it due to the agent's intellectual deficiency. One passage from the end of the *EN* strongly suggests this reading:

Some think people become good by nature, some through habit, and some through teaching (διδαχῇ)... But *logos* and teaching do not have force in every case, but the soul of the hearer has to have been *prepared beforehand* by habits toward rejoicing and hating things in a fine way, just like the earth that is to nourish a seed. For the one who lives according to passion would not listen to a dissuading *logos*, nor again would he understand it... A character proper to virtue must then somehow be there *beforehand* (δεῖ δὴ τὸ ἦθος προυπάρχειν πως οἰκεῖον τῆς ἀρετῆς), loving the fine and being disgusted by the shameful. (*EN* X.9 1179b20-31, emphases mine)⁴⁷

On one reading, this passage says that habituation yields a character which is akin to virtue, but virtue itself comes only with the aid of "*logos* and teaching."⁴⁸ If this is

---

⁴⁵ Ἐνέργεια covers passions as well as actions.

⁴⁶ "A reader of Book II might have thought that virtues of character are acquired by learning to enjoy and want to do virtuous actions... But we must now agree that non-intellectual training is insufficient for real virtue, which requires wisdom" (Irwin 1975, 571; cf. Sorabji 1973-4, 211).

⁴⁷ There are striking similarities here to Plato's description in the *Republic* of the cultural upbringing ("musical education") that is a necessary preparation for virtue: someone raised with the right artistic influences would "praise fine things and enjoy them, and receiving them into his soul would be nourished by them and become fine and good, and would censure shameful things correctly and hate them while he is still young, before he is able to grasp the *logos*, and when the *logos* does come would welcome it, recognizing it through its kinship (οἰκειότητα)" (*Rep.* 401e4-402a4). The *Republic* makes very clear that the upshot of this musical education is a necessary preparation for virtue, but not sufficient for it: to become truly good one needs in addition the *logos*, i.e. the intellectual grasp of the Form of the Good.

⁴⁸ This is not evidence that virtue itself is partly a rational state; it is apparently a version of V/VI.13's claim that there is no virtue without *phronesis*, and the non-Intellectualist can accommodate both claims in the same ways (see below).

indeed Aristotle's view, the "habituated virtue" of our Goal passage is a necessary condition for virtue rather than genuine virtue itself: it is *mere* habit-virtue. The person with mere habit-virtue, like the one with mere natural virtue, is inferior to the truly virtuous person because the truly virtuous person is also *phronimos* (has *phronesis*). This reading seems to fit well with the *Politics*, which distinguishes the virtue of a citizen – a virtue instilled by correct habituation through good laws (see e.g. 1269a20-21) – from "complete" (τελείαν) virtue, the virtue of a ruler or "good man," who is a *phronimos* (*Pol.* 1276b34-35, 1277a15). On the other hand, since this reading of the passage conflicts so strongly with the account of habituation in *EN* II, it is worth considering an alternative interpretation: given that the purpose of the whole discussion of which this passage forms a part is to argue that *logoi* are not sufficient for instilling virtue (see 1179b4 ff.), and given that this discussion nowhere says that they are necessary, Aristotle's view might be that they are simply an optional aid.[49] (I say more about the nature of the *logoi* in question below.)

There is evidence on both sides, then, and I will not try to settle the issue of whether Aristotle's "habituated virtue" is identical with strict virtue itself, or merely a preparation for it. For on either interpretation, the point crucial for my purposes holds: habituated virtue, like natural virtue, is a non-rational state. And thus when Aristotle says that "virtue, natural or habituated, teaches us right opinion about the goal" (1151a18-19), he means that what makes the goal right is solely a state of the non-rational soul.

What about the other Goal passages? These clearly refer to 'strict' virtue, by contrast with natural virtue (and by contrast with mere habit-virtue, if there is such a thing): this is particularly clear for two which come in the context of the very discussion which makes strict virtue dependent on *phronesis* and thereby distinguishes it from natural virtue, in V/VI.12-13 (1144a7-9 and 1145a4-6). The Intellectualist must thus insist that Aristotle changes his mind: in book V/VI he says that what makes the goal right is a partly intellectual state, while in book VI/VII it is a solely non-rational one. But this is a very uncharitable reading indeed: the language of the later Goal passage is so similar to that of the earlier passages that the Intellectualist winds up attributing to Aristotle a stark inconsistency.

Finally, consider an Intellectualist willing to bite this bullet. Even she must accommodate the fact that Aristotle draws sharp contrasts between virtue and *phronesis* – and does so particularly, as we have seen, in the passages which distinguish what makes the goal right from what makes the "things toward it" right. The unreconstructed Intellectualist will have to explain the contrast as part-whole: while virtue is a state of both practical parts of the soul, *phronesis* is just one aspect of this state, the intellectual aspect. The Goal passages certainly do not sound as if they are contrasting a whole with one of its parts.[50] Even if they are, however, "virtue makes the goal right, *phronesis* the things

---

[49] Compare Protagoras' position in the *Protagoras*: an ordinary upbringing is sufficient to instill virtue, but Protagoras' teachings can expedite or embellish the process.

[50] See in particular "*Phronesis* is yoked to virtue of character, and this to *phronesis*" (*EN* X.9 1178a16).

toward the goal" will entail that the non-rational aspect plays a *necessary* role in determining the goal, while the intellectual aspect is sufficient to determine the means. (Compare "That suit makes him look handsome, and the jacket makes him look tall," which clearly implies that the pants as well as the jacket are responsible for making him look handsome.) Thus we would still need an account of how non-rational character contributes to our conception of the goal.

There are Intellectualist strategies for explaining this; in the next section I will argue that they fail.

7.4 Making the goal right

Most Intellectualists belong to the second camp. They accept that virtue is non-rational; what they deny is that it literally supplies the content of one's view of the end. This is a privilege they reserve for *phronesis* (so that, despite the apparent division of labor in the Goal passages, it is *phronesis* task to grasp the end as well as the "things toward it"); virtue's role is purely conative. Aristotle says that temperance (σωφροσύνη) "preserves *phronesis* (σώζουσαν τὴν φρόνησιν)" because "to someone corrupted by pleasure or pain, straightaway the starting-point [i.e. the proper end] does not appear" (V/VI.5 1140b11-20): this allegedly shows that virtue "makes the goal right" only in that the appetites and passions which constitute character determine whether or not the end, which is dictated by intellect, is "preserved" – i.e., whether or not the agent keeps it as an end. Either (a) virtue ensures that one will *want* the goal which one intellectually judges best, or (b) virtue preserves that goal in that non-virtuous desires would prompt intellect to change its view of what is best.[51]

These interpretations are problematic in their own right: why should virtue play this role for ends but not also for "things toward them"? (If I can be easily tempted away from wanting to save a drowning baby, for example, surely I can be all the more easily tempted away from wanting to do it precisely by jumping in myself when deliberation has shown that that is the best means.) But most importantly, they simply do not capture what the Goal passages seem to say. Those passages describe parallel roles for *phronesis* and virtue: whatever it is that *phronesis* does in relation to the "things toward the goal" ("make it right," "make us do it"), virtue does in relation to the goal itself. And surely what *phronesis* does in relation to the things toward the end is literally identify them – tell us what they are. Thus the clear implication of the Goal passages is that virtue dictates what the goal is. This is very nearly explicit in the VI/VII.8 passage, which says that virtue is διδασκαλικός of – teaches us – the goal (1151a15-19).

---

[51] For version (a) see for example Allan 1953, 74-75 (which provides a good history of the dispute between those who accept the straightforward reading of the Goal passages and those who oppose it); for version (b) see for example Irwin's commentary on *EN* 1140b11 ff. But there is a readily available non-Intellectualist reading of the "preservation" passage: without the right end, which can only be supplied by virtue, practical intellect will lack the proper starting-points and so cannot achieve true excellence.

Moreover, that virtue literally supplies the content of the goal is strongly – I would say conclusively – supported by the analogy that Aristotle draws between practical and theoretical reasoning in that passage and others. As we saw in section 2, what Aristotle clearly and explicitly claims is that the role played by *nous* in the theoretical case – laying down the starting-points for reasoning – is played in the practical case by ethical character. In the theoretical case when Aristotle denies that "*logos* is instructive of the starting-points" he assigns that task to *nous*; in the practical case, then, he is assigning the very same task to character. And this means that what virtue is doing in "making the goal right" is *supplying* the goal: giving us the true view of the end at which our actions aim, just as *nous* gives us the true view of the premises from which our theoretical demonstrations follow.

A third plank of support for this reading of 'makes the goal right' comes from Aristotle's systematic correlation of character with views of the end. Recall the passages on wish, character, and how the end appears which we saw above: each person wishes for (has as her end) the apparent good, but only to the virtuous person does the end appear correctly (*EN* III.4 1113a23-31); how the end appears depends on what sort of person one is (*EN* III.5 1114a31-b1); the starting-points of practical syllogisms do not appear except to the good man (V/VI.12 1144a31-36). That is, how the end appears varies with one's ethical character: it is the virtuous person who reliably has a correct view of the end. Of course given the co-dependence of virtue and *phronesis* it is possible to construe these passages as attributing that correctness to the latter, but this is not at all the straightforward reading: had that been Aristotle's point, he should have substituted '*phronimos*' for words like 'virtuous' and 'good.'

That character supplies ends is further supported by a natural reading of a much-debated passage on decision:

[The efficient cause] of decision is desire (ὄρεξις) and the *logos* that is for the sake of something. Wherefore decision requires *nous* and thought, and also a character-state (οὔτ' ἄνευ νοῦ καὶ διανοίας οὔτ' ἄνευ ἠθικῆς ἐστὶν ἕξεως ἡ προαίρεσις). (V/VI.2 1139a31-34)

Decision is the result of a desire for an end – a wish – and deliberation about how to achieve it (see e.g. *EE* II.10 1226b5-6 with 1226a5-8, and less explicitly *EN* III.2 1111b19-20 and III.4 1113a2-12). An Intellectualist reading of the passage must insist that the identification of the end, as well as of the means, is a function of "*nous* and thought," leaving the character-state responsible only for motivation.[52] But if character is the source of wish, and wishes are for ends, then the claim that decision requires "*nous* and thought and also a character-state" is most naturally taken to mean that it requires character as the source of the end, and intellectual cognition (*nous*, in the broad sense, i.e. thought) as the source of the "*logos* for the sake of something" – that is, of the

---

[52] See for example Irwin's (1999) note *ad loc.*: "We need virtue of thought to find the true reasoning, and we need the right sort of character if we are to follow true reasoning in our actions"; cf. Cooper 1975, 63.

deliberation which shows how to achieve the end.[53] In other words, this passage is a version of the Goal passages: compare 1145a4-6.

Thus we have strong support from three sources – the Goal passages' division of labor, the analogy between theoretical and practical reasoning, and Aristotle's consistent correlation of ends with character – for a robust reading of "virtue makes the goal right."[54]

There remains an important question about the scope of "goal." There are more and less general ends, and Aristotle does not make particularly clear which level he has in mind in the Goal passages. Certainly he must think that virtue makes right one's particular goals in particular situations, for it is a mark of doing particular actions virtuously that one decides on them "for themselves" (*EN* II.4 1105a32): contrast, for example, the wasteful person who has an "appetite for giving" with the genuinely virtuous (liberal) person who "aims at the fine" (*EN* IV.1 1121b1-5, discussed below). (As this example brings out, the same action may be aimed at under different descriptions, and so virtue may make the goal right even if a non-virtuous person would have produced the same outcome.) But Aristotle never qualifies the Goal passages by restricting their application to particular goals: he seems to mean that virtue also "makes right" that ultimate goal of paramount importance, namely happiness (*eudaimonia*) as one views it.

Intellectualists try to accommodate this by saying that while happiness as a general, indeterminate goal is an undeliberated starting-point of deliberation, any specification of it (as e.g. pleasure or wealth or virtuous activity) must be the result of deliberation.[55]

---

[53] That the *logos* in question is deliberative, rather than an articulation of the end, should be clear: recall "there is no *logos* of the goal" (*EE* II.11 1227b23-25), and note the equation of deliberation with reasoning (λογίζεσθαι) a few lines before the present passage, at 1139a12-13. Intellectualists will attribute the *logos* to thought (διάνοια) alone, taking *nous* in the putative special sense of intuition of the end (see below). I hope to have shown here that in the absence of evidence from elsewhere, Aristotle uses *nous* in this special sense, this is an oblique reading of the passage; below I will argue that there is no good evidence from elsewhere.

[54] There is one passage from the *EE* which might seem to contradict all this: "Courage is the following of *logos* (ἀκολούθησις τῷ λόγῳ), and the *logos* commands that one choose the fine (τὸ καλὸν αἱρεῖσθαι κελεύει). . . And the *logos* does not command one to endure painful and destructive things unless they are fine" (*EE* III.1 1229a1-9). Aristotle frequently tells us that virtue aims at the fine (see e.g. *EN* III.4 1115b13-14 and IV.1 1120a23-24); this passage seems to say that it is intellect which commands the virtuous person to aim at the fine, while character merely follows intellect's lead. (For this interpretation see Smith 1996.) But this is contradicted not only by all the evidence we have seen above that it is character which sets our goals, but also by the passage quoted above from *EN* X.9, and the lines which follow it: even before he listens to *logos* a properly habituated person "loves the fine" (is φιλόκαλον, 1179b8), and while *logos* urges the decent person to pursue the fine (προτρέπεσθαι τοῦ καλοῦ χάριν, 1180a7), he will obey only because he is *already* "living for the fine" (πρὸς τὸ καλὸν ζῶντα τῷ λόγῳ πειθαρχήσειν, 1180a10-11). Thus we should seek an alternative interpretation of *EE* 1229a1-9, and the last lines of the passage suggest one: intellect's role is to tell us *which* things are fine, i.e. which things count as fine in a given situation. A person with good character will wish for the fine, but without the right *logos* (i.e. without *phronesis*) may wind up (e.g.) pursuing extreme dangers to no one's benefit, and hence acting rashly instead of courageously. (I discuss this role for *phronesis* at length in the next section.) Thus the point of the passage is to show that intellect directs us toward the things that are actually fine, i.e. that are actually fulfillments of the goal; this is compatible with it being virtue, not intellect, which provides the fine as a goal in the first place.

[55] See Irwin and Wiggins, quoted in section 6.

But if I am right that virtue "makes goals right" by literally supplying the content of the goal, this is nonsense: one does not require virtue to be right that the ultimate end is happiness *generally* conceived, for on this point "most people virtually agree" (*EN* I.4 1095a17-18). Where virtuous people differ from others is in having the right specification of the end: in identifying the end as excellent rational activity rather than as e.g. pleasure or wealth (1095a20-25). And it is a very natural inference that they differ in this way precisely *because* they differ in their ethical characters (cf. the passages on wish and the apparent good).

There is one strong piece of evidence in favor of the Intellectualist's line on happiness: Aristotle twice speaks of people "deciding on" (προαιρούμενοι) a specific way of life (the life of pleasure, politics, or philosophy), at *EN* I.5 1095b19-22 and *EE* I.4 1215a35-b1. But there is so much countervailing evidence that views of happiness are instead among the undeliberated starting-points of practical reasoning that I am inclined to treat these as non-technical uses of προαίρεσθαι. Consider a discussion in the *EE*, which begins with the claim that decision (and hence deliberation) is not of ends, and continues as follows:

> But before the process [of deliberation] begins there will be the that-on-account-of-which (ἐκ προτέρου δὲ μᾶλλον ἔσται τὸ δι' ὅ), and this is the that-for-the-sake-of-which, for example wealth or pleasure or any other such thing which happens to be the that-for-the-sake-of-which... And by nature the end is always good... but contrary to nature and by perversion not the good but the apparent good.... And the cause [of this kind of error, i.e. error about the end] is the pleasant and painful. For things are so constituted that (οὕτω γὰρ ἔχει ὥστε) the pleasant appears good to the soul, and the more pleasant better, and the painful bad and the more painful worse. (*EE* II.10 1227a13-b1)

Pleasure, wealth and honor – specifications of happiness – are goals laid down before deliberation begins, not goals reached through deliberation. This is supported by the implication in the last lines that we value these things not on the basis of (faulty) reasoning but simply because we are by nature attracted to pleasure and repelled by pain. (The point is strengthened if we suppose that Aristotle here has in mind, as I have urged that he usually does, the technical meaning of "appears good": we desire pleasure not because we reason that it is good, but because it simply appears good to us through perception and *phantasia*.)

Further evidence comes from a passage from the *Politics*, to which we will return below:

> Well-being (τὸ εὖ) for everyone depends on two things: one is the goal and end of actions being laid down rightly, the other is finding the actions that lead to that end (πρὸς τὸ τέλος φερούσας)... Sometimes people make errors in both, as for example in the medical art: for sometimes doctors neither discern (κρίνουσιν) finely what a healthy body should be like (ποῖόν τι δεῖ τὸ ὑγιαῖνον εἶναι σῶμα), nor hit on the things productive of their undertaken mark. (*Pol.* 1331b26-37)

The example of health as an end is typical (see e.g. *EN* III.2 1111b26-29): Aristotle more than once groups health with happiness as examples of undeliberated objects of wish. The first line of this passage (and the context within the *Politics*) shows that he has that analogy in mind here too. So it is notable that health is here described not as a general and indeterminate end but as a quite determinate one: being right about the end of health is a matter not simply of wanting to produce *whatever* health turns out to consist in, but of "discerning what a healthy body should be like."[56] And thus the health/happiness analogy implies that being right about the end of happiness is a matter of "discerning what a happy life should be like" – of having a fairly fleshed-out view of the good life, such as that it consists in virtuous activity.

Consider also a claim from early in the *EE*:

It would be superfluous to examine all the beliefs (δόξας) that people have about happiness. For many things appear to children and the sick and the insane which no one having any sense would puzzle about: for these people are not in need of *logoi*, but the first need time in which to change, and the second need medical or political discipline... Likewise [it would be superfluous to examine] the beliefs of the many... For it is absurd to apply *logos* to those who have need not of *logos* but of experience (ἄτοπον γὰρ προσφέρειν λόγον τοῖς λόγου μηδὲν δεομένοις ἀλλὰ πάθους). (*EE* I.3 1214b28-1215a3)

It is not *logos* (argument or reasoning) that gives one correct judgment about happiness; instead it is time and experience. And since the relevant experience will surely include the experience of the right kind of activities – that is, habituation – this fits very well with the idea that it is virtue, the product of habituation, which makes the goal right. Two passages confirm this by drawing a direct link between habituation in a certain way of living and the adoption of that way of living as one's ultimate goal:

The many and most vulgar not unreasonably seem *on the basis of their lives* to suppose (ἐκ τῶν βίων ὑπολαμβάνειν) that the good, i.e. happiness, is pleasure. (*EN* I.5 1095b14-19, emphasis mine)[57]

The *that* (τὸ ὅτι) is first and a starting-point. And of starting-points, some are grasped (θεωροῦνται) by induction, some by perception, some by some sort of habituation (ἐθισμῷ τινί), and others in other ways. (*EN* I.7 1098b3-4)[58]

---

[56] Compare an example of deliberation from *Metaphysics* VII: "Since *this* (τοδὶ) is health, if the subject is to be healthy this must first be present..." (*Met.* 1032b6 ff.). Again we have as a starting-point for deliberation something much more specific than "Health is the goal."

[57] The point is made more general if we follow Irwin in transposing 1095b16 with what follows (b17-19): he translates "people quite reasonably reach their conception of the good, i.e., of happiness, from the lives [they lead]; for there are roughly three most favored lives: the lives of gratification, of political activity, and, third, of study. The many, the most vulgar, would seem to conceive the good and happiness as pleasure..."

[58] Some argue that the starting-points Aristotle attributes to habituation at 1098b3-4 are instead claims to the effect that certain actions are fine and just (see Burnyeat 1980, 72-73, following the ancient commentators Aspasius, Eustratius and Heliodorus). I think it more plausible to follow Burnet in holding that the starting-points in question here are those that Aristotle attributes to virtue – views of the ultimate end, i.e. awareness *that* happiness consists in such-and-such a life. The lines come immediately after the famous function argument: the whole context is a determination of what the end is, i.e. of what constitutes *eudaimonia*. In the lines that follow (the start of *EN* I.8) Aristotle says that we should inquire about the starting-point, and

Habituation shapes character (see section 3); in so doing, according to these passages, it also gives one a corresponding view of happiness. (I defend this claim in detail in the next chapter.)

I have argued, then, in this section and the previous, that when Aristotle says that virtue makes the goal right, his statement is neither 'misleading' nor a 'lapse.' He means just what he seems to say: that each person selects her ends, including her ultimate end, not by any intellectual process, but instead through the non-rational habituation of the non-rational part of her soul. In the next sections I turn to consider why this view has seemed so objectionable to many interpreters. I lay out the motives for doubt, and show that they are misguided.

7.5 *Phronesis* and ends

The major motivation for the Intellectualist interpretation of the Goal passages, as we saw above, is the worry that taking these passages at face value saddles Aristotle with a Humean view.[59] But what is so bad about doing that? First, the Intellectualists object that Aristotle holds the very un-Humean view that we desire our ends because we find them *good*. This, as I argued in section 2, is absolutely correct, but does not in fact support the Intellectualist reading over the non-Intellectualist reading at all, for Aristotle may hold that we find our goals good through *phantasia*. But Intellectualists raise a second objection too: they think that Aristotle characterizes *phronesis* in such a way that it must be responsible for more than working out the means to independently given ends – i.e. must also be responsible for setting the ends in the first place. Is there any truth to this? I will argue that there is not.

The Goal passages are not the only evidence that Aristotle restricts *phronesis* to deliberation about "things toward ends." In his discussion of *phronesis* in V/VI Aristotle several times identifies the *phronimos* as the one who is able to deliberate well: see e.g. 5 1140a25-31 (culminating in "so that in general the *phronimos* would be the one able to deliberate (ὁ βουλευτικός)"), and 7 1141b9-10 ("we say that this is the function of the *phronimos* most of all, to deliberate well"). He also claims that *phronesis* is concerned most of all with particulars (8 1142a14), where this means particular actions or objects to be acted on. Other passages go even further. *Phronesis* is "about (περί) things about which there is deliberation (περὶ ὧν ἔστι βουλεύσασθαι)" (7 1141b8-9) – which implies that it is not about things about which there is no deliberation, e.g. ends. And practical intellect, the

---

then launches a defense of the definition of *eudaimonia* he has just given. Moreover he elsewhere claims that *eudaimonia* is a starting-point, not only in the Goal passages but also in *EN* I.12: *eudaimonia* is the starting-point and cause of all other goods, "for it is for the sake of *eudaimonia* that everyone does everything else" (1102a2-4). But even the rival reading supports my general account of the Goal passage, although in a way that only makes a claim about particular goals in particular situations: for the virtuous person recognizing some particular action as fine *is* recognizing it as a (possible) goal, and hence as a starting-point for deliberation.

[59] See for example Allan, Cooper, and Sorabji, cited in note 10.

part of the soul of which *phronesis* is the virtue, gets labeled the λογιστικόν (rational or calculative part), "because deliberation and calculation are the same (τὸ γὰρ βουλεύεσθαι καὶ λογίζεσθαι ταὐτόν)" (2 1139a12-13): the implication is that the function and essence of this part is to deliberate, and nothing more. Finally, when Aristotle explicitly defines *phronesis*, he names as its province "what is good and bad for man" (5 1140b5-6).[60] Intellectualists take this to mean the intrinsically good and bad, i.e. what is good and bad *qua* goal, but this is undermined by comparison with his other statements of this point: what is distinctive of the *phronimos* is "to be able to deliberate finely about the good and advantageous (ἀγαθὰ καὶ συμφέροντα) for himself" (5 1140a25-27), to be concerned with "what is healthy and good (ὑγιεινὸν καὶ ἀγαθὸν) for men" (7 1141a22-23), or to know "the advantageous for himself" (7 1141b5-6). That 'good' is paired in two of these passages with the obviously instrumental 'advantageous' and 'healthy,' and replaced entirely by 'advantageous' in the third indicates that in saying that *phronesis* is concerned with the good Aristotle all along meant the instrumental good rather than the good *qua* goal. All these passages suggest, then, that in the ethical works Aristotle is working with precisely the same definition of *phronesis* which he gives in the *Rhet.*: "The virtue of thought by which people are able to deliberate well about the goods and bads we have mentioned with a view to (εἰς) happiness" (*Rhet.* 1366b20-22).[61]

Against all this evidence that *phronesis*' domain is "things toward ends," there is only one passage which Intellectualists cite as explicitly claiming that *phronesis* gives us our view of the end itself. Aristotle is concluding his discussion of *euboulia* (good deliberation) in V/VI.9:

If then deliberating well belongs to the *phronimoi*, good deliberation would be the rightness that accords with what is advantageous toward the end, of which *phronesis* is true supposition (ἡ εὐβουλία εἴη ἂν ὀρθότης ἡ κατὰ τὸ συμφέρον πρὸς τὸ τέλος, οὗ ἡ φρόνησις ἀληθὴς ὑπόληψίς ἐστιν). (V/VI.9 1142b31-33)

On the standard reading, the claim of the passage is that *phronesis* is (among other things, surely) the state which provides a true view of the end – despite all the implications to the contrary in the Goal passages, and despite Aristotle's silence on any connection between *phronesis* and goals anywhere else (see below). But it is not at all clear that this is what Aristotle means.

For one thing, as is frequently noted, the antecedent of the 'of which' (οὗ) might be 'what is advantageous toward the end,' rather than 'the end,' in which case this passage is consistent with the Goal passages, and makes no claim about *phronesis* grasping the end.[62]

---

[60] *Phronesis* is a "true practical condition, with *logos*, about the good and bad for man (ἕξιν ἀληθῆ μετὰ λόγου πρακτικὴν περὶ τὰ ἀνθρώπῳ ἀγαθὰ καὶ κακά)."

[61] This definition of *phronesis* as restricted to deliberation also has historical precedent: see Democritus, fragment 2, 119, and the other texts cited in Gauthier and Jolif's commentary on 1140a30-31. It is clearly different from Plato's conception of *phronesis*, which includes knowledge of what the Good itself is, but given Plato's lack of distinction between practical and theoretical wisdom this is just what we should expect.

[62] This reading originates with Walter 1874, 470-72. It is worth noting, arguably in its support, that the passage as I have given it above follows what is now the standard text, Bywater's, but Bywater is following only one manuscript; the others all have the indefinite τι τέλος ("some end") rather than τὸ τέλος ("the

Intellectualists argue that this reading cannot make sense of the passage in context.⁶³ This argument is inconclusive, but even if we accept their favored reading the case is not as simple as one might think. For consider Aristotle's use of a phrase very similar to 'true supposition of the end' in a passage earlier in the *EE*, which has not to my knowledge been noted in this connection:

[D]ecision is not present in the other animals nor in people of every age nor of every state. For neither is deliberation [present], nor *supposition of the that-on-account-of-which* (ὑπόληψις τοῦ διὰ τί), but nothing prevents many from being able to opine (δοξάσαι) whether something is to be done or not to be done, while not yet doing this through reasoning (διὰ λογισμοῦ). For the deliberative capacity of the soul (τὸ βουλευτικὸν) is the capacity contemplative of a certain cause (τὸ θεωρητικὸν αἰτιάς τινός). For the that-for-the-sake-of-which (ἡ οὗ ἕνεκα) is one of the causes, because the that-on-account-of-which (τὸ διὰ τί) is a cause... Wherefore those for whom no goal is laid down are not able to deliberate (οἷς μηθεὶς κεῖται σκοπός, οὐ βουλευτικοί). (*EE* II.10 1226b20-30, emphasis mine)

'That-on-account-of-which' is another label for 'that-for-the-sake-of-which,' i.e. the goal;⁶⁴ thus this passage's 'supposition of the that-on-account-of-which' should be taken as a notational variant on 1142b33's 'supposition of the end.' But such supposition, the *EE* passage strongly suggests, is simply *the recognition that one is working towards a given end* – a recognition which is a necessary condition of deliberation, i.e. practical reasoning (λογισμός). "Those for whom no goal is laid down" – animals, children, and wanton adults – do something that resembles deliberation: they opine about whether or not to do something. But they are not actually deliberating, i.e. not "doing this through reasoning," and this is because a crucial part of what it is to do something through deliberation is to recognize what one is doing as being for the sake of an end, and to use that end to guide one's deliberations. (Aristotle goes on to elaborate this point a few lines below, in a passage we saw in part above (1227a13 ff.): deliberation is about means rather than ends, but "before the process [of deliberation] begins there will be the that-on-account-of-which (ἐκ προτέρου δὲ μᾶλλον ἔσται τὸ δι' ὅ), and this is the that-for-the-sake-of-which... For the one who deliberates, if he has carried his

---

end"). If we follow the other manuscripts (with Bekker and Grant), we get: "good deliberation would be the rightness that accords with what is advantageous toward some end, of which *phronesis* is true supposition." 'Toward some end' looks very incidental, simply a way of explaining what 'advantageous' means (what it is to be advantageous, or a "thing toward the end," is to be advantageous with reference to some end or other); if this is right, we should follow Walter's reading.

⁶³ See for example Cooper 1975, 64, note: the immediate context is a distinction between good deliberation toward limited ends (for example technical deliberation) and unqualified good deliberation, which is toward the "unqualified end"; thus the passage is identifying unqualified good deliberation by saying that it is toward "the end of which *phronesis* is true supposition," i.e. the unqualified end. This is reasonable enough, but it may be that Aristotle feels he has made that distinction sufficiently clear in the preceding lines, and is now merely summarizing the whole discussion of *euboulia*.

⁶⁴ Compare the equation in later lines from the same chapter (quoted above): "... the that-on-account-of-which, i.e., the that-for-the-sake-of-which (τὸ δι' ὅ, τοῦτ' ἐστι τὸ οὗ ἕνεκα)..." (1227a14).

inquiry back from the end, deliberates about what is toward it, in order to bring the process back to himself, or what he can do himself towards the end" (1227a13-18, based on Woods' translation).)

Thus 'supposition of the end' in this *EE* passage means not the thought that goes into *identifying* the end, but rather the grasping of the end *qua* end, i.e. the using of the end to guide deliberation. If we bring this passage to bear on 1142b33, then even on the standard construal (*phronesis* is true supposition of the goal), the point is not that *phronesis* supplies the content of the goal. Instead it is that the *phronimos* is one whose excellent deliberation is constantly guided by an excellent goal – a goal supplied, as we are frequently told elsewhere, by virtue.[65]

There is one other passage which talks, indirectly, about supposition of ends: a passage on the starting-points of action which we saw in part at the start of section 3. This may at first sight seem to undermine my reading of 1142b33, but on closer inspection fits it:

Temperance preserves *phronesis*. But it preserves *this* sort of supposition (ὑπόληψιν). For the pleasant and painful do not corrupt or pervert every supposition, such as that a triangle is or isn't equal in degree to two right angles, but only practical ones. For the starting-points of practical things are that-for-the-sake-of-which the practical things are, and to someone corrupted by pleasure or pain, straightaway (i) the starting-point does not appear, (ii) *nor that he should choose and do everything for the sake of and on account of this* (οὐδὲ δεῖν τούτου ἕνεκεν οὐδὲ διὰ τοῦθ' αἱρεῖσθαι πάντα καὶ πράττειν). (V/VI.5 1140b11-19)

As I noted above, Intellectualists read this passage as evidence that *phronesis* identifies ends: they take the claim to be that without *phronesis* the starting-point (the end) does not appear. But the claim is in fact more complex: having the supposition of an end *x* preserved means both (i) having *x* appear to you, and also (ii) knowing that you should be acting for the sake of *x*. We can maintain consistency with the Goal passages, and at the same time explain the idea that temperance "preserves" *phronesis*, if we take it that Aristotle means to attribute (i) to virtue and (ii) to *phronesis*. It is character that ensures (i), making one aware of the *content* of the end – that one should act finely, or that one

---

[65] Broadie suggests an interpretation along these lines (although without the support of the *EE* passage): practical intellect "is active about the goal...by seeing it *as a goal*" (1998, 296). The Intellectualist will object that the proposed interpretation does not sufficiently distinguish *phronesis* from *euboulia*, while the text clearly presents them as distinct. For the Intellectualist the distinction is clear: *euboulia* is one part of *phronesis*, the other part being insight (*nous*) into the end (see for example Gauthier and Jolif, comment *ad loc.*). But there are other ways to draw the distinction. Anthony Price has pointed out (in conversation) that Aristotle presents *euboulia* not as a virtue, like *phronesis*, but instead as a correctness or "rightness" (ὀρθότης) – analogous in the practical sphere not to wisdom but to the correctness it ensures, namely truth (see 1142b11). We know from the Goal passages that *phronesis* "makes right the things toward the goal"; *euboulia* is Aristotle's name for the kind of rightness (correctness) it thereby produces. In support of this reading, note that *euboulia* is not on the list of states (ἕξεις) concerned with particulars at 1143a25-29: unlike *phronesis*, *nous*, consideration (γνώμη) and comprehension (σύνεσις), it is not a "state" at all, and hence not a virtue – and hence need not be distinguished from *phronesis* by assigning the latter a wider province. Greenwood offers a different solution: *euboulia* is the search for practical truth, *phronesis* the state of possessing it (1909, commentary *ad loc.*).

should save the drowning baby, or whatever it may be. What *phronesis* adds is the right "supposition of the end," where this means, as I argued above, being aware of it *as* an end, i.e. using it to guide deliberation – or as Aristotle puts it here, (ii) being aware that one should "choose and do everything for the sake of and on account of it." Even though (i) is a function of character it is necessary for *phronesis*, for without having something as one's end in the first place one of course cannot use it to guide deliberation.

So much, then, for the most explicit piece of alleged evidence that *phronesis* identifies ends. There are however several other passages which have been taken to entail the same claim. First, the discussion of "architectonic" *phronesis* in V/VI.7-8:

> Nor is *phronesis* only of universals, but it must know particulars too: for it is practical, and action is about particulars. Which is why some who don't have knowledge (οὐκ εἰδότες) are more practical than others who do know, and in other cases too the experienced [are more practical]. For if someone knew that light meats are easily digestible and healthy, but did not know which meats are light, he would not produce health, but the one who knows that bird meats are light and healthy will produce health more. But *phronesis* is practical. So one must have both [the universal and the particular], or the latter more. And there would be an architectonic form in this case too. Political science (πολιτική) and *phronesis* are the same state (ἕξις), but their being is not the same. And of the type concerned with the *polis*, the architectonic *phronesis* is legislative science (νομοθετική), but the kind concerned with particulars gets the common name, political science. (V/VI.7-8 1141b14-26)

On the Intellectualist interpretation, architectonic *phronesis* is the excellence by which we identify the highest human good; the universals it grasps are articulations of goals.[66]

The first point to make is that architectonic *phronesis* may not be required for individual virtue and happiness at all.[67] Aristotle emphasizes that in the political sphere it is the non-architectonic type of *phronesis*, the type concerned with particulars, that is practical and deliberative (πρακτική καὶ βουλευτική, 1141b27); meanwhile, throughout his discussion of *phronesis* he has emphasized that it is concerned with action and deliberation (see quotations at the start of this section), and at the start of the present passage he has argued that knowledge of the particular is more important to *phronesis* than knowledge of the universal, precisely on the grounds that "*phronesis* is practical." Moreover, in the *EN*'s final chapter Aristotle seems to say that a grasp of practical universals is needed only for the task of making others virtuous. He begins by praising the Spartan model on which the state attends to the nurture and practices of the citizens; *only* if the state neglects this will the individual need to bring his children and friends to virtue (*EN* X.9 1180a29-32) – which implies that one can be perfectly virtuous without acquiring the expertise needed to make others virtuous. Moreover, he says, if one's task is simply to make a single person virtuous then knowledge of

---

[66] For this reading see for example Joachim 1951, 210, and Greenwood 1909, 44.
[67] See for example Broadie, in her commentary on the *EN* (2002) and (despite his Intellectualism) Hardie 1968.

universals may be of some help, but for the most part knowledge of particulars will suffice, just as it suffices for doctoring a single patient; only if one aims to improve several or many people will one need universals:

> It would seem that presumably the one who wishes to acquire a craft or become a theoretician (τεχνικῷ γενέσθαι καὶ θεωρετικῷ) must progress to the universal, and come to know it as much as possible; for it has been said that the branches of knowledge (αἱ ἐπιστῆμαι) are about that. Then perhaps (τάχα) the one who wants to improve people through care, whether many or a few, must attempt to acquire the legislative art (νομοθετικῷ γενέσθαι), if we become good through laws. (*EN* X.9 1180b20-25)

This implies that individuals who wish only to know how best to live their own lives have no need of these universals.[68] For individual well-being all that is required is the non-architectonic *phronesis*, the kind concerned with particulars; universals are useful only for legislators – and, as we learn elsewhere, political philosophers. (Aristotle calls his subject πολιτική, and says it is the most architectonic of the sciences; he also calls the political philosopher (τοῦ τὴν πολιτικὴν φιλοσοφοῦντος) the architect (ἀρχιτέκτων) of the human *telos*.[69] Presumably political philosophy, which includes ethics, is even more architectonic than legislation; both aim at improving the many.)

This reading is confirmed by what Aristotle says about the practical irrelevance of universals. We can bring this out by considering some lines I elided from a passage we saw above on why *phronesis* is required for strict virtue:

> The natural [virtues] belong also to children and beasts, but are manifestly harmful without *nous*.[70] At any rate it seems this much can be seen: just as it happens to a powerful body without sight that in moving it stumbles heavily, on account of not having sight, thus also here. But if one acquires *nous*, it makes a difference in action.[71] And this state which is similar [to natural virtue] is virtue strictly. (V/VI.13 1144b8-14)

The passage makes very clear that *phronesis* makes a crucial difference in how we act, and this fits with the characterization of *phronesis* throughout the ethical works (see for example "*phronesis* is practical" in V/VI.7). On the Intellectualist interpretation, the point of the passage is to show that without the grasp of the end which *phronesis* supplies, one's passions will lead one astray.[72] *Phronesis* is necessary for acting well because it provides us with the right end, and does so by grasping the first principles of

---

[68] Lest there should be any doubt that the legislative art mentioned in *EN* X.9 is meant to be something different from the kind of *phronesis* Aristotle has been discussing up to this point, the kind necessary for individual virtue and happiness, the passage continues: "Next, then, should we examine whence and how someone might acquire the legislative art?" (1180b28-29), making clear that this is a new topic not already covered in what came before.

[69] *EN* I.2 1094a27; VI/VII.11 1152b1-3.

[70] See note 41 above.

[71] See note 42 above.

[72] "[N]ous is of the first principle or unconditional end, *eudaimonia*. So what natural virtue lacks ... is grasp of the end, grasp of where it is going" (Reeve 1992, 86); cf. (among others) Cooper 1986, 63.

practical reasoning, the universals at issue in the architectonic *phronesis* passage. The trouble is that, as we have already seen from V/VI.7-8, Aristotle denies that knowing universals makes one more practical at all. Further confirmation comes from the *Met.*'s discussion of craft (τέχνη). (We will return to this subject in more detail in Chapter 8, but for now we can note that we should expect Aristotle's view of craft to illuminate his view of *phronesis*, for he defines the two as very similar states in V/VI.)

> With regard to acting experience seems to differ from craft not at all, but the experienced hit the mark even more than those who have a *logos* without experience. The cause is that experience is recognition (γνῶσις) of individual things while craft is of the universal, and actions and becomings are all about the individual: for the doctor does not heal *man* except incidentally, but rather Callias or Socrates or someone else... (*Met.* 981a12-19)

The craftsman is no better at producing the desired effect than the experienced person. Grasping universals in the domain of one's craft makes one wiser – and therefore better able to teach others (*Met.* 981b7-10) – but has no effect on one's own productions; analogously, grasping universals in the domain of action will make one a better writer of ethical and political treatises, and a better lawmaker, but will have no effect on one's own actions. *Phronesis* does of course make us better at acting, but it does so for precisely the reason the Goal passages give: it makes us better at grasping particular "things toward the end." (I argue further for this reading of the natural virtue passage in the next section.)

Others argue, however, that Aristotle thinks political *phronesis* necessary even for one's own virtue and happiness, and there is some evidence in their favor.[73] Moreover, one might argue that V/VI.8's analogy between political and individual *phronesis* implies that there is a form of architectonic *phronesis* concerned only with improving oneself (although Aristotle certainly does not make this clear): knowing the universals as well as the particulars relevant to achieving one's own happiness. But this brings us to a second problem with the Intellectualist interpretation of the passage: nothing Aristotle says about architectonic *phronesis* in either the political or private sphere implies that the universals it grasps are ends.

In its political application, Aristotle tells us, architectonic *phronesis* is law-making (νομοθετική, V/VI.8 1141b25). Laws, however, give guidelines for achieving the goals of a state, rather than setting out those goals. See for example *EN* X.9: laws "prescribe the upbringing and practices" (τετάχθαι τὴν τροφὴν καὶ τὰ ἐπιτηδεύματα) of the citizens, with a view to making them virtuous and thereby happy (1179b34-35) – just as a doctor

---

[73] Arguably this is implied later in the same chapter: in Irwin's translation, "One's own welfare requires household management and a political system" (οὐκ ἔστι τὸ αὑτοῦ εὖ ἄνευ οἰκονομίας οὐδ' ἄνευ πολιτείας) (1142a9-10). Given Aristotle's view that man is a political and social animal, he arguably holds not only what the passage literally says but also the related point that we cannot know what is good for ourselves without knowing what is good for others. Also supporting this view is the fact that Aristotle seems to present his own lectures on ethics, which certainly make universal claims, as an aid to acquiring individual *phronesis*. I return briefly to this point below.

might prescribe a certain type of regimen to a whole population, with a view to making them healthy; one who wants to make the citizens better should study legislative science, because "through laws we become good" (1180b25). And while Aristotle certainly characterizes political science as the science *concerned* with the highest human good, his point is that political science is the science which *aims at* this good – has it as its *telos* – just as medicine aims at health or economics at wealth (*EN* I.2 1094b6-7). Political science is the science not of identifying the human good, but rather of determining which policies and laws will best promote it.

Of course this presupposes having the right conception of the human good, and the political scientist must begin by making a clear statement of it (*EN* I.2 1094a22-25; cf. *Pol.* 1321a14-16). But this does not entail that it is political science which itself furnishes that correct conception: virtue of character is a necessary condition of political as well as of individual *phronesis* – hence Aristotle's insistence that the improperly habituated cannot be good students of political science (*EN* I.4 1095b4-6) – and this because (as I have been arguing) it is virtue that gives one the correct view of the goal.

Thus by analogy with the political case, architectonic *phronesis* about one's own good would consist not in grasping definitions of one's end, but instead in being good at formulating general policies by which one can achieve it.[74] And indeed this interpretation fits the only examples Aristotle gives to show that deliberation is concerned with universals: "light meats are easily digestible and healthy" (V/VI.7 1141b18-19) gives a general guideline for achieving the goal of health, but is no more a statement of that goal than the more particular proposition "poultry is light and healthy"; likewise for the other example he gives, a bit below: "all heavy water is foul" (V/VI.8 1142a23-24).[75] To say that *phronesis* is concerned with universals as well as particulars, then, is simply to say that deliberation involves universal claims as well as particular ones – general rules analogous to laws as well as particular imperatives analogous to decrees. Moreover, this is just what we should expect given the context: as Burnet points out in his commentary, when Aristotle says in V/VI.7 that *phronesis* is "not only about universals, but must also know particulars," this implies that what he has been discussing up to this point is the kind concerned with universals – and what he has been discussing is a state responsible for deliberation. (See for example a few lines before the introduction of architectonic *phronesis*, "We say that this most of all is the function of the *phronimos*, to deliberate well" (1141b9-10).) Thus even if Aristotle does hold that knowledge of universals is required for individual virtue and happiness, this would not show that it is *phronesis*' task to set our ends.

---

[74] See Burnet's note *ad loc.*: it is character that supplies one's end; "What ἡ καθόλου φρόνησις does is, given the true good as an ὀρεκτόν, to frame general rules for its attainment" (Burnet 1900).

[75] These are presumably examples of medical deliberation, not *phronesis* proper, but the point is that they are claims about what promotes health, rather than definitions of health; the analogous universals in the *phronimos*' sphere would be claims about what promotes happiness, rather than definitions of what happiness is.

Further confirmation comes from the discussion of craft in *Met.* I.1. Expert doctors differ from their merely experienced counterparts in grasping the universal as well as the particular, but the universals in question do not look like ends. Instead, Aristotle's claim is that while merely experienced types know only that "this thing was beneficial for Callias when he was ill with this disease, and for Socrates, etc.," craftsmen know the universal truth "that [this cure] benefited all people of this sort, divided off into one type (κατ' εἶδος ἓν ἀφορισθεῖσι), when ill with this disease – for example phlegmatics or bilious people when burning with fever" (981a7-12). This is the medical analogue of a general ethical claim like "Actions of type *x* are to-be-done in situations of type *y*"; the analogue of a definition of happiness would instead be a general definition of health. And while the doctor must of course correctly grasp what health is like, just as the *phronimos* must correctly grasp what happiness is like, what Aristotle here presents as the distinct contribution that medical knowledge makes is not this but instead general rules like the one about fever – that is, about "things toward" the end of health. (See further discussion in Chapter 8.)

So much for Aristotle's discussion of architectonic *phronesis*; the arguments I have given here also count against the related Intellectualist interpretation of two other passages. One is from early in the *EN*:

We must begin from what is known (γνωρίμων) to us. Wherefore the one who is to listen sufficiently about the fine and just and in general about political things should have been finely raised in habits (δεῖ τοῖς ἔθεσιν ἦχθαι καλῶς). For the starting-point is the *that* (τὸ ὅτι), and if this were to appear sufficiently, there will be no additional need for the *because* (οὐδὲν προσδεήσει τοῦ διότι). For this type of person either has the starting-points or can get them easily. (*EN* I.4 1095b3-8)

On a view we find for example in Reeve, Aristotle's point in this passage is that habituated virtue becomes strict virtue when one acquires *phronesis* by grasping the *because*; furthermore, grasping the *because* is grasping the end.[76] But what we have seen above about ethical universals suggests that the passage should be read in one of two ways, neither of which associates *phronesis* with ends. First, if Broadie and Hardie are right that a grasp of universals is not a requirement for individual virtue and happiness, we should take at face value the claim that in ethical matters someone who has the *that* has no need for the *because*.[77] Alternatively, even if they are wrong, we have seen from the *Met.*'s discussion of craft that grasping the *because* in the practical realm (i.e. grasping the universal – *Met.* 981a28-30) means grasping general maxims that relate particulars

---

[76] Reeve 1992, 30; cf. Hardie 1968, 35 and Cooper 2010. Others have thought the *because* crucial to *phronesis* without explicitly identifying it with the end: see Burnyeat 1980.

[77] Compare *EN* I.4 1098a33-b2: "The cause is not to be demanded in the same way in every inquiry, but it is sufficient in some to demonstrate the *that* finely, as for example with starting-points." For a detailed argument that inquiry into universal causes of ethical facts belongs not to ethics itself but rather to metaphysics, physics and psychology, see Achtenberg 2002, 76-95.

to one's end, rather than grasping a definition of the end. (Again, see further discussion in Chapter 8.)

The other passage is one we saw above from *EN* X.9, which arguably implies that *logoi* are necessary to produce full virtue. Those who take the *EN* I.4 passage to imply that *phronesis* involves knowledge of the *because* see confirmation in X.9: they take the *logoi* in question to be something like explanations or reasoned accounts of why the things one has been habituated to admire and desire are good – *becauses* to explain habituation's *thats*, and thereby to provide the intellectual component which allows merely habituated virtue to become strict virtue.[78] But X.9 describes the kind of *logos* in question as one that "dissuades" (ἀποτρέποντος) from wrongdoing, which implies that the *logoi* are exhortations rather than explanations. Moreover, this fits with Aristotle's characterization of the *logoi* relevant to moral education in the chapter as a whole. *Logoi* are not sufficient to make people virtuous because they can "encourage and urge on" (προτρέψασθαι μὲν καὶ παρορμῆσαι) only those who are already on the right track (1179b7); *logoi* are thought useful in bringing about virtue because

...some believe that the legislators should exhort (παρακαλεῖν) people toward virtue, and urge them on for the sake of the fine (προτρέπεσθαι τοῦ καλοῦ χάριν), since those who have been well advanced through habits will listen well (ἐπακουσομένων)...For the decent person, living toward the fine, will be obedient to the *logos* (τῷ λόγῳ πειθαρχήσειν). (*EN* X.9 1180a5-11)

Notably, the language Aristotle uses here to describe the relation between the educational *logoi* and their audience is precisely that he uses to describe the relation between the rational and non-rational parts of the soul in *EN* I.13. The non-rational, passionate part

in the continent person is indeed obedient to (πειθαρχεῖ) the *logos*, and in the moderate and brave person it is probably even better at listening (εὐηκοώτερον)...And admonitions and every reproving and exhorting (παράκλησις) show that the non-rational can be persuaded in some way by *logos* (πείθεταί πως ὑπὸ λόγου τὸ ἄλογον). (*EN* I.13 1102b26-1103a1)[79]

Thus X.9's claim that *logoi* are useful (or even necessary) for virtue does not show that *phronesis* supplies our ends; instead, it confirms what we see in I.13 and elsewhere: intellect (one's own or another's) supplements character by giving specific guidance about what to do.

Even if one accepts my arguments that the passages reviewed above – V/VI.7-8 on architectonic *phronesis*, I.4 on "thats" and "becauses," and X.9 on the role of *logoi* in moral education – do not assign *phronesis* the role of setting ends, one may still feel that they count against my narrow reading of *phronesis* as concerned exclusively with "things toward ends." This is for an important reason which I will touch on only

---

[78] See for example Cooper 2010.

[79] Both this passage and the one from *EN* X.9 go on to compare the relation between exhorting *logos* and exhorted audience to that between father and son.

briefly here: each of these passages has been seen to support the view that the goal of Aristotle's ethical lectures – that is, of the *EN* and *EE* themselves – is to help bring the audience to full virtue precisely by helping them become more *phronimos*. Aristotle says that *phronesis*, as an intellectual virtue, is acquired by teaching (*EN* II.1 1103a15), and given that he calls the subject of his lectures *politikê* (see *EN* I.2-3), which he later pronounces the same as (although different in being from) *phronesis* (V/VI.8 1141b23-24, quoted above), the interpretation is a compelling one. But if *phronesis* is the kind of thing you acquire by studying ethical theory, one might object, then surely it goes beyond excellence in deliberation.

I am not convinced by this argument. We can hold on to a narrow view of *phronesis* by arguing either (a) that Aristotle thinks his lectures useful for the acquisition of architectonic *phronesis*, understood as the kind necessary for teaching and ruling others, while holding that people acquire ground-level *phronesis*, the kind necessary for individual virtue and happiness, in the course of ordinary experience; or alternatively (b) that the aim of the lectures is indeed to make us more *phronimos* with regard to our own lives, but precisely by aiding us in our deliberations – that is, by spelling out the "things toward" the ultimate end. (For a defense of (b) see the close of Chapter 8, in which I argue that the choice between the practical and the theoretical life is a choice of different means to the same end, excellent rational activity.) The issue is thorny, however, and settling it would take us far afield from the main question at issue here.[80] I am thus content to leave open the possibility that *phronesis* involves philosophical understanding in addition to excellence in deliberation, so long as we recognize that this does not automatically entail that it supplies our ends. The *phronimos* might, for instance, be someone with a philosophical understanding of the psychological and metaphysical bases of ethic facts, justifications which secure his grasp of those facts, without for that reason having a different end from his less philosophical counterparts.[81] In the absence of other evidence that *phronesis* supplies our ends we cannot take the possibility that it involves philosophical understanding of ethics to prove that it does.

There is one final piece of alleged evidence for the claim that ends are the province of intellect: an extremely difficult passage on the role of *nous* in practical reasoning. The passage comes at the end of V/VI.11, shortly before the discussion that includes several of our Goal passages. *Nous* in the rest of book V/VI refers unambiguously to theoretical *nous*, the state of grasping universal starting-points for deductions; now, however, Aristotle evidently introduces (without comment or explanation) a technical sense of *nous* in the practical sphere. He has just been emphasizing that *phronesis* is about particulars (1143a26-29); now he says the same of practical *nous*:

And *nous* is of the last things (τῶν ἐσχάτων) in both [the practical and theoretical spheres]. For there is *nous*, and not *logos*, both of the first terms and of the last; and the [*nous*] concerned with demonstra-

---

[80] For good arguments that *phronesis* does not involve philosophical understanding, see Achtenberg 2002, 74-80 and 91-95.
[81] For this kind of view see e.g. Engberg-Pedersen, 1983.

tions is of the unchanging, first terms, while that in practical matters is of the last and changeable [term] and the minor premise. For *these things are the starting-points of the that-for-the-sake-of-which, for the universal is from the particulars* (ἐκ τῶν καθ' ἕκαστα γὰρ τὰ καθόλου). Of these things therefore one must have perception, and this is *nous*. (V/VI.11 1143a35-b5, emphasis mine)

On a widespread reading, this passage shows that we grasp the goal – the "that-for-the-sake-of-which" – on the basis of intellectual induction. The particular facts that we grasp through practical *nous* (which is understood to be an aspect of *phronesis*) form the inductive basis for an intellectual grasp of the goal.[82] But the lines which seem to support this reading – "these things are the starting-points of the that-for-the-sake-of-which, for the universal is from the particulars" – are so compressed that we should be wary of interpreting them in a way so manifestly at odds with everything else Aristotle has said, and in particular is about to go on to say in the Goal passages which shortly follow, about how we acquire our goals. Cooper (despite his own embrace of the view that *nous* grasps practical starting-points) argues persuasively against this reading, citing in his support a passage from the *de An.* which uses very similar language:

The last thing is the starting-point of action (τὸ δ' ἔσχατον ἀρχὴ τῆς πράξεως). (*de An.* 433a16-17)

In this passage Aristotle must mean that the last thing – the particular – is that from which one begins to act towards one goal; thus at 1143b4 too, Cooper argues, Aristotle is saying that particulars are starting-points not for the grasping of ends but rather "for the *attainment* of ends."[83] Thus the passage supplies only very inconclusive support for the view that intellect provides our ends; in the absence of better evidence there is no pressure to read it this way.

Other evidence, however, is not forthcoming. What I have tried to do in this section is to place the textual burden of proof firmly on the Intellectualists' shoulders. There are some scattered, difficult passages which *can* be read as evidence that *phronesis* provides us with our ends, but all these passages admit of alternative readings which fit better with what Aristotle says elsewhere. On the other side, there is copious and explicit evidence that *phronesis*' task is solely to provide us with "things toward the end" – that it is the condition which makes one good at determining how best to achieve goals, goals one has acquired from some other source.

---

[82] See for example Greenwood 1909, 51, Sorabji 1973-4, 214, or Dahl 1984, 44: "... what *nous* grasps are propositions indicating what is to be done or what is good in a particular situation. These propositions are starting points for an inductive inference to universal ends. From propositions of the form 'This Φ is good' or 'This Φ is to be done' one can inductively infer universal principles of the form 'What is Φ is good' or 'What is Φ is to be done'... [O]ne has inductively acquired a universal end."

[83] 1975, 42, note. Broadie argues for a similar reading: particulars are starting-points of the end in the sense that "they give rise to the end (i.e. to its realization) by filling out the general aim so as to convert it into a decision," while the claim that universals come from particulars means that "generalities come into being only as particularized" (commentary *ad* 1143b3-5); for longer arguments cf. her 1998.

7.6 The role of *phronesis*

Even some Intellectualists recognize that nearly all the textual evidence is against them, but balk at drawing the natural inference: witness e.g. Allan's complaint that Aristotle is "for the most part silent about the theoretical insight [i.e. knowledge of the overall goal] of the man of practical wisdom, and seems content to present him as one who... can judge what ought to be done in given circumstances."[84] Why this insistence on privileging a few contested passages above so many clear ones? Aside from the Humean worry that restricting *phronesis* to "things toward the goal" leaves the setting of goals to desire – a worry I have addressed above and will take up again in the next chapter – I suspect Intellectualists are motivated by the corresponding worry that restricting *phronesis* in this way renders it ethically trivial.

Clearly Aristotle thinks *phronesis* of paramount ethical importance: there is no (strict) virtue without it (1144b16-27), and once you have it you have all the virtues (1145a1-2) (and see in general V/VI.12-13). And we should grant the Intellectualists that this strongly implies that *phronesis* is excellence at something that goes beyond what a Humean would recognize as practical reasoning. Someone merely efficient at putting his plans into action – someone who can calculate the quickest route to the river where the child is drowning, or can arrange the most impressive catering for his friend's wedding at the cheapest price – may be smarter and more effective than his bumbling friends, but we would be very wary of calling this a moral difference. But between this ultra-Humean (or sub-Humean) view of practical reason, and the Kantian one which the Intellectualists find in Aristotle, there is room to take up an interesting position.[85] And that, I argue in this section, is just what Aristotle does. Successfully working out the things that promote an end is on his view complex, ethically demanding, and crucial to well-being – and this because "things toward the end" is a category far broader than what we think of as instrumental means.

We can begin by noting that he claims very explicitly that getting the "things toward the end" right *is* of extreme ethical significance. Consider the earliest of the Goal passages again, along with the line which precedes it. Aristotle is arguing, against a putative objection, that *phronesis* is not idle but instead choiceworthy and indeed necessary:

Further, the [human] function is achieved in accordance with *phronesis* and character-virtue: for virtue makes the goal right, *phronesis* the things toward it. (V/VI.12 1144a6-9)

Phronesis is essential just *because* it makes "things toward goals" right, not for some other reason about which Aristotle is "content to be for the most part silent."

---

[84] Allan 1952, 182-83, quoted approvingly by Hardie 1968, 213.
[85] 'Sub-Humean' is Bernard Williams' term, from Williams 1981 – a paper which provides a good model of what I am arguing is an Aristotelian view of deliberation, with "subjective motivational set" corresponding to Aristotle's notion of character.

The ethical significance of "things toward the goal" is further confirmed by the first lines of the passage we saw from the *Politics*: "Well-being (τὸ εὖ) for everyone depends on two things: one is the goal and end of actions being laid down rightly, the other is finding the actions that lead to that end." Being right about the "things toward ends" is crucial to our function, and hence crucial to our happiness.[86]

Thus we should leave off wondering at Aristotle's silence regarding the putative end-setting role of *phronesis*, and instead search his discussions for positive evidence of a suitably broad conception of "things toward ends." One such conception has been proposed by Wiggins and McDowell: *phronesis* is a kind of moral perception, whereby "one rather than another of the potentially practically relevant features of the situation would strike a virtuous person, and rightly so, as salient, as what matters about the situation."[87] This is surely at least in part right, given Aristotle's emphasis on *phronesis*' concern with particulars. But there is another conception – or possibly another way of explaining this conception – much more explicitly supported by the texts. This becomes clear when we focus on a function of *phronesis* which Aristotle evidently thinks extremely important, but which has been largely ignored by those who focus on the debate surrounding the Goal passages: the function of determining the "mean" (μέσον) at which virtue aims.[88]

It is in this capacity that Aristotle first says anything substantive about *phronesis*, in his famous definition of character-virtue in *EN* II.6:

Therefore virtue is a state issuing in decisions, consisting in an intermediate relative to us, determined by *logos* and as the *phronimos* would determine it (ὡρισμένη λόγῳ καὶ ὡς ἂν ὁ φρόνιμος ὁρίσειεν). (*EN* II.6 1106b36-1107a2)

Virtue is an intermediate state (μεσότης) between extremes of excess and deficiency, in that it aims at (is στοχαστική of) the mean (τὸ μέσον) in actions and passions (*EN* II.6 1106b27-28, II.9 1109a20-23). That is, virtue ensures that we aim at the mean – or, to use a less technical formulation which Aristotle frequently presents as equivalent, at acting "as one should" (ὡς δεῖ). But it can be difficult to know just what the mean is: it is one thing to wish to do what is right in a given situation, but quite another to know just what is right – to know "when one should [act, or feel a passion], and about what things, and in relation to whom, and for the sake of what, and how one should" (*EN* II.6 1106b21-22). Hence the need for *phronesis*, whose function, according to this

---

[86] Note also that *EE* II.10 poses as an open question whether virtue makes the goal right or the things toward it; although Aristotle goes on to argue for the former answer, the way that he poses the question shows that he does not think that the latter would obviously give virtue too trivial or non-ethical a task.

[87] McDowell 1998, 29; cf. Wiggins 1975, 232-33.

[88] Greenwood does acknowledge the importance and relevance of this role: see his 1909, 58-59. But on his interpretation (a) determining the mean is only one part of deliberation, and (b) what it is to determine the mean is "to decide what moral states or moral actions are the best means toward the attainment of that final end," the life of excellent contemplation (θεωρία). My interpretation differs significantly, as will become clear below.

passage, is to provide the *logos* which defines or determines (ὁρίζειν) that mean.[89] As Aristotle puts it with regard to some specific examples:

Getting angry belongs to everyone and is easy, and so is giving and spending money; but to whom and how much and when and for the sake of what and in what way no longer belongs to everyone, nor is easy; hence doing this well is rare and praiseworthy and fine.... Presumably hitting the mean is difficult, and especially in particulars: for it is not easy to determine (διορίσαι) how and to whom and about what sort of things and for how long one should be angry. (*EN* II.9 1109a26-30; 1109b14-16)

The 'determine' in b15 reminds us of the role attributed to the *phronimos* in *EN* II.6's definition of virtue; the point of both passages is to show that *phronesis* is necessary for virtue because without it one cannot identify the mean at which virtue aims. And this explains why *phronesis* is ethically so significant – why it makes what we would call a moral difference. Someone who typically gets too angry, or angry at the wrong people or for the wrong reasons, is making an ethical error; he lacks the virtue of mildness. Someone who goes wrong in giving and spending money is making an ethical error too: the generous (ἐλευθερίος) person hits the mean, but the gifts of the wasteful (ἄσωτος) person

...are not as they should be (ὡς δεῖ), but sometimes they make wealthy those who should be poor, and would give nothing to those measured in character, but much to those offering flattery or some other pleasure. (*EN* IV.1 1121b5-7).

Moreover, I want now to show, it is just this sort of thing Aristotle has in mind when he describes *phronesis* in the Goal passages as what "makes right the things toward the end," i.e. as what guarantees good deliberation. One might think – as commentators who ignore *EN* II.6 in their discussion of *phronesis* evidently do – that Aristotle simply forgets about mean-determining when he turns to his head-on discussion of *phronesis* in V/VI. But that discussion opens with a reminder that the mean at which one should aim is "as the right *logos* (ὀρθὸς λόγος) says" and a promise to investigate the deferred question of what the right *logos* is (1 1138b18-25); it ends by identifying the right *logos* first as "the one in accord with (κατά) *phronesis*" and then (in what is presumably an overstatement) as *phronesis* itself (13 1144b23-27). Thus in characterizing *phronesis* as a deliberative excellence that makes the things toward the end right, Aristotle evidently takes himself to have characterized it as what determines the mean. And a careful look

---

[89] More precisely, the passage says that the *logos* determines virtue (or on Bywater's emendation, ὡρισμένη λόγῳ καὶ ᾧ ἄν... determines the intermediate which virtue *is*); some think that this assigns *phronesis* the role of directly monitoring one's character-states. But as I show below, Aristotle elsewhere identifies that which needs wise determination as the mean, where this refers not to what virtue is but instead to that at which it aims. Moreover, just before the definition of virtue at 1106b36 he says that virtue is an intermediate state only in that it aims at a mean (μεσότης τις ἄρα ἐστὶν ἡ ἀρετή, στοχαστική γε οὖσα τοῦ μέσου) – *EN* II.6 1106b27-28, cf. II.9 1109a20-23). Therefore we can put the point as I have done above: the role of *phronesis* is to determine, by *logos*, the mean at which virtue aims. Compare also *EE* II.5 1222b6-7.

at his various characterizations of virtuous action shows him to be, if not a model of clarity, at least plausibly justified in this assumption.

The first point to note is that in saying that virtue "aims at a mean" (is στοχαστική τοῦ μέσου – e.g. *EN* II.6 1106b28), Aristotle is saying that the virtuous person takes the mean as his end or goal. This is implied throughout, but most explicit in a passage from the *EE*:

Every decision is of something and for the sake of something. *That for the sake of which is the mean*, of which virtue is the cause (οὗ μὲν οὖν ἕνεκα τὸ μέσον ἐστίν, οὗ αἰτία ἡ ἀρετή)...[90] (*EE* II.11 1227b36-38, emphasis mine)

This passage repeats the claim of the Goal passages that virtue makes the goal right: because he has a virtuous character, the virtuous person has a good goal – here characterized as "achieve the mean," i.e. "act as one should" (ὡς δεῖ).[91]

The second point to note is that Aristotle characterizes deliberation as a form of determining or defining, ὁρίζειν: deliberation is about things that are as yet "undetermined" (ἀδιόριστον, *EN* III.3 1112b9); "The object of deliberation and the object of decision are the same, but the object of decision is already determined (ἀφωρισμένον)" (1113a4) – i.e. through the preceding deliberation; good deliberation cannot be identical with belief (δόξα), because "everything that is the object of belief is already determined (ὥρισται)" (V/VI.9 1142b11-12).

Thus we can unify Aristotle's various descriptions of virtuous action as follows. In a particular practical situation the virtuous deliberator begins with a goal at which he (for it will always be a he, on Aristotle's view) is aiming, i.e. wishes (has a βούλησις) to achieve. This is a goal which can be described variously as:

(i) the mean (*EE* II.11 1227b36-38, quoted above)
(ii) the fine (e.g. *EN* III.7 1115b13-14, IV.1 1120a23-24, and *EE* III.1 1230a27-29)
(iii) the major premise of a particular practical syllogism: "Avoid all unhealthy things" (or whatever Aristotle intends at VI/VII.3 1147a32) or "I must make

---

[90] The remainder of the sentence is contested: the manuscripts have τὸ προαιρεῖσθαι οὗ ἕνεκα, to which various emendations have been proposed. Woods' translation follows Fritzsche and Susemihl in reading τῷ for τό, yielding "of which virtue is the cause by choosing." This would provide support for version (a) of the Intellectualist interpretation of the Goal passages: virtue makes the goal right in that virtue makes us want the goal. But (as Kenny 1979 persuasively argues) this emendation is misleading and unnecessary. We should instead read with the manuscripts simply that virtue is the cause of the goal, where what this means is explained by passages like *EE* II.11's Goal passage (1227b23-25), which shortly precedes these lines; the remainder of the sentence will then be simply a reminder (albeit both otiose and grammatically awkward) that decision is for the sake of something; or (following Kenny, who thinks we can get this sense either without emendation or by reading τοῦ for τό) the sentence will read "It is the mean that virtue is the cause of the decision's being for the sake of," where this is a clumsy statement of "Virtue is the cause of the decision's being for the sake of the mean" (Kenny 1979, 85-87).

[91] It is worth emphasizing that this is not a universal goal, one like happiness or "doing well" (εὖ πράττειν) which anyone who has any kind of goal has *ipso facto*. There are plenty of people who do not aim at acting as they should: witness for example wasteful people (ἄσωτοι), who "have an appetite for giving, but the how or whence makes no difference to them" (*EN* IV.1 1121b2-3).

something good" (*MA* 701a17) — or, to use the general formula for the starting-points of practical syllogisms,

(iv) "the end and the best" (V/VI.12 1144a31-32).

This goal is his starting-point; now he must deliberate about how to achieve it. His deliberation is (or yields?) a *logos*; since he is *phronimos*, and hence excellent at deliberation, it will be a "right *logos*." And we can describe that *logos* in different ways, depending on which description of the goal we have used, as:

(i) determining the mean
(ii) identifying what is fine in the circumstances
(iii) a minor premise or chain of premises of a particular syllogism: "This is unhealthy," or "a house is good" — or, most generally
(iv) "this will lead to the end and best," i.e. as identifying the "things toward the end."

All these descriptions show that what deliberation does is to make determinate the indeterminate goal with which the agent began. And thus accurately working out how best to achieve that goal — working out the finest "things toward it," i.e. deliberating well — is "determining the mean," i.e. is correctly making specific the worthy but overly general goal of acting as one should. For example, it is characteristic of the generous person to have the right goal: he "will not neglect his possessions, wishing (βουλόμενος) to assist someone through them" (*EN* IV.1 1120b2-3). But in order really to achieve this goal he must deliberate about how much money he should give to whom, and in what way, and so on. And getting this right, as we have seen above, *is* hitting the mean.

This yields an interpretation of *phronesis* with two important advantages. First, it gives us a unified account of *phronesis* by showing that the two apparently disconnected roles which Aristotle explicitly assigns it — determining the mean by the right *logos*, and making right the "things toward ends" — are in fact equivalent. Second, in identifying deliberation with mean-determination, the interpretation shows that *phronesis* as characterized in V/VI is much more than Humean instrumental reasoning, and hence merits the ethical significance Aristotle attributes to it. *Phronesis* is crucial to virtue not because virtue requires mere means-end efficiency, but because without *phronesis* the intention to do what one should cannot reliably be made specific in an appropriate way, and hence cannot reliably be focused onto an appropriate course of action.

Moreover, this allows us to make good sense of Aristotle's claim that natural virtues are harmful without *nous*, because "just as it happens to a powerful body without sight that in moving it stumbles heavily on account of not having sight, thus also here" (V/VI. 13 1144b8-17). This claim comes in the course of an argument that the relation between natural and strict virtue — "not identical, but similar" (1144b3) — is just like that between *phronesis* and cleverness. The clever person differs from the *phronimos* in that her ends may be either good or bad (12 1144a23-36). The naturally virtuous person differs from the genuinely virtuous one, this passage thus suggests – especially given that it comes shortly after one of the Goal passages and shortly before another (the earliest two) – in that her "things toward the goal" may be either good or bad.[92] We saw above that practical *nous* is intellectual quasi-perception of particulars (11 1143a35-b5); this is what the person with merely natural virtue lacks. Just as a blind person may have the strength and will to walk somewhere but stumbles over obstacles because she cannot see her way, so someone with natural courage (for instance) may have the right goal in a given situation, but blunder because she cannot discern what the brave thing to do is in that situation – and thus wind up acting rashly rather than bravely.[93]

After all, even those who wish to do the right thing may find it very hard in a given situation to work out just what the right thing is – and getting it wrong can be a moral failing.[94] This is an idea which a modern Aristotelian, Hursthouse, has forcefully expressed by contrasting practically wise agents with well-intentioned adolescents who harm people they wish to help because they lack the experience necessary for correctly applying ethical concepts in particular situations. Not knowing how to benefit someone most efficiently may be an ethically neutral deficiency; not knowing what sorts of things *are* benefits in a given situation – to take one of Hursthouse's examples, thinking that it would be kind to protect someone from a hurtful truth in a situation where it would in fact be unkind – is an intellectual failing that is at the same time plausibly a moral one.[95]

The interpretation of deliberation I am presenting may look very like one familiar from the literature: the so-called "constituent means" view of deliberation famously advocated by (among others) Wiggins, McDowell, and Irwin. Drawing on a distinction between instrumental means to a goal and constitutive components of it, these interpreters have argued that deliberation can be restricted to "things toward the end" without reducing to mere instrumental reasoning. One notion of "things toward the end" is instrumental means, but:

> The second notion... is that of something whose existence counts in itself as the partial or total realization of the end. This is a constituent of the end... [In the] *constituents-to-ends* case a man deliberates about what kind of life he wants to lead, or deliberates in a determinate context about which of several possible courses of action would conform most closely to some idea he holds before himself, or deliberates about what would constitute *eudaimonia* here and now, or ... about what

---

[92] This reading fits also with the *Politics* passage quoted above (1331b27-38), and *EE* II.11 1227b21-23.
[93] Hence my reading of this passage converges with the Wiggins/McDowell view of *phronesis* as moral perception, as against the Intellectualist reading quoted above.
[94] Gauthier and Jolif's note on 1144b16-17 (from passage 12) makes this point very well; see also Kenny's example of someone who has the worthy goal of justice, but "pursues it under the [let us grant] mistaken belief it consists in taking from each according to his ability and giving to each according to his need" (1979, 107).
[95] Hursthouse 1991, 231. Cf. Hursthouse 2003: "Quite generally, given that good intentions are intentions to act well or 'do the right thing', we may say that practical wisdom is the knowledge or understanding that enables its possessor, unlike the nice adolescents, to do just that, in any given situation."

would count as the achievement of the not yet completely specific goal which he has already set himself in the given situation. (Wiggins 1975, 224-25)[96]

The view is indeed similar to the one I have advanced; Greenwood, one of the originators of the idea of constituent/whole deliberation, recognized determining the mean as one form of it (although Wiggins et al. make no mention of it).[97] Like myself, the constituents-deliberation camp argue that we can do justice to the ethical significance of deliberation while respecting Aristotle's claim that it is of "things toward ends," on the grounds that "making right the things toward ends" is an ethically demanding task which involves giving specific content to a general goal.[98] But if we follow the constituents-deliberation view to its proponents' conclusion, we wind up giving up the game on "virtue makes the goal right" entirely. For Wiggins and Irwin use their notion of deliberation to argue that in an important sense there *is* after all deliberation of ends – and thus that giving content to the goal is an intellectual task:

[P]ractical intellect is not concerned with means *as opposed to* ends. Insofar as it is concerned with constituent 'means,' it is also concerned with ends...A virtuous man's ends are chosen by rational desires resting on deliberation about components of the final good. (Irwin 1975, 571)[99]

But this is simply to obliterate the distinction Aristotle clearly thinks so important: the distinction between being right about the end and being right about the "things toward it." It may be fair to say that Aristotle does not give us much guidance in drawing the line between the two, but we should nonetheless avoid an interpretation which precludes its being drawn.[100] Moreover, to say that practical reasoning can furnish specifications of ends but not ultimate ends themselves is to place a restriction on its powers that is far from arbitrary. Aristotle's claim is that while we can reason about how to live or what to care about, *given* a set of ultimate values, those ultimate values are fixed and determined by our upbringings – that is, by the affective, evaluative dispositions that our upbringings produce: our characters.[101]

We should not, then, take the idea of determining or specifying ends as broadly as the constituents-deliberation camp do. We can nonetheless take it far enough to ensure that deliberation is ethically significant. Deliberation cannot teach us that *eudaimonia*

---

[96] Cf. McDowell 1998, 26. Wiggins and McDowell connect this picture of deliberation to their notion of *phronesis* as the perception of morally salient particulars, mentioned above: to deliberate well is to see what, giving one's goal of acting well, is morally salient in the situation, and this amounts to seeing "what doing well, here and now, is" (McDowell, ibid.).

[97] Greenwood 1909, 58; but see the caveats about his interpretation noted above.

[98] See especially the McDowell passage cited above for an emphasis on ethical significance.

[99] Compare Wiggins, 227: "It is plainly impossible to deliberate about the end if this is to deliberate by asking 'Shall I pursue the end?'...But this platitude scarcely demonstrates the impossibility of deliberating the question 'what, practically speaking, is this end?' or 'what shall count for me as an adequate description of the end of life?'"

[100] As I have urged above, he cannot mean that virtue makes the goal right simply in giving us the right very general end of happiness, for that end is common to everyone.

[101] Compare again Williams' view in "Internal and External Reasons."

consists of the life of virtuous activity – only character can do that – but it can work out the whole substance of that general goal, showing at every point what counts as an achievement of it.

I have attempted in this section to give an account of *phronesis* which allows it the ethical significance which Aristotle clearly grants it despite lacking the end-identifying role which he (almost clearly) denies it. It is compatible with my account that *phronesis* does more than determine the mean at which virtue aims: it might also for example monitor one's character-states to make sure that they remain intermediate between excess and deficiency, or resolve apparent conflicts between the virtues, as some argue; it might also bring with it a philosophical understanding of the end such as enables one to teach others (e.g. by giving lectures on moral philosophy). I see no clear evidence that Aristotle gives *phronesis* these roles, but my main point is simply that what Aristotle explicitly and unequivocally does attribute to *phronesis* – the power to determine the mean at which virtue aims, i.e. the power to "make right the things towards the end" – is sufficient to explain why *phronesis* is so important to happiness and to character. There is neither good textual evidence nor philosophical argument for thinking that it also identifies the ends.

7.7 *Phantasia* and the goal

We are left now with what the Intellectualists rejected as a Humeanizing interpretation of Aristotle: practical reasoning is confined to working out the means toward ends, while the ends themselves are the function of non-rational character. But as I argued in section 2, this view is not in fact objectionably Humean: Aristotle can maintain it while still holding that we desire our ends because we find them good, so long as he holds that we find them good through a non-rational form of cognition, one available to the part of the soul which is the seat of character. Moreover, we have excellent evidence that this is precisely what he does think: the passages with which we began characterize the object of wish – the end as we view it – as what *appears* good, and even as a *phantasia* (*EN* III.4 1113a23-31, *EN* III.5 1114a31-b1, V/VI.12 1144a31-36). Now we have reason to take that language in the technical sense: given all the evidence above that we grasp ends on the basis of a non-rational part of the soul, in conjunction with evidence from Chapter 4 that the appetitive or passionate part of the soul exercises *phantasia* and perception (but not of course reason), a technical use of 'appearance' is precisely what we should expect. Aristotle's view is that one desires something as an end because it quasi-perceptually appears good: the basis of wish – even of the most general wish for happiness as one views it – is, no less than the basis of appetite, an appearance through *phantasia*.

This answers the charge of Humeanism: if this is indeed Aristotle's view, then he can perfectly well restrict practical reasoning to deliberation about what promotes ends while still maintaining that we desire our ends because we find them good. But as we saw above (section 2) it also opens the gates to more Intellectualist objections. How can *phantasia* have the sophistication to grasp ultimate ends? How can this view accommodate the evidence that wish is for what we think good? And why should we accept that there is any non-rational process that can furnish us with a grasp of starting-points?

Here is a very natural suggestion, motivated by Aristotle's parallels between practical and theoretical epistemology. As we saw in section 1, Aristotle attributes the grasp of theoretical starting-points to *nous*, but assigns a crucial role to *phantasia*. Might his view be similar in the practical realm? Perhaps there is some practical equivalent of induction which works through perception and then *phantasia* to give us an unarticulated grasp of the end; perhaps intellect then steps in in some non-deliberative capacity to make this grasp explicit. In the next chapter I argue that this is precisely Aristotle's view.

8

Practical Induction

8.1 Induction and habituation

> Virtue and vice respectively keep healthy, and corrupt, the starting-point, and in actions the that-for-the-sake-of-which is the starting-point, just as in mathematics the hypotheses are. Neither indeed in that case is the *logos* instructive of the starting-points, nor in this case, but virtue either natural or habituated [is instructive] of right belief about the starting-point. (*EE* VI/*EN* VII.8 1151a15-19)

I argued in the previous chapter that we should take this claim very literally: it is ethical character that supplies us with the starting-points of practical reasoning. But how does this work? How does having the right character – where this means having the right non-rational dispositions toward actions and passions – give one the right ends?

The aim of this chapter is to answer this question, and in doing so to resolve the worries left standing at the end of Chapter 7. The key will be to recognize that Aristotle's analogy between the starting-points of theoretical and practical reasoning extends further than he makes explicit.

In the theoretical realm, as we saw in Chapter 7, the starting-points for reasoning are supplied not by reasoning but by *nous* in a technical sense: a special exercise of intellect, sometimes called "intellectual intuition" (*APo.* II.19, cf. V/VI.6). But this is not a mystical process: *nous* does not grasp its objects out of thin air. Instead, *nous*' grasp is the culmination of a process of induction: repeated perceptions are preserved through *phantasia*, yielding first an experience and finally a noetic grasp.

If virtue plays a role parallel to *nous* in the practical realm, might there be some induction-like process in the practical case which explains this power? Many have argued that there is: the process that produces virtue, namely habituation. Indeed, Aristotle explicitly claims that habituation can play a role parallel to induction in furnishing starting-points, in *EN* I.7:

> The *that* is first and a starting-point. And of starting-points, some are grasped by induction, some by perception, some by some sort of habituation (ἐθισμῷ τινί), and others in other ways. (*EN* I.7 1098b3-4)[1]

---

[1] For an argument that the starting-point in question is a grasp of *eudaimonia*, see note 58 in Chapter 7.4.

But if habituation can yield a view of the end, how does this work? Aristotle does not seem worried about the epistemology of practical starting-points in the *EN*: he simply asserts that "we get some starting-points from habituation," as if it were clear that habituation of the kind he describes can have such power.

Some have argued that this must be an intellectual process, basing their arguments on V/VI.11 1143a35-b5, the passage we examined in Chapter 7.5 which says that the particulars apprehended by practical *nous* are "the starting-points of the that-for-the-sake-of-which."[2] I argued that the passage is not in fact concerned with induction, but instead with deliberation. Moreover, the only way to reconcile the view that we reach our ends through intellectual induction with Aristotle's claims that habituation shapes character and thereby determines our ends would be to hold that habituation is in part an intellectual process, and I have argued at length that it is not (see Chapter 7.3).

I will let the arguments of the last chapter stand against any Intellectualist account of practical induction; what we need to find instead is a way that non-rational habituation could yield a grasp of ends. I want to show that Aristotle has the resources for a coherent account of how this works, not one he actually gives in the *Ethics* but one that he could have given, by expanding on his analogies between practical and theoretical epistemology.

Versions of this account (differing at points from mine) have been defended by Burnet, Engberg-Pedersen, and Achtenberg, but the view has not received sufficient attention.[3] I want to show that it is worth taking very seriously, by showing that the parallel between habituation and induction is extremely close indeed. Just as theoretical induction proceeds through repeated perceptions of a certain type of thing, so habituation – which we might call practical induction – proceeds through repeated *practical* perceptions of a certain type of thing, namely virtuous activity (or vicious activity, if the habituation is bad). That is to say, in being habituated into a certain kind of activity we come to take pleasure in it: to perceive it as good. These perceptions are preserved and generalized through *phantasia*, yielding a general appearance – something analogous to an "experience" – of that kind of activity as good. Next some contribution must be made by the intellectual part of the soul; I consider in the final section of this book just what that contribution is, and I argue that it is far less substantial than any Intellectualist would think.

8.2 Habituation and pleasurable perception: an argument from first principles

In an influential article on the role of habituation in virtue, Myles Burnyeat argues that the key to habituation's powers is its connection with pleasure (Burnyeat 1980). There is excellent evidence that this is Aristotle's view:

---

[2] See Greenwood, Reeve, Sorabji, and Dahl, cited in Chapter 7.
[3] See Achtenberg 2002, Burnet 1900 (Introductory Note to Book 2), and, for a more Intellectualist version, Engberg-Pedersen 1983.

Ethical virtue is about pleasures and pains: for on account of pleasure we do base things, and on account of pain hold back from fine ones (τῶν καλῶν). For this reason it is necessary to be brought up straight from childhood, as Plato says, to enjoy and be pained by the things one should. For this is the correct education. (*EN* II.3 1104b8-13)

Virtuous acts, though "by nature pleasant" (*EN* I.8 1099a13-14), will to the person with a bad character be very unpleasant. What ensures that one come to take pleasure in them – and therefore reliably to choose them for themselves, i.e. to be virtuous – is habituation: repeated, supervised performance. This view is perhaps most clearly supported by two passages Burnyeat does not cite:

The absolutely good is absolutely choiceworthy, but for each person what is good for him; and these should be in harmony. And virtue makes this happen... And one who is a human being is suited and on the road for this... but *the road is through pleasure*: it is necessary for fine things to be pleasant [i.e. to become pleasant to the person]. (*EE* VII.2 1237a1-7, emphasis mine)

Upbringing and practices should be ordered by law, for they will not be painful when they have become habitual (συνήθη)... Even when they have grown up they must practice these things and be habituated to them (ἐθίζεσθαι). (*EN* X.9 1179b34-1180a1)

Habitually behaving in certain ways – performing certain actions and undergoing certain passions – makes one take pleasure in that behavior.[4] Moreover, a process that makes one take pleasure in virtuous behavior is a process that molds one's character – for virtue is first and foremost concerned with pleasures and pains. Such is the thesis of *EN* II.3, which launches many arguments for this claim, and concludes by declaring:

The whole affair (πᾶσα ἡ πραγματεία) both in virtue and in the political art is about pleasures and pains. (*EN* II.3 1105a10-12)

What I want to show is that these pleasures which habituation instills, and which are so central to virtue, are properly construed as perceptual pleasures. Habituation is pleasant because it involves pleasurable perception – which is, as we saw in Chapter 2, practical perception, essentially motivating perception of its objects as good.

First, a very quick argument for this conclusion: Aristotle says precisely this, in a passage we have seen twice already from the *Physics*:

Virtue and vice... necessarily arise through the perceptive part of the soul undergoing alteration (ἀλλοιουμένου τοῦ αἰσθητικοῦ μέρους). This part will be altered by perceptibles. For all of ethical virtue is about bodily pleasures and pains, and these are either in acting or in remembering or in expecting. The ones in action are on the basis of perception, so that one is moved by some perceptible, while those in memory and in expectation are from this [i.e. are due to the perception]: for people are either pleased in remembering as they experienced, or in expecting as they will experience. So that it is necessary for all such pleasure to arise from perceptibles. (*Phys.* 247a3-14)

---

[4] See, for a rather different example, *de Sensu* 444a1-2: people who mix scents with their drink "force the pleasure through habit."

The pleasures which give rise to virtue (i.e. the pleasures involved in the process which produces virtue – habituation) are perceptual pleasures: affections of the *aisthētikon*, caused by perceptibles. The passage does refer to these pleasures as "bodily," but as I argued in Chapter 4 (note 23) we should not take this to restrict the claim to the pleasures of eating and sex and the like, for this would attribute to the *Physics* an implausibly narrow view of ethical virtue which obviously clashes with that of the ethical works. In the *de Sensu* Aristotle argues that pleasure and pain, along with all desire, are connected with the body because they are connected with perception (436a6-10 with 436b1-4); given that the *Physics* passage goes on to explain the claim that ethical pleasures are bodily by saying that they arise through perception we should take Aristotle's point here to be the same. More specifically, he may intend precisely the point he makes in *EN* X.8: ethical virtue is connected to the body–soul compound because it involves passions (1178a14-16) – which are, as we saw in Chapter 4, pleasures and pains. I will return in the next section to argue that passions are indeed the pleasures that play the crucial role in habituation.

Here is another quick argument that the pleasures of habituation are perceptual: another passage we saw in Chapters 3 and 4 claims that *all* pleasures are perceptual:

Since to be pleased consists in perceiving a certain affection, and since *phantasia* is a kind of weak perception, and since some kind of *phantasia* of what a person remembers or hopes is likely to remain in his memory and hopes – if this is the case, it is clear that pleasures come simultaneously to those who are remembering and hoping, since there is perception there, too. Thus necessarily all pleasurable things are either present in perception or past in remembering or future in hoping; for people perceive the present, remember the past, and hope for the future. (*Rhet.* 1370a27-35)

If we could take these passages as authoritative, we would be done: the pleasures of ethical habituation are perceptual. But many will protest that the *Rhetoric* and *Physics* represent early or popular views of pleasure that Aristotle rejects in the *Ethics*, where pleasure arises from all manner of different activities – including virtuous behavior.

Bostock has argued to the contrary: the *EN* strongly implies a view that merely emends the earlier one to cover the pleasures of thought (Bostock 1988).[5] Most of Bostock's argument turns on an application of Aristotle's process/activity (*kinêsis/energeia*) distinction that does not wholly succeed.[6] But Bostock is certainly right to

---

[5] Others have noted this implication somewhat in passing: see Broadie's commentary *ad EN* VII.12 1153a2-7, and Gosling and Taylor 1982, 262 (although they seem to ignore this point elsewhere, as at 269, quoted below).

[6] Bostock wants to show that the *EN* view that all pleasure depends on activity (ἐνέργεια) rules out pleasure in actions that are instead processes (κινήσεις) – a category which would include most virtuous actions. Whatever pleasure we take in such actions must therefore lie in some activity associated with the action – namely the perception or contemplation of what one is doing. Sympathetic as I am to Bostock's general conclusions, I think this argument for it is flawed. For there are various passages in which Aristotle speaks of pleasure in activity where 'activity' clearly refers to something other than perception or thought: most strikingly *EN* IX.7 1168a6-7, where performing actions (πράττειν) counts as a pleasant activity. See also *EN* IX.9 1170a5-11, where doing virtuous actions counts as being active (ἐνεργεῖν) in the way relevant to

say that the *EN* gives most attention to perceptual and noetic pleasure, and only shows how his definitions of pleasure work in those cases. As he points out, the famous Book X characterization of pleasure as what perfects or completes (τελειοῖ) activity looks, in context, to apply only to perception and thought:

> But since every sense (αἰσθήσεως) is active in relation to the perceptible, and completely active when the sense is in good condition and its object is the finest in the domain of that sense ... in the case of each of the senses the activity that is best is the one whose subject is in the best condition in relation to the object that is most worthwhile in the domain of that sense. But this activity will be most complete and most pleasant. For there is pleasure in accordance with every sense, and likewise with thought and contemplation; but the most pleasant is the most complete (τελειοτάτη), and the most complete is that whose subject is in good condition, in relation to the most worthwhile of the objects in the domain of the sense; and pleasure is what completes the activity. (*EN* X.4 1174b14-23)

Arguably one could extend this model to other activities, but Aristotle does not do so explicitly; Bostock argues that this is no mere omission but instead a reflection of Aristotle's long-held belief (he cites the *Phys.* passage) that all pleasure is perceptual, here modified to take into account noetic pleasures.

The main objection to this reading is (as Bostock acknowledges) that many pleasures – including most of the ethically significant ones – look neither perceptual nor noetic. Noetic pleasure is a very small species indeed: its paradigm instance is the pleasure of contemplation, touted in *EN* X.8, and although Aristotle may think that practical intellect has pleasures of its own he certainly does not make that explicit. But the pleasures it seems natural to call perceptual are also a very restricted set. I have in mind pleasures taken in things insofar as they directly impact the five senses: the pleasure of tasting something sweet, looking at a beautiful picture, listening to good music, and so on: here one is aware, through one's faculty of taste or sight or hearing, of the pleasant perceptible qualities in the object. But what about the pleasure of filling oneself up when one is hungry? Or of taking a stroll, or having a chat? Or – to come directly to our concerns – the pleasures of doing the right thing, the pleasures of virtue?

Let us return for a moment to the simple claim of *de An.* III.7, the *Rhet.*, and the *Phys.* that pleasure is an activity of perception. Why would Aristotle hold this view? Presumably because he thinks that pleasure is, or at least essentially depends on, some form of awareness of its objects. To take pleasure in filling one's belly involves pleasurable awareness of that filling; to take pleasure in building a house involves pleasurable awareness of the building. If this is indeed his reason for characterizing pleasure as a perceptual activity, then it is natural

---

pleasure, and (against the thrust of a good deal of Bostock's argument) 1170a29 ff., where perceiving that one walks (βαδίζει) counts as perceiving that one is in activity. When Aristotle wants to oppose activity to process (see *Met.* IX.6 and also *EN* X.4), he uses walking as the paradigmatic *kinêsis*; this indicates that – contrary to Bostock's otherwise compelling arguments – Aristotle is not strictly and consistently opposing the two in the *EN*'s discussion of pleasure, and thus not ruling out pleasure in actions *solely* on the ground that they are processes.

to take the ethical works' account only as an expansion of that account, not a radical revision. To feel pleasure in something is to be aware of it in a certain way, which we can describe trivially as a pleasurable way, and more substantively (I have argued in Chapter 2) as being aware of its value. In other words, pleasure is or intimately depends on κρίσις, cognition. As Bostock puts it, "Aristotle's fundamental thought here is that pleasure takes place in the mind" (Bostock 1988, 271). Moreover, as we have seen from the start, there are only three forms of cognition: perception, *phantasia*, and thought (see especially *MA* 700b19-20, quoted in Chapter 1). And since *phantasia* is in essence a kind of perception (the *aisthêtikon* and *phantastikon* are the same although different in being (*Insomn.* 459a16-17), i.e. *phantasia* is an activity of the *aisthêtikon*, although *qua phantastikon*) in a sense these three forms of awareness reduce to two.[7]

If this is right, then all pleasure must be either perceptual or noetic. For any enjoyable thing we do – eating, or drinking, or building a house, or temperately abstaining from sweets, or justly distributing goods – "the place where the pleasure is to be found is in the associated thoughts and perceptions" (Bostock, ibid.).

The ethical works give us a further argument for this claim in some strange passages from the discussions of friendship.[8] In a passage which forms part of a longer argument about the pleasures of virtue which we will consider below, Aristotle says:

4a. To live is defined (ὁρίζονται) for animals by the capacity for perception, and for humans [by the capacities for] perception and thought... It seems then that to live is in the strict sense (κυρίως) to perceive and to think. (*EN* IX.9 1170a16-19; cf. *EE* VII.12 1244b23-25)

What should we take Aristotle to mean when he says that living *is*, in the strictest sense, perceiving and thinking? Surely living also includes things like acting, desiring, speaking, house-building, and so on. We can begin to see why he omits these when we notice that he also omits activities like eating, digesting, sleeping, and growing. These are fundamental activities of our psychic capacities, akin to perceiving and thinking; presumably Aristotle excludes them here because we share them with plants and they are thus in no way distinctively human, while perception, although we share it with animals, has distinctively human uses, or is essentially connected to what is distinctive about us.[9] Thus in 4a Aristotle is talking about what defines us as humans, referring to the idea he develops in the *de An.*: a kind of creature, e.g. human, *is* essentially (has as its soul) a set of fundamental capacities which explain all its essential or characteristic activities. Notably the *de An.* included locomotion along with cognition as what

---

[7] See *de An.* III.9: "The soul of animals is defined by two capacities, the critical, which is the function of thought (διανοίας) and perception [no separate mention here of *phantasia*], and further locomotion..." (432a15-17; cf. 427a17-21).

[8] Bostock notes these but sets them aside as of dubious relevance.

[9] See my arguments in Chapter 4.2: as we saw there, both ethical works treat the activities of the non-rational, passionate part of the soul as part of the human function (by contrast with nutrition and growth), even while describing these activities as ones we share with animals – perception and desire. See especially *EE* II.1 1219b23-38, quoted in Chapter 4.2.

defines human and animal souls (427a17-19; 432a15-17); the *Somn.*, however, concurs with the *EN*: "It is by having perception that the animal is defined" (454b24-25). When we recall that the *de An.* explains locomotion as a function of cognition together with desire, and furthermore declares the desiderative part or faculty of the soul to be "the same as, although different in being from" the perceptive (431a13-14 – passage 3c), the contradiction disappears: there is a case to be made that at the most fundamental level, all animal activity is a function of the *aisthêtikon* – and thus all human activity of either this part or the *noêtikon*. We find confirmation of this idea in a passage from *Pol.* VII.3 which argues that the life of thought is a practical life on the grounds that action (πρᾶξις) is an activity of thought (διάνοια).[10]

To return now to the point relevant for our purposes here: if being alive is fundamentally perceiving and thinking, and therefore all our activities (walking, house-building, getting angry, etc.) are in some sense activities of the perceptive or noetic faculty, then all our pleasures must in some sense be perceptual or noetic. To which class do the pleasures of habituation belong? I argued at length in Chapter 7 that habituation molds only the non-rational soul; therefore its pleasures must be perceptual.

8.3 Pleasure in perceiving the fine

Now we can come down from these very general claims about the nature of pleasure, and look specifically at what Aristotle has to say about the pleasures of habituation. Ethical habituation means repeatedly engaging in virtuous activity – which means both doing virtuous actions and feeling appropriate passions. For the importance of feeling the right passions during habituation, see especially two comments on courage:

> By acting in dangerous situations and being habituated to feel fear or confidence people become either brave or cowardly... By being habituated to scorn (καταφρονεῖν) fearful things and withstand them we become brave. (*EN* II.1 1103b16-17; II.2 1104b1-2).

I argued at length in Chapter 4 that passions are exercises of the perceptual part of the soul, involving *phantasiai* of things as good or bad. A natural suggestion at this point, then, is that the character-shaping pleasures (and pains) of habituation are perceptual because they are the pleasures (and pains) which are or attend passions: appetites, fears, feelings of confidence, pity, hope, and all the rest.[11] This interpretation has the strong advantage of making the character-shaping pleasures of habituation directly related to the constitution of character: by repeatedly feeling certain pleasures and pains (passionate ones) in response to certain objects, one becomes the type of person to feel those

---

[10] "Even in the case of others' actions [the subordinate craftsmen's] the master-builders are most strictly said to act, *through their thoughts* (μάλιστα δὲ καὶ πράττειν λέγομεν κυρίως καὶ τῶν ἐξωτερικῶν πράξεων τοὺς ταῖς διανοίαις ἀρχιτέκτονας)" (*Pol.* 1325b21-23, emphasis mine). This implies that thought is active not only in the forming of plans (deliberation) but also in their execution.

[11] This is close to Burnet's account, although he identifies as the relevant perceptions only those involved in desiring.

pleasures and pains reliably in response to objects of those types – i.e. one comes to have a certain disposition towards passions, which is a major component of what it is to have a certain character (see Chapters 4 and 7). For example, by repeatedly feeling fear in the face of bodily harm, one becomes cowardly. Putting it in the cognitive terms of practical induction, by repeatedly perceiving certain things (noble death, shameful escape, excessive indulgences, etc.) as good or bad, one comes to be the type of person to perceive things that way reliably.

I think this view is clearly on the right track, but it needs refinement. One reason to doubt it is that, as Aristotle himself implies in his discussion of courage in *EN* III.9, the virtuous person's passions will not always be pleasurable: the life of virtue may, depending on one's circumstances, involve a good deal of righteous anger, justifiable fear, friendly pity, and so on. The other reason is that the view as stated does not focus narrowly enough on the content of the virtuous person's view of the goal. The virtuous person, I will argue, is one who sees virtuous activity as good not merely in the various ways involved in feeling the various passions (e.g. as bringing pleasure, or safety, or benefit, or revenge), but very specifically as good "in itself," or to put it equivalently, as fine or beautiful (καλόν).[12]

In what follows I will argue for a restricted version of the passions view: the character-shaping power of habituation lies in one type of passion which attends all virtuous activity, which is always pleasurable, and which furthermore is specifically a response to things *qua* fine: something close to what we would call pride.

To begin with the point about the fine: Aristotle says of the virtuous person, the person who has been correctly habituated, that she chooses virtuous actions for themselves, i.e. for the sake of the fine (see e.g. *EN* II.1 1105a31 with IV.1 1120a23-24).[13] Moreover, she loves such actions, and takes pleasure in them:

And the life of virtuous people is pleasant in itself. For being pleased is one of the [properties/ activities] of the soul, and for each person that thing is pleasant of which he calls himself a lover (φιλοτοιοῦτος), for example a horse to the horse-lover, a spectacle to a spectacle-lover – and in the same way also just things to a justice-lover and in general things in accord with virtue to the virtue-lover (φιλαρέτῳ) ... [i.e. to] lovers of the fine (τοῖς φιλοκάλοις). (*EN* I.8 1099a7-13)

Moreover, we saw at the start of section 2 that habituation works precisely by making us come to take pleasure in fine actions: it is because people do base things on account of pleasure and abstain from fine ones on account of pain that it is crucial to have one's pleasures and pains correctly habituated from childhood (*EN* II.3

---

[12] See citations below. This is forcefully argued by Achtenberg 2002, who sees habituation as depending on perceptions of the fine, although not in quite the same way as I outline below.

[13] It is widely agreed that these are two ways of saying the same thing, in part because this is the only way to save Aristotle from contradiction, and in part because Aristotle defines the fine as one of the things chosen for itself (*EN* II.3 1104b30-31, quoted below, and cf. *Rhet.* 1362b8-9); see also the passage quoted just below in the main text which equates loving virtue with loving the fine.

1104b8-13), i.e. the "road to virtue" must be a process which makes one take pleasure in the fine (*EE* VII.2 1237a1-7).

Thus the crucial effect of habituation is making one take pleasure in the fine; I want now to show that this pleasure is based on awareness of the fine as such, i.e. as virtuous and fine. (The next step will be to show that the awareness involved is perceptual rather than noetic; I will in the process argue that the awareness is self-directed, i.e. is awareness of *oneself* as acting and feeling finely.)

One might object to the claim that the virtuous person takes pleasure in the fine as such, on the grounds that she might love virtue only extensionally: perhaps she loves virtuous, fine acts, but not under that description. This idea has some appeal for modern readers: our notions of humility dictate that one can be virtuous without recognizing oneself as such, and possibly even that one cannot be virtuous while recognizing oneself as such. But this, I will argue, is not at all Aristotle's view.

That "love of the fine" is not meant in the merely extensional sense comes out most clearly in *EN* X.9's discussion of habituated virtue, which we saw in part in Chapter 7.3. Aristotle begins by claiming that *logoi* cannot convert the many to virtue because the many have the wrong motive for doing virtuous actions:

For they do not by nature obey shame (αἰδοῖ) but fear, nor do they hold back from base things on account of the shameful but on account of punishments. (*EN* X.9 1179b11-13)

Where *logoi* do have a chance, as we saw in Chapter 7, is with those who have been correctly habituated:

The soul of the hearer has to have been prepared beforehand by habits (τοῖς ἔθεσι) toward rejoicing in and hating things in a fine way (πρὸς τὸ καλῶς χαίρειν καὶ μισεῖν)... loving the fine and being disgusted by the shameful (στέργον τὸ καλὸν καὶ δυσχεραῖνον τὸ αἰσχρόν). (*EN* X.9 1179b24-31)

Punishments can only give one the right extensional pains: it can make one averse to doing things that are in fact shameful, but not *because* they are shameful (not "on account of the shameful"); likewise, presumably, rewards and incentives can give one the right extensional pleasures but only these, making one want to do the things that are in fact fine but not because they are fine. One might have thought – and some interpreters do – that habituation does the same: it is a kind of conditioning by which one comes to associate pleasure with the right action, but not yet for the right reasons. But Aristotle here contrasts the many's motive with the motive of the well-habituated person, the fine-lover, and therefore he must mean that it is quite a different thing to be one who rejoices in the fine and is disgusted by the shameful. It is only the vulgar who find their pleasure and pains in extrinsic features of virtuous and vicious action; what proper habituation instills, by contrast, is an enjoyment of virtuous actions *as* fine – an enjoyment of them under that description.

Correct habituation thus teaches us to value and aim at the fine *qua* fine, which in the case of actions means valuing and aiming at virtuous actions *qua* virtuous. This is very close to Burnyeat's view:

> [L]earning to do and to take (proper) enjoyment in doing just actions is learning to do and to enjoy them for their own sake, for what they are, namely, just, and this is not to be distinguished from learning that they are enjoyable for themselves and their intrinsic value, namely, their justice and nobility [i.e. fineness – he translates καλόν as 'noble']... [S]omething is desired as noble or just, something inspires shame because it is thought of as disgraceful. The responses are grounded in an evaluation of their object. (Burnyeat 1980, 78; 80)

A paper by Wielenberg (2000) puts the point nicely by making use of the distinction between propositional and sensory pleasures: the pleasures of virtue are pleasures *that* something is the case, namely that one's behavior is fine.[14]

I want now to show that these pleasures are properly construed as perceptual. More precisely, the fully virtuous person takes both intellectual and perceptual pleasure in the fine; the moral habituee takes perceptual pleasure, and it is this that shapes her character. (Since my focus is on habituation I will thus for the most part ignore the intellectual pleasures; that the virtuous person does take intellectual pleasure in the fine is clear from passages like *EN* IX.8 1168b29-30.)[15]

In Chapter 2 I argued that pleasurably perceiving something is perceiving it as good. There we focused on appetitive pleasures like the pleasure of drinking when thirsty: if something agrees with one's bodily nature one will feel physical pleasure in it, and thereby find it good. But this is only one way in which things can be found good – only one guise under which we see things as to-be-pursued. Consider how Aristotle puts the point in the *EN*:

> There are three objects of choice (τριῶν γὰρ ὄντων τῶν εἰς τὰς αἱρέσεις)... fine, advantageous (συμφέροντος), and pleasant[16]... Pleasure follows everything subject to choice (πᾶσι τοῖς ὑπὸ τὴν αἵρεσιν παρακολουθεῖ) – for both the fine and the advantageous appear pleasant. (*EN* II.3 1104b30-1105a1)

Given my arguments in Chapter 2 that Aristotle effectively defines the good (ἀγαθόν) as that which is an end, i.e. chosen for its own sake,[17] we can take this passage's claim that there are three objects of choice as the claim that there are three

---

[14] The distinction between propositional and sensory pleasures comes from Feldman 1988. I thank Sungwoo Um for drawing my attention to these papers, in his own unpublished work on the pleasures of virtue in Aristotle.

[15] Richardson Lear 2006 focuses on intellectual pleasure in the fine, although arguing that there are non-rational – thumoeidic – pleasures as well.

[16] In the *Topics* he says that these are three properties that are αἱρετόν, choiceworthy or to-be-chosen (αἱρετόν ἐστι τὸ καλὸν ἢ τὸ ἡδὺ ἢ τὸ συμφέρον, 105a27-28; cf. 118b27 where these are three things for the sake of which (χάριν) other things are choiceworthy).

[17] See the passages quoted in Chapter 2.3, especially "Let good be [defined as] whatever is chosen (αἱρετόν) for its own sake" (*Rhet.* 1362a21-22); see also "If there is some *telos* of practical things which we want for its own sake... this would be the good and the best" (*EN* I.2 1094a18-22).

species or guises of the good. Moreover, pleasure attends all three ("both the fine and the advantageous appear pleasant") – as we should expect it to if it is (or supervenes on) the awareness of the good in the most general sense.

I want to show that the pleasure the virtuous person, and likewise the habituee, takes in virtuous actions is pleasure in perceiving them as fine. I will not attempt an analysis here of just what it is to find something fine (as opposed to pleasant or advantageous): for a compelling account, see Richardson Lear 2006 (which I follow in much of what I say below).[18] But here is a natural suggestion about the distinctive kind of pleasure we take in the perception of virtuous activity as fine, which will be borne out by the texts we see below: it is something broadly akin to aesthetic pleasure, which is another species of the same genus (since καλόν can mean "beautiful" as well as "fine," and arguably often means some combination of both). It involves admiration, if the fine things belong to others, and if they belong to ourselves, pride.

Moreover, as a perceptual pleasure, it is an exercise of the non-rational part of the soul; arguably (although I will not make that argument here) of the element or aspect of that part which Aristotle follows Plato in calling *thumos* (spirit or spirited passion).[19] Note, however, that it is a pleasure that can only be taken in the course of moral habituation. There may be other non-rational pleasures in fine things: for example, pleasure in such things as gratifying the spirited desire for honor and victory. But such pleasure is not proper to virtue; instead, it is a mere indulgence of non-rational passion (see *EN* IX.8 1168b15-31). Taking non-rational pleasure in the fine *qua* fine must mean in part taking pleasure in it *qua* the kind of thing a *phronimos* would command. Compare my arguments about why virtue cannot exist without *phronesis* in Chapter 7.3: proper habituation trains the non-rational part to obey and wait on the rational part. Thus it trains one to aim at fine things in a special way – namely, in such a way that one's non-rational impulses will wait on the deliverances of deliberation before pursuing them.[20]

We can begin with a comment on the pleasures of virtue which Aristotle makes in the context of the *EN*'s argument that a virtuous person will value virtuous friends:

---

[18] She argues that the pleasures the virtuous person takes in fine activity are noetic as well as non-rational; see note 15 above.

[19] For this view see Richardson Lear 2006, following Cooper 1996b, especially: "the practically wise person has learned to desire the *kalon* with his reason because earlier he desired it with his *thumos*-desires... It is through *thumos* that people are first motivated to experience this kind of value" (Richardson Lear 2006, 279). (Given my arguments below, this view gains some support from Aristotle's claim in the *Pol.* that *thumos* is "that capacity of the soul by which we feel friendship (φιλοῦμεν)" (1328a1). This raises the question of whether or not animals can perceive the fine and feel this special kind of pleasure in it; given that they have *thumos* of some kind it seems that they can, although my arguments in Chapter 4 about how intellect expands our perceptual range leave it open to Aristotle to argue that they cannot.

[20] See Smith's (1996) arguments about pursuing the fine vs. living according to passion, although I think he overstates the role of intellect.

The virtuous person's activity... will be pleasant in itself... For the virtuous person, insofar as he is virtuous, delights in (χαίρει) actions in accordance with virtue, and is disgusted by those that come from vice, just as a musical person is pleased by beautiful/fine (καλοῖς) melodies and pained by base ones. (*EN* IX.9 1170a7-11)

Enjoying virtuous acts – one's own or a friend's, the context implies – is like listening to good music: a perceptual pleasure taken in the fine. This is an idea Aristotle elaborates in *Pol.* VIII.5, where pleasure in artistic representations of virtue is made a crucial part of moral education:

And since it is the case that music is one of the pleasant things, and since virtue has to do with being delighted (χαίρειν) correctly and loving and hating correctly, it is clear that there is nothing one should learn and become habituated in (συνεθίζεσθαι) so much as discerning correctly and delighting in virtuous characters and fine actions (τὸ κρίνειν ὀρθῶς καὶ τὸ χαίρειν τοῖς ἐπιεικέσιν ἤθεσι καὶ ταῖς καλαῖς πράξεσιν); but the best likenesses of the real things – of anger and calmness, and further of courage and temperance and all their opposites and the other character-traits – are found in rhythms and melodies... And habituation (ἐθισμὸς) in feeling pain and delight at likenesses is close to feeling them towards the real things... From these things therefore it is apparent that music has the power to form the character of the soul (δύναται ποιόν τι τὸ τῆς ψυχῆς ἦθος ἡ μουσικὴ παρασκευάζειν), and if it has this power, it is clear that the young must be directed to music and must be educated in it. (*Pol.* VIII.5 1340a14-b14)

The education described here works to shape character by habituating people to take pleasure in virtuous actions and characters. It does so by what we would call aesthetic means: through music. One might think that the pleasure we take in music is obviously different from anything properly called ethical pleasure, but the project of using music to shape character shows that Aristotle (following Plato, who prescribed just this kind of musical education in *Republic* II-III and *Laws* II) clearly did not. "Habituation in feeling pain and delight at likenesses is close to feeling them towards the real things": by frequently experiencing pleasure in musical representations of courage, one will come to feel the same kind of pleasure in one's own courageous acts: perceptual pleasure, or as we might say, using the Greek word, aesthetic pleasure.[21]

In the *Ethics* there is no explicit mention of musical education: moral education takes place entirely through habituation in virtuous activity.[22] But the comparison we saw above from *EN* IX.9 of the virtuous person with the lover of music at least suggests

---

[21] Aristotle does hold that there are intellectual pleasures to be gained from art, but his argument that education must first address the non-rational part of the soul, in *Pol.* VII.15, together with his characterization of musical education as shaping the characters of children (see especially *Pol.* VIII.5), implies that the relevant pleasures are non-intellectual.

[22] Arguably this is due to a difference in focus rather than to any change of mind. Aristotle's focus in the *Ethics* is on what an individual can do to achieve virtue and happiness, and in the *Politics* on what the state can do to make the citizens virtuous and happy. Habituation can happen at home (although it is influenced by the laws – see *EN* X.9), but musical education must (the *Pol.* argues, following Plato's *Rep.* and *Laws*) be prescribed by the state.

that the mechanism is the same: in both cases, one is learning to take pleasure in the perception of virtue.

This is confirmed by the rest of that chapter's discussion. Aristotle is arguing that the virtuous person needs friends in order to be happy:

> If then happiness is in living and being active, and *the activity of the good person is virtuous and pleasant in itself*, just as was said in the beginning; and what is one's own (τὸ οἰκεῖον) is one of the pleasant things; and we are more able to observe (θεωρεῖν) those close to us than ourselves, and their actions than our own; and the actions of the virtuous who are friends are pleasant to the good (for they have both the things pleasant by nature):[23] therefore the blessed person will have need of such friends, *since he chooses to observe actions decent and his own*, and such are the actions of the good [i.e. virtuous] friend. (*EN* IX.9 1169b30-1170a4)

The first line might imply that the simple *doing* of virtuous actions is pleasant in itself, independent of any awareness of it; insofar as there is any standard interpretation of the Aristotelian pleasures of virtue, this is certainly it.[24] But the rest of the argument shows that this cannot be quite what Aristotle means. Virtuous friends contribute to our happiness because we take pleasure in observing (θεωρεῖν) their good character, their good actions and good passions; but we need friends only because it is easier to observe others than ourselves.[25] This implies that *being* virtuous is pleasant because *observing* virtue is pleasant. That is, being virtuous is pleasant not precisely because one enjoys doing virtuous actions, but rather because one enjoys observing them.

This still leaves open the question of what kind of awareness Aristotle has in mind: one might think that θεωρεῖν indicates that the virtuous person takes pleasure in the contemplative thought that she is acting virtuously – that this is an instance of θεωρία in Book X's sense. But the word can be used for perception as well as thought (its original meaning is "to look at"), and what Aristotle says in the next lines should leave no doubt that at least one kind of observation he has in mind is literal perception.

Here he makes one of his fresh starts, arguing again for the conclusion that the virtuous person needs friends by "examining the question more from nature" (1170a13); the argument begins with a passage we saw above:

---

[23] This is explained by what comes just below: the things pleasant by nature are things "decent" (ἐπιεικεῖς) and "one's own" (οἰκεῖα).

[24] The account fits naturally with the *EN*'s definitions of pleasure as either being or perfecting activity (VII.12 1153a13-15, X.4 1174b14 ff.), if one ignores Bostock's arguments that 'activity' refers only to thinking or perceiving. The thought goes: actions like distributing goods or fighting in battle are themselves activities; when one does them virtuously (justly, bravely) these activities are perfect or complete, and therefore pleasant. See e.g. Gosling and Taylor: "A good man must take pleasure in his good actions... For... they are actualizations of a well-developed nature in relation to the proper objects. But in that case the actualizations are perfect, and so pleasant" (1982, 269).

[25] Why should this be so? Angela Chew has suggested to me that Aristotle's idea is the following: when one is acting virtuously oneself, one is caught up in the situation, attending to external events, and thus not fully able to reflect on one's own state. (As a bonus, this interpretation is compatible with the pleasing suggestion of one of my undergraduates: that Aristotle would never have made this claim had he known about things like camcorders!)

4a. To live is defined for animals by the capacity for perception, and for humans [by the capacities for] perception and thought (νοήσεως)...It seems then that to live is in the strict sense to perceive and to think.

It continues as follows:

4b. If then being alive itself is good and pleasant (which seems likely from the fact that everyone desires it, and especially the decent and blessed; for to these life is most choiceworthy (αἱρετώτατος), and their living is the most blessed),

c. and if the one who sees perceives that he sees, the one who hears perceives that he hears, the one who walks perceives that he walks, and similarly in the other cases there is something that perceives that we are active (ἐνεργοῦμεν), so that if we perceive, [we perceive] that we perceive, and if we think, [we perceive] that we think, and the fact that we perceive and think is the fact that we are (for being is perceiving or thinking),

d. and if perceiving that one is alive is one of the things pleasant in themselves (for being alive is something naturally good, and perceiving what is good as being there in oneself is pleasant), and being alive is choiceworthy, and especially so for good people, because *being is good for them and pleasant, for perceiving together/being conscious of (συναισθανόνεμοι)*[26] *what is in itself good they are pleased,*

e. then as the virtuous man is disposed toward himself, so is he disposed toward his friend – for his friend is another self.

f. Therefore, just as for each his own being is choiceworthy, so his friend's is too. *But as we saw, the good man's being is choiceworthy because of his perceiving himself, that self being good; and such perceiving is pleasant in itself.* (*EN* IX.9 1170a25-b10, emphases mine)

What makes the virtuous life pleasant, according to this passage, is the pleasurable awareness that one is virtuous. One thing to note right away is that this renders the pleasures of virtue strikingly self-referential: on a straightforward reading, one takes pleasure not merely in the fact that one's actions or states are good (where one might take equal pleasure in someone else's actions and states being such), but that the good actions and states are one's *own*. Indeed this was already implied in the earlier lines of the chapter, quoted above: the actions that please the virtuous person are those "decent and *one's own* (οἰκεῖον)." This self-reference will seem offensive to modern readers, who may try to downplay. I return to the topic at the end of this section, but another point emerges from passage 4 that is more important for my purposes: the pleasurable awareness that renders the virtuous life pleasant – the awareness that one is virtuous – is characterized as a form of perception. From this it will follow that the pleasures of virtue are indeed perceptual pleasures.

One might protest that this is an overly literal reading of passage 4: perhaps Aristotle is using αἰσθάνεσθαι in the loose sense of 'be aware,' and he means that the virtuous person takes pleasure in believing (thinking, knowing) that he is good, rather than in literally seeing (let alone smelling or tasting!) his good qualities. But there is good reason to take the talk of perception in the narrow sense. First, in 4a Aristotle clearly contrasts perceiving

---

[26] On the translation of this term see below.

with thinking, and attributes it to animals as well as people, so he must there be using αἰσθάνεσθαι in the narrow and technical sense; if he uses it in a looser sense when he speaks of perceiving that one perceives and thinks, in 4c, he will be switching between two senses of the word within a few lines. Second, he strongly implies that he has literal perception in mind in a similar passage a few pages on, which characterizes the perception one enjoys of oneself and of one's friends as belonging to the same genus as sight:

> Just as seeing (τὸ ὁρᾶν) is most welcomed by lovers, and they choose this form of perception (ταύτην τὴν αἴσθησιν) more than the others... in the same way living together is most welcomed by friends. For friendship is a sharing, and we are related to our friend as we are related to ourselves. Hence, *since the perception of our own being is choiceworthy, so is the perception of our friend's being*. Perception is active when we live with him; hence, not surprisingly, this is what we seek. (*EN* IX.12 1171b29-1172a1, emphasis mine)

Third, and most important, we have very good evidence from outside the ethical works that Aristotle treats self-awareness as a form of literal perception. This comes out most explicitly in his treatise on sleep and waking:

> We consider the one who is perceiving to be awake, and every waker to be perceiving either something external or some movement within itself. If then being awake consists in nothing other than perceiving (τὸ ἐγρηγορέναι ἐν μηδενὶ ἄλλῳ ἐστὶν ἢ τῷ αἰσθάνεσθαι), it is clear that by the very thing with which one perceives, wakers are awake and sleeping things sleep. (*Somn.* 454a2-7)

In this passage Aristotle is clearly using 'perceive' (αἰσθάνεσθαι) in the narrow and technical sense: in the lines that follow he alludes to the psychic divisions of the *de An.* and argues that plants do not wake or sleep because they lack τὸ αἰσθητικὸν μόριον, the perceptive part (454a12-17), and later he reminds us that "it is by having perception that animals are defined [viz., distinguished from plants]" (454b25). What he attributes here to the perceptive part (or faculty) is a power we would call consciousness – what makes for the difference between waking and sleeping.

In the following pages Aristotle claims more specifically that the power of sleeping and waking – of consciousness – belongs to what is known as the "common sense," in a passage which reminds us strongly of 4c:

> Now to every sense there belongs something special to it, and also something common. Thus, seeing is special to the sense of sight... But all are attended also by a certain common capacity (κοινὴ δύναμις), whereby one perceives that one is seeing or hearing. For it is not by sight, after all, that one sees that one is seeing, nor is it by taste or sight, or both, that one discerns (κρίνει) or is able to discern that sweet things differ from pale ones, but by some part that is common to all the sense-organs. For there exists a single sense (αἴσθησις), and the controlling sense-organ is single... Given this (τοίνυν) it is manifest that waking and sleeping are an affection of this thing [the common sense]. (*Somn.* 455a12-26)[27]

---

[27] Some take this passage to be discussing only an aspect of sensory perception, something like the awareness of the change in the sense-organ that constitutes perception: see e.g. Everson 1997, 143. But given Aristotle's argument that *because* we perceive that we perceive by the common sense it is *therefore* this

Returning now to the ethical works, we see that 4c uses precisely this same language of second-order perception: the one who sees perceives that he sees. Here Aristotle extends the idea to cover perception of other activities as well: we perceive that we are (4c), where this means that we perceive not only that we perceive but also that we think. Thus we should conclude that the kind of self-awareness or self-observation is literal perception: an activity of the *aisthêtikon*. Some may doubt that consciousness or self-awareness is properly conceived of as a form of perception, and it is not my purpose here to defend Aristotle on this point (although the idea seems sensible enough). The crucial point for my account is that Aristotle *does* treat self-awareness as a form of perception, both in the psychological works where he clearly means to be giving a technical account of perception, and in this passage from the *EN*. Therefore the pleasures of self-awareness count for him as perceptual pleasures; and therefore, given 4f, the pleasures of virtue count for him as perceptual pleasures. (This allows for the possibility that one may also, as on Richardson Lear's view, take pleasure in the intellectual contemplation of one's goodness; the point is simply that this would be something beyond the essential pleasure of virtue, the one which 4f characterizes as rendering the life of virtue choiceworthy.)

Returning now to the objection against Bostock's view which we saw in the previous section – that many pleasures cannot be construed as either perceptual or noetic – we see that the self-awareness aspect of perception can extend *EN* X.4's account of perceptual pleasure to cover cases that do not fit into the "tasting sweetness" schema. Eating when hungry is pleasurable because one perceives the inner replenishment.[28] Being healthy is pleasurable because one feels the good condition, the smooth functioning, of one's own body. In general, we feel pleasure when we perceive good things in ourselves (4d, f). And it is clear how this applies to the pleasures of virtue: the virtuous person takes pleasure in perceiving his own good psychic condition, the excellence of his ethical state (4f).

A passage from the *EE* loosely corresponding to passage 4 makes this even clearer. There, as in *EN* IX.9, Aristotle argues that being alive is choiceworthy because it is choiceworthy to know (γνωρίζει) oneself, where this turns out to mean to be aware of oneself when one is in good condition, i.e. virtuous (*EE* VII.12 1244b33-1245a5). The

---

sense which is responsible for waking – i.e., as we saw from the earlier passage, for consciousness – it is very natural to take the idea of "perceiving that we perceive" in a broader sense: as being conscious or aware of one's own perceptual activity. (For this interpretation see e.g. Kahn, who uses 4c to argue that even in the psychological works perception of perception is a broad phenomenon: "Now this 'common power which accompanies all the senses, in virtue of which one perceives that he is seeing and hearing' [*Somn.* 455a], would not seem to be so very different from the modern notion of consciousness as defined by Locke, 'the perception of what passes in a man's own mind'" (1966, 59).)

[28] Bostock implies this account of bodily pleasures: bodily replenishments are processes, and cannot in themselves be pleasant; what is pleasant instead is the perception of the replenishment (1988, 269). This is a view that comes straight from Plato's *Philebus*, and there should be no surprise in Aristotle adopting it without much comment.

next premise is the famous claim that a friend is "another self" (1245a30). From this he concludes:

> To perceive [and to know] a friend, therefore, is necessarily in a manner to perceive and in a manner to know oneself. Consequently to share even vulgar pleasures and ordinary life with a friend is naturally pleasant... but more so to share the more divine pleasures [e.g. virtuous activity], the reason of which is that *it is always more pleasant to observe (θεωρεῖν) oneself enjoying the superior good, and this is sometimes an action (πρᾶξις), sometimes an affection (πάθος)*. (EE VII.12 1245a35-b2)

To be virtuous is to be disposed to feel the right passions and do the right actions. Recall a worry we raised above, as to how being virtuous can be pleasant when the virtuous actions and passions themselves are unpleasant (self-sacrifice or anger, for example). This passage makes the answer clear: the pleasure comes from observing these fine, appropriate, virtuous actions and passions in oneself. It is what we would call a pleasure of pride – and one can be pleasantly proud of one's pains.[29]

In fact, pride seems precisely the right general term for the pleasures of virtue as Aristotle describes them. Recall the first long passage we saw above from EN IX.9 (1169b30-1170a4): one enjoys one's friends' virtuous actions because "they have both the things pleasant by nature": they are good, and they are οἰκεῖον, one's own; this is very close to Hume's definition of the things which excite pride (*Treatise* II.i.v). Aristotle offers the same explanation for why the virutous person's own existence is pleasant to him, in 4d: "perceiving what is good as being there in oneself is pleasant" (cf. 4f). Thus a version of the account on which the pleasures of virtue are pleasurable passions is correct: one pleasurable passion always accompanies virtuous activity, namely pride. (One might object that if this were Aristotle's view he should have said so; so far as I can tell, however, he does not have a word for pride as a *pathos*, presumably because all the words at his disposal have connotations of excess.[30])

---

[29] Consider as an example the odd phrasing of Gordon Brown's apology to the late Alan Turing, on behalf of the British government: "I am *pleased* to have the chance to say how deeply *sorry* I and we all are for what happened to him... I am very *proud* to say: we're *sorry*, you deserved so much better" (emphasis mine; quoted in "PM's Apology to Codebreaker Alan Turing: We Were Inhumane," *The Guardian*, 11 September, 2009).

[30] The *pathos* opposed to shame in the *Rhet.* is the clearly pejorative "shamelessness" (ἀναισχυντία), with no mention made of fitting or blameless pride. He does elsewhere come up with labels for the attitude, although not ones that sound like passions, and does characterize it as pleasurable and passion-like: the EE's discussion of greatness of soul (*megalopsuchia*) calls the thing of which vanity is an excess and self-belittling a deficiency "valuing oneself" (ἀξιῶν αὑτόν) (see EE II.3 1221a31, with 1221a13 implying that this counts as a *pathos*); in the EN he says that the *megalopsuchos* takes pleasure in hearing about his deeds (ἡδέως ἀκούειν – IV.3 1124b15), implying that there is a pleasurable passion involved, but not giving it a name. Thus he seems to think that there is a passion that plays this role, but not to label it as such, and this would be well explained by the lack of a non-pejorative term. (In fact, I am not sure that English speakers had a non-pejorative word for pleasure in one's own perceived goodness until fairly recently; and I am told that even now it is only Americans who can speak of feeling proud without squirming.) Arguably if my account is correct Aristotle should have described the pleasures of virtue as pleasures of *thumos*, but he says much less about this passion than does Plato.

I have argued, then, that the primary pleasure of Aristotelian virtue is that of prideful self-perception. Despite all the evidence presented, however, one might object that something has gone wrong: this cannot be Aristotle's view of the pleasures of virtue, for it seems morally repellent. Aristotle's virtuous person now appears intensely self-conscious, outrageously vain, and lacking in appreciation for the genuine value of his actions – a fair match, in fact, for a character like Emma Bovary:

> ... The pride (*orgueil*), the joy of saying to herself "I am virtuous," and of looking at herself in the mirror striking poses of resignation, consoled her somewhat for the sacrifice she believed she was making.[31]

Is this complaint justified? At least not entirely. On the account I have given, the virtuous agent need not have the explicit thought that she is virtuous, merely the pleasurable perception of her good qualities as good. So her awareness of her behavior as good could in principle be less explicit, and certainly less intellectual, than Emma's awareness of her own (putative) virtue. Using the analogy which Aristotle (following Plato) makes between virtue and physical health, we can explain the difference as follows. I have claimed that on Aristotle's view, just as being healthy is pleasurable because one perceives the good condition of one's body, being virtuous is pleasurable because one perceives the good condition (actions and passions) of one's soul. Now, one can easily imagine a Mme Bovary-type pleasure of health: the pleasure of working out in front of the mirror, all the time saying to oneself "I'm getting so buff!" But there are other ways of taking pleasure in health too: one can simply be pleasurably, confidently aware of the good functioning of one's own body, without pausing to think "That's health, and I'm proud of it." It seems open to Aristotle to hold that the pleasures of virtue come closer to the latter.

There are also even less self-conscious pleasures of health: one can simply feel good, where the cause of the feeling is the smooth functioning of one's body, without any awareness that this is the cause. Such pleasure can arise without the kind of perception we exercise in observing or reflecting on ourselves the way a third person might. It might come from something more like proprioception: *feeling* one's good condition from the inside. If this is the closest analogue to Aristotle's view then his virtuous person can be very modest indeed. Moreover, this account erodes the difference between the view on which pleasure is in the doing of virtuous actions and the view on which pleasure is in the perceiving of them (after all, no one claimed that we could take pleasure in doing things without being in any way aware that we were doing them) – and thereby throws us back on what I called the standard interpretation.

But can Aristotle hold that the pleasures of virtue are so unreflective? There is good reason to think not. First, fully virtuous acts are chosen on the basis of deliberation; as

---

[31] Flaubert 1992, 86. Of course part of what is repellent here is that we think Emma not merely vain but self-deluded: she thinks she is virtuous but really she is not. But we tend also to think that if she *were* virtuous, she wouldn't be sitting in front of the mirror rejoicing in the fact.

we saw above they are chosen "for themselves," i.e. "for the sake of the fine" (*EN* II.1 1105a31, IV.1 1120a23-24). Thus Aristotle's virtuous agent need not be as self-conscious as Mme Bovary, but she has to be aware that what she is doing is virtuous and fine, and has to choose her behavior for that reason. (This does not in itself show that she has to value it as *her* fine behavior, as opposed to as fine in itself, but I have argued separately for that claim above.)

The texts on friendship provide another strong argument that proprioception is the wrong model here: that would make nonsense of the claim that it is easier to observe virtue in those close to us than in ourselves (*EN* IX.9 1169b30, quoted above) – and would thereby undermine Aristotle's most extensive argument, an argument he makes at length, for why the virtuous person needs friends.[32]

But the main argument against the deflationary proprioception interpretation, and in favor of the robust self-perception interpretation, is that the latter is precisely what we should expect to find in Aristotle. We should expect Aristotle's virtuous person to be proud of his own excellence, and even to rejoice in it – and not at all to be unwittingly virtuous, humble, unconsciously prompted by his feelings to do the right thing without any awareness of it as right, or of himself as good.

Consider the virtue of *megalopsuchia* ('greatness of soul') and its special relation to the other virtues. The great-souled person is not merely worthy of being valued, but "values himself greatly (μεγάλων αὑτὸν ἀξιῶν) while being worthy" (*EN* IV.3 1123b2). This is clearly an extreme of pride: as Russell puts it, "One shudders to think what a vain man would be like."[33] But in fact Aristotle's vain man may be no more prideful than the great-souled one: vanity is a vice not because extreme pride is bad in itself, but because the vain man's pride is misplaced – he overestimates his own worth (*EN* IV.3 1125a27-28). If he were as good as he thinks he is there would be nothing wrong with his pride; and indeed, vanity is better than its opposite, under-valuing oneself (the vice of the "little-souled," 1125a24). Moreover, this is not a one-off case of Aristotle indulging pride, for *megalopsuchia* is not merely one virtue among others: "It seems to be a kind of adornment (κόσμος) of the virtues, for it makes them greater" (1124a1-2). His view is not that pride does not diminish virtue – instead it is that it enhances it.

Finally, the above picture of the pleasures of virtue fits very well with the egoistical underpinnings of Aristotle's theory of virtue. Virtue enters Aristotle's ethical theory by way of the function argument: the reason he gives for caring about virtue is that being virtuous is crucial to one's own flourishing. Virtuous actions often benefit others, and possibly benefiting others is even a condition on an action's being virtuous, but Aristotle makes it perfectly clear that the ultimate value of virtue is, like the value of everything else in life, eudaimonistic: it is good to be virtuous because that is a part or condition of one's functioning well and thereby living a happy life. And while one

---

[32] I am grateful to Antony Eagle for helping me to see this point.
[33] Russell 1945, 176, quoted in Hardie 1968, 119.

could construct a theory on which even the most rational agents take pleasure in virtue on the basis of some features other than what makes virtue valuable, Aristotle gives no sign of doing so. So it should be no surprise that the pleasures of virtue are pleasures taken in the awareness of one's own good condition, in a robust and literal – if not fully repugnant – sense.[34]

Thus the foremost pleasures of virtuous activity – the pleasures that make one's life worth choosing when one is fully virtuous – are pleasurable perceptions of oneself as fine. Furthermore, it is a very natural inference from here to the conclusion that these are the same pleasures that attend the virtuous actions and passions of the moral habituee, the pleasures that shape her character, especially given that Aristotle describes the effect of habituation as making one take pleasure in virtuous action as fine (see *EN* X.9 quoted above).[35] And thus the process of habituation has a very important cognitive aspect. Through habituation, as through the musical education described in the *Pol.*, one comes to take pleasure in perceiving virtuous passions and actions – which is to say that one comes to perceive them as good, or more specifically, as fine.

To return to the main argument of this chapter, we can now see that habituation is indeed a close analogue of induction. It is what we might call practical induction, since the cognition involved is practical (pleasurable, evaluative) cognition. Through habituation, one acquires not only many perceptions of virtuous activity, but many pleasurable perceptions of it – many perceptions of it as good. Now let us consider how the process continues.

8.4 *Phantasia* of the goal

Recall my brief summary of Aristotle's account of theoretical induction at the start of Chapter 7:

i) One perceives triangles many times.
ii) The perceptions are preserved in memory, via *phantasia* (*APo.* 100a3; cf. *Met.* 980a28–29).

---

[34] Note that the complaint we have been considering about Aristotle's view of the pleasures of virtue is similar to one that critics make about contemporary virtue ethics: that it attributes to the virtuous person excessive concern with her own virtue. This is sometimes presented as a point about *reasons*: virtue ethics claims that the reason a person has to help a friend, for example, is that *doing so is virtuous*, while (the critics say) a really virtuous person's reason would be *that doing so will benefit the friend*. As Hurka puts it, "[I]t is not virtuous – it is morally self-indulgent – to act primarily from concern for one's own virtue" (2001, 246; cf. Keller 2007). The criticism here is parallel: Aristotle says (I have argued) that the pleasure one properly takes in benefiting a friend is pleasure *in being virtuous*, while (the objection goes) it ought to be pleasure *in the beneficiary's well-being*. It is certainly not clear that this charge against contemporary virtue ethics is fair – but if I am right about Aristotle's view, it looks like the parallel charge against him is.

[35] Moreover, the person becoming physically fit will normally take the same sort of pleasure in her nascent fitness as she will take in her full fitness once she has acquired it, and likewise for the one becoming wealthy, or famous, or skilled in a craft; thus the person becoming virtuous can take the same sort of pleasure in his nascent virtue as he will take in his full virtue once it comes. According to *EN* X.4 the pleasures will be better (more perfect (τελεία)) when the relevant capacities and objects are, but they need not be different in kind.

iii) From many memories of triangles arises one experience (ἐμπειρία) (*APo.* 100a5-6; *Met.* 980b29-981a1), which implicitly contains a universal (*APo.* 100a6-7), i.e. a cause explaining why triangles have the properties they do (*Met.* 981a28-30).

iv) One achieves an explicit grasp of this explanatory universal, which will then serve as the starting-point for demonstrations (*APo.* 100a6-9; cf. *Met.* 981a5-7); the state one is now in is called *nous* (*APo.* 100b12).

Induction begins with perception but requires *phantasia* to move forward. Repeated perceptions of triangles do not on their own provide a grasp of triangles sufficient to supply the starting-points for deductive reasoning, for although the universal is somehow in the perceptions one cannot grasp it solely by perceiving. To get to the point where one can grasp it explicitly (stage iv), one must be able to generalize from one's perceptions, and this presupposes that one remember triangles one has perceived (stage ii), and that one be able to recognize new things as triangles on the basis of one's memories (stage iii). Memory is certainly a function of *phantasia*. As to the next stage, as we saw in Chapter 7.1 an experience *is* (perhaps the same as although different in being from) many memories, and animals have a little of it, which implies that it is at least largely or even wholly the work of perception and *phantasia*.[36]

If habituation is the practical analogue of induction, then we should expect *phantasia* to play a role here too. Repeated perceptions of virtuous activity as good on various occasions do not on their own provide a grasp of virtuous activity as the goal sufficient to serve as the starting-point for practical reasoning; *phantasia* is required too. (This is not to say that *phantasia* is enough; I turn to that issue in the next section.)

This is in part for a reason familiar to us from Chapter 3: practical perception cannot on its own furnish goals of any action, human or animal, because goals are by definition things not yet present to perception. To have virtuous activity as one's goal is not simply to enjoy doing the virtuous thing one is doing now, and thus the wish to perform virtuous activity, just like the appetite for a drink or the fear of an imminent blow cannot be based merely on perception: one must preserve one's previous pleasurable perceptions in memory, and reproduce them as representing something to-be-pursued. And we saw in Chapter 3 that the preservation and reproduction of perception, pleasurable perception included, is the work of *phantasia*.[37]

But in this particular case *phantasia* is necessary in a different way, too, which corresponds to one difference between wishes and passions. Someone who wants to live a life of virtuous activity does not merely want to live a life in which she repeats various actions

---

[36] *APo.* 100a5-6 and *Met.* 980b26-27, quoted in Chapter 7 note 4. For arguments that experience is wholly a product of perception and *phantasia* see e.g. Engberg-Pedersen 1983, 156 and Charles 1995.

[37] Aristotle emphasizes that pleasurably perceiving virtuous activity will go with pleasurably remembering and expecting it: the virtuous person "wishes to spend time in his own company; for he does so pleasantly, since he has both delightful memories of things he has done and good hopes for things he will do in the future, and such things are pleasant" (*EN* IX.4 1166a23-26).

more or less identical to those she has already performed; instead, she wants to live a life of *that kind* of activity. She thus needs to be able to recognize particular excellent and fine actions open to her as being the kind of actions she finds good. This requires that she have at least the practical equivalent of stage iii, a grasp of virtuous activity as the good parallel to an experience (I am for now bracketing the question of whether she also needs some practical equivalent of stage iv). This will be not just a pleasurable memory or expectation or imagination of some particular virtuous activity, but a pleasurable general representation of that kind of activity – a general representation of it as good.

We saw that in the theoretical realm stage iii involves *phantasia*; this fits with all our evidence from Chapter 7 that in the practical realm it must. It is "virtue, either natural or habituated" which teaches us the goal: that is, our view of the end is a function of the non-rational soul, which exercises *phantasia* and perception but not reason. Moreover, when Aristotle speaks of our view of the goal in positive terms, he speaks of it as something which *appears* quasi-perceptually to us – in fact, as a *phantasia* (Chapter 7.2). The parallel between theoretical induction and habituation has given us strong reason to take that language in the technical sense: just as induction yields, through perception and *phantasia*, an ability to recognize certain shapes as triangles (where that does not yet include an explicit grasp of the feature one is recognizing), so habituation yields, through pleasurable perception reproduced by *phantasia*, an ability to recognize virtuous activity as to-be-pursued (with the same caveat). Someone who has acquired this ability is someone to whom virtuous activity now appears good, i.e. someone subject to a general appearance of virtuous activity as good.

This does not mean that thought plays no role in the formation of this general appearance: we saw in Chapters 3 and 4 that the contents of our perceptions can be influenced by thought, and therefore a thinking creature will have a broader range not only of perception but therefore also of memory, and therefore also of experience – or of its practical counterpart, the generalized appearance of a certain kind of activity as good. Thus thought may influence the content of this appearance. Perhaps thought also plays a role in making that appearance suitably general: there is after all some evidence that in ordinary induction thought plays a role in constructing a general experience from specific memories (for after all animals have it only "a little," and perhaps this is even an understatement for "not at all").

What I want to emphasize, however, is that activities of a certain type can only appear good as a goal on the basis of previous pleasurable perceptions and *phantasiai* of that type of activity. Moreover, the relation between the perceptions and *phantasiai* on the one hand, and the general stage iii appearance on the other, is fairly direct: one acquires such a general appearance not by inferring from or reasoning about what one has perceived, but instead by making implicit generalizations of a kind arguably available even to lower animals. (This raises the question of whether or not animals can have such a general *phantasia*. I suspect that Aristotle's answer would be that, as with stage iii in the theoretical realm, they can "a little," for they are susceptible to habituation. See *Pol.* 1332b3-4: "the other animals live mostly by nature, and some also a little by habits (μικρὰ δ' ἔνια καὶ τοῖς ἔθεσιν)"; various passages in the *HA* illustrate this, for example 573b27 on sheep who are habituated (συνεθίζουσι) from youth to act as leaders of the flock.

Thus at the practical equivalent of stage iii someone who has been correctly habituated has a general appearance of virtuous activity as good, an appearance which is at least in the main part the product of her non-rational cognitive capacities. But is this the end of the process? Has she now fully acquired the starting-points of practical reasoning? Or is there, as in the theoretical case, a need for intellect to convert this appearance into something else? In the theoretical realm only those who reach stage iv have the starting-points for theoretical reasoning, and thus only they can perform genuine demonstrations and achieve genuine knowledge (ἐπιστήμη) – and thus only they can have wisdom (σοφία), the excellent state of theoretical intellect. Is the practical case parallel – does *phronesis* involve or presuppose an intellectual grasp of the end?

Recall one species of Intellectualist we encountered in Chapter 7: Intuitionists, who think that intellect provides our grasp of the end not on the basis of deliberation but rather through an intuitive grasp – namely, *nous*.[38] They hold, that is, that *nous* furnishes the starting-points of practical reasoning in the same way that it furnishes those of theoretical reasoning. This view would certainly seem to be a natural fit with the analogy between habituation and induction I have proposed here: as the final stage of practical induction, *nous* uncovers substantive, hitherto undetected truths about virtuous activity, and only now does the agent have a correct view of the end. In fact there are a few Intuitionists who have presented just this view.[39] But my arguments in Chapter 7 count strongly against it: it is not intellect's task to provide us with goals.

Indeed, if Aristotle thinks that *nous* furnishes practical starting-points he seems to go out of his way to obscure the point. As we saw at length in Chapter 7, the role that *nous* plays in the theoretical realm – grasping the starting-points – gets attributed in the practical realm to virtue instead, even in passages that explicitly mention the analogy between practical and theoretical reasoning (e.g. VI/VII.8 1151a15-19). Moreover, far from saying that *phronesis* includes *nous* as a part he explicitly contrasts the two: *phronesis* "lies opposite to (ἀντίκειται) *nous*," because *phronesis* is of the "last thing," i.e. the particular (while *nous* is of universal starting-points) (V/VI.8 1142a23-25). Likewise, in the one passage where he introduces a technical sense of *nous* in the practical sphere – V/VI.11 1143a35-b5, quoted and discussed in Chapter 7.5 – *nous*'s role is to grasp not the end of action, but rather the opposite: the "last thing" or "second [i.e. minor] premise" – the particular facts of a situation in which one acts.[40]

---

[38] See among others Greenwood 1909, Hardie 1968, Cooper 1975, Dahl 1984 and Reeve 1992.

[39] See Greenwood 1909 and Reeve 1992, 86, although their views of the earlier stages of practical induction are very different from mine, and more intellectualist. Burnet's view is nominally Intuitionist, but I think his version is in fact closer to what I propose below.

[40] Cooper emphasizes this: although he is an Intuitionist he recognizes that this passage does not support that view, for the passage is very explicit in describing what it calls *nous* as a perception-like apprehension of particulars (Cooper 1975, 42, note).

Nonetheless, there seem to be some important considerations in favor of this reading. First, the theoretical analogy would seem to entail it. Second, it would resolve an important worry about wish left hanging at the end of the previous chapter: if goals are grasped through intellect, albeit on the basis of *phantasia*, then wish is indeed a distinctively human, thought-based kind of desire.

In the next section I will argue that neither of these considerations necessitates the strong Intuitionist version of the practical induction account: there is a cheaper solution, and one which accommodates all the evidence we saw in Chapter 7 that it is character rather than intellect which furnishes our goals.

8.5 Beyond *phantasia*: true supposition of the end

We need to distinguish carefully between three quite different questions. First, does the fully virtuous, *phronimos* person have *any* intellectual grasp of happiness? Second, if so, does this grasp play a necessary role in her practical life? And third, if so, does this undermine my arguments in Chapter 7 that it must be non-rational cognition which provides the content of our goals?

As to the first question, the answer is surely Yes. As we saw in Chapter 4, a *phantasia* as of *p* will normally and by default trigger the belief that *p*. Therefore if habituation has led someone to have a generalized *phantasia* of virtuous activity as to-be-pursued, then so long as he sees no reason to question or doubt that *phantasia* (as he might were he for example to come under the influence of malicious sophists), he will automatically also *believe* that virtuous activity is to-be-pursued. Likewise for the more specific goal-appearances which habituation will also give him: if in a given situation it appears to him good to eat temperately, or stand firm in battle, he will normally also believe that this is so. (That when we wish for and deliberate toward an end we also have the belief (δόξα) that we should pursue it is particularly explicit in *EE* II.10, where Aristotle distinguishes decisions from beliefs on the grounds that the latter align with wishes rather than decisions: "One wishes most of all for the end, and believes (δοξάζει) that one should both be healthy and act well" (1226a13-16).) But this leaves open the possibility that the beliefs are epiphenomenal: perhaps the *phantasia* does all the work, forming the starting-point for deliberation and the basis for wish (in which case the answer to the second question is No).

In the remainder of this chapter I want to show first that beliefs of this kind (beliefs that inherit their content from the appearances to which they are assents) do play a necessary role in furnishing the starting-points of practical reasoning, and second that they also suffice. Intellect makes no more substantial contribution, and therefore the content of our goals comes entirely from our characters: the answer to both the first and second questions is Yes, but the answer to the third is still No.

There is a simple reason to accept that it must be the belief rather than the *phantasia* that is strictly speaking the starting-point for practical reasoning. The starting-points of practical reasoning are cognitions or statements of the end that can be used as the bases for inference: as Aristotle puts it in a passage we have seen several times, "Practical syllogisms are equipped with a starting-point: 'Since (ἐπειδή) the end and the best is of such a sort...'" (V/VI.12 1144a31-33).[41] Therefore, one's grasp of the end has to be the sort of thing which can play a role in inferences: "*Since* the end is...". And Aristotle's (plausible) view is that only intellectual cognitions can perform that task. As the discussion of the akratic's reasoning in VI/VII.3 shows, he thinks that non-rational cognitions must if they are to play a role in reasoning be taken up as beliefs: the minor premise "this is sweet" is a δόξα about something perceptual, rather than a mere perception (1147a25-26, cf. 1147b9). If awareness that *x* is the end is to serve as a basis for deliberation, then, it too must be grasped by intellect.[42]

Thus we should concede this much to the Intellectualist: the virtuous person will have a correct intellectual cognition of the end, which is not epiphenomenal but instead a crucial condition of correct deliberation. Moreover, it would be very natural to take this correct grasp to be a part of *phronesis*.[43] Let us grant, then, that it is a requirement of *phronesis* that one believe that the life of excellent rational activity is the good life.

But this is not much to grant: in fact, I have already granted it. Recall my interpretation in Chapter 7.5 of the claim that *phronesis* is "true supposition of the end" (V/VI.9 1142b31-33) (and recall that belief is one species of supposition, according to *de An.* 427b25). Part of *phronesis* is having a grasp of the end *qua* end, i.e. recognizing it as the goal toward which one is deliberating (cf. *EE* II.10 1226b20-30, discussed in 7.5); part of *phronesis*, then, will be having an explicit intellectual cognition that *x* is the end. But this in no way entails that intellect *adds* anything to the view of the end supplied by character. Instead, it suggests that intellect's grasp of the end consists merely in agreeing with – assenting to – what character supplies. If this is indeed Aristotle's view then he can sometimes refer to the end as appearing good through *phantasia*, and sometimes as our believing it good – as he does in shifting between talk of the apparent and seeming (τὸ δοκοῦν) good in *EN* III.4 – without thereby committing any grave equivocation: the content of intellect's belief is the same as that of character's appearance. One of the Goal passages, the one with which I began this chapter, fits this reading very well:

---

[41] There is a debate here as to whether the statement of the end is to be understood as the major premise of the syllogism, or instead as something which comes before the syllogism proper. For the latter position see Cooper 1975 and Hardie 1968, 228-31, who points out that we need not take οἱ συλλογισμοί τῶν πρακτῶν as a technical term, as the translation 'practical syllogism' implies: it might instead mean simply reasoning about practical things; for the former see Allan 1953, Joachim 1951, and indeed the majority of interpreters. I have accepted the standard view, which I do think supported by our passage 1c from the *MA*, but in either case the crucial point remains: we reason *from* the end.

[42] As Greenwood puts it, "Since the actual stating of any proposition is an intellectual and not a moral act, the actual stating of the end... must be the work not of moral virtue but of practical wisdom" (Greenwood 1909, 51); my view here is also very close to Engberg-Pedersen 1983, 152.

[43] Aristotle arguably implies that *phronesis* includes everything that counts as a virtue of practical intellect, at V/VI.5. Some, like Reeve 1992, take intellect's grasp of the end to be distinct from but a necessary condition for *phronesis*; my arguments in what follows count against this view as well.

Neither indeed in [mathematics] is the *logos* instructive of the starting-points, nor in [the practical case], but virtue, either natural or habituated, [is instructive] *of right belief* (τοῦ ὀρθοδοξεῖν) about the starting-point. (VI/VII.8 1151a17-19, emphasis mine)

Non-rational character teaches us the starting-points by yielding correct *beliefs*.[44] Thus, strictly speaking, our cognitions of the starting-points of practical reasoning are rational, exercises of intellect – but their content derives from character, i.e. from the generalized *phantasia* that is produced through habituation.

What about wishes, desires for the end? We can resolve the tensions we saw in the previous chapter if we take it that when one wishes for what appears good to one, the wish is based directly on an evaluative belief which arises from the appearance without adding any content to it.[45] This will accommodate the evidence that wish is distinctively human desire for what one thinks good, while still respecting the evidence that wishes are determined by non-rational character, and are for what appears good in the technical sense. Wishes, like passions, normally track both appearances and beliefs, but unlike passions are based directly on beliefs.

We would have good evidence that this is Aristotle's view if it turned out that one can have a wish for something one believes good without having the corresponding appearance – i.e. that one can get the belief by testimony or reasoning or some other way. In fact, this seems to be precisely Aristotle's view of the akratic and enkratic, who have correct wishes but lack good character.

Aristotle says that the akratic is better than the intemperate person because he has the right end: "the best thing in him, the starting-point, is preserved" (VI/VII.8 1151a25-26). But this comes directly after he has told us that it is "virtue, either natural or habituated" which makes the goal right. Surely the akratic has neither kind of virtue: she has unruly, intemperate appetites.[46] Correspondingly, the arguments of *EN* III.4-5 imply that she lacks a correct appearance of the end: only the virtuous person has that. How then can the akratic have the right goal, and the right wishes (and therefore make the right decisions)? Aristotle's thought must be that her character is good enough to make her responsive to arguments about the good life, or to make her admire virtuous

---

[44] Gabriel Richardson Lear has pressed on me that Aristotle must hold that the *phronimos*' grasp of ends is a form of knowledge rather than mere belief (in which case this passage mentions only one stage in the acquisition of that grasp). I think there is something to this, but it is notable that he calls *phronesis* "true supposition (ὑπόληψις)" of the end, perhaps deliberately leaving it open whether it is knowledge or mere belief. I suspect the right thing to say is that by contrast with theoretical *epistêmê*, *phronesis* counts as mere belief (being about changeable things, and being a state of the *doxastikon* rather than of the *epistêmonikon*). On the other hand, the *phronimos*' grasp of the goal is as good as any such grasp could be, and so by contrast with other people's grasp of the goal – the enkratic's and akratic's, most saliently – it should count as knowledge.

[45] This talk of content may seem problematic: arguably the content of a conceptualized belief necessarily differs from that of a perception or *phantasia*. But recall that Aristotle thinks beliefs can contradict appearances (*Insomn.* 459a6 and 460b20, discussed in Chapter 5.4), and thus presumably also that they can agree with and confirm them; that is what I have in mind.

[46] Burnyeat argues that the spirited akratic has been well habituated but lacks *phronesis* (1980, 84); I disagree, for reasons to do with my understanding of *phronesis* laid out in Chapter 7, but this is anyhow beside the point, for the present passage is concerned with the appetitive akratic.

people, and thus acquire correct beliefs about the goal in these ways.[47] This is not the normal, proper way to acquire such beliefs: in a well-functioning human, virtue makes the goal right (since that is how virtue helps to complete our function: see V/VI.12 1144a6–9, one of our Goal passages). Thus our akratic is like someone who knows her eyesight is sometimes unreliable and so accepts other people's judgment about what colors things are: she acquires the right belief, but not in the usual way. As a result, there is dissonance between how she believes things are and how things appear to her to be. (This is obviously similar to the cognitive dissonance I attributed to the akratic in Chapter 5, but it is a more general phenomenon. There we were considering the akratic's state during particular episodes of *akrasia*, and I argued that she has conflicting rational and non-rational cognitions about some particular object or course of action, e.g. eating this piece of cake now. But I raised the possibility that the particular *phantasia* of the cake as good might arise from the general *phantasia* of bodily pleasures as good, and we can see now that it does: her uneven upbringing has involved enough self-indulgence to yield a generalized appearance of bodily pleasures as good, and this stands in conflict with her general belief that they are not. Note that this conflict is found in the enkratic as well, and is therefore not enough (*contra* interpretations like e.g. Charles' (2009)) to explain akratic episodes – unless the agent's intellect is "covered over" by passion the general belief will hold sway and she will act in accordance with her wishes and decisions rather than with her appetites – but it does explain why she is prone to conflicts between decisions and appetites.)

Thus we have good evidence that wishes are based not directly on appearances but instead on beliefs. It is not immediately clear why Aristotle should hold this view, however: given that he thinks that wishes are not based on practical reasoning (see my arguments in Chapter 7), what is his motivation for holding that they are based on intellectual cognitions at all? Here is a suggestion: wishes are for ends, as decisions are for "things toward ends," and just as to decide on something one must be able to see it as a means to an end, so to wish for something one must be able to see it as an end toward which there could be means.[48] To put it another way, the content of any wish is something that could in principle be expressed as the starting-point of practical reasoning. But we saw that only intellectual cognitions can play a role in reasoning, and thus in order to want something as an end one must *believe* that it is good, rather than merely being subject to an appearance of it as good.[49]

There is another reason to hold that wishes are based on intellectual cognition: Aristotle more than once characterizes wishes as desires for the good rather than for the pleasant, and many take this to entail that they must be based on intellect because only

---

[47] Aristotle arguably has this possibility in mind at *Pol.*1332b6–8: "people do many things contrary to their habits and their nature on account of *logos*, if they are persuaded that it is better...".

[48] This is compatible with the fact that we can, as Aristotle stresses, wish for the impossible: "I wish I could fly" would mean, "I wish there were something I could do to bring about the end of my flying, even though I know there isn't" – by contrast with an appetitive urge to fly, perhaps!

[49] Compare Tuozzo 1994, 541.

intellect can grasp the good *qua* good. Despite my arguments in Chapters 1 and 2 that all desire is for things *qua* good in a substantive sense, there is something right in this, and the present view of wish can account for it. (Here I follow Tuozzo 1994, although he does not treat beliefs as assents to appearances.) In rationally assenting to an appearance of something as square one no longer merely perceives it as square but also thinks it square; one explicitly applies the concept 'square.' I argued at length in Chapter 2 that feeling perceptual pleasure in something is perceiving it as good – perceptually discriminating it as to-be-gone-for – without thereby applying the concept 'good.' In assenting to such a perception, however – or to a generalized *phantasia* arising from many such perceptions – one does apply the concept. Thus it makes sense to introduce a strict sense of 'desire for good' that applies only to desires based on conceptualized cognitions of the good. As Tuozzo puts it, as objects of desire the good and the pleasant "differ only in their mode of cognition: the one [the good] is conceptualized, and so involves thought, while the other [the pleasant] is unconceptualized, and so involves perception (or *phantasia aisthêtikê*) ... " – and therefore "the distinction between *epithumia* and *boulêsis* does not turn on a distinction between two kinds of attractiveness in things that can motivate us to action, but rather on the two different ways we can cognize the attractiveness of things."⁵⁰ (Note that this does not entail that appetites are desires for the pleasant conceptualized *as* the pleasant.)

Thus our minimal concession to the Intellectualist resolves the apparent contradictions in Aristotle's account of wish: if wishes rest on conceptualized assents to non-rational cognitions, then Aristotle can hold that they are distinctively human, based on thought, and for the good rather than the pleasant; and he can do all this without thereby undermining all his arguments that our ends – the objects of our wishes – are not reached on the basis of *logos*, but determined instead by non-rational character. *Phantasia* supplies the content of the goal; intellect merely accepts and in the process conceptualizes it.⁵¹

Is there any reason to go further? On the Intuitionist view, for intellect to grasp the end is for intellect to supply the end – to reveal virtuous activity as the good for the first time. Those who combine Intuitionism with practical induction thus hold that while

---

[50] 1994, 542; 543. Tuozzo furthermore sees this conceptualization as the culmination of a process of what I have been calling practical induction, although his view here differs from mine. Something like habituation plays a role: when babies appetitively desire and enjoy pleasant food, "This nonconceptualized cognition of the good serves as the experiential basis for the child's coming to possess the concept 'good,'" and thus one will come to have wishes for bodily pleasures unless moral education intervenes (ibid., 547). I think he goes wrong, however, in ignoring the power of correct habituation to give us rival appearances of goodness, and thus that his view gets the belief/appearance relation backwards: "Once one has the concept of the good, one can, under the influence of parents, etc., come to *believe* that some things are good which do not *appear*, through perception or *phantasia*, good to one ... The moral education of most people progresses only this far; hence most people are incontinent ... or continent ... Moral education need not stop there ... [B]oulêsis can influence the objects that appear to one as pleasant. Sensible appearances of the good can be modified by sincerely held opinions about the good" (ibid., 548).

[51] I take this view to be roughly in line with Achtenberg's (2002, 133–34) and Burnet's (1900, 67), and perhaps also McDowell's (1988, 31-33).

habituation gives us the right general orientation, only with the intervention of *nous* do we come to have the right end: the last stage of practical induction, just like the last stage of theoretical, really teaches us something new. Reeve, for example, interprets V/VI.13's claim that natural virtue without *nous* is potentially harmful, like strength without sight (1144b4-14), as follows:

> Now *nous* is of the first principle or unconditional end, *eudaimonia*. So what natural virtue lacks, as the analogy of the blind person makes clear, is grasp of the end. (Reeve 1992, 86)[52]

I argued in Chapter 7.5 that this is a misreading: what practical *nous* supplies is a grasp of the "things toward the end" (so the person without it is like a blind person who stumbles over things in her way); the whole content of our goal comes from character. I want to defend that claim now by looking at Aristotle's analogies between *phronesis* and another broadly speaking practical expertise, craft. My aim is to show that reaching stage iv in the practical realm does not give one a new goal, but only makes what one was already implicitly going for, in stage iii, an explicit and conceptualized goal.

I take the Intuitionist view to be that in moving from an experience-like grasp of virtuous activity to a *nous*-like grasp (that is, in moving from stage iii to stage iv), what one grasps is the *because* underlying the *that* one had at stage iii, and in doing so one comes, for the first time, to have virtuous activity as one's goal (cf. the Intellectualist reading of *EN* I.4 1095b3-8, on ethical *becauses*, discussed in Chapter 7.5). At stage iii one often performed virtuous actions, but, on this view, without recognizing their excellence or fineness as the thing about them that made them worth choosing. Now one grasps that such actions are worth choosing *because* they are excellent and fine, and therefore means to the end of living excellently (rather than because they feel good, or are socially approved, etc.), and this makes a major difference to how one acts – as if a blind person had acquired sight.

I want to show that grasping the *because* in the practical realm does not make this kind of difference. It does make a difference, of precisely the kind discussed above: when one has an explicit, articulate goal, grasped as a goal, one can use it to guide one's deliberations. But grasping the goal in this way does not make one aim at something new. It gives one an end in the strict sense for the first time, and so in that sense gives one a new end, but what is new is the status of the end as a full-blown starting-point for practical reasoning, rather than its content. This explains why Aristotle refers to this grasp as a "true supposition," rather than employing the more elevated term he uses for its theoretical parallel, *nous*.

This emerges from Aristotle's discussion of the *becauses* involved in a state that is broadly like *phronesis*: craft. Aristotle emphasizes that *phronesis*, as a condition of

---

[52] Although what he goes on to say is close to what I defend below (although I do not use the term *nous*, which I think out of place here for reasons given above): "It is natural or habituated virtue, then, that 'teaches true opinion about the first principle' (1151a17-19). *Nous* simply grasps the universal implicit in what they teach" (ibid.).

practical intellect rather than theoretical, differs significantly from scientific knowledge (ἐπιστήμη) and wisdom (σοφία), which have as their province necessary, eternal truths (V/VI.5 1140a35-b3, 7 1141a22-25). There is however another truth-grasping condition (ἕξις) much more similar to *phronesis*: craft (τέχνη – skill, art, craft-knowledge). The definitions Aristotle provides of these two in V/VI.5-6 imply that they differ only in their ends: *phronesis* guides action (πρᾶξις), which has its end in itself, while craft guides the production (ποίησις) of some product. Like *phronesis*, craft is contrasted with scientific knowledge as being practical in the broad sense – concerned with doing things rather than merely thinking – and hence concerned with "things that can be otherwise." Therefore while it is true that craft, like scientific knowledge, comes about through a grasp of universal causes – *becauses* to explain experience's *thats* (*Met.* 981a24-30) – these are quite unlike the universal causes at issue in scientific knowledge. The latter are definitions or accounts of essences, but Aristotle evidently denies those to the craftsman. What then are the universal *becauses* that belong to craft? I argued briefly in Chapter 7 that they seem to be general, lawlike claims that subsume the particulars of experience under universal categories. I quote again (cf. Chapter 7.5) the one clear example Aristotle gives of a *because* that differentiates stage iii from stage iv in the realm of production:

Craft comes to be whenever from many experiential concepts (πολλῶν τῆς ἐμπειρίας ἐννοημάτων) one universal supposition (ὑπόληψις) comes to be about similar things. For to have the supposition that this thing was beneficial for Callias when he was ill with this disease, and for Socrates, and in the same way individually for many belongs to experience; but that it benefited all people of this sort, divided off into one type (κατ' εἶδος ἕν ἀφορισθεῖσι), when ill with this disease – for example phlegmatics or bilious people when burning with fever – belongs to craft. (*Met.* 981a5-12)

The expert doctor grasps the starting-points of productive reasoning, the universal causes which the merely experienced doctor (the one who reaches only stage iii) lacks; the important difference that this makes, according to this text, is simply that he is now able to make explicit the generalizations implicit in experience, with the help of explicit concepts (phlegmatic, feverish, etc.).

We can infer, although Aristotle notably does not bother drawing attention to the point here, that he will also have an explicit grasp of his end, and indeed Aristotle says as much in *Met.* VII.7: the essence (οὐσία) or form (εἶδος) of health is in the doctor's soul (for the medical craft *is* the form of health (1032a32-b14)). But if we are to respect Aristotle's distinction between producers and theoreticians, and the claim in *Met.* I.1 that the latter are wiser than the former, which entails that they have a higher grasp of causes (981b31-982a1), we must take the craftsman's grasp of the end to be fairly minimal. The doctor grasps *that* health is e.g. the right balance of the hot, cold, wet, dry and so on, and uses this in deliberating about how to cure a fever, but in grasping these facts he is only making explicit and articulate what was already implicit in his experiential grasp on health, rather than acquiring a substantially new view of health – and therefore is not acquiring a new goal.[53]

The practical analogue should be clear. Someone who fully grasps the starting-points of practical reasoning, i.e. the ends of action – that is, the *phronimos* – is like someone who has a craft, and thus differs from the analogue of the merely experienced worker (namely the person with the non-rational conditions for virtue but without *phronesis*).[54] But because *phronesis* is concerned with what can be otherwise, and thus is more like a craft than a science – more like carpentry than math – one can be *phronimos* without delving into the most fundamental causes relevant to action.[55] What someone gains when he grasps the starting-points of practical reasoning is merely an articulated, explicit awareness of the generalizations he was already making on the basis of his habituation. Earlier he could say only "This action is to-be-done in this circumstance, and this similar one in this similar circumstance"; now he can say things like "All fine actions are to-be-done," (or, at a lower level of universality, "All temperate actions are to-be-done") – and this is because he now recognizes the goal, the *because* and explanation for why other things are to-be-done, as fine, excellent activity.

In other words, when someone goes beyond having a stage iii *phantasia* of a certain type of activity as good, and becomes able to conceptualize that type of activity as excellent, fine activity, the main thing he gains is the ability to deliberate appropriately, subsuming particular actions under the universal categories that show how they promote the end. Once again, this is the account dictated by Aristotle's claim that *phronesis* is "true supposition of the end," on the interpretation I argued for in Chapter 7.5. I explained that claim on the basis of *EE* II.10 1226b20-30, where Aristotle argues that deliberation requires being aware of one's goal as such, and therefore that the deliberative part of the soul is the part that contemplates final causes. Thus what it is to have a true grasp of the ultimate *because* in the ethical realm – a true supposition of the end – is to be guided by the end in one's deliberations. The person at stage iii has the right goal, but only implicitly, and so is not yet correctly guided by it: she cannot yet connect up particular actions to the end of excellent rational activity

---

[53] Compare *EN* I.7 1098a26-b2, which says that craftsmen do not need the *because*, but only the *that*. *De Sensu* 436a19-21 says that the "more philosophical" doctors (τῶν ἰατρῶν οἱ φιλοσοφωτέρως) do engage in the study of the same first principles that engage the natural scientist; but this implies that there are many doctors who do not, and even that insofar as a doctor does study such causes he is acting not *qua* doctor but instead *qua* philosopher. After all, Aristotle can hardly mean in *Met.* VII.7 that the carpenter has a philosophical understanding of his products, although the language of form and essence does seem to imply that. We should compare Plato's claim in *Rep.* X that the carpenter looks toward the form (ἰδέα) of the bed (596b), which clearly means not that he has philosophical understanding of beds – indeed, Plato goes on to say that he merely has correct belief (δόξα, *Rep.* 602a4) – but instead that he works with an eye to their function.

[54] This will be the person with mere habit-virtue, if there is such a thing, and if not the person who is on the way to full virtue but not yet there.

[55] As to what these causes are, this is not entirely beyond dispute, but the passage we saw from *EN* I.7 very strongly suggests that they at least include the explanations of the *that* outlined in the preceding lines: explanations of the fact that *eudaimonia* is the life of excellent rational activity. (See my arguments about the reference of 'the *that*' in Chapter 7, note 58.)

(nor to more local goals) by means of excellent deliberative syllogisms. The person who has reached stage iv is precisely the person who has acquired this ability. He can say not merely (with the stage iii person) "This act of abstention was to-be-done on this occasion, and this similar action on this one," but rather, explicitly, "Temperate acts are to-be-done"; in articulating this he is guiding his deliberations by the goal of acting temperately. Thus the full syllogism would be: "Virtuous activity is the goal; acting temperately is a way of acting virtuously; therefore temperate acts are to-be-done; this particular action *a* is temperate in this circumstance; therefore *a* is to-be-done," where the last clause represents his decision.

Note that we get a version of this type of syllogism, although from a third-person perspective, in the *APo.*:

We seek the that-on-account-of-which up to this point, and we think we know something [when we have grasped this cause] . . . For example: for the sake of what did he come? In order to get the money. And that in order to pay back what he owed; and that in order not to do something unjust. (*APo.* 85b27-32)[56]

The person with *phronesis* – the person who has reached stage iv and has an intellectual grasp of the end – knows *becauses* for why his actions are to-be-done, because he can relate his actions to their cause: their final cause, namely his end. It is good to come and get the money, and thereby pay back the money, *because* acting in this way is an instance of acting justly, and therefore is a way of achieving the end, excellent activity. *Met.* I.1 equates grasping causes with having the *logos* (τὸ λόγον ἔχειν, 981b6). In the theoretical realm having a *logos* means being able to give a demonstration from one's starting-points; in the practical realm, as I argued in Chapter 7, it means being able to deliberate correctly.

If this is what it means to acquire an intellectual grasp of the starting-points of practical reason, then in moving from stage iii to stage iv one merely acquires concepts for the kind of activity one was already pursuing, and thereby becomes able to use such activity thus conceptualized to guide one's deliberations, i.e. to use it as a goal. And therefore we should reject the Intuitionist's robust account of stage iv in favor of the minimalist one: character supplies the content of the goal, and intellect merely conceptualizes it. Aristotle's discussion of *phronesis*, his analogies between practical and productive reasoning, and the contrasts he draws between practical and theoretical reasoning, all count against the Intuitionist version of the practical induction account.

A final point on this subject: it may seem that there is one major advantage to be gained by expanding the account of practical induction to include a robust final stage closer to what *nous* does in the theoretical sphere. For that would give us a clear way to reconcile all the evidence for the face-value reading of "virtue makes the goal right"

---

[56] The passage is noted in a similar context in Allen 2012, which has a very helpful discussion of the parallels between deliberation and demonstration, and an analysis of "practical knowledge" largely in accord with what I say here.

with an important complication I have hitherto ignored: Aristotle's claim that the ultimately right goal is the life of excellent contemplation (θεωρία) (*EN* X.7-8; *EE* VIII.3). Habituation in virtuous activity cannot on its own give us any experience of contemplation, and thus cannot yield an appearance of the life of contemplation as good. It might however furnish an appearance of ethically virtuous activity as good, in which intellect can somehow discern the life of contemplation as the underlying cause.[57] If this is right then *phronesis* does play a role in supplying the end: it supplies the ultimate end – the view of *eudaimonia* – for those few who recognize the life of contemplation as the highest human good. This concession to the Intellectualist would be an important one, but a very limited one too: even if intellect does provide the content of the contemplator's ultimate goal in this way, it reaches this content not as the conclusion of pure practical reasoning, but only by abstracting from a non-rational appearance furnished by character.

In fact, however, there is compelling evidence that Aristotle treats the contemplator as having the same goal at least at a general level as the person who lives the life of ethically virtuous activity. Recall that the function argument identifies the correct end as excellent activity of the rational part of the soul, a definition that applies both to the life devoted to the exercise of ethical virtue and to the life devoted to the exercise of intellectual virtue. Some reconcile this with *EN* X by arguing that both contemplators and those who live the practical life of ethically virtuous action are achieving the correct goal, although the former only "secondarily" (*EN* X.8 1178a9).[58] Although I do not think it has been noted, this interpretation gains confirmation from the *Pol.*, where Aristotle identifies the correct end as "the activity and use of excellence [ἀρετή, i.e. virtue in the broad sense that leaves open whether he has in mind character-virtue or intellectual virtue or both]" (see for example 1328a38 and 1332a9). Here he treats this as an end shared by contemplators and practical types alike, by contrast with popular but incorrect ends like military power or wealth. In speaking of the disagreement between contemplators and practical types, for example, he says,

> Let us now address those who, while they agree that the life with virtue is most choiceworthy, disagree about the use of it (περὶ τῆς χρήσεως αὐτοῦ). (*Pol.* 1325a16-17; cf. 1324a25-28)

The implication is that both share the same goal: excellent, fine activity – "the life with virtue." Aristotle does imply that they disagree about the goal, at 1324a34, so perhaps we need here to distinguish between generic and specific goals. If this is right, then even contemplators get their generic goal through correct habituation. Intellect cannot work out that excellent rational activity is to-be-pursued – that task is reserved

---

[57] Here is one way in which this might work, perhaps implied by the final chapter of the *EE*: ethical habituation molds the non-rational part to defer to reason, and to take pleasure in letting it lead; one then grasps through *nous* that this is good *because* the very best life is the life of pure (vs. practical) exercise of the rational part – the true flourishing of this part of the soul.

[58] See for example Purinton 1998; I was persuaded of the merits of the view by an unpublished paper by Hille Paakkunainen.

for character – but it can show that the best and finest species of excellent rational activity is contemplation.

And therefore, to return at last to the main claim of this chapter and the previous, the contents of our goals are at least largely a function of *phantasia*. Despite all the differences between wishes and passions, and despite the mediation of intellect in particular, when Aristotle says that we wish for the apparent good, just as much as when he says that appetite is for the apparent good, he means that we desire what we pleasurably represent through *phantasia*, and he means that this representation is derived from previous pleasurable perceptions.

Conclusion: Aristotle's Practical Empiricism

In Chapter 1 we saw that practical intellect has two roles, detailed in our passage 1c from the *MA*: identifying something as an end – the "premise of the good" – and determining the means to achieving it – the "premise of the possible." We have now seen in Part III that intellect depends on evaluative *phantasia* – and thereby, indirectly, on pleasurable perception – at both stages.

Identifying an end is the result of a process parallel to induction. The thought "x is a triangle" is made possible by the perception of many triangles, and the eventual grasping, mediated by *phantasia*, of the universal property they all have in common. So too, I have argued, the thought "x is the good, i.e. the end" is made possible by the *pleasurable* perception of many activities, and the eventual grasping, mediated by *phantasia*, of the universal property they all have in common. On an empiricist epistemology like this, one will not come to make intellectual judgments about triangularity which apply to things radically different from triangles one has actually seen, because it is those triangles which inform the concept. (More precisely, one might come to do so, but this would be an abnormal process; it is not the natural, correct way to reach such judgments.) Neither, the analogy shows, will one come to make intellectual judgments about goodness which apply to things radically different from things one has actually pleasurably perceived, because it is those things which inform the concept. That is why habituation is so important: the perceptions it involves determine one's eventual conception of the good. This is how we should understand Aristotle's idea that habituation shapes character, which in turn determines one's *phantasia* of the end, which in turn forms the basis of wish.

Deliberation, meanwhile, the rational process that generates the premise(s) of the possible, makes use of *phantasmata* as it proceeds: we conjure up images of the various options and choose one we imagine pleasurably. Thus just as one cannot make calculations about triangularity without imagining a triangle, which in turn requires having perceived triangles in the past, one cannot make calculations that a certain action is to be done without pleasurably imagining that type of action, which in turn requires having pleasurably perceived that type of action in the past. This is a second reason why habituation is so important: without past pleasurable perception of one's own virtuous activity, one cannot pleasurably imagine the virtuous option in a given episode of deliberation, and therefore cannot be counted on to decide upon it.

Thus Aristotle is a thoroughgoing empiricist in the practical realm as well as in the theoretical: practical thought depends on practical *phantasia*, and thereby ultimately on practical perception. And thus we have seen that his moral psychology has the two features I mentioned in the Introduction as the most radical consequences of my arguments in the book.

First, Aristotelian practical thought is far less sovereign and self-standing than its Kantian or Platonic counterparts. Although it is superior to non-rational cognition, and although non-rational cognition exists in us partly for its sake, reason does not rule in us as an independent force inserted as it were from above (on the model for example of Plato's *Timaeus*). Instead, it is dependent on non-rational cognition, both in genesis and in operation.

Second, Aristotelian practical thought has its content largely determined by pleasure. Aristotle says that "*The whole affair* both in virtue and in the political art is about pleasures and pains" (*EN* II.3 1105a10-12, emphasis mine). We have seen that not only non-rational character-virtue but also *phronesis*, not only non-rational passions but also wishes and decisions, all depend on past pleasurable perceptions. Therefore we should take it that this is precisely what he means.

Bibliography

Ancient and Medieval Works

ALEXANDER OF APHRODISIAS, *De Anima Liber cum Mantissa*, ed. I. Bruns (Berlin, 1887).
——*De Fato*, ed. and trans. R.W. Sharples (London, 1983).
ARISTOTLE, *Ars. Rhetorica*, ed. W.D. Ross (Oxford, 1959).
——*De Anima*, ed. and trans. R.D. Hicks (Cambridge, 1907).
——*De Anima*, ed. W.D. Ross (Oxford, 1961).
——*De Motu Animalium*, ed. and trans. M.C. Nussbaum (Princeton, 1978).
——*Ethica Nicomachea*, ed. I. Bekker (Berlin, 1831).
——*Ethica Nicomachea*, ed. I. Bywater (Oxford, 1894).
——*Eudemian Ethics*, ed. and trans. H. Rackham (Cambridge, MA, 1935).
——*Parva Naturalia*, ed. W.D. Ross (Oxford, 1995).
——*Physica*, ed. W.D. Ross (Oxford, 1956).
——*Politica*, ed. W.D. Ross (Oxford, 1957).
——*Topica et Sophistici elenchi*, ed. W.D. Ross (Oxford, 1958).
ASPASIUS, *In Ethica Nicomachea quae supersunt commentaria*, ed. G. Heylbut (Berlin, 1889).
EUSTRATIUS, *Eustratii et Michaelis et Anonyma in Ethica Nicomachea Commentaria*, ed. G. Heylbut (Berlin, 1892).
MICHAEL OF EPHESUS, *In Libros De Partibus Animalium, De Animalium Motione, De Animalium Incessu Commentaria*, ed. M. Hayduck (Berlin, 1904).
PHILOPONUS, *In Aristotelis De Anima Libros Commentaria*, ed. M. Hayduck (Berlin, 1897).
PLATO, *Opera*, ed. J. Burnet (Oxford, 1900–1907).
SIMPLICIUS, *In Libros De Anima Commentaria*, ed. M. Hayduck (Berlin, 1882).
THEMISTIUS, *In Libro Aristotelis De Anima Paraphrasis*, ed. R. Heinze (Berlin, 1899).
THOMAS AQUINAS, *In Aristotelis librum De anima commentarium*, ed. A.M. Pirotta, 2nd edition (Turin, 1959).
——*In decem libros ethicorum Aristotelis ad Nicomachum expositio*, ed. A.M. Pirotta and R. Spiazzi (Turin, 1934).

Modern works

D. Achtenberg (2002), *Cognition of Value in Aristotle's Ethics: Promise of Enrichment, Threat of Destruction* (Albany).
D.J. Allan (1952), *The Philosophy of Aristotle* (Oxford).
——(1953), "Aristotle's Account of the Origin of Moral Principles," *Actes du XIe Congrès Internationale de Philosophie*, Vol. XII, 120–7; reprinted in J. Barnes, M. Schofield, and R. Sorabji (eds.), *Essays on Aristotle*, vol. 2, *Ethics and Politics* (London, 1977), 72–78.
J.V. Allen (2012), "Practical and theoretical knowledge in Aristotle," in D. Henry and K.M. Nielsen (eds.), *Bridging the Gap between Aristotle's Science and Ethics* (Cambridge).

G.E.M. Anscombe (1965), "Thought and Action in Aristotle. What is Practical Truth?" in R. Bambrough, (ed.), *New Essays on Plato and Aristotle* (London), 143–58.

J.L. Austin (1961), *Philosophical Papers* (Oxford).

J.I. Beare (1906), *Greek Theories of Elementary Cognition from Alcmaeon to Aristotle* (Oxford).

D. Bostock (1988), "Pleasure and Activity in Aristotle's Ethics," *Phronesis* 33: 251–72.

S. Broadie (1991), *Ethics With Aristotle* (Oxford).

——(1998), "Interpreting Aristotle's Directions," in J. Gentzler (ed.), *Method in Ancient Philosophy* (Oxford), 291–306.

——and C. Rowe (2002), *Aristotle, Nicomachean Ethics: Translation, Introduction, and Commentary*, (Oxford).

J. Burnet (1900), *The Ethics of Aristotle* (London).

M. Burnyeat (1980), "Aristotle on Learning to be Good," in Rorty (1980), 69–91.

S. Cashdollar (1973), "Aristotle's Account of Incidental Perception," *Phronesis* 18: 156–75.

V. Caston (1996), "Why Aristotle needs Imagination," *Phronesis* 51: 20–55.

——(1998), "Aristotle and the Problem of Intentionality," *Philosophy and Phenomenological Research* 58: 249–98.

D. Charles (1984), *Aristotle's Philosophy of Action* (London).

——(1995), "Aristotle and Modern Realism," in R. Heinaman (ed.), *Aristotle and Moral Realism* (London), 135–72.

——(2006), "Aristotle's Desire," in V. Hirnoven, T. Holpainen, and M. Tuominen (eds.), *Mind and Modality: Studies in the History of Philosophy in Honour of Simo Knuuttila* (Leiden).

——(2009), "*Nicomachean Ethics* VII.3: Varieties of *Akrasia*," in C. Natali (ed.), *Aristotle: Nicomachean Ethics Book VII, Symposium Aristotelicum* (Oxford), 41–71.

W. Charlton (1991), trans., *On Aristotle on the Intellect (de Anima 3.4–6)* (Ithaca).

J. Cook Wilson (1879), *Aristotelian Studies I: On the Structure of the Seventh Book of the Nicomachean Ethics, Chapters I–X* (Oxford).

J.M. Cooper (1975), *Reason and Human Good in Aristotle* (Cambridge); reprinted Indianapolis, 1986.

——(1982), "Aristotle on Natural Teleology," in M. Schofield and M.C. Nussbaum (eds.), *Language and Logos* (Cambridge), 196–222.

——(1996a), "An Aristotelian Theory of the Emotions," in Rorty (ed.) (1996), 238–57.

——(1996b), "Reason, Moral Virtue and Moral Value," in M. Frede and G. Striker (eds.), *Rationality in Greek Thought* (Oxford), 81–114.

——(1998), "Some Remarks on Aristotle's Moral Psychology," *Southern Journal of Philosophy* 27 Supplement: 25–42; reprinted in Cooper (ed.) (1999), *Reason and Emotion* (Princeton), 27–251.

——(2010), "Political Community and the Highest Good," in J.G. Lennox and R. Bolton (eds.), *Being, Nature, and Life: Essays in Honor of Allan Gotthelf* (Cambridge), 212–64.

K. Corcilius (2011), "Aristotle's Definition of Non-rational Pleasure and Pain and Desire," in J. Miller (ed.), *Aristotle's* Nicomachean Ethics: *A Critical Guide* (Cambridge), 117–43.

N.O. Dahl (1984), *Practical Reason, Aristotle, and Weakness of the Will* (Minneapolis).

D. Davidson (1970), "How is weakness of the will possible?" in *Moral Concepts*, J. Feinberg (ed.).

R. Demos (1961–2), "Some Remarks on Aristotle's Doctrine of Practical Reason," *Philosophy and Phenomenological Research* 22: 153–62.

P. Destrée (2007), "Aristotle on the Causes of *Akrasia*," in C. Bobonich and P. Destrée (eds.), *Akrasia in Greek Philosophy: from Socrates to Plotinus* (Leiden and Boston), 139–66.
J. Dow (2009), "Feeling Fantastic: Emotions and Appearances in Aristotle," *OSAP* 37: 143–75.
F. Dretske (1981), *Knowledge and the Flow of Information* (Cambridge, MA).
T. Engberg-Pedersen (1983), *Aristotle's Theory of Moral Insight* (Oxford).
S. Everson (1997), *Aristotle on Perception* (Oxford).
F. Feldman (1988), "Two Questions about Pleasure," in D. Austin (ed.), *Philosophical Analysis: A Defense by Example* (Dordrecht), 59–81.
G. Flaubert (1992), *Madame Bovary*, trans. G. Wall (London).
W.W. Fortenbaugh (1964), "Aristotle's Conception of Moral Virtue and Its Perceptive Role," *Transactions and Proceedings of the American Philological Association* 95: 77–87.
——(1970), "Aristotle's *Rhetoric* on Emotions," *Archiv für Geschichte der Philosophie* 52: 40–70.
——(2002), *Aristotle on Emotion*, 2nd edition (London).
K. Foster, S. Humphries and R. McInerny trans., (1994), *Aquinas: Commentary on Aristotle's De Anima* (South Bend).
A.P. Fotinus (1979), *De Anima of Alexander of Aphrodisias: a translation and commentary* (Washington D.C.).
D. Frede (1992), "The Cognitive Role of *Phantasia* in Aristotle," in M.C. Nussbaum and A.O. Rorty (eds.), 279–98.
M. Frede (1986), "The Stoic doctrine of the affections of the soul," in J. Schofield and G. Striker (eds.), *The Norms of Nature: Studies in Hellenistic Ethics* (Cambridge), 93–110.
——(1996), "Aristotle's Rationalism," in M. Frede and G. Striker (eds.), *Rationality in Greek Thought* (Oxford), 157–73.
C. Freeland (1994), "Aristotle on Perception, Appetition, and Self-Motion," in M.L. Gill and J.G. Lennox (eds.), *Self-Motion* (Princeton), 35–63.
D.J. Furley (1980), "Self-Movers," in Rorty (ed.) (1980), 55–68.
D. Gallop (1991), *Aristotle on Sleep and Dreams* (Peterborough, Ontario; reprinted Warminster 1996).
R.A. Gauthier and J.Y. Jolif (1958–9), *L'Éthique à Nicomaque: Introduction, Traduction et Commentaire*, 3 vols. (Louvain).
T.S. Gendler (2008), "Alief and Belief," *Journal of Philosophy* 105: 634–63.
J.C.B. Gosling and C.C.W. Taylor (1982), *The Greeks on Pleasure* (Oxford).
A. Gotthelf (1989), "The Place of the Good in Aristotle's Natural Teleology," *Proceedings of the Boston Area Colloquium in Ancient Philosophy* 4, 113–39.
A. Grant (1874), *The Ethics of Aristotle*, 2 vols., (London).
L.H.G. Greenwood (1909), *Aristotle, Nicomachean Ethics Book VI* (Cambridge; reprinted New York, 1973).
R. Hackforth (1945), *Plato's Examination of Pleasure: A Translation of the Philebus, with Introduction and Commentary* (Cambridge).
A. Hackmann, J. Bennett-Levy, and E.A. Holmes (eds.) (2011), *The Oxford Guide to Imagery in Cognitive Therapy* (Oxford).
D.W. Hamlyn (1968), *De Anima, Books II and III*, translation and commentary (Oxford).
W.F.R. Hardie (1968), *Aristotle's Ethical Theory* (Oxford).
M. Heath (2008), "Aristotle on Natural Slavery," *Phronesis* 53: 243–70.
R.D. Hicks (ed.) (1907), *Aristotle, De Anima* (Cambridge).

E.A. Holmes and A. Mathews (2010), "Mental Imagery in emotion and emotional disorders," *Clinical Psychology Review* 30: 349–62.
S. Hudson (1981), "Reason and Motivation in Aristotle," *Canadian Journal of Philosophy* 11: 111–35.
T. Hurka (2001), *Virtue, Vice and Value* (New York).
R. Hursthouse (1991), "Virtue Theory and Abortion," *Philosophy and Public Affairs* 20: 223–46.
——(2003), "Virtue Ethics," *Stanford Encyclopedia of Philosophy*, revised 2007.
T. Irwin (1975), "Aristotle on Reason, Desire and Virtue," *Journal of Philosophy* 73: 567–78.
——(1990), *Aristotle's First Principles* (Oxford).
——(1998), "Some Rational Aspects of Incontinence," *The Southern Journal of Philosophy* s.v. 28: 49–88.
——(1999), *Aristotle, Nicomachean Ethics*, translation and commentary, 2nd edition (Indianapolis).
H.H. Joachim (1951), *Aristotle: The Nicomachean Ethics* (Oxford).
T. Johansen (forthcoming), *The Powers of Aristotle's Soul* (Oxford).
C. Kahn (1966), "Sensation and Consciousness in Aristotle's Psychology," *Archiv für Geschichte der Philosophie* 48: 43–81.
——(1992), "Aristotle on Thinking," in Nussbaum and Rorty (eds.), 359–79.
S. Keller (2007), "Virtue Ethics is Self-Effacing," *Australasian Journal of Philosophy* 85: 221–31.
G. Kennedy (1991), *Aristotle, On Rhetoric: A Theory of Civic Discourse* (Oxford).
A. Kenny (1966), "The Practical Syllogism and Incontinence," *Phronesis* 11: 163–84.
——(1979), *Aristotle's Theory of the Will* (London).
J.-L. Labarrière (2004), "Désir, sensation et altération," in A. Laks and M. Rashed (eds.), *Études sur le De motu animalium* (Lille), 149–65.
S. Leighton (1996), "Aristotle and the Emotions," in Rorty (ed.) (1996), 206–37.
C. Litzinger (1964), trans., *Aquinas: Commentary on Aristotle's Nicomachean Ethics* (Chicago).
A.A. Long and D.N. Sedley (1987), *The Hellenistic philosophers* (2 volumes) (Cambridge).
H. Lorenz (2006), *The Brute Within: Appetitive Desire in Plato and Aristotle* (Oxford).
——(2009), "Virtue of Character in Aristotle's *Nicomachean Ethics*," *Oxford Studies in Ancient Philosophy* 37: 177–212.
J. McDowell (1998), "Some Issues in Aristotle's Moral Psychology," in McDowell, *Mind, Value and Reality* (Cambridge, MA), 23–40.
D. Modrak (1986), "Φαντασία Reconsidered," *Archiv für Geschichte der Philosophie* 68 (1986), 47–69.
——(1987), *Aristotle, The Power of Perception* (Chicago).
J. Moss (2006), "Pleasure and Illusion in Plato," *Philosophy and Phenomenological Research* 62: 503–35.
——(2008), "Appearances and Calculations: Plato's Division of the Soul," *OSAP* 34: 35–68.
——(2009), "*Akrasia* and Perceptual Illusion," *Archiv für Geschichte der Philosophie* 91: 119–56.
——(2010), "Aristotle's Non-Trivial, Non-Insane View that Everyone Always Desires Things under the Guise of the Good," in S. Tenenbaum (ed.), *Desire, Practical Reason and the Good* (Oxford), 65–81.
——(2011), "'Virtue Makes the Goal Right': Virtue and *Phronesis* in Aristotle's Ethics," *Phronesis* 65: 204–61.
——(2012), "Pictures and Passions in the *Philebus* and *Timaeus*," in R. Barney, T. Brennan, and C. Brittain (eds.), *Plato and the Divided Self* (Cambridge), 259–80.
T. Nagel (1970), *The Possibility of Altruism* (Princeton).
A. Nehamas (1992), "Pity and Fear in the *Rhetoric* and the *Poetics*," in Rorty (1992), 291–314.

P. Nieuwenburg (2002), "Emotions and Perception in Aristotle's *Rhetoric*," *Australasian Journal of Philosophy* 80: 86–100.

M.C. Nussbaum (1978), *Aristotle's De Motu Animalium* (Princeton).

——(1996) "Aristotle on the Emotions and Rational Persuasion," in Rorty (1996), 303–21.

——and H. Putnam (1992), "Changing Aristotle's Mind," in Nussbaum and Rorty (1992), 27–56.

——and A.O. Rorty (eds.) (1992), *Essays on Aristotle's De Anima* (Oxford).

G. Oddie (2005), *Value, Reality, and Desire* (Oxford).

M. Pakaluk and G. Pearson (eds.) (2011), *Moral Psychology and Human Action in Aristotle* (Oxford).

M. Pickavé and J. Whiting (2008), "*Nicomachean Ethics* VII.3 on Akratic 'ignorance'," *Oxford Studies in Ancient Philosophy* 34: 323–71.

A. Price (1995), *Mental Conflict* (London and New York).

J. Prinz (2004), *Gut Reactions* (Oxford).

J. Purinton (2008), "Aristotle's Definition of Happiness (*NE* I.7, 1098a16–18)," *Oxford Studies in Ancient Philosophy* 16: 259–97.

C.D.C. Reeve (1992), *Practices of Reason: Aristotle's Nicomachean Ethics* (Oxford).

H.S. Richardson (1992), "Desire and the Good in *De Anima*," Nussbaum and Rorty (1992), 381–453.

G. Richardson Lear (2006), "Aristotle on Moral Virtue and the Fine," in R. Kraut (ed.), *The Blackwell Guide to Aristotle's* Nicomachean Ethics (Oxford).

A.O. Rorty (ed.) (1980), *Essays on Aristotle's Ethics* (Berkeley and Los Angeles).

——(ed.) (1996), *Essays on Aristotle's Rhetoric* (Berkeley).

W.D. Ross (1949), *Aristotle* (5th edition) (London).

——(1961), *Aristotle: De Anima* (Oxford).

B. Russell (1945), *A History of Western Philosophy* (New York).

G. Santas (1969), "Aristotle on Practical Inference, the Explanation of Action, and *Akrasia*," *Phronesis* 14: 162–89.

S. Schiffer (1976), "A Paradox of Desire," *American Philosophical Quarterly* 13: 195–203.

M. Schofield (1978), "Aristotle on the Imagination," in G.E.R. Lloyd and G.E.L. Owen (eds.), *Aristotle on Mind and the Senses: Proceedings of the Seventh Symposium Aristotelicum* (Cambridge), 99–130; reprinted in Rorty (1992), 249–77.

——(2011), "*Phantasia* in *De Motu Animalium*," in M. Pakaluk and G. Pearson (eds.), *Moral Psychology and Human Action in Aristotle* (Oxford), 119–34.

H. Segvic (2002), "Aristotle's Metaphysics of Action," in *Logical Analysis and History of Philosophy, Volume 5: Focus: Medieval Philosophy*: 23–53.

J. Sihvola (1996), "Emotional animals: do Aristotelian emotions require beliefs?" *Apeiron* 29: 105–44.

A.D. Smith (1996), "Character and Intellect in Aristotle's *Ethics*," *Phronesis* 51: 56–74.

R. Sorabji (1973–4), "Aristotle on the Role of Intellect in Virtue," *Proceedings of the Aristotelian Society*, n.s. 74: 107–129; reprinted in Rorty (1980), 201–20.

——(1993), *Animal Minds and Human Morals: The Origins of the Western Debate* (Ithaca).

——(1996), "Rationality," in M. Frede and G. Striker (eds.), *Rationality in Greek Thought* (Oxford), 311–34.

——(1972), *Aristotle On Memory, Translation and Commentary* (London).

G. Striker (1996), "Emotions in Context: Aristotle's Treatment of the Passions in the *Rhetoric* and his Moral Psychology," in Rorty (1996), 286–302.
C.C.W. Taylor (2006), *Aristotle, Nicomachean Ethics Books II–IV* (Oxford).
——(2008), "Aristotle on the Practical Intellect," in *Pleasure, Mind, and Soul: Selected Papers in Ancient Philosophy* (Oxford), 204–222; reprinted from T. Bucheim, H. Flasher, and R.A.H. King (eds.), *Kann man heute noch etwas anfangen mit Aristoteles?* (Hamburg, 2003), 142–62.
T. Tuozzo (1994), "Conceptualized and Unconceptualized Desire in Aristotle," *Journal of the History of Philosophy* 32: 525–49.
J.J. Walsh (1963), *Aristotle's Conception of Moral Weakness* (New York).
J. Walter (1874), *Die Lehre von der praktische Vernunft in der griechischen Philosophie* (Jena).
M. Wedin (1988), *Mind and Imagination in Aristotle* (New Haven).
A.R. White (1990), *The Language of Imagination* (Oxford).
J. Whiting (2002), "Locomotive Soul: the Parts of Soul in Aristotle's Scientific Works," *Oxford Studies in Ancient Philosophy* 22: 141–200.
E. Wielenberg (2000), "Pleasure as a Sign of Moral Virtue in the *Nicomachean Ethics*," *Journal of Value Inquiry* 34: 439–40.
D. Wiggins (1975), "Deliberation and Practical Reason," in Rorty (1980), 221–40.
B. Williams (1981), "Internal and External Reasons," in Williams, *Moral Luck* (Cambridge), 101–13.
M. Woods (1982), *Aristotle: Eudemian Ethics Books I, II, and VIII* (Oxford).
J. Yurdin (2009), "Aristotelian Imagination and the Explanation of Behavior," in *Ancient Perspectives on Aristotle's De Anima*, G. Van Riel (ed.) (Leuven), 71–88.
E. Zeller (1897), *Aristotle and the Earlier Peripatetics*, 2 vols., trans. B.F.C. Costelloe and J.H. Muirhead (London).

Index

Achtenberg, D. 32 n.17, 37 n.34, 42 n.43, 69 n.1, 159 n.15, 187 n.77, 189 n.80, 201, 207 n.12, 227 n.51
action *see* locomotion
akrasia 7, 18, 19, 94, 170, 100–33 *passim* 225–6
    illusion account of 118–21
Alexander of Aphrodisias 17, 35, 117
alief xiii
Allan, D.J. 157 n.10, 174 n.51, 179 n.59, 191, 224 n.41
Allen, J.V. 158 n.12, 231 n.56
anger 26 n.8, 69, 73–6, 78–83, 85, 88–9, 95, 99, 118, 193, 206–7
animals
    appetites 40
    cognition 3, 6, 12, 19, 29–31, 37–42, 54–6, 56 n.23, 61–5, 72–4, 89, 92–4, 97, 105 n.8, 137–8, 145–6, 154, 181, 205–6, 210 n.19, 220–1
    passions 93
Anscombe, G.E.M. ix n.2, 18 n.29
apparent good *passim*
    defined 63–4
    extensionalist reading 6–8, 10, 12–14, 18, 20, 22, 32–3
    and *phantasia* ix–xi, 48–9, 63–4
appetite (*epithumia*) 30, 38, 40–1, 45, 46 n.50, 69, 72 n.6, 80 n.26, 82, 85–6, 88, 93, 100, 101 n.3, 103–5, 110–11, 118–20, 122–8, 132–3, 139, 147–8, 168–9, 225–7
    for the apparent good 4–9, 13–16, 18–21, 33, 46 n.50, 104, 110
    human vs. animal 40
    see also *akrasia*; parts of the soul
Aquinas, Thomas 3 n.3, 32 n.20, 43, 130 n.49, 139, 150, 168 n.37
Aspasius 72 n.10, 80 n.26, 98 n.53, 178 n.58
assent 92–8, 116–19, 149, 224, 227
Austin, J.L. 132

Beare, J.I. 37 n.35
belief (*doxa*)
    and *phantasia* 96–8, 142–3, 223–6
    role in passions *see* passions, role of belief in and starting-points 123–7
    see also assent; wish
Bostock, D. 203–5, 212 n.24, 215
boulêsis see wish

Broadie, S. 30, 32 n.17, 101 n.3, 102, 131, 152 n.24, 157, 182 n.65, 183 n.67, 187, 190 n.83, 203 n.5
Burnet, J. 159 n.15, 169 n.39, 178 n.58, 186, 201, 206 n.11, 222 n.39, 227 n.51
Burnyeat, M. 178 n.58, 187 n.76, 201–2, 209, 225 n.46
Bywater, I. 3 n.2, 180 n.62, 193 n.89

cake 110–31, 147–8, 226
Cashdollar, S. 37 n.36, 40 n.41
Caston, V. 50 n.6, 52 n.12, 54 n.20, 64 n.34
character 39, 64, 72 n.6, 75, 80 n.25, 152, 155, 157–61, 163–74, 175–9, 182–3, 186, 188, 191–4, 197–8, 200–2, 206–7, 211, 224–5, 227–8, 231–3, 234–5
    see also habituation; virtue
Charles, D. 6 n.7, 17 n.26, 32 n.17, 36 n.30, 45 n.48, 48 n.1, 101 n.1, 103 n.7, 126 n.45, 131 n.50, 131 n.51, 140 n.4, 220 n.36, 226, 237
Charlton, W. 31 n.16
cognition (*krisis*)
    defined 3–4
    evaluative 3–21, 34–5, 41–7; *see also* pleasure, as cognition of value
    instrumental 10–11, 13–15, 17–20, 23, 28–9, 50, 62
    pleasurable 14–15, 22–3, 26–9; *see also* perception, pleasurable
    practical vs. theoretical 9–10, 17, 22–3, 27–8, 46; *see also* cognition, evaluative; practical reasoning; ends, cognition of; perception; *phantasia*; rational vs. non-rational; thought
cognitive therapy xiii
common sense 32, 114 n.25, 145, 214
    see also perceptibles, common
consciousness 213–15
constituent means 196–7
continence *see enkrateia*
Cook Wilson, J. 102
Cooper, J.M. 30, 34, 69 n.1, 90 n.38, 157, 158 n.11–12, 158 n.14, 160 n.18, 171 n.44, 175 n.52, 179 n.59, 181 n.63, 184 n.72, 187 n.76, 188 n.78, 190, 210 n.19, 222 n.38, n.40, 224 n.41
Corcilius 6, 7, 30, 32, 44
craft (*technê*) 153 n.1, 184–5, 187, 228–30

Dahl, N.O. 101 n.2, 102, 122, 131, 157 n.9, 158 n.11, 190 n.82, 201 n.2, 222 n.38
Davidson, D. ix n.2, 132
decision (*prohairesis*) 5, 45, 66, 119, 122, 124, 129 n.48, 138–40, 162, 165–7, 170–1, 175, 177, 194, 223, 225–6
  in the *de Anima* 124 n.41, 138 n.2, 162
  and *phantasia* 148–52
deduction 144, 156, 189, 220
  see also *phantasia*, role in
deliberation 175–87, 229–31
  as determining the mean 192, 194–6
  not of ends 156, 177–8, 197; see also constituent means; starting-points
  and *phantasia* 61, 95–6, 105 n.9, 144–52, 234–5
  and pleasure 151–2
  Williams' account of 191 n.85
Demos, R. 45 n.48
desire (*orexis*)
  for the good or apparent good 3–9, 19–20, 227
  relation to evaluative cognition 19, 36
  role in locomotion 9–20
  see also appetite, decision, rational vs. non-rational, wish
Destrée, P. 17 n.26, 48 n.1, 102 n.6, 105 n.9, 120 n.33, 129 n.48
Dow, J. 69 n.2, 77 n.20, 88 n.33, 90 n.38
doxa see belief
dreams x, 51, 53, 64 n.34, 70, 73, 78, 86, 87, 90–1, 107, 114, 115–16, 126 n.44
Dretske, F. 39 n.40

emotion see passion
empiricism xi, 234
  see also induction; practical empiricism
ends (*telé*)
  cognition of 49–62, 199, 221–33
  and the good 33–4
  see also constituent means; Goal passages; starting-points
Engberg-Pedersen, T. 164 n.23, 189 n.81, 201, 220 n.36, 224 n.42
enkrateia 19, 65, 101, 103–4, 106, 118, 225–6
Epictetus 92, n.43
epithumia see appetite
euboulia (deliberative excellence) 180–2
eudaimonia 155, 163, 178–9, 184, 196–7, 200, 228–32
Eustratius 72, 178 n.58
Everson, S. 40 n.41, 50 n.6, 51 n.10, 52 n.12, 97 n.50, 108 n.17, 214 n.27
expectation (*elpis*) 26, 56 n.23, 58–60, 71, 75, 78, 79–83, 81 n.27, 85–6, 120 n.32, 147–8, 202–3, 206, 220 n.37
experience (*empeiria*) 153–4, 178, 185–7, 196, 200–1, 220–1, 228–30

fear 25, 38, 60, 69–70, 74–7, 79 n.23, 80, 82–3, 85–7, 90–1, 93–4, 98, 115, 148, 206–8
Feldman, F. 209 n.14
fine (*kalon*) see pleasure in the
Flaubert, G. 217 n.31
Fortenbaugh, W.W. 69 n.2, 72–4, 75 n.14, 159 n.15
Foster, K. 139
Frede, D. 61 n.31, 91 n.39, 142 n.5, 146–7, 154 n.5
Frede, M. 42 n.42, 89 n.36, 92 n.43
Freeland, C. 17 n.26, 38 n.17, 48 n.1
Furley, D.J. 55

Gallop, D. 97 n.50, 107 n.13, 116, 126 n.44
Gauthier, R.A. 157 n.10, 162 n.21, 169 n.39, 180 n.61, 182 n.65, 196 n.96, 238
Gendler, T.S. xiii n.5, 94 n.46, 112 n.22
Goal passages 157–8, 163, 170, 173–4, 176, 190, 193–4
good
  cognition of see cognition, evaluative
  perception of see perception, evaluative
  thought of derived from *phantasia* 46–7, 139–41, 144–52, 227–8, 234–5
  without qualification (*haplós*) 4, 7–8, 16, 105 n.10, 108–12, 119–20, 125, 129–30, 147
  see also apparent good, desire for the; ends, and the
Gosling, J.C.B. 203 n.5, 212 n.24
Gotthelf 33 n.23, 34
Grant, A. 32, 130 n.49, 180 n.62
Greenwood, L.H.G. 129 n.48, 157, 168 n.36, 182 n.65, 183 n.66, 190 n.82, 192 n.88, 197, 201 n.2, 222 n.38, 222 n.39, 224 n.42

habituation
  and the goal 178–9, 234–5
  as non-intellectual 158 n.14, 171–2
  and pleasure 201–3, 206–11, 219
  as practical induction 155, 200–1, 219–22, 225, 227–8, 230, 234–5
  see also virtue, habituated
Hackforth, R. 85 n.31
Hamlyn, D.W. 32 n.20, 51 n.9, 145 n.13
Hardie, W.F.R. 157, 183 n.67, 187, 191 n.84, 218 n.33, 222 n.38, 224 n.41
hatred 79 n.22, 81 n.27
Heath, M. 11 n.16, 56 n.23, 73 n.12
hedonism 66, 141, 150, 152
Hicks, R.D. 97 n.50, 127 n.46, 143 n.7, 144 n.8, 145 n.10, 145 n.13, 150
Holmes, E.A. xiii n.5, 107 n.12
hope (*elpis*) see expectation
Hudson, S. 17 n.26, 18 n.29, 48 n.1
Hume, D. 9 n.13, 10 n.15, 66 n.36, 94, 158, 216
Humean theory of motivation 10

Humean theory of practical reasoning 158–60, 163–4, 179, 191, 195
Hurka, T. 219 n.34
Hursthouse, R. 196

illusion
  evaluative 100, 108–12
  perceptual 53, 90, 97, 100, 106–8, 114–15
  see also *akrasia*, Illusion account of; *phantasia*, role in
imagination 50, 63, 71, 86, 90–1, 94, 108, 148–9, 221
incontinence see *akrasia*
induction 153–7, 159, 163, 190, 200–1, 203, 207, 219, 220–3, 227 n.50, 227–9, 231, 234
  see also *phantasia*, role in
intellect see *nous*
Irwin, T. 6, 7 n.10, 14 n.21, 32 n.18, 37 n.33, 50 n.4, 57 n.25, 61 n.31, 101 n.2, 124, 131, 157, 158 n.11–12, 164 n.23–24, 165 n.26, 29, 167 n.33, 172 n.46, 174 n.51, 175 n.52, 176 n.55, 178 n.57, 185 n.73, 196–7

Joachim, H.H. 101 n.2, 131, 157, 183 n.66, 224 n.41
Johansen, T. 57 n.24, 154 n.5

Kahn, C. 37 n.35, 37 n.36, 214 n.27
Keller, S. 219 n.34
Kennedy, G. 75 n.15, 120 n.32
Kenny, A. 101 n.1, 122, 131 n.50, 194 n.90, 196 n.94
krisis see cognition

Labarrière, J.-L. 11 n.17
Leighton, S. 69 n.2
Litzinger, C. 168 n.37
locomotion 9–17, 23–8, 48–64, 138–40, 150–1, 205–6
  and action 9 n.14
  see also *phantasia*, role in
Long, A.A. 89 n.37, 117 n.29
Lorenz, H. 37, 50 n.4, n.6, 55, 56 n.23, 57 n.25, 60–2, 72 n.8, 85 n.31, 86 n.32, 96 n.48, 113 n.23, 131 n.51, 149 n.18, 164 n.23, 164 n.24, 165 n.27, 165 n.29, 168 n.38, 169

McDowell, J. 101 n.2, 111, 129–31, 148 n.17, 157, 192, 196, 197 n.96, 227 n.51
mean (ethical) 166, 168, 192–8; see also *phronesis*, determines the
medicine 186–7, 229, 230 n.53
megalopsuchia 216 n.30, 218
melancholics 106–7
memory 38, 42 n.42, 51, 58–60, 62–3, 71, 78–9, 81–3, 143, 146, 153–4, 202–3, 219–21

Michael of Ephesus 25 n.6
Madame Bovary 217–18
Modrak, D. 38 n.37, 50 n.4, 55, 57 n.25, 61 n.32, 114 n.25, 126 n.44
motivational internalism 8–9

Nagel, T. 9 n.12
natural slaves 73–4 n.2
Nehamas, A. 69 n.1
Nieuwenburg, P. 69 n.1, 71 n.4
nous
  broad sense (intellect) 11–12, 105 n.10, 175; see also thought
  practical 176 n.53, 182 n.65, 189–90, 195–6, 222, 228, 232 n.57
  theoretical (narrow sense) 153–8, 189, 200 175, 222
Nussbaum, M.C. 11 n.17, 11 n.18, 24 n.1, 37, 50 n.6, 51 n.9, 54, 60, 69 n.2, 70 n.3, 74 n.13, 90 n.38

Oddie, G. 34 n.25

parts of the soul 71–4, 93, 98, 126, 173, 188, 210
  and virtue 158–9, 164–5, 167–9
  appetitive (in Plato) 46 n.50, 86–7
  passionate 71–4
passions
  characterized 75–84
  role of belief in (doxastic interpretation of) 70–1, 77–94
  Stoic account see Stoics
  see also anger; *phantasia*, role in; fear; pity; pride; shame; *thumos*
perceptibles
  common 37, 41, 43, 53–5, 58, 65, 88; see also common sense
  incidental 37 n.35, 39–40, 41, 53–5, 56 n.23, 58, 65, 88, 89
  proper 37–8, 53–5, 58, 65, 88
perception
  contents of 41–2, 88–9
  evaluative 30–45, 88–9, 209–10; see also pleasure, as cognition of value
  pleasurable see pleasure, perceptual
  propositional structure 88
  second-order 213–18; see also perceptibles; *phantasia*, derived from
phantasia
  and the apparent good see apparent good
  as cognition 3
  calculative/rational/deliberative 129 n.48, 105 n.9, 140, 145–52
  defined ('the basic conception') 50–7
  derived from perception 6 n.8, 22, 51 n.9, 52–7

phantasia (cont.)
  of ends *see* ends, cognition of
  evaluative/practical 57–64
  general/generalised 120, 221–3, 225–7
  role in deduction 142–3
  role in deliberation 142–52
  role in illusions 106–12
  role in induction 153–4, 219
  role in locomotion 48–50, 57–63
  role in passions 69–71, 76–84
  see also belief and; decision and; good, thought of derived from; wish and
phantasma 50 n.8, 51–3, 59, 61–2, 65, 85–6, 95–6, 106, 108–12, 142–52
Philebus 36 n.31, 58–9, 78 n.21, 81 n.28, 85–6, 96, 149 n.18, 215 n.28
Philoponus 31, 36 n.30
phronesis
  architectonic 183–7
  and craft 228–30
  and deliberation 179–83, 186, 192–8
  determines the mean 192–8
  and grasp of ends 180–90, 224, 225 n.44, 228–30
Pickavé, M. 116, 121 n.34, 131 n.50, 131 n.51
pity 69, 72, 74–7, 80 n.26, 83, 91, 93, 99 n.55, 206–7
plants 3, 34, 73, 205, 214
Plato 5, 36 n.31, 106 n.11, 131 n.51, 172 n.47, 180 n.61, 210, 211, 230 n.53, 235
  on the apparent good xii–xiii
  on appetite 46 n.50, 86–7
  on passions 85–7
  on *phantasmata* 85–7, 96
  on pleasure 58, 81 n.28, 215 n.28
  on rationality 116–17
  see also Philebus; *Protagoras*; *Republic*; *Timaeus*
pleasant without qualification (*haplōs*) 7, 16, 29, 39 n.39, 108–12, 119–20, 125, 129–30, 147
pleasure
  as cognition of value 22–47
  in the fine 207–19
  intellectual 27–8, 31, 80, 203–6, 209, 211, 215
  perceptual 29–47, 59, 63–4, 79–80, 151–2, 203–6, 209–19, 234–5
  of virtue 202, 204, 207, 210–19
  see also habituation and
Practical Empiricism xi–xii, 22, 46–7, 140, 152, 234–5
practical reasoning
  parallels with theoretical 13, 141–6, 153–7, 159, 175, 200–1, 219–22, 228–9, 234
  starting-points of *see* starting-points
  see also cognition, practical vs. theoretical; deliberation

practical syllogism 14–15, 17, 29, 34–5, 101–2, 123–30, 138, 141, 149, 156–7, 159, 175, 194–5, 224, 230–1
practical wisdom *see phronesis*
praxis see action
Price, A. 46 n.50, 182 n.65
pride 76, 80, 84, 207, 210, 216–18
Prinz, J. 39 n.40
prohairesis see decision
Protagoras 102 n.5, 106 n.11, 121, 150 n.20, 173 n.49
Purinton, J. 232 n.58

rational vs. non-rational
  cognition and desire xiii, xiv, 5–10, 20, 30, 33, 42, 66, 70, 104–5, 118, 137–41, 160–2, 224–7, 234–5
  parts of soul 6, 71–74, 86, 188
  phantasia 145
  virtue 163–74
  see also akrasia, passions, thought
rationality
  and assent 92–3, 96–8, 226–7
  and appearance-scrutiny 112–18
Reeve, C.D.C. 157 n.9, 158 n.11, 184 n.72, 187, 201 n.2, 222 n.38, 224 n.43, 228
Republic 101–2, 106 n.11, 172 n.47
Richardson Lear, G. 209 n.15, 210, 215, 225 n.44
Richardson, H.S. 17 n.26, 18 n.28, 48 n.1, 54 n.19
Ross, W.D. 3 n.2, 51 n.9, 102, 121–2, 124, 145 n.13, 149
Russell, B. 218

Santas, G. 101, n.1, 102 n.6, 124 n.40
Schiffer, S. 9 n.12, 9 n.13
Schofield, M. 11 n.17, 50 n.6, 51 n.9, 54 n.19
Segvic, H. 17 n.26, 48 n.1
self-control *see enkrateia*
Sextus Empiricus 92 n.41, 97 n.49
shame 69, 72, 75–6, 80, 84, 93, 172, 207, 208–9, 216 n.30
Sihvola, J. 69 n.1, 73 n.11, 75 n.14, 95
Simplicius 18 n.28, 31
Smith, A.D. 168 n.37, 176 n.54, 210 n.20
Socrates 85, 100, 121, 130, 132
sophia see wisdom
Sorabji, R. 69 n.1, 88 n.34, 92 n.42, 98 n.53, 158 n.12, 158 n.14, 172 n.46, 179 n.59, 190 n.82, 201 n.2
starting-points (*archai*)
  of practical reasoning 17, 141–2, 155–63, 174–7, 178 n.58, 182, 189–90, 194–5, 200–1, 220, 222–31
  of theoretical reasoning 141–2, 144, 153–6, 175, 199, 220

Stoics 73, 78, 89, 92–8, 114, 116–18, 142, 143 n.7
Striker, G. 69 n.1
supposition (*hupolêpsis*) 90, 96–7, 98 n.53, 106, 143 n.7, 180–3, 224, 225 n.44, 228–30
System 1 and System 2 xiii

Taylor, C.C.W. 158 n.14, 169 n.39, 203 n.5, 212 n.24
technê see craft
telos see ends
thumos 11, 72, 73 n.11, 74, 80 n.24, 85, 89, 95, 122, 125, 162, 170, 210
Themistius 45–6, 97
theoretical reasoning *see* cognition, practical vs. theoretical; practical reasoning, parallels with; starting-points of
theória (contemplation) 27, 30–1, 80, 143, 155, 192 n.88, 204, 212, 215
  as the happy life 232–3
thought
  as a broad term 30, 60
  dependence on *phantasia* 61, 64, 95–6, 143–5; see also *phantasia*; *nous*
Timaeus 85–7, 131 n.51, 235
Tuozzo, T. 34 n.25, 36 n.30, 41, 43 n.44, 88 n.34, 226 n.49, 227

virtue
  habituated 171–3
  intellectualist account of 163–91, 194 n.90, 198–9, 201, 222–4, 227–8, 231–2
  makes the goal right 155–63, 174–9; *see also* Goal passages
  natural 111, 167–8, 170–3, 184–5, 195–6, 228
  as non-rational 163–74
  relation to decision 166
  strict 167–8, 170–3
  'with *logos*' 169
  see also pleasure of

Walsh, J.J. 102 n.6
Walter, J. 101 n.1, 158 n.13, 180 n.62
weakness of will see *akrasia*
Wedin, M. 50 n.6, 51 n.9, 54 n.20
White, A.R. 50 n.7
Whiting, J. 32 n.17, 38 n.37, 57, 116, 121 n.34, 131 n.50, 131 n.51
Wielenberg, E. 209
Wiggins, D. 101 n.2, 111, 129, 130, 131, 157 n.10, 158 n.11, 176 n.55, 192, 196–7
Williams, B. 191 n.85, 197 n.101
wisdom (*sophia*) 222, 229
wish (*boulêsis*) 17, 66, 124 n.41, 138–40, 166 n.31, 175, 198–9, 233–5
  and belief 223–7
  and the good/apparent good 4–5, 7, 19, 48, 104–5, 158–63
  and *phantasia* 64, 66, 140, 158–63
  rational 162
Woods, M. 72 n.7, 182, 194 n.90

Yurdin, J. 61 n.31, 64 n.34

Zeller, E. 32, 152 n.24, 158 n.13

Index Locorum

ARISTOTLE

Analytica Posteriora
85b27–32 231
87b37–39 42
99b36–37 154

Topica
100a3 153, 219
100a4–6 154 n.4
100a5–6 153, 220
100a6–7 153, 220
100a8–9 153, 220
100a17–b1 153 n.3
100b4 154
100b5 154
100b12 153, 220
105a27–28 209 n.16
111b17 20
118b27 209 n.16
126a13 162 n.20
146b9–12 14
146b36–147a4 7
146b36–147a8 5
146b37–a8 139

Physica
194a32–33 33
195a23–25 33
198a25–26 36
247a3–14 202
247a7–14 58, 80
247a16–17 43, 44, 59
247a 81 n.28
247b13–247a6 122, 131 n.52

de Anima
403a5–18 74
403a7 ff. 118
403a7 74
403a16–403b1 79 n.23
403a18 81 n.27
403a31–b1 26 n.8
406b25 124 n.41, 138 n.2, 162 n.22
413b23–24 26, 27 n.11, 38
414b1–6 26, 38
414b5–6 14
414b15–16 55 n.22
415b24 43
417b22–28 154 n.5
418a21–22 88
421a10–15 38
427a17–19 206
427a17–21 205 n.7
427a17–22 3 n.2
427b14–16 52, 96, 143 n.7
427b16 51
427b17–20 90
427b17–24 148
427b18–19 84
427b21–22 98
427b21–24 70, 90
427b24–26 96
427b25 224
427b27 51 n.9
427b27–28 96, 143 n.7
428a1–2 52
428a1–5 91 n.39
428a3 ff 3 n.2
428a8 78
428a10 3 n.2
428a14–15 54 n.19
428a20–22 92
428a20–24 70, 97
428a22 ff. 105 n.8
428b2–4 90 n.38, 106
428b3–4 53 n.18
428b10–17 53
428b11 50 n.8
428b12–13 52
428b25–30 53 n.17
428b25–429a2 54
429a1–2 52
429a4–6 53, 56, 57
429a4–8 91
429a5–8 61 n.32, 113, 117, 129
430b29–30 88
431a8–10 (**3a**) 26, 31, 32, 35
431a8–11 (**3a-b**) 37
431a8–14 (**3a-c**) 45, 144
431a8 57
431a8–9 27 n.11
431a8–12 55
431a8–12 3 n.1
431a10–11 (**3b**) 32–36, 36 n.31, 39, 43–45
431a11 6
431a12 36 n.28, 36. n.31
431a12–14 (**3c**) 36, 45, 72, 206
431a13–14 72, 72 n.7, 206
431a13–17 143 n.7
431a14–17 (**3d**) 25 n.5, 51, 61, 65, 95, 139, 140, 142, 144, 145, 145 n.12, 147
431a14–b10 145

431b2 96
431b2–5 (3e) 144 n.8, 145, 145 n.12
431b3–5 144 n.8
431b5–6 (3f) 145 n.12
431b6–8 (3g) 145, 145 n.12, 149
431b8–10 (3h) 139, 149, 150
432a3–9 61, 95, 25 n.6
432a3–10 143, 145 n.12
432a3–11 143 n.7
432a8–9 65
432a8–14 51
432a15–17 205 n.7, 206
432a16 3
432a23–25 162
432b5 105, 162 n.20
432b15 49
432b15–16 49, 139, 105 n.9
432b26–433a8 103
433a9–10 (2a) 16, 17, 19, 104
433a9–12 (2a-b) 138
433a9–b12 16, 104
433a10–11 113
433a11 61 n.32
433a10–12 (2b) 17, 18, 113, 117
433a13–20 (2c) 17, 28, 34, 224 n.41
433a15 55 n.21
433a16–17 190
433a20–25 (2d) 17, 104, 124 n.41
433a20-b12 (2d-g) 104
433a21 16 n.24
433a23–25 162
433a24-b12 91
433a25–29 (2e) 17–19, 48, 105, 105 n.10, 139
433a25-b10 (2e-f) 18, 50
433a26–29 139
433a27–29 4
433a27–30 33
433a28–30 27
433a29 105 n.9, 145
433b5–10 (2f) 18–20, 104, 105,
    109–11, 118–20, 123, 127,
    127 n.46, 129, 147
433b8–10 7, 36 n.32, 147
433b9 33
433b10–12 (2g) 9, 17, 138
433b11–12 138
433b12 10, 61 n.32
433b22 41
433b27–29 10, 55 n.22, 105 n.9
433b27–30 140
434a5–7 105 n.9, 145
434a7–8 146 n.14
434a7–10 61, 129 n.48
434a7–11 145
434a12–14 101, 105
434a16–19 12 n.27
434b22–27 37

de Sensu
436a6–10 203
436a9 43 n.45
436a19–21 230 n.53
436b1–4 203
436b15–17 29
436b15–437a2 37
436b16–18 14, 38
438a1–4 50
438a3 3 n.2
443b22–23 29
443b24–26 38
443b29 27
444a1–2 202 n.4
447a14–17 113 n.24

de Memoria
449b13–15 58 n.28
449b30–450a9 96
449b31 51
449b31–450a13 143
450a1–11 114 n.25
450a5 84
450a12–13 79
450a27–32 53
451a3–4 52
453a13 149 n.19
453a21 107

de Somno et Vigilia
454a2–7 214
454a12–17 214
454b24–25 206, 214
455a12–26 214
455a 214 n.27

de Insomniis
458b15–26 126 n.44
458b17–18 126 n.44
458b18 126 n.44
458b18–25 126 n.44
458b20 ff. 84
458b29 116, 162
459a6 115 n.28
459a6 225 n.45
459a6–7 114
459a6–8 114, 126 n.44
459a8 116
459a15 129
459a15–17 36 n.31
459a16–17 72
459a17–18 52
459a24–28 52
459a26–28 107
459b6–7 107
459b7–23 108 n.14
460b2–3 52, 107
460b3–16 115
460b4 ff. 118

de Insomniis (cont.)
  460b6 116
  460b7 52 n.16
  460b7–8 108 n.15
  460b16–18 114 n.25
  460b16–20 ix, 53 n.18, 106, 114
  460b20 50 n.8, 65, 225 n.45
  460b20–21 108
  460b23–25 53, 107
  460b25 108 n.14
  460b28 ff. 52 n.11
  461a6–7 52 n.11
  461a19 52
  461b5–7 116
  461b6–8 126 n.44
  461b21–22 52
  461b26–29 114 n.25
  461b29–462a8 115
  461b31–462a2 97
  462a5 114
  462a8 114
  462a28–29 126 n.44

de Divinatione per Somnum
  463b17 107

Historia Animalium
  573b27 222
  588a18–26 73 n.11
  608b10 73 n.11
  612a12 56 n.23
  619b27–31 73 n.11

de Partibus Animalium
  661a6–8 14, 38
  666a11–13 26 n.8, 43
  669a18–21 56 n.23

de Motu Animalium
  700b10–11 9, 11
  700b15–23 (**1a**) 11, 12, 19, 60, 138
  700b15–29 (**1a-b**) 48, 50
  700b15–701a33 (**1a-d**) 13
  700b17–20 91
  700b17–21 10
  700b18–20 138
  700b19–20 205
  700b19–21 3 n.2, 12 n.25
  700b20 3 n.2, 12
  700b23–29 (**1b**) 12, 13, 20, 138
  700b23–700b29 4
  700b25–26 5, 27
  700b28–29 138
  701a4–5 10
  701a6–25 11
  701a7–25 (**1c**) 11, 13, 15, 17, 141, 234
  701a13 34
  701a17 195
  701a25–33 (**1d**) 13–15, 23, 29, 32, 53, 62, 65, 125

  701a25–b19 (**1d-f**) 60
  701a27 34
  701a28 14, 125 n.42
  701a29–30 33
  701a29–36 91
  701a31 15
  701a32–33 54
  701a33–36 (**1e**) 9 n.14, 14, 23, 55 n.22, 60
  701a34 9 n.14
  701a34–36 10
  701a35–36 55 n.22
  701b1–19 23
  701b2–19 (**1f**) 23, 24, 60, 150, 151
  701b2–702a1 (**1f-g**) 151
  701b2–702a7 (**1f-h**) 66
  701b13–19 59
  701b16–19 91, 150
  701b19–702a1 (**1g**) 24–26, 59, 151
  701b20–21 25
  701b24–32 24 n.3
  701b33–35 59, 91
  702a2–7 26, 60
  702a3–7 (**1h**) 25, 26, 26 n.8, 60
  702a15–19 10, 61, 36 n.32, 146
  702a17–19 23, 49, 61 n.32, 91, 105 n.9, 139
  702b21 24 n.4
  702b21–5 26 n.8
  702b21–25 23, 60
  703a5 9
  703a32–33 33 n.22
  703a34–36 36 n.32
  703b8–11 49
  703b14–20 25

de Generatione Animalium
  735a9–11 122 n.37

Metaphysica
  980a27–981a7 42 n.42
  980a28–29 153, 219
  980b26–27 154 n.4, 220 n.36
  980b29–981a1 153, 220
  981a5–7 153, 220
  981a5–12 229
  981a7–12 187
  981a12–19 185
  981a24–30 229
  981a28–30 153, 187, 220
  981b6 231
  981b7–10 185
  981b12–13 42
  981b31–982a1 229
  983a31–32 33
  1032a32–b14 229
  1032b6 ff. 178 n.56
  1072a27–28 6, 36 n.32, 138
  1072a27–30 4

INDEX LOCORUM   251

Ethica Nicomachea
1094a18–22 209 n.17
1094a22–25 186
1094a27 184 n.69
1094b6–7 186
1095a17–18 177
1095a20–25 177
1095a22–23 155
1095b3–8 187, 228
1095b4–6 186
1095b14–16 178
1095b16 178 n.57
1095b19–22 177
1096b28–29 113 n.23
1097b26–27 33
1097b33–1098a5 72
1098a26-b2 230 n.53
1098a33-b2 187 n.77
1098b2–4 178, 200
1098b3–4 178 n.58
1099a7–13 207
1099a13–14 202
1102a2–4 178 n.58
1102a30 72, 72 n.6
1102b13 72 n.10
1102b14 168
1102b14–25 101
1102b26–1103a1 188
1102b27–28 110, 119
1102b31–33 71
1103a1 72
1103a3–5 71 n.5, 164
1103a14–b2 171
1103a15 189
1103a18–26 168 n.37
1103a25–6 171
1103b3–4 171
1103b16–17 206
1103b16–22 172
1104a33–b2 172
1104b1–2 206
1104b3–5 80 n.25
1104b8–9 80
1104b8–12 172
1104b8–13 202, 208
1104b14–15 26 n.8
1104b30–31 207 n.13
1104b30–1105a1 209
1105a10–11 235
1105a10–12 202
1105a31 207, 218
1105a31–32 165, 167
1105a31–b5 171 n.43
1105a32 152 n.23, 176
1105b4–5 167
1105b21–23 43 n.45, 80 n.24, 81 n.27
1105b23 74 n.13

1106a3–4 165
1106b16–17 72
1106b21–22 192
1106b27–28 192
1106b27–28 192, 193 n.89
1106b28 194
1106b36 165, 193 n.89
1106b36–1107a2 192
1109a20–23 193 n.89, 192
1109a26–30 193
1109b14–16 193
1111b11–13 138
1111b12–13 73 n.11, 163
1111b17 5, 14, 139
1111b19–20 175
1111b26–29 178
1112b9 194
1112b11–16 156
1112b33–34 156
1113a2–4 194
1113a2–12 175
1113a15–31 4
1113a21 162
1113a23–24 4, 5
1113a23–31 7, 110, 159, 175, 198
1113a23–33 161
1113a33-b2 30, 109
1113a912 165
1114a31-b1 159, 175, 198
1114a31-b20 161
1114a32-b3 77 n.20
1115b13–14 176 n.54, 194
1117a4–5 170
1117b23–24 169 n.39
1118a23 56 n.23
1118a24–26 40
1119a12 39
1119a14 111
1119b10 113 n.24, 131 n.52
1119b15–18 110, 119
1120a23–24 176 n.54, 194, 207, 218
1120b2–3 195
1121b1–5 176
1121b2–3 194 n.91
1121b5–7 193
1124a1–2 218
1124b15 216 n.30
1125a24 218
1125a27–28 218
1138b18–25 193
1139a6–8 27 n.12
1139a12 167 n.34
1139a12–13 162, 167 n.34, 176 n.53, 180
1139a20 9 n.14
1139a22–23 165
1139a23 124 n.41

Ethica Nicomachea (cont.)
1139a31–34 175
1139a35–36 28 n.13
1139b4–5 138
1139b5 124 n.41
1139b29–31 156
1139b31–32 166 n.30
1140a6–8 168 n.38
1140a25–27 180
1140a25–31 179
1140a30–31 180 n.61
1140a35–b3 229
1140b4–6 166 n.30
1140b5–6 180
1140b11 ff. 174 n.51
1140b11–19 182
1140b11–20 174
1140b20–22 168 n.38
1140b25–28 105 n.8, 114 n.26
1140b26–27 167 n.34
1140b33 168 n.38
1141a22–23 180
1141a22–25 229
1141b5–6 180
1141b8–9 179
1141b9–10 179, 186
1141b14–26 183
1141b18–19 186
1141b23–24 189
1141b25 185
1141b27 183
1142a9–10 185 n.73
1142a14 179
1142a23–24 186
1142a23–25 222
1142a23–30 129
1142b11 182 n.65
1142b11–12 194
1142b18–20 18
1142b31–33 180, 224
1142b33 181, 182
1143a25–29 182 n.65
1143a25–b5 129
1143a26–29 189
1143a35–b5 158 n.11, 190, 196, 201, 222
1143b3–5 190 n.83
1143b4 190
1143b5 41
1143b27–30 41
1144a6–9 41, 166, 226
1144a7–9 157, 173
1144a23–36 195
1144a24–27 168 n.36
1144a31–33 17, 156 n.6, 224
1144a31–36 159, 175, 198
1144a32–33 195
1144a33–36 110 n.19
1144b2–17 170

1144b3 195
1144b4–14 228
1144b8–14 184
1144b8–17 165, 195
1144b10–12 113 n.23
1144b14–16 167, 170
1144b16–17 196 n.94
1144b16–27 167, 191
1144b23–27 193
1144b26–27 165
1145a1–2 191
1145a4–6 157, 173, 176
1145b26–27 121
1146a16 ff. 105 n.10
1146b8–9 121
1146b22–24 119
1146b31 121
1146b31–35 121
1146b35–1147a10 121
1147a8 121, 121 n.35
1147a10–18 118, 122
1147a11–12 122
1147a12–13 122
1147a12–15 103
1147a20 123
1147a21–23 122
1147a24–b5 123
1147a25–26 224
1147a25–28 123
1147a31–35 123
1147a32 194
1147a35–b3 125
1147b1 125
1147b2–3 123
1147b3–5 127, 127 n.46
1147b6–8 124
1147b6–9 121
1147b9 224
1147b9–12 128
1147b9–17 130
1147b13–17 130
1147b16 131 n.50
1148a9 124
1149a9–10 73 n.12
1149a32–34 89
1149a32–35 125 n.43
1149a34–b1 125
1149b1–3 127 n.46
1150b19–22 128
1150b25–26 107
1150b27–28 127
1151a4–5 119
1151a15–19 157, 172, 174, 200, 222
1151a17–19 225, 228 n.52
1151a18–19 170, 173
1151a19 171
1151a20–24 119
1151a25–26 225

INDEX LOCORUM   253

1151a35 19
1152a2–3 110
1152b1–3 184 n.69
1153a2–7 203 n.5
1153a5–6 29 n.14, 169 n.39
1153a13–15 212 n.24
1153a14–15 31, 44
1153a22–23 27
1154b11–15 107
1154b15–20 29 n.14
1156b22–23 109 n.18
1166a23–26 220 n.37
1166b7–8 101 n.3
1166b8–9 119
1166b9 5
1168a6–7 203 n.6
1168b15–31 210
1168b29–30 209
1169b30 218
1169b30–1170a4 212, 216
1170a5–11 203 n.6
1170a7–11 211
1170a13 212
1170a16–19 (**4a**) 205, 213
1170a16–b1 74
1170a25–29 (**4b**) 213
1170a25-b10 (**4b-f**) 213
1170a29 ff. 203 n.6
1170a29–b1 (**4c**) 213–15, 214 n.27
1170b1–5 (**4d**) 215, 216
1170b7–10 (**4f**) 215, 216
1171b29–1172a1 214
1172a20–25 80
1173b18–19 58 n.30
1173b20–25 29 n.14, 39
1174b14 ff. 212 n.24
1174b14–15 32
1174b14–23 204
1174b20–23 30, 44
1174b33 44
1175b30–35 44
1176a10–22 29 n.14
1176a13–22 39, 39 n.39
1176a15–19 110 n.19
1176a15–22 111
1178a9 232
1178a14–16 74, 79 n.23, 80, 203
1178a16–17 173 n.50
1178a16–19 157
1179b4 ff. 173
1179b7 188
1179b8 176 n.54
1179b11–13 208
1179b20 ff. 165
1179b20–31 172
1179b24–31 208
1179b34–35 185
1179b34–1180a1 202

1180a5–11 188
1180a7 176 n.54
1180a10–11 176 n.54
1180a29–32 183
1180b20–25 184
1180b25 186
1180b28–29 184 n.68

Magna Moralia
1185b5–12 165 n.26

Ethica Eudemia
1214b28–1215a3 178
1215a35–b1 177
1218b4–6 33
1219a8 33
1219b21–25 73
1219b23 72, 73
1219b23–38 205 n.9
1219b27 168
1219b30 71
1219b37–38 72, 73
1220a3–4 169
1220a4–12 168 n.38
1220a8–11 71 n.5, 164
1220b7–10 80 n.25
1220b12–14 26 n.8, 80 n.24
1220b14 81 n.27
1220b18–19 165 n.27
1220b37 80
1221a13 216 n.30
1221a31 216 n.30
1221b28–31 71 n.5, 164
1221b31 72
1221b36–39 80 n.25
1221b39 80
1222b6–7 193 n.89
1222b9–10 80 n.25
1123b2 218
1223b6 162
1224a28–30 9 n.14
1224a33 101 n.3
1224b16–21 148
1224b24 ff. 101
1224b24 113 n.24, 131 n.52
1225b25–26 162
1225b26–27 73 n.11
1226a5–8 175
1226a13–16 223
1226b5–6 175
1226b9–10 156
1226b20–30 181, 224, 230
1227a7–8 156
1227a13 ff. 181
1227a13–18 182
1227a13-b1 177
1227a14 181 n.64
1227a18–23 166 n.31
1227a18-b1 109

254   INDEX LOCORUM

Ethica Eudemia (cont.)
  1227a27–31 166 n.31
  1227a39 30
  1227b1–5 166 n.31
  1227b8 166
  1227b9 165
  1227b12–1228a3 166
  1227b21–23 196 n.92
  1227b22–25 157
  1227b23–25 176 n.53, 194 n.90
  1227b28–32 141, 156
  1227b36–38 194
  1228a24 165
  1229a1–2 168
  1229a1–9 176 n.54
  1229a20–28 170
  1229b13–18 76 n.17
  1230a27 165
  1230a27–29 194
  1230a27–32 166
  1231a5–10 56 n.23
  1232a35–38 161
  1234a29–30 170
  1235b25–27 4, 6, 8, 36 n.32
  1235b26–29 xi, 30, 48, 50, 106
  1235b27 33, 109
  1235b32–33 109 n.18
  1236a9–10 109, 110
  1236b27 109 n.18
  1236b39–1237a7 202
  1237a1–7 172, 208
  1237a3–7 29
  1244b23–25 205
  1244b33–1245a5 215
  1245a30 216
  1245a35–b2 216

Politica
  1252b34–35 33
  1253a9–18 39, 45
  1253a10–18 89 n.35
  1253a15–18 6
  1254b9 72 n.6
  1254b22–24 73 n.12
  1260a13 73 n.12
  1269a2–1 173
  1269a20–21 171 n.43
  1276b34–35 173
  1277a15 173
  1281b35–38 40
  1312b33–34 81 n.27
  1321a14–16 186
  1324a25–28 232
  1324a34 232
  1325a16–17 232
  1325b21–23 206 n.10
  1328a1 210 n.19
  1328a10–12 89 n.35
  1328a38 232

  1331b26–37 177
  1331b27–38 196 n.92
  1332a9 232
  1332b3–4 221
  1332b6–8 226 n.47
  1334b8 ff. 171
  1334b17–25 162, 162 n.20
  1340a14–b14 211

Rhetorica
  1354a24–26 99 n.55
  1356a14–16 99 n.55
  1362a21–22 209 n.17
  1362a21–23 33
  1362a21–28 34
  1362b8–9 207 n.13
  1363b13–17 34
  1366b20–22 180
  1369a1–4 5, 138
  1369a3 162
  1370a18–27 168
  1370a27–35 58, 203
  1370a28–35 78
  1370a35–b11 81
  1370b1–11 83
  1370b10 82 n.29
  1370b13–15 82 n.29
  1370b16–17 82
  1370b21–22 82
  1370b23–1371a20 82
  1370b32–34 76, 84
  1371a8–9 76, 84
  1371a18–20 76
  1377b24 99 n.55
  1377b31–1378a5 120 n.32
  1378a19–20 99 n.55
  1378a19–22 26 n.8, 80
  1378a30–31 26 n.8, 75, 83
  1378b1–10 78, 87
  1380a24–26 73 n.11
  1380b16–17 95
  1382a10 79
  1382a10–12 79 n.22, 40
  1382a12–13 81 n.27
  1382a21 25 n.6, 38 n.38
  1382a21–23 70, 82
  1382b29–33 77, 97
  1382b33 95, 96, 98
  1383a16–19 75
  1383a17–19 82
  1383b12–13 75
  1383b13 84
  1384a22 75
  1384a22 84
  1384b32–35 84
  1385b13–16 76, 83
  1385b13–17 97
  1385b14 83
  1385b16–18 77

1385b24 95
1386a1–3 83
1386a29–b7 83
1386b5–7 77 n.19
1387a8 84
1387a8–9 76
1387a24 95
1387a24–25 77 n.18
1387b23 84
1387b23–24 76
1388a32 84
1388a32–34 76

PLATO

Philebus
  32c1 59, 81 n.28
  39a–b 85
  39d4 ff. 59, 81 n.28
  40a9 85
  40a10–12 85
  40e2–4 85
  47c–d 36 n.31
  47d5–9 85
  47e1–2 85
  47e 85

Timaeus
  45b–c 87
  45d–46a 87
  69c–d 86
  71a1–2 87
  71a3–d4 86
  71a 87
  71d–72b 87
  86b–c 131 n.52

Republic
  401e4–402a4
    172 n.47
  596b 230
  602a4 230

Laws
  645d–e 131 n.52
  645e2, 131
  649d–e 131 n.52

The manufacturer's authorised representative in the EU for product safety is
Oxford University Press España S.A. of el Parque Empresarial San Fernando de
Henares, Avenida de Castilla, 2 – 28830 Madrid (www.oup.es/en or product.
safety@oup.com). OUP España S.A. also acts as importer into Spain of products
made by the manufacturer.

www.ingramcontent.com/pod-product-compliance
Ingram Content Group UK Ltd.
Pitfield, Milton Keynes, MK11 3LW, UK
UKHW022230230426
12048UKWH00016BA/1178